A Metaphysics for Freedom

A Metaphysics for Freedom argues that agency itself—and not merely the special, distinctively human variety of it—is incompatible with determinism. For determinism is threatened just as surely by the existence of powers which can be unproblematically accorded to many sorts of animals, as by the distinctively human powers on which the free will debate has tended to focus. Helen Steward suggests that a tendency to approach the question of free will solely through the issue of moral responsibility has obscured the fact that there is a quite different route to incompatibilism, based on the idea that animal agents above a certain level of complexity possess a range of distinctive 'two-way' powers, not found in simpler substances. Determinism is not a doctrine of physics, but of metaphysics, and the idea that it is physics which will tell us whether our world is deterministic or not presupposes what must not be taken for granted—that there could be no irreducibly top-down form of causal influence. Steward considers questions concerning supervenience, laws, and levels of explanation, and explores an outline of a variety of top-down causation which might sustain the idea that an animal itself, rather than merely events and states going on in its parts, might be able to bring something about. The resulting position permits certain important concessions to compatibilism. A convincing response is also offered to the charge that even if determinism is incompatible with agency, indeterminism could be of no possible help. The whole is an argument for a distinctive and resolutely non-dualistic, naturalistically respectable version of libertarianism, rooted in a conception of what biological forms of organization might make possible in the way of freedom.

Helen Steward is Professor of Philosophy of Mind and Action at the University of Leeds.

A Metaphysics for Freedom

Helen Steward

OXFORD
UNIVERSITY PRESS

UNIVERSITY PRESS

Great Clarendon Street, Oxford, OX2 6DP,
United Kingdom

Oxford University Press is a department of the University of Oxford.
It furthers the University's objective of excellence in research, scholarship,
and education by publishing worldwide. Oxford is a registered trade mark of
Oxford University Press in the UK and in certain other countries

Published in the United States of America by Oxford University Press
198 Madison Avenue, New York, NY 10016, United States of America

British Library Cataloguing in Publication Data

Data available

Library of Congress Cataloguing in Publication Data
Library of Congress Control Number: 2012933422

ISBN 978–0–19–955205–4 (Hbk)
ISBN 978–0–19–870646–5 (Pbk)

Contents

'It is strange that philosophers have been able to argue endlessly about determinism and free-will, to cite examples in favour of one or the other thesis without ever attempting first to make explicit the structures contained in the very idea of action.'

(Jean-Paul Sartre, *Being and Nothingness*, tr. Hazel E. Barnes,
(London: Methuen, 1958: 433))

Preface

I have always thought that the free will problem is the most interesting problem in philosophy. It is the most interesting partly because it already includes so many of the others—it is perfectly obvious from the outset that its solution demands getting straight about some of the most difficult philosophical concepts there are: causation, explanation, the self, the mind, the physical, power, possibility, conditionals...I could go on. For this reason, it is an enormously challenging problem but also endlessly fascinating: it provides, easily, a lifetime's work in philosophy and probably many lifetimes' worth.

I do not suppose that I have got properly straight, in what follows, about all or even some of these difficult concepts. Nor do I think I have provided knock-down arguments for the view for which I have attempted to argue; and I am very conscious that I have made only a poor beginning on some of the tasks that need to be accomplished if that view is to be defended against objections. But I hope to have described in the pages that follow a view I believe to be distinctive, unusual and—to my mind—really rather appealing, a view which I think has been undeservedly under-explored in the past, for a mixture of unconvincing reasons. It is also one which, if it does not itself constitute a solution to the free will problem, might at least be the beginnings of such a solution.

I have many people to thank for help with the development of the ideas that are set out here and for encouragement and support along the way. Thanks of both sorts are due, first and foremost, to Jennifer Hornsby, who has been an unfailing source both of intellectual inspiration and support throughout my entire academic career. I owe to her early book, *Actions*, a range of basic ideas about how action ought to be conceptualized, which forms part of the framework of this book. To her later work I owe a sense of the fruitfulness of hard, detailed thought about the assumptions made by physicalists, and of imaginative exploration—although always within a framework that is naturalistic, in the best sense of that word—of what the world might look like with those assumptions discarded.

Thanks are due also to all the other members of the Leverhulme-funded 'Rethinking the Philosophy of Action' network—Maria Alvarez, John Hyman, Ralf Stoecker, Thomas Spitzley, Carlos Moya, Monika Betzler, and Hanjo Glock—for a constant stream of interesting exchanges over a period of several years, as well as a very thorough and useful grounding in the work of Anscombe, whose ideas have proved invaluable to me. A timely meeting with Sarah Broadie on a train convinced me that my views on action were not insane, and subsequent reading of her work gave me grounds for thinking they might even deserve further development. Denis Noble deserves a special mention for the 'systems biology' group he formed at Balliol while I was still there; an interdisciplinary environment in which I first began to think about the possible relevance of developments taking place elsewhere in the natural sciences for the philosophy of action. I still do not really know the answer to the question of what the relevance of those developments might be and have made less progress with that particular issue than I would have liked, but it was extremely helpful to be able to explore the question with such a range of interesting people working in disciplines as varied as computer science, physiology, physics, and mathematical biology.

On the opposite side of the Atlantic, both John Fischer and Michael McKenna have been friendly encouragers of my efforts to engage with a free will literature, the presuppositions of which I mostly do not share. I would particularly like to thank Michael for a timely recommendation not to take rejection by a journal too much to heart, but simply to put rejected articles 'right back in the post'. Many a paper that might otherwise have languished in a bottom drawer, including some whose contents have found their way into this volume, are now out in print as a result of his wise advice. I have also learned a great deal from the work of Wayne Wu, whose empirically informed approach to the philosophy of action I cannot yet hope to emulate. However, he has made me see the importance and relevance of reading the psychological literature carefully.

The first draft of a substantial portion of this work was written under the Arts and Humanities Research Council Research Leave Scheme; Balliol College provided matching leave. The Leverhulme Fund and the Centre for the Study of Mind in Nature in Oslo have also provided financial support for activities, conferences, and workshops from which this book has benefited greatly.

Two anonymous readers for OUP provided exceedingly astute and helpful feedback on the first draft of the material that has now become the first four chapters of this work; without their comments, this book would have been very much worse than it is now (though it might also have appeared a bit sooner). Two further readers provided immensely useful comments on the entire draft. I do not think I have fully responded to all the hard questions that all these people have raised about the views I try to defend here, though I have done my best with some of the more manageable-looking ones. Thinking about some of the more difficult issues is going to occupy me for some time to come.

I would like to thank my parents, Cathy and Ernie Steward, and also John and Maureen Hesmondhalgh for love and support over the years and also their help with looking after the children, which has given me the freedom to write and think. My children's incredulity at the amount of time it has taken me to complete this book has been a helpful spur to its eventual completion. Thanks to them both—Rosa and Joe—for their love, humour, and forbearance; and also special thanks to Joe for letting me use his bedroom as a study during the year in which I began this book. My partner Dave Hesmondhalgh, who seems to have written about three books in the time it has taken me to complete mine, has mostly avoided the temptation to mock my slow progress. Thanks to him for resisting and for always being there for me through thick and thin.

Some of the material in this book is reworked from the following articles. Acknowledgement to the relevant journals and publishers is duly given:

'Moral Responsibility and the Irrelevance of Physics', *Journal of Ethics* 12 (2008): 129–45.

'Animal Agency', *Inquiry* 52 (2009): 217–31.

'The Truth in Compatibilism and the Truth of Libertarianism', *Philosophical Explorations* 12.2 (2009): 167–79.

'Fairness, Agency and the "Flicker of Freedom"', *Nous* 43: 64–93.

'Perception and the Ontology of Causation'. In: Naomi Eilan, Hemdat Lerman and Johannes Roessler (eds.), *Perception, Causation and Objectivity: Issues in Philosophy and Psychology* (Oxford: Oxford University Press, 2011).

Overview

Having completed the manuscript, I have realized that although there is quite a lot of signposting throughout of the overall structure of the argument, there is no single place in which an overview is offered of what is attempted by each chapter. Here, then, I attempt such an overview, so that readers can orient themselves in advance and direct themselves to the individual chapters that might interest them.

Chapter 1 outlines the free will problem as I see it and explains why I intend to tackle here a rather non-standard version of the questions generally asked under the 'free will' head. It outlines the libertarian position for which I wish to argue, a position that I call 'Agency Incompatibilism', and also provides a general introduction to my distinctive claim that the agency of many non-human animals is just as difficult to square with determinism as is our own. In Chapter 2, I set out the concept of agency that underpins the rest of the book—a conception according to which an action is to be thought of as an input into the course of events such that it is essentially up to its agent whether or not it occurs—and argue that if this is indeed what an action is the existence of actions must be inconsistent with determinism. In passing, I also explore Van Inwagen's Consequence Argument, which, like mine, exploits the idea that nothing that is already settled by the past and the laws of nature could be up to the agent. I suggest, however, that Van Inwagen's argument is inconclusive, and argue that he makes a crucial mistaken concession to the compatibilist in appearing to accept that there could be such things as actions which were not 'up to us'. It is also in this chapter that the notion of 'settling' is first introduced. An action, I suggest, is a means by which agents generally settle, for at least some values of φ, at least some of the following questions: whether they will φ, and if so, how, when, and where they will do so. Chapter 3 explores some possible objections to my account of settling and considers the case for a deflationary compatibilist understanding of what settling involves, concluding eventually, however, that there are good reasons for thinking that such compatibilist manoeuvres are bound to be unsatisfactory, for a number of important reasons.

In Chapter 4, I move to consider animal agency and defend the view that many animals are indeed agents in my sense. I argue in this chapter, using the work of cognitive psychologists, that agency is a highly robust and distinctive concept that ought to be accorded a central role in our basic categorization of entities, a role that has not generally been properly recognized for what it is. The concept of agency is an outgrowth, I suggest, of the concept of animacy and I argue that the concept applies unproblematically to many animals. I consider the difficult question of how it is to be decided which animals are to be accounted agents and why, making use of some aspects of Dennett's work on the intentional stance. Chapter 5 then diverts a little from the main line of argument of the book to meet a particular sort of objection to the general idea that agency is inconsistent with determinism, which stems from the worry that determinism might one day be shown to be true by physics. I argue that this conception of determinism already presupposes what must not be taken for granted; that is to say, the assumption that physics settles everything else.

In Chapter 6, I confront what I call the 'Challenge from Chance', which has always been the main difficulty faced by libertarianism. The problem is that it is difficult to see how the mere truth of indeterminism might make room for the kind of control over the future we feel we might not have if determinism is true. In some ways, indeed, indeterminism appears to make things even worse. In this chapter, I argue that the libertarian should make an important concession to the compatibilist, and that having made it the way is clear for a better understanding of the sorts of alternative possibilities that really are required for agency and therefore for freedom. The incompatibilism that results, I argue, can meet the Challenge from Chance. Chapter 7 deals with various objections to my solution to the Challenge from Chance, including those stemming from so-called 'Frankfurt-style' examples.

The conception of agency for which I have argued gives the agent (rather than events occurring inside the agent, states or properties of the agent, or facts concerning the agent) centre stage and might therefore be thought to be a version of agent causationism. In Chapter 8, I try to say in what sense my view is, and in what sense it is not, a version of agent causationism, and then respond to those criticisms of agent causationism that might seem to be applicable to it. I argue, against some critics of agent causationism, that there need be nothing problematic or incoherent about the very idea of substance causation, insisting on a pluralistic understanding of the sorts of thing that can be causes. I do concede, however, that there is a very difficult issue to be faced about how the causation of effects by a complex, highly organized agent such as an animal could fail to reduce to causation of effects by the parts of that same animal; and in the second part of the chapter, I try to indicate, by means of a discussion of the phenomenon of top-down causation, where I think the solution to this problem may lie.

I hope the whole constitutes an argument for the view that there really could be such a thing as the power of agency as I have characterized and defined it. In order for such a power to exist, the world must be indeterministic, to be sure. But I am as confident of that indeterminism as I am of, for example, the existence of the external world or of other minds, and the reason has nothing to do with quantum mechanics. Just as it is a basic presupposition of our conception of the world that it contains mind-independent entities, or that it contains other persons, so indeterminism is, I think, a basic presupposition of our world view, for that world view embraces the existence of agents: entities things can be up to. The task of this book is to show why we need not fear that this idea will lead us into confusion, obfuscation, or mystification.

1

The Problem

The traditional problem of free will asks whether human freedom (or sometimes 'free action', 'free agency', or 'free will') is consistent with a thesis that is called 'determinism'. This book will be about a set of interconnected issues that are at the heart, so it seems to me, of this traditional problem. But I shall not frame my enquiry in the traditional way. In the terms of the traditional debate, I am, I suppose, an incompatibilist, in that I do not believe there could be anything worthy of the designation 'free agency'—nor indeed, worthy to be called 'agency' at all—in a universe that was completely deterministic. In this chapter and the next, I shall try to say what I think it is possible to say in defence of this claim. But the particular footing on which I shall attempt to rest my incompatibilism will be unusual in a number of respects, and I want to begin by saying something about the ways in which it differs from some of the other versions of incompatibilism that are prominent in the literature.

The first, and most important point, as I have already hinted, is that I wish to claim that it is agency itself (and not merely some rather specialized form or selectively occurring feature of it) which is inconsistent with determinism. For ease of reference, I shall refer to this view in what follows as 'Agency Incompatibilism'. Obviously, the clarification of this view requires that a good deal more be said about the conception of agency which is in play, but it may suffice for the time being to show the distinctiveness of the view for which I wish to argue if I say that I regard agency, at any rate, as a power, or set of powers, that can be safely ascribed to a wide variety of non-human animals. The agency incompatibilist therefore makes a strong claim, and to the extent that the relevant form of incompatibilism might be thought to be more radical than most other incompatibilist theories, it might be supposed that it is bound to be correspondingly less plausible. But radicalism can sometimes disrupt tired alignments and reveal alternative combinations of views whose possibility was not evident prior to the disruption. One of the distinctive and perhaps surprising virtues of my approach, I shall later argue, is that it allows for serious concessions to certain of the more appealing lines of thought propounded by the traditional compatibilist. My hope is that the view I mean to offer might be a version of incompatibilism unencumbered—paradoxically, because of its very radicalism—by the supply of implausibly feeble responses to the best of the compatibilist's arguments.

New answers can sometimes only be seen, though, by asking new questions. The traditional free will debate, I noted above, begins by posing the question whether something called 'freedom' is compatible with universal determinism. But I believe that *neither* of the concepts in terms of which the traditional compatibility question has been framed—that is, neither 'freedom' nor 'determinism'—is really the right concept on which to fasten in order to formulate the oppositions and tensions as it seems to me they ought now to be formulated, in the light both of scientific and of philosophical developments since the seventeenth and eighteenth centuries, when the problem of free will first assumed the contours which are now so familiar to us. John Bishop once claimed that the serious problem which underlies the debates about freedom and determinism '*has nothing essentially to do either with freedom or with determinism*. Rather, it has to do with the possibility of accommodating *actions* within the natural universe'.[1] This seems to me exactly right, and I shall now attempt to explain why.

1.1 Freedom

Freedom first. Sometimes the word 'freedom' is used in the free will literature to do no more than denote the power of any agent to have done otherwise than she did—and in so far as that is intended as its meaning, I have no quarrel with the claim that freedom is one of the concepts at the heart of the serious problem of free will. But the word also connects very readily with aspirations that are distinctively human, and the traditional debate certainly often proceeds as though the thing with which determinism is or is not to be found compatible, whatever else it is, is a possession unique (at any rate, so far as we know) to human beings. The form of agency thought to be in potentially problematic tension with determinism is characterized by such things as rationality, deliberation, and forethought; is susceptible to moral considerations and to the dilemmas typical of situations in which the demands of principle, or of far-sighted prudence, compete with those of self-interest or immediate gain; is capable, indeed, of creativity and even of self-development. In an era which had yet fully to embrace the idea that human nature is continuous with that of the rest of the animal kingdom, perhaps it was unsurprising that human agency should be singled out in this way for special consideration. And in view of the fact that the free will question is often approached as a topic, primarily, in ethics, of interest mainly for its consequences for the idea that persons may be held morally responsible for their actions, perhaps it is unsurprising still. But the assumption that it is only something utterly distinctive of this relatively complex, intelligent, conscious, and deliberative form of agency that could possibly create worries about its compatibility with deterministic conceptions of the universe is surely questionable. Is it really plausible, in view of what we already know about the continuities between our own nature and that, at least, of the higher animals—other primates, for instance—that while all their activities—whatever they go in for in the

---

[1] Bishop (1989: 1–2).

way of planning, deliberating, choosing, acting, etc.[2]—can be safely accommodated without difficulty within a deterministic conception of reality, our own status as agents presents utterly distinctive metaphysical problems?[3] There is surely something suspiciously Cartesian about the idea that cats, bats, and the rest are readily assimilable by deterministic models of reality which threaten, however, to obliterate the most vital aspects of our own form of agency. I shall try to argue, indeed, in Chapter 4, that determinism is falsified just as surely by what it is utterly natural to think about the meanderings of a goat as it is by the ethical agonizings and deliberate human choices on which the tradition has tended to focus as instances of places where the future has to be thought of as open.[4] Thus, 'freedom', in so far as that word tends to suggest a level of sophistication, rationality, creativity, and self-consciousness which it may not be plausible to accord to animals much less intelligent and deliberative than ourselves, already overestimates, I believe, the complexity of the phenomena required to make potential trouble for determinism. My view, to put it very crudely, is that *animals* make trouble for determinism[5] and, moreover, that some natural objections to incompatibilism are very much easier to meet once it has been made clear that it is not only humans whose agency is hard to square with the idea that there is only a single physically possible future.

In some respects, then, I mean to buck a trend which I believe it is possible to discern in recent writings on the free will debate. If anything, there has been, in recent years, a tendency for the 'freedom' side of the freedom/determinism opposition to be conceived of in ever more lofty and sophisticated terms. There has been a resurgence of interest, for instance, in 'free will' envisaged somewhat more literally than has been presupposed by my liberal and unguarded talk of 'the free will problem'. Robert Kane, for example, speaks of wishing to retrieve a traditional sense for the term 'free will', in which it designates 'the power of agents to be the ultimate creators (or originators) and sustainers of their own ends or purposes'.[6] Galen Strawson clearly also has powers similar to those mentioned by Kane in mind when he speaks of our wish to be 'truly self-determined' where one can be truly self-determined 'only if one has somehow or

---

[2] Those who are sceptical about whether any of these concepts really has any application at all to non-human animals will have to await the arguments of Chapter 4.

[3] One might also mention *children*, of whom it can scarcely be doubted that their nature is continuous with our own, although they lack many of the capacities sometimes singled out as crucial to the paradigmatic free agent.

[4] And even if one is sceptical about the goat, the extent to which our own daily lives are dominated by activities in which conscious deliberation plays either no role whatever or at best a very minor one should give us reason to wonder whether an account of freedom focused only, or mainly, on choices made following a careful weighing of pros and cons is really likely to capture the entirety of what it is we think we have in having freedom.

[5] Only *very* crudely. For not all animals are agents, and it is only those that can sensibly be so regarded whose existence is inconsistent with determinism. I shall discuss in Chapter 4 the hugely important, interesting, and extremely difficult question which animals fall into the relevant category, and why.

[6] Kane (1996: 4).

other *determined how one is in such a way that one is truly responsible for how one is'.*[7] Thomas Pink, like Kane, again stresses the centrality of the will, conceiving of it as a capacity for decision-making that is informed by practical reason, a capacity which he explicitly denies any non-human animal could possess.[8] And incompatibilists in general, I think, under pressure, perhaps, from arguments purporting to show that moral responsibility does not in any case require that one could have done otherwise,[9] have tended to reconceive their idea of what it is, precisely, that determinism is supposed to be incompatible with, moving away somewhat from the suggestion that mere choice-making *per se*, with its apparent connections to the need for alternate possibilities and open futures, is what makes for the difficulties, and towards the idea that it is rather something about, say, the power of self-creation, or thoroughgoing self-determin-ation, or autonomy, powers which surely do not extend (on earth, at any rate) beyond the compass of humanity, that presents the real problem.[10] Harry Frankfurt and Gary Watson, writing in the compatibilist tradition,[11] have also moved away from the classical compatibilists' concern with the reconciliation of mere free *action* with deter-minism and have characterized the freedom in which they are interested in terms of powers which it is plausible to suppose that only a human being might enjoy—the capacity to form second-order desires, for instance, or to possess an evaluational standpoint.[12]

I do not want to deny, of course, that such powers as these are of great philosophical importance and interest. But I do want to insist that problems of reconciliation with determinism arise in connection with much simpler and more widely shared powers than any of these, and also that seeing that this is so can help put incompatibilism on a more solidly naturalistic footing than has sometimes been thought available to it. The supposition that agency itself—the capacity to move oneself about the world in purposive ways, ways that are in at least some respects up to oneself—is unproblematic, and that it is only something rather more special, given, perhaps, the honorific appellation '*free* agency' or '*free* will', that creates potential difficulties, inevitably gives rise to the suspicion that the incompatibilist must mean to insist upon the operation, in connection solely with human powers, of types of causality or disruptions in the natural unfolding of events not generally found elsewhere in the world, and it is

---

[7] Strawson (1986: 26).   [8] Pink (2004: Ch. 2).

[9] For arguments in this vein, see, for example, Frankfurt (1969) and Fischer and Ravizza (1998). These arguments will be considered in Chapter 7.

[10] One sign of this tendency is the recognition in much recent work that one ought to distinguish between two distinct varieties of incompatibilism: 'source incompatibilism' (or sometimes 'causal history incompatibilism') alongside the more traditional 'leeway incompatibilism'; see, for example, Pereboom (2001; 2003). I shall be arguing, though, that there is a sense of 'sourcehood' relative to which non-human animals have just as strong a claim to be regarded as the source of their actions as humans have to be the source of theirs.

[11] I hope it is safe to say that they are writing 'in the compatibilist tradition' whether or not it is safe to say they are compatibilists; see Watson (1987: 165 n5) for some doubts about Frankfurt's position.

[12] See, for example, Frankfurt (1971) and Watson (1975).

reasonably supposed by many that this simply cannot be acceptable. In such a context as this, compatibilism must surely be the position to which anyone at all naturalistically inclined is bound to default. But if it could be successfully shown that much larger swathes of reality are in potential conflict with the deterministic or near-deterministic visions of the universe we are sometimes encouraged to think that science has shown us to be mandatory, the hope might arise that incompatibilism would be able to represent itself not as a lunatic thesis which insists that human agents be permitted uniquely to escape the grip of an otherwise more or less universal mechanism, but rather as a more general claim about how we must think about causality and the evolution of reality over time in a world in which animals, and their distinctive powers of self-direction, are present. It is not anything so grand as what is usually understood by 'freedom', therefore, but what I shall call *animal agency*, a collection of powers that are remarkable enough, despite the fact that they are not unique to humanity, and which might themselves be thought of as representative of a *variety* of freedom—albeit, admittedly, a far more lowly sort than we are used to encompassing with that term—which will be the main focus of my concern in this book.

Methodologically speaking, my approach will therefore be quite different from that of many writers on the free will problem. Many writers on free will begin by noting that 'freedom' is a term with many meanings, and attempt to zero in on the conception of freedom in which they are interested by means of the question what kinds of freedom are 'worth wanting'[13] or which kinds might be important for moral responsibility. One can see the appeal of these strategies—one does not want to debate the question whether or not something called 'freedom' is compatible with determinism in a complete void—and these might seem to be sensible ways of making an unhelpfully indeterminate notion more determinate. But these are recipes which are likely immediately to deliver a notion, or notions, of freedom that are much richer, and generally much more deeply connected with the idea of rationality, than the one in which I shall mainly be interested. It would be surprising if anyone thought the freedoms available to a shark or a horse or even to a chimpanzee, in and of themselves, were really terribly desirable from the point of view of a human being, were 'worth wanting'. But for all that, it is evident that in order to be a human being, one has to be an animal. In order to exercise the forms of agency that we value so highly—moral choice, exercises of taste and skill, communication, self-disciplined attention to duties, personal development, creativity, etc.—we have to be able also to exercise forms that in themselves almost escape our notice—we have to be able to move our bodies in such a way as to make them carry out plans of our own devising, in the service of our ends. My claim will be that these humble abilities, which are widely possessed throughout the animal kingdom, are themselves already incompatible with universal determinism. I take it that if this can be made out, it will be enough already to show that no freedom that it would

---

[13] See Dennett (1984) for this phrase.

be worth our wanting can be compatible with determinism either, since all significant human freedoms depend for their existence on such basic capacities as these.[14] It is enough to show also, I shall argue, that the thesis of universal determinism is false.[15] The challenge I shall hope to meet in this book, therefore, is that of trying to understand how we are to conceive of the therefore necessarily *in*deterministic universe that could support such powers as these.

For a book which purports to be about free will, there will, then, be perhaps surprisingly little attention to the notion either of specifically 'free' action or of moral responsibility in what follows. It is not that I do not think that the existence of either of these things depends upon the truth of indeterminism. On the contrary, I am sure that the falsity of universal determinism is a necessary condition of the possibility of any freedom or moral responsibility there might be. But the best reason for thinking that is so, in my view, is that the falsity of universal determinism is a necessary condition of *agency*—and agency is, in its turn, a necessary condition both of free action and of moral responsibility.[16] There are, of course, other ways in which determinism—or indeed other features of the world—might appear to rule out freedom or moral responsibility. There is, for example, a familiar line of thought which insists that something may be an action only if it is chosen for a reason—and that in order for action to be free, that reason must itself be chosen according to principles of choice which are themselves chosen, and so on, so that free action must be impossible because such a regress can never be terminated except with an eventually unchosen principle.[17] Or it might be said that it could never be *fair* to blame a person who could not have done otherwise, or that true moral accountability demands that our characters not be

---

[14] I thus depart sharply from the position of libertarians like Kane (1996), who concede that many valuable kinds of freedom can be analysed without supposing that determinism is false, and claim only that 'there is *at least one* kind of freedom that is incompatible with determinism, and it is a *significant kind of freedom worth wanting*' (1996: 15).

[15] This claim is likely to prompt an immediate worry about my approach, a worry which I shall address further in Chapter 5. It will be said that the thesis of universal determinism is an empirical thesis that one ought not to be able to *show* to be false by means of a fairly straightforward argument to the effect that it is incompatible with the indisputable fact of agency. In some ways, I believe, this line of thinking has done more than any other to encourage the thought that compatibilism of some sort just *must* be correct—for if it has to be allowed that determinism might *turn out* to be true, then anyone who thinks that agency (or perhaps even 'free' agency) is an undeniable given will want to ensure that it is not going to be endangered by possible future scientific developments. The question is, though, whether the thesis of universal determinism really *is* a thesis which might yet turn out to be true. And it can be argued that it is not—and not merely for the reason that current physics makes its truth seem unlikely. Perhaps it must ultimately be conceded that no one can prove absolutely that determinism is not true, but then there are not many things which one can prove absolutely. I shall try to show, at any rate, that the falsity of determinism is a fairly straightforward consequence of commitments concerning the nature of agency and the future which it would be deeply problematic for us to give up (intellectually, as well as emotionally). That is, perhaps, not a proof of indeterminism, but it is a very good reason for believing in it.

[16] Cf Wolf: '...only an agent who has a will—that is, who has desires, goals or purposes, and the ability to control her behavior in accordance with them, can be responsible for anything at all' (1990: 7).

[17] For a modern version of this worry, see, for example, Strawson (1994). Thanks to an anonymous reviewer for OUP for alerting me to the need to make it clear whether or not I intended to address this line of thought.

the ineluctable upshots of heredity and environment, or that moral responsibility requires that we not be under the deterministic influence of merely self-interested desires. Some of these reasons for thinking that free action and moral responsibility are impossible, or inconsistent with determinism, might also be good ones, of course—and I do not claim to have addressed them here. But in as much as the lines of thought involved import relatively sophisticated conceptions of rational action, or else reasoning which is of itself distinctively *moral*, resting on intuitions concerning fairness, character-formation, and the like, they seem to me in various respects less *basic* than the line of argument which contends simply that since there can be no agency in a deterministic world, there can be no 'free' action or moral responsibility either.[18] They tend to make presuppositions I regard as questionable (and will later question)— such as that the concept of action is best defined via the idea of reason or that there might be agents under the supposition of determinism—agents who could not have done *otherwise*, to be sure, but agents who (being agents) could certainly have *done*. But perhaps to concede these things is already to have made a mistake.

Secondly, and perhaps even more importantly, the less basic, morally focused lines of argument for incompatibilism require a particular conception of what needs to be the case if it is to be true that an agent could have done otherwise, a requirement which, I shall later argue,[19] makes the resulting positions vulnerable to what has always been, in my view, the most serious of the compatibilist's objections. Because the available alternative possibilities are intended to ground the thought that the agent can be fairly praised and blamed for what she does, they are conceived of as robustly alternative *courses of action*—things which might, for example, be differentially judged from the moral point of view. But to the claim that such alternative possibilities as these are necessary for moral responsibility, and that therefore determinism must be rejected, the compatibilist has always had a powerful response. She will agree that it is indeed normally evident, in the usual sorts of non-constraining circumstances, that agents have these kinds of alternative possibilities available—that such an agent generally could, absent specific varieties of physical or psychological coercion or constraint, have done other than she did. But, she will say, in the sense in which this is evident, surely nothing incompatible with determinism can be being presupposed. For a substantially different course of action would have required a different set of antecedent motivations if it is not to be an absurd and irrational exploit with no connection whatever to the agent and her antecedent psychological state. Freedom and moral responsibility cannot depend on a capacity to act in a way which is utterly unjustified and unmotivated by any of the beliefs or desires one has. As it is generally meant, then, the compatibilist insists, the claim that

---

[18] Cf Sarah Broadie: 'doubt whether determinism can allow for agency is logically prior to doubt whether it can allow for moral responsibility…If it turns out that determinism makes nonsense of agency, then there is nothing for moral responsibility to be responsibility *for*, and so questions whether determinism threaten moral responsibility, and how, if so, we should respond to the threat, must lapse for lack of a subject.' (Broadie, 2002: 119).

[19] In Chapter 6.

an agent 'could have done otherwise' must surely be innocent of any commitment to the claim that she has the ability to undertake an alternative course of action, *even given a set of motivations and beliefs that can, at the relevant moment in time, make no rational sense of it.* For such a capacity would be pointless, and not at all the sort of thing that one might think could subserve freedom or moral responsibility. I shall have a good deal more to say about this compatibilistic claim in later chapters, for there is much justice in it. But for now, I wish merely to note that the incompatibilistic commitment which is judged absurd by this strand of compatibilist thinking arises directly out of a conception of alternative possibilities that is generated by a focus on the deliberative situation, the rational choice, the potentially morally significant decision. I shall later claim that my very different focus—on abilities which are shared by humans with many kinds of animal—makes it possible for my version of incompatibilism to do proper justice to what the compatibilist gets right, and the incompatibilist often gets wrong, about the kind of power to do otherwise which is a necessary condition of freedom.

There is also a third reason why I prefer not to begin from moral responsibility. This reason is well-captured by Bernard Williams:

The truth is that we have other reasons to worry about many of our moral notions, and if we have come to have difficulty in understanding ideas such as 'moral responsibility', this is not simply because of our suppositions, hopes and fears about naturalistic explanations of action...we have reasons *anyway* for being doubtful about moral responsibility.[20]

Williams' point, I take it, is that one might have good reasons for being sceptical about the notion of moral responsibility which were utterly independent of worries concerning determinism (or, more broadly, concerning naturalistic explanations of action).[21] Many writers seem to begin from the assumption that whatever else we may or may not know, we know, at least, that we are morally responsible agents, and so that we may begin from there. But this assumption seems to me very far from secure. It seems at least possible that the whole framework of concepts and practices within which the notion of moral responsibility has its place—those of praise and blame, punishment and reward, and the range of associated reactive attitudes (pride and shame, gratitude and resentment, contempt and admiration, etc.)—however impossible it may be to conceive of doing without it—is deeply ungrounded and ungroundable in anything we should be able to recognize as proper justification.[22] It is perhaps not even clear how culturally or historically specific the notion of moral responsibility might be—it is often alleged that no form of life which was recognizably human could manage without it, but without proper anthropological support I would be disinclined

---

[20] Williams (1985: 6–7).

[21] I shall come later to the very important question whether it is really determinism *per se* or rather some other thesis (such as, for example, the thesis that I think Williams means to gesture towards when he speaks of our fears about 'naturalistic explanations of action') that is really the problem.

[22] See, for example, Strawson (1986: Ch. 2) and Klein (1990) for arguments to the effect that this framework cannot properly be defended, whether or not determinism is true.

to take this claim merely on trust. If there are worries about whether we may justifiably apply our concept of *agency*, on the other hand, it is hard to see what they might be if they are not just the very worries about determinism (or the naturalistic explanation of action) with which the free will problem has traditionally been concerned. One can, of course, envisage the possibility of scepticism here too—eliminativism in the philosophy of mind is, I take it, a view which supposes that the concepts in terms of which we construct ourselves and other creatures as agents are (or eventually will be) brought into disrepute by the advance of the neurobiological sciences. But at least such scepticism as there may be in connection with agency arises only out of the very debates and controversies with which I intend in any case to be concerned, whereas moral responsibility is potentially vulnerable, so it seems to me, on multiple fronts. I am hoping, therefore, that it will be possible to leave moral responsibility safely to one side for the time being—and to focus directly on agency.

1.2 Determinism

'Determinism' traditionally meant *universal* determinism, the thesis that whatever happens anywhere in the universe (where 'whatever happens' is intended to cover not merely every event, but every aspect of every event—every state of affairs)[23] is necessitated by prior events and circumstances, in combination with the laws of nature.[24] But there are reasons for wondering whether this thesis really captures precisely enough what it is that we ought to be worrying agency might not be compatible with. One sign that it clearly does not do so is the fact that the free will problem has not simply disappeared as a result of the now fairly widespread acceptance by many philosophers and scientists that universal determinism is not true. No one supposes that the mere existence of, say, quantum level indeterminacies, would in and of itself lead to the dissolution of the free will problem. A related point one might make here is that a thesis rather weaker than universal determinism seems to present all the same problems for agency as its universal cousin. As Galen Strawson notes, commenting on the view that determinism is a *requirement* for freedom, 'even given a view according to which free actions must be determined, a few random events, or even a great many in the right (not in the wrong) places, would not do any harm to freedom of action or freedom of will'.[25] Likewise, then, for the incompatibilist, the problem would seem to be not so much universal determinism, but rather, at most, determinism in what Strawson calls 'the wrong places', the places, presumably, at which humans (or animals) undertake the activities constitutive of deliberation, choice, and action. It is only these things, it would seem, or perhaps some crucial subset of them, which the incompatibilist will require not to be determined inexorably by their antecedents.

---

[23] See Sorabji (1980), Introduction, p. ix, for the formulation in the brackets.
[24] Perhaps, it is sometimes uncomfortably added, with the exception of the Big Bang.
[25] Strawson (1986: 8).

It is worth asking, then, why anyone would suppose that the causal relationships involved in the generation of action, whatever they are, must be deterministic ones. Presumably, it is much less attractive than once it was to want to derive one's commitment to determinism in the realm of action merely from a quite general commitment to universal determinism, since it now seems over-bold, in the light of developments in physics, to suppose that any such general commitment can be safely maintained. So the deterministic convictions which one still finds so very prevalent in the free will literature must have other, and deeper, roots.

What are these roots? There is, I think, quite a range of sources for deterministic thinking about action. One such source is no doubt supplied by the idea that actions must be identifiable with bodily movements, or neural antecedents of bodily movements, or mereological sums of such things, together with the not unreasonable thought that the transmissions of causality which relate such things as these to one another must be deterministic. Causal theories of rational action, according to which an agent's strongest desire always prevails, provide further grist to the determinist's mill, as does the increasingly large body of empirical evidence which seeks to root the explanation of an ever larger proportion of the things human agents do in sub-personal phenomena such as hormonal levels or neurally-based predispositions. The huge success of molecular biology is another important factor, providing evidence, as it does, that at least some of the complex, higher-level phenomena associated with life in all its manifestations are susceptible to reductive explanation at the lower level represented by chemistry. It is really these ideas, I believe, about what actions and their antecedents *are*, about how they are to be causally explained, and about how biological phenomena in general ought to be thought of as relating to the simpler chemical and physical processes which in some sense or other indisputably underlie them, rather than any generalized commitment to determinism, that truly motivate the intuitions which keep compatibilism in business. And so it is to these theses that the incompatibilist who wishes to carry any conviction is going to have to look. It is not universal determinism *per se* which really constitutes the thing with which agency is most specifically in tension. It is rather a more localized variant of the thesis, born of a conception of agency itself as a phenomenon which must be neatly superimposable over, or at least very straightforwardly supervenient upon, the various intuitively lower-level and impersonally describable phenomena that we know have something very important to do with it, which generates the real problem. Chapters 6, 7, and especially 8 will each attempt, therefore, in a different way, to provide the elements of a challenge to this conception.

The fact that it does not seem necessary to presuppose absolutely *universal* determinism in order to create potential problems for agency is doubtless connected to the often-made observation that quantum indeterminacy, even if we grant it, seems not to *help* very much with the free will problem. It is apparently essential to a satisfactory indeterministic resolution of the free will problem not merely to make place for indeterminacy in the universe, but to make the *right* place for it. Some have tried to argue that making the right place for it is bound to be impossible, since no quantum-level indeterminacy could ever manage to surface in such a way that its effects might be manifest in such large things as our own actions and decisions.[26] And even if, as has sometimes been argued, micro-indeterminacies might be able to precipitate (by way, for example, of chaotic amplifications) indeterministic effects on the sort of scale which would seem to be required if agency is to be affected,[27] it might be said that it remains inevitably obscure how the possibilities left open by the micro-indeterminacies manage to coincide properly with such possibilities for choice as we might wish to have—how the 'openness' made possible by microphysical indeterminacy could translate into the sort of openness we need as agents. But if what I have said above about the real source of the problem of agency is correct, it should be unsurprising that the existence of quantum indeterminacy, by itself, is inadequate to make the problem disappear. It will certainly be insufficient, if that diagnosis turns out to be accurate (though it will, I think, still prove to be necessary), merely to replace a microphysically deterministic vision of the universe with a microphysically indeterministic one. For the problem lies as much with the conception of the relation between agency and the microphysical that is often involved in our thinking, as it does with the determinism. It is as much about the way in which we suppose the different levels of reality relate one to another, as it is about the idea that each momentary state of the universe inexorably necessitates the next. So microphysical indeterminism will 'help' with the problem only by removing one preliminary obstacle to the possibility of agency—the one that would be represented by the truth of an entirely universal determinism. It will not by itself supply the answer to the question how agency is possible. An answer to *that* question will require also an understanding of what could lead us to want to say that an *organism* rather than merely some part of one, or some process within one, has brought something about, and of how the causality thereby effected (the causality that is agency) relates to the causality involved in the sub-personal processes that make it possible.

This point has an important corollary. Supposing it does prove possible (as I hope it will) to argue successfully for the view that universal determinism is in conflict with the existence of agency, we will need to ensure that the *in*determinism one needs to posit, in order to escape the threat, is thought of, at any rate in the beginning, merely as the negation of the problematic thesis.[28] No positive conception of the indeterministic universe should be allowed to gain a foothold at this initial stage, unless it can prove its title to be the only one available. It may be tendentious to surmise immediately, for instance, that the wanted indeterminism must necessarily involve such suppositions as

---

[26] See, for example, Honderich (1988: Vol 1, Ch. 3) and Weatherford (1991: 114–15).

[27] For an admirable attempt to develop this suggestion in serious detail, see Kane (1996: Ch. 8).

[28] Cp William James (1968: 43): 'The sting of the word "chance" seems to lie in the assumption that it means something positive, and that if anything happens by chance, it must needs be something of an intrinsically irrational and preposterous sort. Now chance means nothing of the kind. It is a purely negative and relative term, giving us no information about that of which it is predicated, except that it happens to be disconnected with something else—not controlled, secured, or necessitated by other things in advance of its own actual presence.'

these: that all the motivational antecedents of some given φ-ing might have been in place, and yet the agent might, at the very instant at which she in fact φ-ed, have ψ-ed instead, or that humans have a special power to intervene between their reason-determined decisions to act and their initiations of action in such a way as to enable them to do something other than what could be plausibly justified and motivated by those desires and beliefs,[29] or that something it would be right to regard as randomness would have to be involved in the aetiology of action. For to assume any of these things may be unwittingly to import into the characterization of indeterminism ideas that are not in fact essential to it, and thereby cut ourselves off from what may be the best versions of libertarianism. The incredulity of compatibilists on contemplating the question how such suppositions as those above could ever help to establish that we have anything we could possibly want in the way of freedom is understandable. But it must be shown, before the compatibilist is allowed to prevail, that the mere denial of determinism in fact entails any of them.

Though I shall begin by offering my own answer to the question whether animal agency is compatible with strictly universal determinism, therefore, this will really be merely a preliminary to an extended discussion of what I regard as more important questions. I shall be interested in trying to understand the emergence of agency as a phenomenon in the natural world and to locate those features of it which seem particularly difficult to reconcile with deterministic visions of reality. And I shall be *especially* interested in trying to understand the challenges that the idea of indeterministic causal connections has been alleged to create for the possibility of agency. It is, as I have noted, a commonplace in discussions of the free will problem that it is just as difficult to see how indeterminism could be consistent with real agency as it is to see how determinism could consist with it. But if indeterminism is merely the denial of universal determinism, there are likely to be many and varied conceptions of the ways in which a universe might satisfy the description 'indeterministic'. I shall try to argue that it is not indeterminism *per se* that is in potential conflict with agency, but rather a particular *conception* of the indeterministic universe, which is by no means obligatory. I shall hope to suggest that there are alternative conceptions, and moreover that it is possible that some of these might be accurate conceptions of the universe we ourselves inhabit.

1.3 An argument against universal determinism

Here is an argument for the falsity of universal determinism.

1. If universal determinism is true, the future is not open.
2. If there are self-moving animals, the future is open.
3. There are self-moving animals.
4. Therefore, universal determinism is not true.

---

[29] See Strawson (1986: 51) for this formulation. I address the question how to avoid conceiving of the necessary indeterminism in this way in Chapter 6.

In the course of the next three chapters, I should like to develop an argument that has something like this basic form. Despite its apparent simplicity, its exposition and defence will not be a straightforward matter; indeed, to clarify it properly and render it invulnerable to objections will be a complex and time-consuming business. But before delving into the complexities, it may be useful to offer here, at the outset, a brief and informal elucidation of the nature of the thinking behind the argument in an attempt to make clear what the basic intuitions are which motivate the thinking behind it.

The two concepts utilized in the argument which most cry out for further elaboration and clarification are those of the 'open future' and of a 'self-moving animal'. To say that the future is 'open', as I shall use that phrase, is to say that more than one future is genuinely physically (and not merely epistemically)[30] possible, from the perspective of the present; that is to say, that there is more than one way, even granted the supposition that the laws of nature will remain constant, in which things might unfold from now on. Despite the fact that the concept of physical possibility (and the associated notion of a law of nature) is contentious, I suspect that its contentiousness would not prevent most philosophers from granting that there is at least some reasonable understanding of (1) on which it is true. Determinism is quite often directly characterized these days as the thesis that there is at any instant exactly one physically possible future,[31] and even when it is not thus characterized directly, it is usually described in such a way that it would not be a difficult matter to derive this thesis from the definition of determinism which is given, together with a suitable understanding of the notion of 'physical possibility'. The thesis that there is exactly one physically possible future can be regarded, I think, then, for present purposes, as equivalent to the thesis that the future is not open—and therefore (1) as a thesis with which there is little room to quibble. I shall, then, say no more about the idea of openness that is involved, supposing it to be sufficiently clear to get the argument off the ground.

The concept of a self-moving animal that is needed for the argument, though, is, by contrast, surprisingly difficult to characterize with sufficient precision to give the wanted *prima facie* plausibility to (2), the premise which expresses the thesis I call Agency Incompatibilism. For it might quite reasonably be asked why one should think that there is any relationship at all between self-movement and the open future. Surely there are all sorts of self-moving entities (cars? robots? planets?) whose operations have no particular tendency to subvert whatever confidence we might antecedently have had in

[30] It is a standard compatibilist idea that in so far as we are inclined to take it for granted that there is more than one possible future, it may perhaps be an epistemic notion of possibility that is really in play—that the relevant truth is really just that *for all we know* the future might unfold in any one of a number of ways. For this idea, see, for example, Dennett (1984: Ch. 6).

[31] See, for example, Van Inwagen (1983: 3) and Dennett (2003: 25).

determinism. Why should self-moving *animals* be different? What has the animal capacity for self-movement to do with indeterminism?

The notion of self-movement enters into the premise in the first place because there seems no reason to accord anything like agency to a creature which spends all or most of its life rooted to the spot, feeding only on what comes directly into contact with it, and reproducing asexually, say, or by means of the random release of sperm which are then carried on current or tide perhaps to meet one day by sheer good fortune with an appropriate egg. Sessile sponges, for instance, live the whole of their adult lives permanently rooted to a location in the water, obtaining nourishment and oxygen from water flowing constantly through thousands of tiny pores, and reproducing by a variety of means, none of which ever requires a sponge actively to seek out a mate. There seems to be nothing in the life of a sponge which ever requires anything like a plan or a choice, anything which we need to think of as an *action* on the part of a sponge. One might think, then, at first, of supposing that the capacities constitutive of agency must be restricted to self-moving animals, and moreover are required to be possessed by such self-movers.[32] But the trouble with this beautifully simply hypothesis is that there seem to be certain animals which might appear at first sight to qualify as self-movers, but do not appear to be much better candidates for agency than the sessile sponge. Consider a paramecium, for instance.[33] A paramecium is a single-celled animal, just visible to the naked eye, which propels itself through the water by means of cilia on the outside of its body, which beat very fast. If it encounters an obstacle, it backs up, turns, and then progresses forward until another stimulus is encountered. It prefers warmer temperatures and a slightly acidic environment, and will move away from cooler water and towards the acidic surroundings in which the bacteria on which it feeds are usually to be found. It is, I think, very natural to think that a paramecium is a self-moving creature. And yet it would be unsurprising to discover that its movement needed nothing more than a few fairly basic types of physico-chemical reactions to explain it. There are indeed, in the scientific literature, papers which suggest that fairly simple equations govern the relation between a few basic features of the paramecium's environment and the direction and speed of its movement.[34] No particular threat to determinism, surely, can lurk in the beating of its cilia and its engulfment of its bacterial prey.

If the concept of a self-moving animal is to be developed in such a way that it might come to bear weight in the argument against determinism, therefore, more must be said to elucidate the relevant conception of self-movement, and to distinguish it from the more basic concept of self-movement which applies unproblematically to such

---

[32] Although there would, of course, be room for debate about what constitutes a self-moving animal in the requisite sense, whether, for example, locomotion of the whole body from place to place is necessary or whether the controlled motion of a body *part* might be sufficient.

[33] Thanks to Rowland Stout for this example.

[34] See, for example, Glaser (1924) and Chase and Glaser (1930).

entities as robots and paramecia. On one intuitive understanding of self-movement, an entity is a self-mover if and only if it can move *by* itself—that is to say, without being pushed or pulled into motion by some sort of external source, in particular by another object. It is of course a difficult matter, in many cases, to decide what does and does not count as such an 'external' source. To take one example: a planet moves in its orbit without the need first to be impacted by any other body or to be dragged along on any kind of cord, and thus might be thought to move 'by itself'. But its orbit can be thought of as due to the gravitational 'pull', as we say, of the body being orbited, which might then be regarded as an external source of its motion. Reflection on such examples, indeed, might make one wonder whether one can really make the internal/external distinction perfectly clear, but it is not important for my purposes, in fact, to argue that this first conception of self-movement can be made entirely perspicuous. What I am talking about is an idea that plays a rather rough-and-ready role in our everyday thinking about the world, not one that can necessarily survive in the testing environment of modern (or even not so modern) physics. It is quite enough for my purposes if it can be conceded, at least, that we are able to make a crude division of entities into those that never appear to move from a position of rest except when made to do so by an external impetus of some sort (e.g. a rock, a table) and those that may do so (animals, and perhaps also robots and machines of various kinds).[35] The latter are self-movers in one perfectly usable and familiar sense.

But what is crucial for my purposes is that it is possible also to understand the idea of self-movement in a second, stronger way. On this second conception, an entity is a self-mover if and only if it is able to *make itself (or parts of itself) move*. And it is this second, stronger conception of self-movement that is needed for the argument. There can be entities which can move *by themselves* yet cannot *make themselves move*. The paramecium, I think, would be an example. It is a self-mover in the weaker sense, since its relation to its environment is not that of mere flotsam and jetsam—it is not merely buffeted about by the currents and eddies in the water in which it resides. It makes a contribution, of a kind, to its own progress through the world, in virtue of the fact that at least some important parts of the processes which cause it to respond to such things as obstacles, detected sources of light, food, warmth, etc. are internal to the cell that constitutes it. It is therefore a self-mover in the first, weak sense—it can move by itself. But, I would maintain, it does not make itself move. There is insufficient ground, in the case of a single-celled creature, to make the distinction that is a natural accompaniment to this second, stronger conception of self-movement, between the creature and its body, an entity to which the creature itself stands in the relation of controller and director.[36] Something that can make its body do various things must be a thing of

---

[35] Machines must, of course, usually be *switched on*, which might be thought to be a kind of external impetus. It is not important to me to insist that it is not.

[36] It may not be absolutely obligatory to accept the distinction between an animal and its body in order to make sense of this stronger conception of self-movement. (Indeed, if we take talk of self-movement literally,

which it at least makes sense to say that it 'has' a body—something that can reasonably be regarded as an 'owner' of its body.[37] And it is only of some sorts of entity that it makes sense to say that they 'have' bodies, thereby separating what is moved (a body or a body part) from what is doing the moving (an animal). It is these entities that are potentially sufficiently complex to sustain an owner/body distinction which I call 'agents' and the power of self-movement in question is the 'agency' which figures in Agency Incompatibilism. In their case, we seem faced with a kind of agency that belongs in a deeper way to the entity concerned such that the entity is no longer merely the thing that *houses* the relevant mechanisms of movement production, but is thought of as itself a crucial contributor to those mechanisms. The crucial determinant, for me, of whether a creature truly can be said genuinely to be a self-mover has to do with whether there is any irreducible role to be played in the explanation of that organism's motor activity by a certain kind of *integration* which I believe is part and parcel of the functioning of most animals of a certain degree of complexity, a type of integration which I shall be attempting to characterize towards the end of this book. This integration is missing from the paramecium. Although different factors can contribute to the explanation of the way in which a paramecium moves through the water (e.g. obstacles, temperature, acidity), the way in which these different factors combine to produce paramecium movement seems to require for its understanding nothing more complex than a kind of vector addition—temperature effects might produce a tendency to move in direction X, while acidity effects might produce a tendency to move rather in direction Y, and the resultant movement will be a simple function of these two inputs (or of those, together with some further relevant inputs). There is no need to suppose that the paramecium is anything but an *arena* for the playing out of these functional dependencies of its movement upon variations in these local environmental factors. It need not be thought of as making any contribution to what occurs in respect of the movement of its body which amounts to anything over and above that of the contribution of a few simple, chemically controlled processes occurring inside the cell which *is* its body. But the same, I shall argue, is not true with respect to those creatures I want to call true self-movers. Most animals of any appreciable degree of complexity, I shall argue, are possessors of a capacity for a kind of top-down determination of what will occur with respect to the movement of their

what the animal moves should really be the animal!) It is rather that the same types of complexity which justify the thought that the animal not only moves by itself but also makes itself move are the same types which make an animal/body distinction feasible and natural.

[37] It should not be—but probably is—necessary to say at this point that the kind of animal/body dualism on which I rely here needs to be sharply distinguished from Cartesian dualism. That animals are not to be identified with their bodies (because, for instance, they *move* their bodies while their bodies do not move them) has no tendency whatever to imply that animals consist of an immaterial soul together with a material body. I look to utilize a conception of the species terms which fall under the sortal 'animal' ('cow', 'dog', 'spider', etc.) that looks upon these terms rather as Strawson looks upon the concept of a person in his (1959), i.e. as a unified bearer of both psychological and material predicates, not a bipartite construction out of two distinct entities.

own bodies, in such a way that their contribution *does* amount to something over and above the contribution of the processes inside them which eventuate in the resulting bodily movements—and it is *these* creatures I mean to refer to when I say, in (2) above, that if there are self-moving animals, the future is open. My thesis, then, can be more accurately expressed as follows: that if there are things which can *make their bodies move*—i.e. agents—the future is open.

Which sorts of entity may be said to 'have' bodies, to be potentially distinct from them in a way which makes sense of this second, stronger conception of self-movement? Entities with a mind, it is tempting to say—and indeed, in a sense I think the question which entities have minds and which have bodies ought properly to be regarded as the very same question.[38] Only a creature which can have a mind—i.e. to which certain sorts of mental predicates can be applied—can really 'have' (own) a body—and *vice versa*. There is no *point* in the distinction between an entity and its body, without the correlative idea of that entity as an initiator, director, and discretionary controller of the movements of its body—otherwise, we default, and are right to default, to a one-object ontology without further ado. We do not think that rocks or tables have bodies. Nothing 'has' a body (except by analogy, as in the case of dolls, mannequins, humanoid-shaped robots, etc.) that we do not conceptualize as the owner also of a set of powers pertaining to that body. And the most crucial, the most basic member of the set of powers in question is the power of self-movement of which I am speaking—the power to make that body move in various ways, as we say 'at will'—a power which, I shall suggest in Chapter 4, involves at least the applicability of the rudimentary psychological ideas of a goal, an attempt and a subjective point of view on the world. This power of self-movement defines the class of willed entities, a class for which (rather extraordinarily) we have no ordinary word.[39] Children, I think, sometimes express their need for a word here when they say, for example, that a blackbird or a lion or a salmon is 'a person'. We know they are wrong to say this—the concept of a person is of course much too specific to apply comfortably to these sorts of animals. But we know what they mean, and there need be no foolish anthropomorphism involved in the thought. The claim represents a recognition that the conditions for making an owner–body distinction are satisfied in the case of these and many other animals—and what the claim reveals is the fact that the cognitive mechanisms which govern our application of concepts to things demand special recognition for these entities. I shall

---

[38] This is not to say, note, that having a mind is *merely* a matter of having the relevant power of self-movement. It is rather that having the relevant power of self-movement is a necessary condition of having any of the other powers that we think of as mental. For even what is normally thought of as pure thought involves the capacity to move parts of one's body (although these are parts one does not normally know about), e.g. to make certain neurons fire. And although I do not propose to defend the thesis here, I also believe that there are deep conceptual connections between perception and action, such that one can doubt that perceptual capacities would be available to a creature not able to move itself.

[39] As Frankfurt has observed (1971: 11).

have a good deal more to say in Chapter 4 about what these mechanisms are, and what we ought to make of the fact that they make the various demands upon us that they do.

If we ask the further question, which entities are such as to be self-movers in the relevant stronger sense which I have tried to characterize, I venture to suggest that the answer is: quite a large number of species of animal (though not all) and (at present) nothing else that we know of.[40] One might doubt this. One can imagine saying of a humanoid-shaped robot, for instance, that it was raising its arm or turning its head—that it was moving its body in various ways—thereby using the sort of propriety language we use in the case also of animal control of bodily motion. But I think we could be rapidly brought to agree, on reflection, that this is hyperbole—robots do not really 'have' bodies. A robot does not truly control its own body, though it might perhaps make a sort of sense to say that a *part* of the robot did so, for example the part which stored the programme according to which it functions. But robots do not have the sort of functioning we suppose many higher animals to have whereby execution of a great many of their own movements are conceived of by us as being *at their discretion*. Even if we can imagine building a 'choice module' into the design of a robot, so that its 'decisions', for example, concerning whether to go right or left at some particular juncture were tied to the outcome of some genuinely random event, that would have no tendency to imply that anything had been truly in the robot's power—for in the case of the robot there is nothing to *have* the power. We might say metaphorically, perhaps, that the decision whether to go right or left was 'up to' the choice module. But the choice module no less than the robot itself is not the sort of thing that something could really be up to. Things happen within it, and those happenings have certain effects, and that is all.

There will be those, of course, who will say that it is the same with us at the end of the day. But this I shall deny. It is not the same with us, and it is not the same with a great many other animals. And to say this is not, as is often assumed, merely to indulge in anti-naturalistic speculation on the basis merely of a foolish confidence in what introspection seems to tell us about the way in which we operate when we act—an inchoate sense that we 'could have done otherwise'. My suggestion, indeed, is not based primarily on the deliverances of introspection at all, but rather on some interesting features of the conceptual scheme we apply to animals, and reflection concerning the likely reasons why this scheme serves us so well. I shall be arguing for what I believe to be the naturalistically respectable view that the capacity for discretion which I shall be maintaining is the hallmark of true agency is an *evolved* capacity, crucially important for creatures which need to make decisions based on a very large number of complex

---

[40] It is no part of my claim that it is anything other than a contingent truth (if it is a truth at all) that only creatures which have a biological origin are self-movers in my strong sense. It is perfectly possible, for all I shall say, that true self-movers might eventually be produced by artificial means, and indeed that true self-movers of a non-biological sort already exist elsewhere in the universe. But I do assume that we do not *yet* know how to create them.

and often incommensurable factors, about how to distribute their efforts through space and across time, and how to respond as they move to a constantly changing environment. Deterministic programming could have been—but in fact is not—the way in which nature has solved the problem of how to provide a creature which needs to negotiate a very complex environment with the means to do so—and only the extraordinarily powerful grip of certain metaphysical ideas could have led us to think that there is really no properly conceivable alternative.

Much more, of course, needs to be said about what exactly it takes to be a self-moving animal in this more exiguous sense, and to rebut what is likely to be the natural objection that *no* creature can be capable of a truly top-down form of determination of its own movements—but it would be inappropriate to pre-empt the detailed arguments of later chapters at this stage. Rather, I shall content myself here with rehearsing some commonsense thoughts which, I think, are curiously absent from the current free will literature, in order to give some substance, colour, and, I hope, support to (2).

Here is a simple and, I think, attractive picture of what animal agency introduces into the universe. Where animal agents exist in a world, the unfolding of that world through time must wait upon decisions and choices[41] which have to be made by those animals—not just temporally, in that the effects of those decisions and choices can, naturally enough, only *follow* the prior occurrence of their causes—but also metaphysically. By this, I mean something like the following: nothing in the universe which exists prior to the period of time *t* in which a given animal undertakes the sequence of activity that is constitutive of a given process of acting by the animal can *determine* (that is, necessitate) precisely what the animal is going to do because precisely what will happen then is up to the animal, which has not yet acted. *Influence* is another matter— the idea that what an animal does bears no causal relation whatever to the state of the universe prior to the time of its acting would be a denial, so it seems to me, of the

---

[41] I do not mean to suggest, by using these words, that all intentional animal activity has to be preceded by a distinct event or process of choosing or deciding what to do, although doubtless some is. Deciding can be *constituted* by acting—and perhaps is always thus constituted in certain simpler animals, of which it might be implausible to suppose that they go in for anything that could be regarded as *prior* 'choosing' or 'deciding'. However, it should be borne in mind that ethologists and biologists appear to be increasingly happy with the attribution to relatively simple creatures of capacities for such things as choice, decision, and planning. I shall offer some considerations in Chapter 4 in support of the view that a picture of animal agency involving a certain sort of capacity for advance planning is very naturally thought of as applicable to animals that we are used to think of as relatively humble creatures, earthworms and spiders, for instance. I am disposed to believe, indeed, that these concepts are serviceable in connection with pretty much anything which is a self-moving animal in my strong sense, for they are concepts which come into their own in connection with creatures which must utilize environmental information in order to achieve their ends, by solving problems, to which there is not necessarily any unique best answer, about how to move through space. And that, roughly, is what my self-moving animals *are*. (I shall postpone the detailed argument for this claim until Chapter 4.) None of this need be to deny, though, that certain of these capacities take on a very special form in human beings because of the way in which they are integrated with such things as our powers of conceptualization and rationality, our moral sense and our vast potential for learning. It is only to insist that it can be worth thinking philosophically about what these capacities have in common with those possessed by non-human animals, as well as about the ways in which our powers outstrip theirs.

possibility that rationality should characterize any such activity.[42] All that is being claimed is that it is not true that everything relating to the relevant set of movements and changes in the animal's body is determinately *settled* by the universe prior to the time of the animal's activity, for at least some things have to be settled by the *animal* at the time of its period of activity, if it is to be an agent in respect of that activity at all. And the animal's decision might, for all that the unfolding of the universe (and its laws) thus far dictates, go in any one of a number of ways. Animals are therefore in a sense *originators* of certain chains of events because the initiation of those chains depends upon them, and so the chains in question cannot be deterministically extended back in time beyond the relevant period of the animals' activity (though it does not follow that chains of *causality* cannot be thus extended backwards, since causal relationships need not be deterministic).[43] Animals are true authors of their actions—not merely the loci at which certain deterministically caused events give rise to others.

To forestall any possible misunderstanding, let me say at once that I do not mean to suggest for a moment that animals (even humans) have any very grand capacity to transcend such things as the promptings of instinct. A deer is clearly not free not to run from a lion it has spotted running towards it, a spider not free not to bother with spinning any webs for a few weeks. It is utterly undeniable that all animal agency takes place within a framework which constrains, sometimes very tightly, what can be conceived of as a real option for that animal. (This is no less true of human beings than it is for other creatures—I am sure I could not, under the normal sorts of circumstances, jump off a cliff to my certain death or leave my children to starve). What I wish to insist upon is only that there is much flexibility *within* these constraints, even for very simple creatures, for such things as different orderings of the actions necessary to complete a complex task or set of such tasks, the taking of alternative spatial routes to a place, different chosen strategies for achieving a given goal, different timings (an animal can carry out some activity now instead of later, for instance, or later instead of now because it is enjoying basking in the sun at the moment)—different ways, in short, for an animal to go about its business, even if, broadly speaking, the nature of that business, in many respects, must be a given. Doubtless, the precise degree of flexibility which is possible depends upon the sophistication of the animal. The better its memory, its spatial awareness, etc., the more impressive are likely to be its abilities to organize itself according to a flexible schema. But what seems so implausible to me about *universal* determinism is that absolutely all these details of execution, down to the last wiggle, flap, and scamper, are supposed in principle to be fixed and settled already by the initial condition of the universe together with the laws of nature. This is

---

[42] Cp Timothy O'Connor's suggestion that the term 'unmoved movers' is less apt than 'not wholly moved movers' to describe what he called 'the commonsense view of ourselves as fundamental causal agents' (1995: 174). See Chapters 6–8 for further elucidation of how it might be possible to make sense of this idea of causal influence, without presupposing determinism.

[43] See Steward (2008) for some further reflections on this idea of origination.

only a datum and not an argument, but I find myself quite unable to believe that this is so—it is literally incredible.[44] It seems to me to be an utterly basic part of our everyday commonsense metaphysics that the universe is, as it were, loose at those places in it where animals act—that they are free, within limits, at those junctures, to make it unfold as they will. But if they are indeed free (within limits) to make it unfold as they will, it cannot also be true that there is at any instant only one physically possible future. Multiple futures must be available, if the alternative unfoldings which we all ordinarily believe that animals are able to produce are genuinely capable of happening.

I believe this is an appealing and commonsensical metaphysical picture of animal agency, and an appealing and commonsensical argument about what it entails in the way of indeterminism. It is, however, conspicuous only by its more or less complete absence from the contemporary philosophical literature. There is, to be sure, an increasingly vocal minority of so-called 'agent causationists', who are keen to insist that *human beings* are the authors of their actions in something like the way I have indicated above.[45] But the privilege is rarely (or never?) extended to other creatures; indeed, if anything, it appears to be regarded almost as a touchstone of the plausibility of agent-causal views that it *not* turn out, according to such views, that other animals are 'agent-causes'.[46] On my view, though, more or less exactly the opposite is true. If there is agent causation, then it had better be something that pertains to animals as well as humans, on pain of postulating an absurd and inexplicable discontinuity in the natural order.[47]

---

[44] Those who are in general inclined towards indeterminism may wonder whether the very same implausibility might not attach to events whose occurrence has nothing to do with agency—that it is just as hard to believe, for instance, that it has always been settled that the last leaf would fall from the crab-apple tree in my garden precisely at the time it did as that it has always been settled that I would, right at this moment type the letter 'r'. And being myself, in general, inclined towards indeterminism, I sympathize with the intuition that it is very hard, in fact, to believe of *most* events that their inevitable occurrence has been settled since the dawn of time. But the reasoning associated with these intuitions is, I think, somewhat different, and even more powerful, in the case of agency.

[45] Amongst the most prominent defences of agent causationism, one might mention Thomas Reid (1858), Roderick Chisholm (1966, 1971, 1976a,b), Richard Taylor (1966, 1992), Timothy O'Connor (1993, 1995, 1996, 2000), and Randolph Clarke (1993, 1996a). Agent causationism will be discussed further in Chapter 8.

[46] Timothy O'Connor, for example, who has done as much as anyone in recent years to articulate the agent-causal view, notes that 'the notion of a particular actively...bringing about an effect is intelligible only on the supposition that the particular be an agent capable of representing possible courses of action to himself and having certain desires and beliefs concerning those alternatives' and that 'this simple observation is sufficient to dismiss the derisive query of Watson...as to whether it is conceivable that spiders should turn out to be agent-causes in Chisholm's sense.' (1995: 197). But what justifies O'Connor's assumption that a spider is *not* capable of representing possible courses of action to itself, and having certain desires and beliefs concerning those alternatives? I shall argue in Chapter 4 that there is no reason not to suppose that a spider can perfectly well do some version of all these things.

[47] Of course, that there are important distinctions between human and other animals is incontrovertible. But there are more and less plausible places to locate these distinctions, and to suggest that event causation is somehow suspended altogether when a human being acts is what I judge—and I think many others would judge—hugely implausible.

What explains the absence of the kind of incompatibilist position I have briefly outlined from the philosophical scene? One explanation is to be found in the unfortunate legacy of behaviourism. Although I think we have, by and large, worked ourselves largely free of behaviouristic influences when it comes to thinking about the psychology of human beings, the same cannot be said for our thinking about animals. We have been encouraged to regard as unscientific and perhaps dangerously anthropomorphic conceptions of animals according to which they are cognitive beings, to be regarded, alongside us, as thinkers, planners, deliberators, etc. I shall consider and attempt to debunk this inheritance a little in Chapter 4. But another explanation stems from a feature of the philosophical literature on which I have already had occasion to remark—that is, its tendency to begin with a characterization of freedom which derives first and foremost from an idea about what it is we might *want* in the way of freedom if we are to salvage such notions as moral responsibility, creativity, dignity, and so on. That starting point is likely to make the brand of incompatibilism that I have tried to make seem appealing look peculiar, and perhaps beside the point. For it is likely to be said that such freedoms as I have highlighted here are worthless freedoms—that it is not much comfort to be told that one is free (within limits) to choose merely the detailed means to ends that are imposed by a complex mix of evolutionary and cultural factors, say. One wants to be able to choose between different kinds of *life*—not merely to choose, say, whether one will turn one's head to the left or the right to ease a stiffness in one's neck, or to scratch one's ear now rather than in a couple of seconds when one has finished typing the current sentence. But here I hark back to a point made previously. It may be true that there is nothing which, in and of itself, could satisfy our yearning to be, say, the creators and sustainers of our own ends and purposes, in a view of ourselves as animals determining merely the small and insignificant details of a picture whose broad outline is externally imposed. Such freedom as this is clearly not *sufficient* for anything like moral responsibility or dignity or creativity. A libertarian who wishes to show not only that moral responsibility is incompatible with determinism, and that determinism is false, but also that we *are* thus morally responsible, therefore, is going to have to add a great deal to what I have to say here if she is to justify that conclusion. But for all that, it is surely very plausible that this capacity to settle these details of how we shall move through the world is absolutely *necessary* in order for us to be in a position in the first place to have anything grander. If these very basic powers are inconsistent with universal determinism, as I believe they are, then it is certain that the more impressive powers to which we might also hope to aspire are also inconsistent with it. This book, then, aims at a 'metaphysics for freedom' only in the sense that it aspires to provide a view about some of the conditions necessary for the phenomenon of action, surely a prerequisite for the existence of such phenomena as responsibility, creativity, origination, etc. It does not attempt the more ambitious task of explaining what might constitute *sufficient* conditions for the applicability of these more sophisticated and demanding notions, nor does it have ambitions to show that such sufficient conditions are in fact instantiated.

Is it possible to offer something that looks more like an *argument* for the view that animal agency implies an open future, rather than merely to *say* that it does? At this point, it is necessary to face the fact that I need to combat two quite different types of opponent, if this claim is to be made out successfully. One is, of course, the compatibilist, who will want to say that even *human* agency does not imply a future that is open *in the requisite sense*. The compatibilist will insist that even if it is true that there is some sense in which the existence of agency implies that the future is open, it is not the sense given by the notion of physical possibility—that the future can perfectly well be open relative to one conception of possibility, but closed relative to others—and that it is a confusion to suppose that the sense in which futures must be open if there are to be self-moving animals is a sense which requires the falsity of universal determinism. The other type of opponent, on the other hand, might well concede that specifically *human* agency requires the falsity of determinism. However, he or she will not allow that any of the phenomena found in the rest of the animal kingdom are sufficiently impressive to motivate incompatibilism with respect to their activities.

It seems inadvisable to try to fight simultaneously on two fronts at once. I intend, therefore, to postpone until Chapter 4 the considerations with which I hope to persuade the second of these types of opponent that they have underestimated our animal relations. For now, then, I wish to leave on one side the issue of whether it is animals in general, or merely *human* animals, whose nature implies the falsity of universal determinism. I shall begin, therefore, by considering what may be said in favour of the weaker claim that at any rate, the existence of *human beings*, with their characteristic abilities and capacities to act, implies the openness of the future. I shall look at what I think is currently probably regarded as the best argument there is for a conclusion of something like this sort—the argument which has come to be known as the Consequence Argument.[48] I shall suggest, as others have done, that this and other similar arguments in the literature[49] cannot be regarded as decisive—it is fairly clear, in general terms, how the compatibilist must respond to them. However, I shall also try to make a suggestion about where the incompatibilist might turn in order to try to articulate a line of argument that might provide fewer opportunities for resistance than the Consequence Argument itself, an argument that does not make what I regard as the crucial concession made by the Consequence Argument, that agency *per se* is consistent with determinism.

---

[48] See Van Inwagen (1983).
[49] For similar arguments, see Ginet (1966), Wiggins (2003), and Lamb (1977).

2

'Up-to-Usness', Agency, and Determinism

In the last chapter, I suggested an argument for the falsity of universal determinism, which went as follows:

1 If universal determinism is true, the future is not open.
2 If there are self-moving animals, the future is open.
3 There are self-moving animals.
4 Therefore, universal determinism is not true.

In this chapter and the next, I want to explore further what can be said in justification of the crucial second premise of this argument. As explained at the end of the previous chapter, I intend to leave until later my discussion of the extent to which non-human animals share with human beings the powers that (on my view) make difficulties for determinism. In these next two chapters, then, I should like to discuss *in general* the question why the capacity to make oneself move might be thought inconsistent with determinism, without as yet making specific claims about whether animals, as well as humans, might be thought to possess the relevant capacity.

The idea that I think is at the intuitive heart of the particular conception of self-movement that we require for the defence of premise (2) is that of some matter—in particular here, some matter pertaining to the distribution and arrangement of at least some of its bodily parts—being 'up to' a given creature or system. It has become something of a commonplace in the philosophy of mind that we can make the philosophically hugely important distinction between conscious and non-conscious beings by reference to the idea that there is 'something it is like to be' a conscious being—something it is like 'from the inside'. But the conscious/nonconscious divide is not the only one that is of crucial metaphysical importance to the philosophy of mind. The agent/nonagent divide is another equally significant, though less often examined distinction. My suggestion is that the idea of 'up-to-usness' might be used to play the same sort of role with respect to the philosophy of agency that 'what-it-is-like-to-be-ness' has come to play with respect to the philosophy of consciousness—that is, that it is an everyday locution, which, despite its everydayness, serves rather well to capture something quite crucial about the distinctions we make between different sorts of entity. Agents are entities that things can be up to—and that there are such things is a crucial assumption of our conceptual scheme.

It is very natural to think that nothing is ever really 'up to' a car or a robot or a planet—that their movements and the other changes which occur within them are entirely dictated by the way things are locally in various respects just prior to the time of that movement or change, together with appropriate laws of nature—or at any rate, if their movements are not entirely so dictated (because, for example, the laws in question are probabilistic only), the eventual result is, to that extent, a chance matter, not something which is truly up to the individual entity in question. Planets do not what they will but what they must, and likewise, we tend to think, for many other varieties of inanimate entity. It is true that some of the complicated objects of human design can *mimic* the self-directedness one finds exemplified in higher animals—a robot might *look* as though it were deciding or choosing where to go—and we might well even find it very useful to speak of it in these ways, as Dennett has emphasized.[1] But I think we have great difficulty taking seriously the idea that anything could truly be up to a robot—or at any rate, to any robot of the kinds with which we are currently familiar. Certain outcomes indeed may *depend* on the way things are with the robot at a given moment, but this sort of dependence is insufficient to qualify the robot as the sort of thing that something could be 'up to'—as argued in the previous chapter, it is not a self-mover in the relevant sense, because it *is* its body—it does not *have* one. But that things are up to *persons* is a mainstay of our conceptual scheme. I shall be arguing in Chapter 4 that the idea that things are up to many kinds of animal is also a mainstay of that conceptual scheme, even if it takes work to persuade people that they might be committed to a scheme the implications of which they claim to reject. But for now, I shall focus on human persons, about whom agreement should be easier to reach.

A compatibilist will be likely to think that the idea that certain things are up to us, though correct, has nothing in particular to do with the claim that the future is metaphysically open. She will tend to suppose that something's being up to someone is a matter merely of that thing's being causally dependent on such things as her desires or choices or intentions. She will claim that this is an idea we have no difficulty making sense of within the confines of a perfectly deterministic model of the world, according to which actions are the causal upshots of such prior mental events and states. But in the present chapter and the next, I want to challenge this compatibilist take on the idea of 'up-to-usness'. For a start, I shall argue that an outcome need not be dependent on such things as anyone's desire, choice, or intention for it to be up to a given person whether or not it occurs—there are instances of agency, I claim, and hence instances of outcomes that are 'up to the agent' such that it is implausible to suppose that any desire, choice, or intention (or anything similar) on the part of that agent has caused that outcome. And this implies that, although it is true that where a creature is such that

[1] Dennett (1971, 1987).

various outcomes may depend on its desires, choices, intentions, etc., it must be the sort of creature that things can be 'up to', the connection between the influence of psychology and the exercise of agency is not the simple reductive one that the compatibilist tends to suppose. Being an agent in respect of some particular action, that is, cannot simply be a matter of possessing certain internal states that bring about some relevant type of bodily movement 'in the right kind of way'. For it is simply not necessary, in order that some question or matter be up to me, that I should want a given outcome or intend it or choose it. What I have to be able to do, I shall argue, is to *settle* that matter. And moreover, from this necessary condition flows the argument we need to make the connection between agency and the open future. Since I cannot settle what is *already* settled, it is only if the future is open that I can be an agent at all.

I am not, of course, the first person to have spotted the enormous fertility of the idea of 'up-to-usness', nor the first incompatibilist to have supposed that the idea might be made to bear some weight in an argument for incompatibilism. Indeed, the idea of 'up-to-usness' is at the heart of what is arguably the most important argument for incompatibilism in the literature—the Consequence Argument. In the next section of this chapter, therefore, I shall need to consider this argument. I shall argue, as many others have argued, that it does not establish its conclusion beyond reasonable doubt; it is clear enough what the compatibilist ought to say in response. However, in the remainder of the chapter, beginning with some reflections on where the Consequence Argument may have gone wrong, I try to develop my own argument for Agency Incompatibilism—the view that agency itself is inconsistent with determinism.

2.1 Van Inwagen and the Consequence Argument

Van Inwagen summarizes the informal thinking behind the Consequence Argument as follows.

If determinism is true, then our acts are the consequences of the laws of nature and events in the remote past. But it is not up to us what went on before we were born, and neither is it up to us what the laws of nature are. Therefore, the consequences of these things (including our present acts) are not up to us.[2]

Van Inwagen does not, of course, wish to draw the conclusion of this argument; rather, it is intended as a *reductio* of the supposition that determinism is true. The idea is that since our present acts *are* up to us, determinism must be false. In one important respect, then, Van Inwagen's argument uses an idea that connects it to mine—the idea that up-to-usness is inconsistent with determinism. But note that Van Inwagen appears to concede that the truth of determinism would not rule out the existence of 'our acts'. It is just that those acts would not, if determinism were true, be 'up to us'. The peculiarity of the idea that there might be such things as 'our acts', which yet were not 'up to us', is

---

[2] Van Inwagen (1983: 86).

one to which I shall later return, for I believe it holds the key to seeing how to present a better argument for incompatibilism than the one Van Inwagen provides.

Van Inwagen offers three different formal versions of the Consequence Argument. For brevity's sake, I shall consider just one version here—what he calls the Third Argument—in order to explain why I am so tentative about what can be hoped for from it in the way of conclusive reasoning. The Third Argument involves a modal operator 'N', where 'Np', Van Inwagen tells us, can be thought of as reading 'no one has, or ever had, any choice about whether p'. Van Inwagen suggests that the following two inference rules ought to be valid rules of any plausible logic for 'N':

(α) $\Box p \vdash N p$
(β) $N(p \supset q), N p \vdash N q$

'P_0' is used as an abbreviation for a sentence expressing the proposition that gives what Van Inwagen calls 'the state of the world' at some arbitrarily determined time T_0, which is specified, however, to be earlier than the birth of any agent in whose activity we might be interested. For the purposes of the Third Argument, it is easiest to assume that T_0 is a time prior to the birth of any agents. 'L' is an abbreviation for a sentence expressing the proposition constituted by the conjunction of all the laws of nature. 'P' serves as a dummy for which one can substitute any sentence one likes that expresses a true proposition. The Third Argument now proceeds as follows:
If determinism is true, it follows that:

(1) $\Box(P_0 \ \& \ L \supset P)$,

i.e. that it is a necessary truth that the truth of P is implied by the truth of P_0 and L together. From (1), we may deduce that

(2) $\Box(P_0 \supset (L \supset P))$

by elementary modal and sentential logic. Applying rule (α) to (2), we can derive:

(3) $N(P_0 \supset (L \supset P))$.

We now introduce the premise:

(4) $N P_0$,

which is presumably true, since no one has or ever had any choice about whether P_0 is true, it being a sentence expressing a proposition about the state of the world at a time before there were any agents. From (3) and (4), together with rule (β), we can obtain:

(5) $N(L \supset P)$.

We then introduce a second premise:

(6) NL,

which is also very plausible, since it seems true that no one has, or ever had any choice about whether the laws of nature are true. Then from (5) and (6), together with (β), we obtain:

(7) NP.

If it is sound, this argument shows that if determinism is true, then no one has ever had any choice about anything, since any sentence that expresses a true proposition can stand in for 'P'. Roughly, the idea is that since no one has ever had any choice either about what the laws of nature are, nor about what the state of the world was at any time before there were agents, no one can ever have had any choice about any of the necessary consequences of these things either. Suppose, for instance, we let 'P' be 'Helen Steward went for a bike ride on 5 March 2006', which is a true sentence. If determinism is true, then I can derive, by means of the argument above, the conclusion that 'no one had, or ever had, any choice about whether Helen Steward went for a bike ride on 5 March 2006', since, according to determinism, this is a necessary consequence of the laws of nature together with the state of the universe at T_0, a time before there were any agents. But this seems absurd—surely Helen Steward, at least, had such a choice. By *reductio*, therefore, it cannot be that determinism is true, since that supposition leads to an obviously false conclusion.

Like Van Inwagen, I find this line of reasoning intuitively very persuasive. But the trouble with the argument—and also with others of the same ilk—is that compatibilists are likely to deny that Rule (β) has to be accepted. Slote, for example, has argued that certain kinds of necessity may possess a feature that he calls *selectivity*, which results in the relevant operator's failing to be agglomerative (that is, it fails to sustain the inference from 'Np' and 'N($p \supset q$)' to 'N($p. \, p \supset q$)' (which is a sub-inference needed for the move from 'Np' and 'N($p \supset q$)' to 'Nq') and failing also to be closed under entailment (which is the other sub-inference needed for the move from 'N($p. \, p \supset q$)' to 'Nq').[3] Slote furnishes a number of examples of notions that have sometimes been thought of as types of necessity, and which will not sustain either inference principle due to the phenomenon that he calls 'selectivity'. Obligation is alleged to be one—Slote argues that it is not agglomerative because although one can be obliged to φ and also obliged to ψ (since, for example, one has promised to do both these things), one is not necessarily obliged to (φ & ψ)—since obligations are owed to particular persons and there need be no one to whom the obligation to (φ & ψ) is owed. There is perhaps room for debate about whether Slote is correct about the nonagglomerativity of obligation—does the fact that obligations are owed to particular persons really stand in the way of its agglomerativity?—but Slote certainly seems correct to insist that the obligation operator fails closure: it does not seem to follow from the fact that I am under an obligation to φ, together with the fact that φ-ing entails that I meet some

---

[3] Slote (1982).

other condition, that I am under an obligation to meet that other condition. For instance, Slote argues, if I promise to meet you at 3 o'clock tomorrow, I do not seem also to be under an obligation to you to stay alive until tomorrow. If I die tomorrow before 3 o'clock, I shall fail to fulfil my promise to meet you—but surely I have not, additionally, failed to fulfil a second, separate obligation to stay alive until then.

Another notion that displays the same recalcitrance, slote argues, is the interesting notion of nonaccidentality. From the fact that it is not an accident that A is at the well and the fact that it is not an accident that B is there, it does not follow that it is not an accident that A and B are there *together* (so agglomerativity fails). And it does not seem to follow from the fact that it is no accident that I am, for example, in a certain place right now (my boss sent me to Glasgow on business), together with the fact that my being in that place entails that I am not somewhere else (e.g. Edinburgh), that it is no accident that I am not in that other place (my boss tossed a coin to decide which of the two Scottish representatives of the firm I was to visit), so closure fails, too.[4]

Others have also argued against Rule (β) by way of a challenge to agglomerativity. McKay and Johnson offer the following counterexample.[5] Suppose I have a coin that was not tossed yesterday. But I was able to toss it yesterday, and no one else was. Suppose, moreover, that if I had tossed it, it might have landed heads and it might have landed tails—and it would have had to land in one or other of these ways since we exclude its being caught and not landing at all, its landing on its side, etc. In this case, I would have had no choice about which way it landed. Hence, it seems natural to endorse both:

N The coin did not land 'heads' yesterday; and
N The coin did not land 'tails' yesterday.

But the proposition

N (The coin did not land 'heads' yesterday and the coin did not land 'tails' yesterday)

seems false. I did have a choice about whether the conjunctive proposition is true—since I could, by tossing the coin yesterday, have rendered it false. This seems then to be a counterexample to Rule (β), and indeed Van Inwagen has conceded that it is so.[6]

The trouble, is, however, that it seems to be quite easy to avoid the counterexample by utilizing a different understanding of the operator 'N'. What is needed, as O'Connor argues, is a notion of 'having a choice about whether p' that applies even in a case where, though one does not have reliable control over whether p, one at least has open to one the possibility of acting in such a way that p *might* then obtain.[7] For example, to take a case offered by Van Inwagen, we need an understanding of Np on which it

---

[4] Interestingly, I shall have reason to exploit these features of the notion of nonaccidentality in a central argument of this book—see Section 8.8.
[5] McKay and Johnson (1996). Similar examples are offered in Widerker (1987) and Vihvelin (1988).
[6] Van Inwagen (2000).   [7] O'Connor (2000: 11)

would be false in the following case: someone's life depends on a coin's landing 'heads' (p = the coin did not land 'heads') and I simply don't toss it. That is a case in which I *did* have a choice about whether p in the relevant sense, for I could have tossed the coin and, if I had, it *might* have then landed 'heads'. The correlative notion of having *no* choice about whether p is then correspondingly strong: an agent at a time t has no choice about whether p if and only if there is no possibility for that agent to act at t in such a way that p *might* then be rendered false. But this interpretation of 'N' should be unproblematic as far as the argument against determinism is concerned, since all such propositions are thought by the incompatibilist to be things about which no agent has any choice in just this strong sense. This understanding of N seems sufficient to protect Rule (β) against the suggested counterexample.

It cannot be said, then, that Slote or anyone else has managed to establish that Van Inwagen's argument is invalid (given a suitable reading of the operator 'N'). But we have at least been given some reasons to wonder how much faith to place in Rule (β). Slote has offered examples of plausible instances of various sorts of necessity that flout principles akin to Rule (β), in order to 'weaken the feeling of inevitability and obviousness that...initially attends the modal principles used in the recent arguments for incompatibilism'.[8] He has tried to present a framework within which to understand the failure of principles like (β)—the framework provided by his notion of 'selectivity'—and into which the failure of (β) itself, it is alleged, can be fitted. And that seems enough, at least, to have cast doubt on Van Inwagen's Third Argument. Slote has not of course *established* that Van Inwagen's argument is invalid; and neither, as I have argued, have McKay and Johnson. But I think it can reasonably be claimed that neither has Van Inwagen established that it *is*. The result, I believe, is a rather frustrating stalemate.

Very similar conclusions have been reached by others who have reflected upon the various versions of Van Inwagen's Consequence Argument and similar incompatibilist arguments in the literature. Kane, for example, discussing the first of Van Inwagen's three arguments for incompatibilism (which makes use of the idea of rendering a proposition false) and objections to it by Lewis[9] and Fischer,[10] concludes that the result is an impasse, which can only be broken by looking more deeply into the intuitions that lead compatibilists and incompatibilists to disagree about the meanings of *can* and *power*.[11] Gary Watson, also considering this argument in the light of Lewis's objections that there are alternative strong and weak readings of the claim that you can render false a proposition about the past or about the laws, concludes that 'there is room for the reasonable suspicion that the argument trades on these different readings',[12] which suggests that he, too, regards the matter as essentially unresolved. It does not seem as though we will make further progress merely by poring over the details of the Consequence Argument. Everything depends on whether we have reason to accept

---

[8] Slote (1982: 22).   [9] Lewis (1981).   [10] Fischer (1983).
[11] Kane (1996: 52).   [12] Watson (1987: 178).

the inference rules on which it trades, and this is itself a matter that does not seem likely to be resoluble by means that are clearly independent of the very claims at issue.

I mentioned earlier, however, that Van Inwagen's summary of the thinking behind the Consequence Argument had a curious feature. The curious feature was that in Van Inwagen's view, determinism would imply that our acts would not be up to us. Presumably, Van Inwagen takes it for granted that there are such things as 'our acts'; the question with which he is concerned is merely whether or not these acts are or are not 'up to us'. But this, I want next to argue, is quite the wrong way of looking at the matter. If nothing is up to us, then there simply are no such things as actions. If the universe is merely a series of inexorably unfolding events, in which everything that is to happen is settled from the start, it leaves no room for actions. Actions, I shall argue, are things which, of their very nature, cannot be the inexorable consequence of what has gone before.

I shall begin by saying something about the conceptions of action and of agency that will be at the heart of my discussion, for the appeal of Agency Incompatibilism is often missed, I think, because many philosophers are operating from the start with an inadequate idea of action. I shall then lay out my argument for the claim that agency is inconsistent with universal determinism, before going on to try to clarify its central concept: the difficult and crucially important concept that I shall call 'settling'. When an agent acts, I shall suggest, various matters are thereby *settled* by that agent at the time of action. This concept bears close relations to others that are often found in the free-will literature: the idea I have already mentioned of something being 'up to' an agent, for instance, and also the concept of 'determination' as it is used by R. E. Hobart, for example, when he claims that for an action to come from the self it must be determined *by* the self whether or not that action will occur.[13] But I prefer 'settling' to these other concepts, for reasons that will become clear. I shall explain shortly one particular ontological confusion that can arise in connection with the idea of something's being 'up to' someone; the concept of 'determination' is, I think, especially dangerous because of its etymological connections with the concept of determin*ism*. This etymological relation encourages the thought that when we speak of an *agent's* determining something we are using the concept of determination in the same sense as we use it when we speak of a set of circumstances or events determining (i.e. necessitating) an outcome. That idea can make it seem as though there is a quicker route than is really available to the conclusion that the purposes of freedom and rational action are best served by a deterministic world. I shall try to show in a later chapter, indeed, how this etymological relation has served the purposes of one kind of

---

[13] Hobart (1934). The concept of settling, as I shall use it, is also a close relative of the operator that Belnap, Perloff, and Xu (2001) call the 'stit' ('sees to it that') operator, which they use in laying out their formal theory of agents and choices in branching time.

fallacious argument for the view that freedom is not only compatible with determinism but requires it.[14]

Having clarified the concept of settling, which is at the heart of my main premise, I shall then move on, in Chapter 3, to examine what I imagine will be the two main forms of objection to the argument that I base on that premise. The first kind of objection simply denies that there is any sense one can give to the claim that all actions are settlings of matters by agents such that the claim comes out true on that reading. The second, by contrast, proposes that although it is true, as I claim, that there is a sense in which all actions involve the settling of certain matters by agents, this is a claim that can perfectly well be accommodated by the determinist, so that the inference—from the claim that actions are settlings to the conclusion that universal determinism cannot be true—is faulty. I shall try to show that neither kind of objection can, in the end, be sustained. By the end of Chapter 3, then, I shall hope to have provided a strong argument for supposing that universal determinism is false. Later chapters will consider and respond to two reasons for thinking that however plausible the argument may look, there must be something wrong with it. The first alleges this on the ground that no argument of the kind I have attempted to supply can be possible, because universal determinism is a basically empirical thesis that no armchair philosopher should presume to defeat. The second insists, rather, that the conclusion of the argument cannot be squared with what we know already about the place that agency must have in the natural world.

2.2 Actions and agency

Before embarking on my argument, which attempts to show that agency is inconsistent with determinism, it will be necessary to say something about what I shall mean when I speak of an 'action'. As suggested earlier, for me, an agent is an entity that has a body and can make that body move in various ways[15] and, correlatively, an action is an exercise of this power to make the body (or particular parts of the body) move. But a number of clarifications are in order. The first is that this focus on the body does not mean that I ignore so-called 'mental' actions, such as those performed when one obeys an instruction to form a mental image of the Eiffel Tower or to mentally add 24 and 38. For it is plausible, I believe, that these too are exercises of an agent's power to make parts of the body move, although it may not be obvious to the agent that this is what

---

[14] See Section 6.4.2.

[15] I do not defend here my large and controversial assumption that an agent must be embodied. Many will doubt that this is so. They will insist that whether or not we are right to suppose that any immaterial entities exist, we can at least make sense of the idea of an immaterial entity. I suspect this is not in fact so: what appears to make sense when one is not thinking very hard can be seen to make very much less sense when one is. But it would take me too far away from my central concerns here to examine the arguments for thinking that the idea of an entirely immaterial agent falls to pieces on closer inspection. There is a beautiful summary of some of them at the beginning of Chapter 25 of Ayers (1991: 278).

they are.[16] When one actively thinks or undertakes mental operations of any kind, one exercises a power to effect movements and changes in one's own brain (although one need not be aware that the action has such a description). It is true that the *structure* of mental agency is somewhat different from that of bodily agency.[17] But in essence, I do not think there is any difficulty in extending to mental actions, which are in fact at the same time bodily actions, the account of bodily agency that I shall give.

Another very important point is that the fact that an agent's actions are movings of that agent's body does not imply that actions are bodily movements, as that claim is frequently interpreted. Hornsby (1980) offers the tools we need to disambiguate the notion of a movement in such a way that we can be clear about which kinds of movements actions may be identified with, and which kinds it is imperative to distinguish them from. Hornsby points out that many English verbs, of which 'move' is one, occur both transitively and intransitively, in such a way that the two sorts of occurrence are systematically related to one another. For example, someone can move something (a chair, their leg); and when that person moves that thing it moves as a result. Hornsby uses the subscripts '$_T$' and '$_I$' to differentiate these two different kinds of verb-use and then notes that there is a resulting ambiguity in certain noun-phrases deriving from these special verbs. If, for example, I refer to 'the melting of the chocolate' it may not be clear whether I am talking about the melting$_T$ of the chocolate, which was a person's doing of something (the 'melting' which is derived from nominalization of the verb in the base sentence 'She melted$_T$ the chocolate') or the melting$_I$ of the chocolate which is something that, as it were, merely happened to the chocolate as a result of its being melted by the person or other agent (the 'melting' that is derived from nominalization of the verb in the base sentence, 'The chocolate melted$_I$'). The word 'movement' may demonstrate a similar ambiguity; when we speak of someone's bodily movement, it may be unclear whether we mean to speak of a movement$_T$ (their moving of their body or, equivalently, their causing of their body to move) or the movement$_I$ that results from this. But if actions are to be identified with bodily movements, it can only possibly be movements$_T$ of which we are speaking or, as I shall sometimes say, *movings*. Actions cannot be identified with bodily movements$_I$ for bodily movements$_I$ are not doings, they are rather the results or effects of such things. The argument for this conclusion is given by Hornsby:

---

[16] Indeed, the unobviousness of the fact that this is what they are may help to contribute to the thought that we can make sense of the idea of a non-embodied agent.

[17] In particular, mental actions do not seem to have 'results' in the technical sense of that word, where 'a result is a change of a sort an instance of which is logically required for an action of the kind in question to have occurred at all' (McCann, 1974). Thus for instance, it is logically required that my arm rise if I am to raise my arm. But while there are doubtless all sorts of events that must occur if I am to mentally add 24 and 38, none stands in the same sort of logical relation to my act of mental addition as my arm's going up stands to my act of raising my arm. ('24 and 38's being added' seems to refer most naturally only to the action *itself*—to their being added by me, as it were—not to a *result*. And '24 and 38 are added' is indeed a result, but it is a result that is a fact and not an event).

The sort of answer we expect to the question 'What did he do?' is not 'His body moved' ('His arm rose', 'His knee bent') but rather 'He moved his body' ('He raised his arm', 'He bent his knee'). It is the same when we go beyond the agent's body to describe his action: what he did, we say, was melt_T the chocolate; and we cannot say that what he did was the chocolate melted_I. So it appears that if there is to be any hope of truth in an identification of actions with bodily movements, then they must be movements_T, not movements_I, that are actions.[18]

It will already be apparent, I think, from the stress I have already laid on the concept of bodily movement, that on the question of action individuation, I adopt (broadly speaking) the Anscombe–Davidson approach,[19] according to which when an agent φ-s by ψ-ing, her φ-ing may normally be identified with her ψ-ing; that is, there is one action with a variety of descriptions, at least one of which will generally be a description in terms of the agent's moving of her own body or a part of it ('Her raising of her arm', 'Her crooking of her finger', etc.). For example, I shall assume that, when an agent turns on a light by flicking a switch her turning on of the light is to be identified with her flicking of the switch and that both of these can in turn be identified with the agent's moving of her finger. But I shall not make what is the very common additional assumption of the Anscombe–Davidson view that an action has to be intentional under at least one of these descriptions (nor that an action has to be done 'for a reason'). It might, of course, be perfectly legitimate to adopt, for certain philosophical purposes, a conception of action which *did* limit the class to those movings that can be regarded as identifiable with intentional doings. However, for reasons that I hope will become clear in due course, I am seeking a conception of action that is broader than this.

It might be thought that the reason I am seeking this broader conception of action is that I am looking for an account of agency on which it can be accorded to animals, but in fact that is not the reason. I shall be arguing later that animals, even quite lowly ones, no less than humans do various things intentionally, so the Anscombe–Davidson conception of action would certainly not present any automatic bar to their inclusion in the class of agents. It is rather that the concept on which I shall centrally rely—the concept of settling—can be more readily disambiguated and seen for what it is in a context in which it is being allowed that there are certain actions that are not intentional under any description at all— 'sub-intentional' actions, as O'Shaughnessy calls them.[20] Thus, when I absent-mindedly scratch my head, slightly shift position in my chair, or jiggle my foot as I type, I shall count as having acted on the conception of action in which I am interested, for although I am doing none of these things intentionally, it seems right to say that they are all movings of my body *by me*—the owner–body distinction applies. They therefore count as settlings by me, I shall claim, of how matters are to be in respect of my body at certain times, despite the fact that

---

[18] Hornsby (1980: 3).   [19] See Anscombe (1957) and Davidson (1971).
[20] O'Shaughnessy (1980, Volume 2, Chapter 10).

they are not movements that are intentional under any description whatever.[21] What this claim comes to, given that I am not involved in the production of the relevant bodily movements$_1$ as *intender* of those movements, will of course have to be examined; this task will be undertaken in the next chapter.

2.3 The argument: agency is inconsistent with universal determinism

The idea that our actions themselves—our movings of our bodies—are things that *had* to occur, something that is an evident consequence of determinism in at least *some* important sense of 'had to' is, I submit, an idea that is in extreme tension with what we ordinarily think about them. It is easy not to feel the full impact of this tension if one is thinking of actions as bodily movements$_1$, for of course there is nothing immediately peculiar about the idea that events of *this* sort might be determined by certain antecedents. Indeed, it is our normal assumption that such things *are* determined (at any rate, in the absence of external interference) by certain antecedents: neural firings, muscle contractions, etc. That is one reason it is so important to be clear from the start that actions are *not* bodily movements$_1$. But once we are clear that it is not these of which we are speaking when we speak of actions, but rather that we are speaking of bodily *movings*—of causings of movements which are *by us*—the tension becomes readily palpable. It is a tension that is recognized, of course, by the incompatibilist who worries that determinism is inconsistent with the claim that the agent *could have done otherwise*. But the incompatibilist who puts his worry in this way often appears at the same time to concede a claim that is, by my lights, unacceptable; that is, that there could still be such things as agents, and such events as their intentional doings of various things, under the assumption of determinism. Though the agent could not have done *otherwise*, if determinism is true, it is generally conceded by the incompatibilist that she could, all the same, have *done*: that she could have acted. Recall, for instance, Van Inwagen's informal presentation of the Consequence Argument. For ease of reference I reproduce it here:

---

[21] It might be said (and was said by a reviewer for OUP) that without the concept of intention, we have no way to ground our intuitive preference for some descriptions of actions over others, when it comes to characterizing 'what the agent is doing'. That is true. But there are many ways of explaining why we prefer descriptions that characterize actions in ways that would be accepted and recognized by the agent as capturing her intention or goal which do not imply that where no such description can be had there can be no action at all. Perhaps it might be said that, even remaining within the realm of the sub-intentional, we intuitively want to prefer some descriptions over others (e.g. 'jiggling my foot', rather than 'wearing out my socks'—thanks to the reviewer for this example). But given a case in which I am not aware I am doing either of these things, I am not sure I any longer have the preference in question, or at any rate, in so far as I do, I think that is because the former and not the latter is a description in terms of what I am *directly* bringing about—viz., a movement of my body.

If determinism is true, then our acts are the consequences of the laws of nature and events in the remote past. But it is not up to us what went on before we were born, and neither is it up to us what the laws of nature are. Therefore, the consequences of these things (including our present acts) are not up to us.[22]

I mentioned earlier that Van Inwagen here appears to presuppose that even if determinism were true, there might still be things which counted as 'our acts'; it is merely that they would not be things which were 'up to us'. But how could something which was not 'up to me' count as my act? How could it count as an act at all? Is it not part and parcel of the concept of an act or action that it is a thing which, whatever else it is, is 'up to' the agent?

I shall suggest in a moment that the answer to this question, properly speaking, is in fact 'no', but the argument I shall offer will lead only to a reframing and not a rejection of the point being pressed above against Van Inwagen's assumption that agency is conceivable under the supposition of determinism. There might be sorts of reason for returning a negative answer other than the one I shall discuss. In particular, it might be thought that there are certain sorts of *counterexample* to the claim that an action must be up to its agent. Perhaps it will be said that there are all sorts of things that we count unhesitatingly as actions, although they are not 'up to' the agents of those actions, for example when a drug addict takes a drug to which he is addicted or a mother rushes instinctively into a burning house to rescue her children. Or perhaps so-called 'Frankfurt-style examples' will be thought to present instances in which an action occurs that was not 'up to' its agent. But once the relevant notion of action and the relevant notion of something's being 'up to' the agent are characterized, these alleged counterexamples will be seen, I believe, to melt away. There is a conception of what an action is, and a conception of what it is for something to be 'up to' an agent, that are correlative, so that something's being an action in the relevant sense *just is* a matter, not precisely indeed of *its* (the action's) being up to the agent (for reasons I shall shortly explain), but rather for that action to be the settling of at least one from a range of possible *other* things that are up to the agent. It is moreover not necessary, in order that an action occur, that it be up to the agent whether or not an act of some specific *type* to which the action belongs occur (e.g. whether a drug-injecting or child-rescuing act by that agent occur), nor even, as certain sophisticated Frankfurt-style cases have shown, that it be up to the agent whether an act of that specific type occur at that particular *time*. But when an agent acts, she must settle *something*.

It is not correct, however, to say that particular actions must be 'up to' their agents. If one asks oneself the question what are the sorts of things which are (or are not, as the case may be) 'up to' an agent, the answer seems best given by a list of clauses that would normally function as embedded questions. The sorts of things that I normally suppose to be up to me are, for example, *whether* I shall φ, *when* I shall φ, *how* I shall φ, and *where* I

---

[22] Van Inwagen (1983: 86).

shall φ. If I do indeed φ intentionally, then it can perhaps be said, as a reasonable extension of this primary usage, that the *fact that I φ-ed* was up to me, meaning roughly just:

(i) that it was up to me whether I would φ or not
(ii) that I (in fact) φ-ed.

There is no harm in conceding, similarly, that the fact that I φ-ed at time t, in way W, at place P, etc., can also be things that were up to me, meaning thereby that:

(i) it was up to me when, how and where I φ-ed respectively
(ii) I (in fact) φ-ed at time t, in way W, at place P.

But to say that the particular φ-ing which occurred when I φ-ed was also 'up to me' is, I think, grammatically uncomfortable and conceivably even philosophically confusing. What, properly speaking, is up to me in the usual sort of action situation is not a particular event, but rather the answers to a whole range of questions that are settled by my action when I act. That this is so will perhaps become clearer if one substitutes for the general talk of 'actions' in which I have engaged so far, the kind of more specific noun-phrase that is normally supposed to refer to a particular action. To say that, for example, 'my buttering of the toast was up to me', is rather peculiar and if it means anything, presumably means merely that the fact that there *was* such a buttering around the relevant time was up to me.[23] The claim that the particular action itself was also 'up to me' is, I submit, a category mistake. Particular things are not the *sorts* of things that can be 'up to' anyone. Just as a particular table could only be said to be 'up to me' if I were using that expression as shorthand for some other claim, e.g. to the effect that its *existence* was up to me (because I was the carpenter who made it) or its *location* (in my house) was up to me (because I was the person who bought it), so one could only mean by saying that a particular buttering was up to me that *whether or not* to butter was up to me (as well perhaps as where, when, and how to butter). The buttering qua particular event (if particular event is indeed what a buttering is) cannot have been up to me. Perhaps it will be said that the mistake is, in the end, only a benign one, and that there is not much, if anything, to be gained by this kind of fussing about grammatical propriety. But I am inclined to think that the idea that particular actions are 'up to us' is a manifestation of a way of thinking about them as things essentially characterizable in separation from agents, which prevents us understanding properly what actions really *are*. Thinking of actions like particular butterings as things that are 'up to' their agents rather suggests that they are particulars that an agent may or may not choose to bring

---

[23] Confusion here is facilitated by the fact that gerundive nominals like 'my buttering' can serve to refer both to particular actions and to facts concerning the occurrence of actions of particular kinds. Compare e.g. 'My buttering (of) the toast was hasty' with 'My buttering the toast was perhaps surprising; for I had eschewed dairy products for years'. In the latter case, but not the former, 'my buttering the toast' could be readily replaced with 'the fact that I buttered the toast'. See my (1997, Chapter 4).

about. But of course an agent never chooses with respect to a *particular* action whether or not to bring *it* about; the choices that relate to actions are always, rather, of such general things as what to do (and when and how and where). Particular actions are not objects of choice in advance of their occurrence. And the idea that particular actions are 'up to' their agents might also encourage the thought that an agent must be the *cause* of any action he chooses to undertake. But it is fatal to a proper understanding of actions to suppose that they are caused by agents. Agents cause things, at any rate when they do so qua agents,[24] *by acting*. So it cannot be that they also cause their actions, unless we are to suppose that for each caused action there is another action by means of which it is caused. The only alternative to this nasty regress would seem to be the supposition that there is an irreducible causal relation between agents and their actions, such that actions are indeed caused by agents, but not by means of any actions of those agents.[25] But this particular version of agent causationism has been accused many times of mystification, and even agent causationists now often eschew the idea that agents cause their actions, preferring other ways of making the claims about the specialness of agency that are important to them.[26]

We ought not, then, to say that actions (qua particulars) are 'up to' their agents. However, what is undoubtedly true is that by means of acting I normally settle a variety of questions whose answers are indeed 'up to me'. By means of my buttering action, for instance, I settle not only whether there shall be a buttering, but also when, precisely, it will occur, in what manner (with which hand, with which knife, fast or slow, etc.), and in what place. Moreover, even agents whose actions are of a type paradigmatically supposed to be 'unfree' still settle various matters when they undertake the relevant actions, and therefore also count as having acted. The kleptomaniacs and drug addicts who pepper the philosophical literature on free will are unable, perhaps, to avoid undertaking activity of a certain relevant type (stealing, drug-taking) under the conditions of temptation in which we are to suppose them placed. But they continue to settle, nevertheless, such matters as what in particular will be stolen, how, and where it is to be concealed, or whether the drug will be smoked or injected and in which arm. These actions, then, considered as particulars, are settlings of matters by their agents in the relevant sense, even though it may not have been up to their agents whether an action of some given *type* would occur within a given timeframe.

Actions, then, I should like to say, are the particular engagements with the world by means of which, at the time of action, I typically settle such matters as whether or not

---

[24] Agents can of course cause things though not in virtue of having acted—e.g. I may cause a vase to break when I faint and collapse on top of it.

[25] The classic source of this dilemma is Davidson (1971: 52).

[26] See for example O'Connor: '...on the agency theory, rather than there being a causal relation between agent and action, the relational complex [between agent, immediately executive intention and resulting sequence of bodily movements] *constitutes* the action' (1995: 182). Also Maria Alvarez and John Hyman: 'We shall argue that the concept of agent causation, although widely disparaged, can be rehabilitated by detaching it from the doctrines that agents cause their actions and that actions are events (Alvarez and Hyman, 1998: 222).

I shall φ and, if I do, when, how, and where I shall do so. If there really are actions, therefore, it has to be possible that I *should* settle such matters as these; that the answers to those questions should be open until by acting I close off all possibilities except one. And now it is possible to recast the worry expressed earlier about Van Inwagen's suggestion that my acts, under determinism, would fail to be things that were 'up to me'. Even if we are chary, for the reasons given, of supposing that actions themselves have to be up to me, we can at least insist that if there are to be actions, there have to be *other* things that are up to me. In most normal and non-contrived cases, the answers to certain questions about, for example, whether I shall φ at all and, if so, when, how, and where I shall φ, have to be up to me. And in *every* case of agency, I shall later claim, the answer to *some* such question must remain up to me if what has occurred is to count as an instance of agency at all.[27]

We can now put the worry about determinism a little more precisely. If universal determinism were true, it would seem that I would not be able genuinely to settle any of these matters at the time of action. If determinism were true, the matters in question would already be settled, long before it even occurred to me that I might, by acting, come to settle any of them. And surely it is a condition of being truly able to settle something that it has not already been settled in advance of one's potential intervention. If determinism were true, then, I would not be able to settle matters that it is essential for me to be able to settle, if I am to be an agent. And so, if determinism were true there could not be agents and there could not be actions.

That is the core of my argument for supposing that agency is inconsistent with determinism. I now want to try to clarify some of its central concepts. In the next chapter, I shall attempt to defend it against some likely objections.

2.4 Settling

The concept of 'settling a matter' is evidently central to the argument I have laid out above. I want to insist that as I move through the world, performing the various activities of which my life consists, I am constantly settling the answers to a variety of questions whose answers are (therefore) not *already* settled long before the time at which my actions take place, such as whether I shall φ, when and how I shall φ (if I do), and so on. The core idea at the heart of this notion of settling a matter is that of a question that is capable of being resolved in different ways at all times up until a certain moment—the moment of settling—at which point something that happens causes it to become resolved in one particular way. We can think of each matter that is subject to settling as expressible by means of a question the form $[p \lor \neg p]$, whose answer is (metaphorically) decided at a certain point in time, when it becomes impossible either that p should obtain or that $\neg p$ should. p will normally be a proposition that contains

---

[27] My detailed defence of the claim that even in Frankfurt-style cases, something is always left to be settled by the agent is given in Chapter 7.

some reference to a particular time, which may be either a period or an instant. Not all matters, therefore, are subject to settling. It is plausible to suppose that necessary truths fall outside the realm of questions that are subject to settling—and perhaps many sorts of contingent truth do too. *General* truths, in particular, do not seem to be the sorts of thing with respect to which one should always expect there to be an answer to the question when it was settled that *p*—for instance, when it was settled that all men are mortal or that pandas eat bamboo—perhaps partly because it is not utterly clear that these matters *are* settled for all time. But I shall not attempt the difficult task of trying precisely to delineate which kinds of matters, precisely, can be the subject of 'settling'—no doubt there is quite a long list of types of propositions which do not bear the right sort of relation to time. Suffice it to say that in general, at least, the wanted class will contain particular questions concerning the occurrence of certain sorts of *events* at particular times (e.g. whether there will be an avalanche on Mont Blanc at *t* (where *t* can be a period, as well as an instant)) or the obtaining of particular kinds of circumstances at times (for example, whether I shall still be sitting in this chair at 3pm this afternoon). Perhaps there are other kinds of question that may get settled, too, but for the purposes of my argument, nothing will be lost if we focus, for the time being, on questions (and related propositions) of these two basic sorts.

Though I shall be attempting to insist that the actions of agents represent one means by which matters often come to be settled, I do not mean to suggest that it is the only means. There may be types of occurrence other than actions which are able to settle certain matters; in particular, if there are events which bear only an indeterministic relation to their antecedents, then these will be events which settle certain matters at the time of their own occurrence, both matters whose settling is *constituted* by the occurrence of those very events (e.g. that atom A emitted a particle at *t* is settled by atom A's emission of a particle at *t*) or matters which are deterministically connected to the occurrence of those indeterministic events (e.g. that detector D lit up in response to the emission of the particle at *t* + 1 may be settled by atom A's emission of a particle at *t*). But it is important to see that on this rich conception of settling, not just any cause of an event, or of the obtaining of a circumstance, counts, merely in virtue of its role in the causation of a phenomenon as something which also *settles* any associated matters. For example, if an utterly deterministic process leads via a successive chain of causes $c_1 \dots c_n$ to effect e, then c_n cannot count as having settled that an event of any of the types that e instantiates occurs, even though c_n is essential to the occurrence of e, since it was *already* settled at the time of c_1's occurrence that e would occur. An event can only settle a matter at the time at which it occurs, if that matter is not already settled before that time. And it is this feature of the concept of settling on which my argument against universal determinism depends. If there is ever any settling of matters *in time*, then universal determinism cannot be true, since according to universal determinism, everything is already settled at the start (whatever exactly we are to understand by 'the start'). So if to act is indeed to settle a matter at the time at which that action occurs, and action is a real phenomenon, universal determinism cannot be true.

I do not want to deny that it would be possible to use the word 'settle' in a different and less metaphysically committed way. I do not want to deny, for instance, that it might be reasonable to speak of some person or event's having settled a matter which was nevertheless determined to occur well in advance of that person's intervention or that event's occurrence. One might perhaps speak, for instance, of the fall of the third domino's having settled that the fourth would fall, even in a context in which one took it for granted that the fall of the fourth was already guaranteed by the fall of the first (or indeed by events and circumstances occurring long before the fall of the first), meaning by this merely that had the third not fallen, the fourth would not have fallen either. But even if it has to be conceded that such a conception of settling can be made sense of, there is clearly available also a much stronger conception of what it is for a matter to be settled by some event: one according to which, as time goes by, certain matters which were hitherto open questions become no longer open, either because some happening occurs which itself (given the context in which it occurs) *constitutes* the closing of that matter (as, for example, the question whether my foot will move at t is closed by my moving it then) or else because some happening occurs which brings a particular resolution of that matter inevitably in its train (as, for example, the question whether a particular ant will die at $t + 1$ may be settled by my moving my foot as I do at t). On this stronger conception of what it is for a contingent matter to be settled, there is a definite time at which a matter becomes settled, even if we cannot generally know when that time is—a definite time at which it becomes no longer possible for there to be a different resolution of that matter. Often, perhaps, a matter which concerns what is to be the case at a particular time t will not be settled until t itself. But it is *possible* for a matter to be settled somewhat in advance, where an entirely deterministic process links a set of prior circumstances to an outcome, or else (and perhaps more usually) where it is obvious that *no* process exists which could lead from the circumstances of the present to a given outcome. Matters which are characterized negatively are likely frequently to be settled in advance in this second way—for instance, even if it is not settled now what I shall be doing at 11 o'clock this morning, it is certainly already settled that I shall not be doing anything which requires that I be in Barbados, in Australia, or on the moon, since there is no possible means of my getting to any of these places before then.

This stronger conception of settling is clearly distinct from the weaker one. On the weak conception of settling, on which one matter can settle another merely because a certain causal relation holds, there is no particular reason to single out any particular point in time as *the* time at which a particular matter was settled. That the fourth domino would fall was settled by the fall of the third, but equally (and in the same sense) by the fall of the second and the first…and indeed by any of the large number of prior events and circumstances of which it might truly be said that had they not occurred/obtained, the fall of the fourth domino would not have occurred either. The idea of the settling of a matter as *itself* something which has a particular temporal location, which may or may not be identical with the time that the matter concerns, belongs only to the stronger conception of settling that I have outlined. And though there is nothing preventing the universal determinist from conceding that this stronger conception represents, as it were, a legitimate idea, she cannot concede that settlings of matters, thus understood, actually occur for different matters at different times. For the believer in universal determinism, who assumes the immutability of the laws of nature, and who contemplates the application of this conception of settling to his vision of the universe, all matters are settled together at the same time. Laws and initial conditions being fixed, so is everything else. Matters themselves can unfold in time, but the settling of them cannot. It is only the indeterminist who can lay claim to the thought that settling itself (in this second sense) is an ongoing process.[28]

The claim I would like to make is that we normally conceive of our actions as interventions by means of which we not only *cause* certain further events to happen and thereby cause certain things to be or not to be the case, but also *settle* certain matters in this strong sense of 'settle', thereby closing off certain possibilities that until the time of our action had remained open. In particular, when I move my body, I settle certain questions concerning *how* it will move that until then had not been settled. I move right rather than left, for instance, or I move at t rather than at $t + 1$, or quickly rather than slowly. It was *possible* until the time of action that I should have moved left rather than right, or at $t + 1$ rather than at t, or slowly rather than quickly. But as I move, I close off these possibilities and settle what is to be the nature of actuality, in respect of that particular portion of it which concerns my own body and its movements and whereabouts, together with the inevitable consequences of these things. But in order for this to be possible, it has to be true that the nature of actuality is not already settled prior to my intervention. And so, if actions are what we generally take them to be, the future must be metaphysically open.

In this chapter, then, I have attempted to present an outline of the conception of agency that motivates the view I have called Agency Incompatibilism. But clearly, the compatibilist will want to deny that the strong conception of settling that I have outlined here is genuinely part and parcel of our concept of agency. In the next chapter, therefore, I shall turn to consider some natural objections both to the conception itself and to the claim that it justifies the assumption that agency is incompatible with determinism.

---

[28] Cf Peirce (1892: 333): 'Very well, my obliging opponent, we have now reached an issue. You think all the arbitrary specifications of the universe were introduced in one dose in the beginning, if there was a beginning, and that the variety and complication of nature has always been just as much as it is now. But I, for my part, think that the diversification, the specification, has been continually taking place'.

3

Action as Settling: Some Objections

In the last chapter, I argued that if actions necessarily involve the settlings by their agents of at least some hitherto unsettled matters, then the existence of actions must imply the falsity of determinism. In this chapter I want to consider some objections, both to the premise that actions are indeed settlings by agents of hitherto unsettled matters and also to the inference from that premise of the falsity of determinism. I shall begin with a look at two objections to the claim that actions are settlings that might occur even to those who might be otherwise sympathetic to the claim that actions involve settling in the richer, option-closing sense that I have tried to characterize. I shall call these, respectively:

(i) the objection from the impossibility of ensuring success
(ii) the objection from imperfect execution.

My responses to these objections will help, I hope, to clarify and disambiguate my claim that actions are necessarily settlings. I shall then turn to examine what I imagine will be the main compatibilist line of response to my suggestion about settlings: that although there is indeed a sense in which actions may be said to be settlings of the unsettled, it is not a sense that requires the falsity of determinism.

3.1 The objection from the impossibility of ensuring success

Both of the first two objections may be approached initially by way of the preliminary question whether it is really true that there is very much at all that I can really *settle* when I act. Suppose, for instance, that I φ, where φ is 'score a goal'. By merely kicking the ball at t, it might be said, I cannot normally settle whether a goal is scored at $t + 1$ and so I cannot settle either (at t) whether I shall have scored a goal by $t + 1$. Whether I shall or not usually depends on things other than the nature of my action at t, in particular on the actions of the defenders on the other team, none of whom is under my control. So it is wrong to say, in general, that when I φ, I always settle the question whether or not I shall φ. In particular, in cases where 'φ-ing' describes my action in terms of one of its distal consequences, then the settling of the question whether I shall φ may only occur later, at a time subsequent to the time of my action.

This seems correct. But there are two points to be made in response. The first is that it is not obvious that I might not be able at least *sometimes* to settle such a matter as whether a goal is scored at the very time at which I act, despite the fact that it must be admitted that I cannot always do so. For there might be occasions on which my shot is simply unstoppable by anyone or anything in the vicinity; once the ball has left my foot there might just be nothing and no one near enough to do anything about its subsequent trajectory, so that once I have acted it is simply physically determined that the ball will go into the back of the net. And in such a case it seems correct to say that I settle, with my action and at the time of my action, the question whether or not a goal is scored at a slightly later time. Even where an action is described in terms of distal consequences, therefore, it need not *always* be the case that the agent fails to settle at the time of action whether an action of that type occurs. But the second, more important, point to which it is immediately natural to appeal in responding to the present objection is that each kind of physical action I perform is performed by means of moving or altering my body in some particular way. For instance, I scored the goal *by moving my leg*—so that, even if it cannot be said on every occasion on which I try to score a goal and succeed that in that case I settled at the time of my action the question whether or not a goal was scored, it can at least be said that I settled at that time whether, when, and precisely how my leg would move. So it can still be maintained that actions always involve the settling of things; one merely needs to be more cautious in one's account of what those things might be. Generally speaking, what one *always* settles when one acts is (at least) how one's body will move or change in some respect. One will doubtless usually thereby settle certain other things too, e.g. that certain air molecules will move in such and such ways or that an ant will die (as I tread on it, say).[1] But the important point for present purposes is that, provided all actions have descriptions as bodily movings, all will likewise count as settlings of *something*, even though they may in addition have descriptions—as φ-ings, say—such that the agent does not settle, at the time of action, that a φ-ing will occur.

Someone might worry, though, that there are certain sorts of reasons for supposing that we are not able even to settle this limited question how our bodies will move when we act. The main concern I have in mind here stems from the thought that the movements of our bodies, no less than movements of footballs, are *consequences* of our actions: where something is a consequence of something else there is always the possibility of some unforeseen disruption in the chain of causality the agent is hoping to effect. I might, for example, mean to kick a ball and try to do so, but in the event I might be unable to move my leg because it is suddenly paralysed by cramp. Someone might say, therefore, that actions cannot be settlings because it is impossible for a human agent to guarantee that nothing will go wrong between the attempt to move

---

[1] Mental actions, perhaps, may be an exception to the rule that some such extra-bodily consequences are generally settled by our actions.

and the bodily movement itself, which is, strictly speaking, no less than the movement of a kicked football, the *consequence* of my action.

There is, however, a view of actions implicit in this objection that I do not want to accept. According to this view, actions are the prior causes of what Hornsby calls bodily movements₁. But on my view, actions are rather the *causings* of bodily movements by their agents, not the (wholly prior and separate) causes of them. They are processes, not events. And in cases such as those envisaged, where a bodily movement is not produced at all because of some disruption in the causal chain leading to the bodily movement, there is no causing of such a bodily movement, and so no action in the first place, or at least no action of the sort originally intended. It is true that there may, under such circumstances, be an *attempt* to act, and true also that an attempt to bring about an action may be regarded as a kind of action in its own right. But the settling necessary for the *attempt* to have occurred has indeed occurred: the movements and changes in the brain that are presumably necessary for an attempt have indeed occurred under the conditions imagined. And so we are able to say, on my view, precisely what I think we ought to want to say about such cases, namely that where there is no overt movement of a particular part of the body by the agent, there is no causing of that part of the body to move and so no action of that kind (no raising of an arm, no moving of a leg, or whatever). But the agent will nevertheless have success-fully settled that movements and changes of certain *other* kinds have occurred (e.g. she will have settled questions concerning the occurrence of certain brain events) and her causing of those movements and changes may constitute an attempt to bring about some further type of movement, an attempt that, on this occasion, has failed. So we have not yet been given an example of an action that is not at the same time a settling of anything by the agent.

It might be said in response, though, that if (as I have suggested) to act is necessarily to move a part of one's body, and if (as the ever-present possibility of bodily non-cooperation might suggest) I cannot often settle in advance at *t* whether my body will move at *t* + 1, I cannot settle in that case the question whether I shall *move* my body, because I am unable to make it impossible that it should *not* move. Actions (if actions are indeed to be identified with movings of my body by me) cannot therefore be settlings. But this is where the claim that actions are processes and not events becomes particularly important. It is true that what is possible in the way of *advance* settling by an agent is, on my view, tremendously circumscribed. For quite apart from the objector's point about possible disruptions in the chain of physical causality, it is in fact very important for my own view of action that very little in the way of advance settling be possible. I insist upon the presence of alternative possibilities *throughout the duration* of an action and so it is important to my view that nothing that happens during the action's earlier stages must compromise an agent's ongoing power to move in a variety of different ways during what may be the later ones, or indeed to cease to move. This means that nothing that happens early on in any temporally extended action is able to settle anything that happens appreciably later. There might, I think, be settling-in-advance across very short stages of an action (because, for instance, a message having gone out to a motor neuron there may be a point at which there is nothing I or anyone else can do to prevent the relevant muscle from then moving in some particular way). However, one need not insist that an agent settle the character, as it were, of the whole causing in which her action consists with some advance initiatory thrust in order to count as having settled it: the settling on which I insist does not have to be advance settling. The idea need not be that by doing something at one time I am able to ensure that certain *other* things will occur later on (though I may indeed be able to do a small amount of this across certain very short temporal intervals; so short as to make unforeseen interference or indeed retraction by me impossible). The settling of which I insist action mainly consists may be thought of as taking place alongside, and at the same time as, the movements and changes that are thereby being effected, and since, at the time of settling, those movements are already being effected, there is no question of the bodily systems on which the settling relies being out of order: they are already in operation and their operation is part of the process that *constitutes* my settling how my body will move. My action is the whole, embodied process by means of which the movement is brought about, not just an initiatory push at the beginning of the causal chain, because my role in the relevant causation extends far beyond the role played by the initiatory portion of the chain. This is because I settle things not only by initiating motor activity but also by continuing it; by refraining, for example, from vetoing the original instruction or from altering it in any of the multifarious ways that are constantly open to me. Because these powers of refrainment and alteration are present throughout the whole duration of the action, I am *constantly* settling what happens from moment to moment, even if I do not in fact exercise those powers of refrainment and alteration. The point is that I *could* exercise them. The whole action is permeated by the possibility of the agent's making movements and changes of a different character from those she in fact ends up making. And that is what makes this causation constitute at the same time, a *settling*. As the relevant causation occurs, matters are settled that hitherto were unsettled; and it is the agent who settles them.

Perhaps it may be thought that experiments such as those conducted by Libet[2] cast doubt on the question whether agency could be the kind of contemporaneous settling of effects on which I have insisted, since it may be suggested that these experiments indicate that how we shall move is settled in at least some cases by prior causes of which we have no knowledge. These experiments appear to show that participants in a study who were asked to move a finger spontaneously, while noting the position of a clock hand at the time when they became consciously aware of the decision to move, underwent an increase in brain activity known as the 'readiness potential' about 300 ms *before* they were aware of the decision to move their finger. Many have suggested

---

[2] See Libet et al. (1983) and Libet (1985, 1993).

that this experimental finding has hugely important consequences for the free will debate; it might perhaps be thought that the apparent evidence of prior neural activity in advance of a conscious decision to move might suggest the operation of a hidden, neural variety of determinism, which would be problematic for my view of actions as settlings. But in fact, there is nothing in the Libet experiments to trouble my view of agency; indeed my view is much *better* placed than many more familiar conceptions of agency smoothly to accommodate the Libet findings. For even if it were to turn out that the onset of such a readiness potential brings about a given finger movement entirely inexorably in some cases (and note that this is not normally claimed, it being usually allowed that the agent may 'veto' the action, even after the activity represented by the readiness potential has occurred), that would simply show that the production of the readiness potential (and the production, conceivably, of even earlier changes) is an early and crucial part of the *action*, since it (or even earlier happenings) would in that case be the locus of settling. In describing the 'readiness potential', Wegner says that it peaks 'about 90 ms before the action', but of course what he should really say is that it peaks about 90 ms before the *bodily movement*. On my view, the experimental evidence makes it natural to suppose that, in cases of the type in question, the readiness potential is simply *part* of the activity on which the action depends, for it is natural to think that it is part of the embodied process by means of which the agent ultimately settles that her finger will move in such cases. And the fact that it occurs prior to the agent's becoming consciously aware of a decision to move is, on my view, neither here nor there. On the view I wish to endorse, it is entirely unnecessary for a conscious decision to precede an action in order for the action to count either *as* an action or as *mine*, and so it does not matter in the least if it turns out to be true that in many cases the awareness of conscious 'decision' is subsequent to the initiation of action. What has happened can remain an action (provided it is a settling), even if conscious decision has nothing to do with the production of the movement in question.

The idea that agency must be a kind of conscious, *advance* settling of matters if it is to be any kind of settling at all is related to ways of thinking about agency to which we have grown very used, but from which I think we need to disentangle ourselves if we are ever going to come by an adequate account of action. The concept of an agent as a settler-in-advance of what will happen to her body and then to the world beyond it is related to a picture of the agent as primarily a mental being (a pure will); her capacity for agency is conceived of as an unconditional capacity to bring the world into conformity with a thought-of and wished-for representation of how things should be. Despite the manifest inapplicability of this conception of agency to any denizen of the natural world, I believe that it has nevertheless exerted an extraordinarily powerful influence on the philosophy of action, as I shall shortly try to show. For even if we are physicalists (and therefore eschew completely the idea of a purely mental being) we may nevertheless continue to suppose that the settling of which action consists is constituted by the causation of bodily movements by events and states which, for all their admitted physicality, nevertheless are thought of as themselves elements that take some kind of place, if only sometimes a submerged one,[3] in our conscious mental life: our wishings, intentions, beliefs, desires, decisions, and the like. *Our* settling of things is thought of, as it were, on this conception, as *their* settling of things, and since the settling of things by events and states can presumably only be a matter of their *causing* things (and moreover deterministically so causing them, if we want the greatest possible degree of assurance that the wanted effects will occur), we rapidly arrive at the idea that an agent's settling things is the same thing as the causation of bodily movements by these conscious, or at any rate potentially conscious, states and events.

This is a conception of what the settling inherent in agency consists in that accords very well with compatibilism, of course, for it reduces the settling inherent in agency to mere causation of movement by a privileged class of events and states. It also provides an obvious resource for those wanting to argue that human agency is of a different kind from that of other animals, since it may well be unclear whether we may attribute these sorts of mental states to other creatures. If we are worried about the extent to which other creatures can be regarded as possessors of these sorts of state, then we will be worried too about the prospect of regarding those other creatures also as agents. But the second, contemporaneous conception of settling, the one I should like to try to elaborate during the course of this book, effectively loosens the relation between the power of agents to settle things and the efficacy of events and states that are to be found either actually present in or potentially available to consciousness, events, and states of the sort classically regarded as 'mental'. For me to be able to settle whether my body will move in a particular way is merely for me to be able, in the actual context in which I find myself, both to bring about that particular movement of my body and to be able not to bring it about. But nothing is said or implied specifically by this conception of settling about any antecedent thinkings, wishings, plannings, or the like. The first person pronoun is of course used. It is I who settles the relevant matters when I act: whether my body will move, for example, and if so, when and how. However, in this picture of what settling involves there is nothing as yet to imply that something that genuinely counts as *my* settling things cannot take place by means of bodily systems that do not involve any antecedent role in the voluntary causation of bodily movement for mental states, as those things are usually conceived. This conception attempts to take more seriously the thought that the 'I' who is doing the settling is a bodily, as well of course as a mental being, equipped in fact with a multitude of means by which to effect its own movements, not all of which are equally deeply connected to that agent's conscious life, including the exercise of skills and the deployment of learned and perhaps even some partially innate habits, etc.

---

[3] Those who adhere to a causal theory of action according to which an action occurs when a bodily movement is brought about by something like an intention or a belief/desire pair, 'in the right kind of way' usually meet the objection that we are not always aware of such prior intentions, beliefs, and desires when we act, by appealing to the fact that these phenomena can sometimes be unconscious. I consider some of the problems with this general approach in Section 3.6.

The animal body, on this conception, is not merely the instructed instrument of that animal's will. On the contrary, the complex set of embodied systems that enliven it are constitutive themselves of the phenomenon of willing. The 'I' that settles things in my sense, is therefore not to be conceived of as a pure will, not even one that can be located, roughly, in the physical brain. It is to be conceived of as a whole, functioning animal whose systems of agent control are various and only some of which involve the paradigmatically mental phenomena often said to be essential to the causation of action. I shall return in due course to this idea, which will play a crucial role in the arguments to come. First, though, I want to address the second objection to the idea that actions are settlings. I call this the objection from imperfect execution.

3.2 The objection from imperfect execution

This second kind of worry about the claim that actions are settlings relates to the fact that we are often very imperfect controllers of the movements of our bodies. We often want them to do things (dance, ski, skateboard, etc.) that require movements that we find it difficult to bring off and can only attain, if at all, with considerable practice. And in these circumstances, it might be said, surely I do not settle what my body does. If I could do *that*, it might be said, there would be no need for practice! But this point can be met, like the objection from the impossibility of ensuring success, by appealing to the distinction between the two different conceptions of settling outlined above. When I try to execute a complicated dance move and fail to bring off what I hoped to achieve, I clearly cannot be said to have exercised a capacity to guarantee to bring the world (or the bit of it constituted by my body) into conformity with my will, for that is something, clearly, that I have failed to do on this occasion. But I can still be said in fact to have made it the case, with respect to my body, that things went a certain way rather than some other way in which I might equally have made them go at the time of my action. As I go through the painstaking process of attempting to learn the new skill, I am settling all the time which movements my body will make, for it is me and not someone or something else who is moving my body, even if my body is not always doing precisely what I would ideally have liked it to do. The fine details are no doubt mostly outside the scope of my conscious will: I do not consciously will with milli-metre-fine precision exactly which limbs will move where. Sub-personal systems are certainly in charge of most of the minutiae, and indeed it is because they have not properly habituated themselves to make the moves I want to make that I cannot perform many kinds of movement without practice. But the sub-personal systems in question are still part and parcel of an agency which is mine. It does not follow at all from the fact that a movement is controlled and orchestrated in large part by sub-personal systems that it is not a movement that *I* make—otherwise it would certainly be impossible for me to make any movement at all. The class of actual movings of which I can genuinely be said to be agent is simply not identical with the class of actual movings I can be said to have wanted, wished, decided, chosen, or intended to have occur; it is a far bigger class. This point, indeed, should be obvious to anyone who bothers to take note for even a minute of the movements she makes during the course of that time. During any reasonably extended period, one will be moving around in various ways, slightly rearranging oneself, leaning a bit more this way or that, turning one's head slightly, jiggling one's foot. What Brian O'Shaughnessy calls the 'sub-intentional act' is an utterly omnipresent feature of human life.[4] However, I regard it as implausible to suppose that we are not agents of these acts, despite the fact that they occur, on the whole, well below the level of our conscious notice and cannot really sensibly be thought of as the products of intentions. These movings are *our* movings, but if we are indeed their agents, if they are settlings by us of whether, when, and how our bodies shall move, it is already clear, is it not, that we must not identify our settlings of things with the causation of bodily movements by fully-fledged decisions, choices, intentions, conscious desires, and the like. It must be possible for *us* to settle things without *their* settling things, as I put it earlier. The challenge, then, is to say in virtue of what, if not in virtue of direct conscious control, these movings really do count as ours and therefore are to be distinguished from the many other unintended movements that occur in and around my body of which I am clearly *not* the agent (heartbeats, peristaltic motions of the gut, reflex responses, etc.)

Why do I insist that it is right to say of the former kinds of movings, but not the latter, that they are indeed *mine,* thereby counting as genuine agential movings rather than as mere movements$_i$? My answer to this question is roughly as follows. Though I make many movements that I do not specifically intend to make and which are not produced by means of any causal process in which conscious or other types of thought-involving states play an active role, I am nevertheless *able* to bring these movements under the control of genuinely intentional processes at a moment's notice. What makes it right, it seems to me, to attribute the movements to *me*—what makes them voluntary movings by me rather than, say, reflex responses over which I have no meaningful control—is that the relevant systems are ultimately subordinated to personal-level, conscious ones in a well-integrated hierarchy whose purpose generally is to ensure that they function overall to serve my conscious aims, although of course it may happen on individual occasions that there is no point or purpose to a given individual output from such a system. The subordination has many aspects. I can choose at any time to make the workings of the relevant subordinate systems the focus of conscious will. For example, while learning a dance I can attend to particular aspects of my movement in an attempt to correct problems, trying very consciously to keep my back straighter or to go through the dance moves more slowly in order to try to learn them better. Conscious memory is likely to be required, at any rate at the beginning, to help me recall which moves are required in which order. If the dance is at all complex, I will probably count to keep myself in time. I may use consciously acquired *methods* to help

---

[4] O'Shaughnessy (1980: Vol II, Chapter 10).

me gain overall competence, for example I may practise the arm movements on their own until I have them perfected, before adding in other parts of the body. And ultimately, of course, the whole exercise is something which I consciously initiate. It is I who allows, or not, the relevant sub-personal systems to go into operation in the first place. I decide whether or not to dance and, if I do, when I shall stop. It is the actual or possible interweaving of conscious decision, focus, planning, and attention with the relevant movements that makes those movements constitutive of actions that are mine, even in cases when I pay them no particular mind at all. The crucial point is that I *could* pay them mind and, by so attending, change what happens. I control them, not in the sense that I directly and consciously produce the movements[5] from moment to moment, but rather in the sense that I *could* alter what occurs and in particular could desist from or change the nature of the movements (e.g. from dancing to running) if it became at all important for me to do so. I am in charge in the way that a government minister is in charge of a department. No minister directly controls all the work of a particular department or knows all the details of what is going on within it: tasks are delegated to particular civil servants who in turn delegate further work to more junior officials, and so on. But if it becomes important, a minister can step in to take a more direct interest in a particular matter. She can more closely monitor the work of the civil servants beneath her, issue directives, insist on changes in working practice, or even, in *extremis*, take on some of the necessary work herself. And of course it is the minister who sets the overall agenda and ultimately determines the tasks on which her subordinates are to be engaged. She is in control, even though she is not doing all the work. And so even when she has *not* been paying particular attention to some matter or other, we may nevertheless hold her responsible for what has happened in respect of that matter. She *could* have intervened to change things, even though she did not. And in just the same sort of way, I want to claim, an agent can count as the agent of a movement which was not in fact directly effected by any conscious state or process of hers. Provided she could, by way of a conscious state or process, have seen to it that the movement did *not* occur, she has the power to settle whether or not it will, and that is the power that constitutes agency.

Agents do not have a similar kind of control over the peristaltic movements in their gut or the reflex knee-jerk that occurs when someone taps their knee with a hammer. There is no means by which they are able to bring these things directly under a conscious form of supervision. These things are beyond the power of the agent to influence in the direct way that is characteristic of willed action.[6] My claim, then, is that the answer to the question what makes it right to think of a sub-intentional act as

---

[5] Indeed, as one of the reviewers of this work pointed out, there may be some sorts of action that can only be produced in the absence of the focus provided by the conscious will, in the sense that once I attend to what I am doing I can no longer produce the movements at all.

[6] It should go without saying, of course, that there may still be *indirect* means of affecting what happens in such cases, for example by taking drugs to slow down peristaltic motion or tying oneself up to prevent one's knee responding in the normal way to the hammer.

genuinely an *act*—to think about the relevant movements as things that *I* bring about—is ultimately one which makes essential reference to the position in a hierarchy of the system of movement control that brings the movement about. It is not in virtue of the occurrence of any special sort of causal antecedent or component that the movement counts as the result of a moving by me. Instead it is in virtue of my possession of an ongoing *capacity* to prevent altogether, stop in its tracks, reverse, alter, change the direction and speed of, or otherwise affect the motion in question. It is this power that means that my activity constitutes a settling by me of what in fact occurs with respect to my body as I dance, even when the movements are not the ones I should really have liked to be able to make, and even when the details of exactly how I move are not necessarily under direct, conscious supervision. The crucial point is that they *could* at any instant have come under that direct supervision; that the movements were within the scope of the powers of what it is natural to think of as the top-level system in the hierarchy: the conscious mind.

It must not be thought that the sorts of case on which I have been focusing—cases in which we find it difficult to make our bodies do what we want them to do without considerable practice—are special in this respect. *All* intentional bodily agency, I should like to suggest, involves this interweaving of conscious systems of bodily control with more basic, effectively automated or partly automated systems. When I type, for instance, although I decide consciously which words I shall use, I do not need to engage in any conscious supervision of my fingers—they just get on with the job by themselves, as it were, now that I have learned to type. An enormous amount of the settling that we do as agents is delegated, inevitably, to processes that are very ill-described as the causing of motions by mental states, such as choosings, intendings, and the like. But this does not imply that what is settled by those processes to which the agent delegates is not at the same time settled by the agent. An agent's settling of things can perfectly well be constituted by processes to which she pays no mind whatever, provided they are processes that she is able to control, if she chooses to do so, by attending to them.

I have been trying to defend the claim that when we engage in bodily action, we settle certain questions and, in particular, that we settle certain questions about whether, when, and how precisely our bodies will move. It might be objected at this point that even if it is granted that we can settle such matters of detail as these, it would not follow from our possession of such capacities that we could settle any of the *other* sorts of surely more important matters with which the traditional incompatibilist has tended to be concerned: whether, for instance, to raid the poor box or to resist temptation,[7] or whether to inject heroin today or not. For it is perfectly possible, it might be said, that an agent might possess the capacity to settle exactly which movements to make and at precisely what speed and in which order, for instance, while

---

[7] This example is Van Inwagen's. See his (1983: 144ff).

lacking the more general (and intuitively higher-level) capacities in which the moral philosopher may be more likely to be interested. Take Van Inwagen's example of robbing a poor box, for instance; it might be said that someone might find it impossible, given the character and structure of her motivations, not to make some movement or other within the next few days that would constitute a robbing of the poor box—even if it remained up to her when precisely to rob it, with which hand, and how to conceal the money about her person. This is perfectly true. But this is the point at which to repeat a claim made in Chapter 1, namely that, although it is by no means a sufficient condition of an agent's being able to settle important moral matters that she be able to settle questions about how precisely and when and whether her body will move, it is without doubt a necessary one. If determinism were indeed incompatible with this capacity to settle how one's body will move, therefore, we would have a very quick route to incompatibilism concerning the kinds of power to do otherwise with which the traditional incompatibilist has been concerned. Moreover, it is by no means obvious that the case for incompatibilism is best pursued by focusing on the high-level settlings that are represented by such things as the resolution of moral dilemmas and the making of life-choices. Indeed, in connection with such choices as these, the compatibilist's counterargument that different motivations would surely have been required in order for a different rational outcome to have ensued seems at its strongest. My suggestion, which will be more fully elaborated in Chapter 6, is that the best case for incompatibilism is made by focusing not on such crucial moments of meaningful decision as these, but rather on the basic powers (which we share with other self-moving animals) to make our bodies move, as we say, 'at will', in any one of a vast number of possible ways. These powers, I shall be arguing, are not easy to accommodate within a deterministic picture of the universe. And if these simple powers to settle what occurs in the world cannot be thus accommodated, there is certainly no possibility of accommodating the more significant kinds of power for moral choice and self-development in which the traditional moral philosopher is likely to be interested.

Here may be the place also to note that my strategy undermines the relevance to the incompatibilist about determinism and moral responsibility of so-called 'Frankfurt-style counterexamples' to the Principle of Alternate Possibilities. That principle states that a person is morally responsible for what she has done only if she could have done otherwise; the counterexamples therefore purport to show that it is possible for an agent to be morally responsible for φ-ing even though she could *not* have done other than φ. Suppose, for the sake of argument, that these counterexamples do show this. Does that mean that it is possible for an agent to be morally responsible for φ-ing even if determinism is true? Not at all. For even if the agent could not have done other than perform some φ-ing or other (could not, for example, have done other than rob the poor box) it is questionable whether she could have done *anything at all* had she lacked the power to settle which precise movements her body would make as she robbed it. If the power to settle which movements are made by one's body is essential to the very possibility of agency, and if this power is inconsistent with determinism (as I shall be arguing), then it will not matter to the truth of incompatibilism about moral responsi-bility if there are counterexamples to the Principle of Alternate Possibilities. For there will not be counterexamples to the following principle: that the agent is morally responsible for her φ-ing only if she *is* an agent in respect of the particular φ-ing that she undertakes. I shall return to this claim (and to a more detailed discussion of Frankfurt-style examples) in Chapter 7.

Having thus clarified somewhat the concept of settling that is involved in my claim that an agent can, by acting, settle various matters, and having defended the claim that actions are settlings against some possible objections, I want now to return to the central argument against universal determinism. That argument, recall, alleges that if there are to be such things as agents and actions, it must be possible for the phenome-non that I have called the settling of matters by agents at the time of action to exist. And it further alleges that the settling of matters by agents at the time of action can only exist if those matters are not *already* settled in advance of the time of the agent's action. I have already defended the first of these claims against some possible objections. I want now to consider what I imagine is going to be the *other* main line of objection to the argument. The objection I have in mind insists that there is an equivocation on the notion of 'settling' involved in the argument: that an agent can perfectly well settle something by acting, *in the only way in which it is legitimate to insist that she must be able to settle it if action is genuinely to occur,* without its being true that the matter is not, as it were, *metaphysically* settled at the time of action, and so without its being true that settling is incompatible with determinism.

3.3 Settling: the compatibilist's conception

The present objection is rather like those objections to more traditional varieties of incompatibilism, which insist that determinism does not rule out the truth of claims of the form 'S could have done otherwise', because claims regarding agential powers of the sort expressed by the words 'can' and 'could' are not impugned by the merely physical impossibility that the course of events necessary for the alleged alternate possibility to be actualized should occur. The current suggestion is that an agent can settle (in the relevant sense of 'settle') the answer to any of a wide variety of questions, such as whether or when and how he shall φ, say, even if the answer is, in another sense, *already* settled. This is because there are simply two different conceptions of settling at work here. For an agent to settle some matter *in the relevant sense*, it will be said, is simply for certain of her mental states or events to be among the causes of a bodily movement that settles the matter, in the limited sense that that movement's occurring either causally brings it about that, or perhaps constitutes the occurrence of conditions intrinsically sufficient for, its being the case that the matter is resolved in a certain way. For instance, in order for me to settle the question whether some toast is buttered at t, it is only necessary for my body to perform toast-buttering movements at t and for those buttering movements to be caused in the right sort of way by an intention to butter toast that was, in turn, perhaps caused by a desire to eat buttered toast and a belief that it would be necessary for me to butter some toast if I am to eat any. All this is perfectly possible, it will be said, under determinism. It is not additionally necessary that the agent *metaphysically* settle the matter at the time of action by foreclosing possibilities that the world, as it were, had left open until that point.

The compatibilist's hope, here, is to try to argue that in so far as it can be regarded as simply obvious that agents settle things when they act, their settling of those things can be understood to consist in a network of ordinary causal relations amongst various special sorts of state and event: things like desires, beliefs, intentions, etc., and the bodily movements that result from them. The settling of things by agents is alleged to be just a matter of certain special sorts of states and events causing things, specifically their causing bodily movements. However, there are a number of serious problems with this suggestion. By raising the issue of sub-intentional actions, I have already tried to cast doubt on the idea that causation by specifically *mental* events and/or states could really be what, in the end, provides the key to understanding the nature of action in the way that this strategy proposes. I want now to go on to consider three further sources of concern about this general approach. Two of these have already become prominent in the literature; the third is a particular worry of my own, which one rarely finds adequately addressed. I shall conclude by suggesting that there are strong reasons for supposing that it is indeed impossible properly to characterize agency without making use of the robust, metaphysical conception of settling, which I have characterized above.

3.4 Deviant causal chains

It should already be obvious that what the compatibilist hopes to offer by way of an account of the settling of matters by agents is, in effect, a version of what has come to be known as the Causal Theory of Action. For an agent to act is roughly, on the causal theory, for the bodily movements that are intrinsic to the relevant action to be caused by certain of that agent's own mental states. And the compatibilist I am currently imagining wishes to respond to my claim that agents must be settlers of matters by saying: 'Of course! But for an agent to settle a matter (in the relevant sense), it is not necessary that that matter should remain unsettled (in your metaphysically robust sense) until the agent acts. All that is necessary is that suitable mental states of that agent should bring about the relevant bodily movements. If such causal chains do indeed occur in the world, then these chains simply *constitute* the settlings of matters by agents. But there is nothing inconsistent with determinism in this picture of what action requires. On the contrary, deterministic causation is at the very heart of the picture.'

If there are problems, then, with the Causal Theory of Action, they are likely to present problems also for the compatibilist strategy I am currently considering. More-over, the Causal Theory of Action has indeed faced one particularly intractable obstacle to its satisfactory formulation over the years. This is what has come to be known as the problem of deviant causal chains. The difficulty is that, for an action of a certain kind to have occurred, it does not seem to be sufficient for mental states of the relevant agent to have brought about a bodily movement of a kind that might be thought of as intrinsic to an action of that particular type. For it is possible for this type of causal relation to obtain when no action occurs. Davidson (1973) offers a classic example to illustrate the point. He imagines a climber who wants to be rid of the weight and danger of holding another man on a rope and who also knows that merely by loosening his grip he could rid himself of this weight and danger. This belief and desire might cause him to become so nervous that he loosens his grip inadvertently without having meant to do so. In such a case, the relevant bodily movement, the loosening of the climber's grip, was caused (and rationalized) by relevant beliefs and desires of the agent. But the agent nevertheless did not act. The causation in this case did not operate in the right sort of way to constitute agency.

But what *is* the right sort of way? The challenge for the causal theorist is to say what more would need to be added to mere causation of bodily movement by rationalizing beliefs and desires (or perhaps intentions) in order that conditions sufficient for an action to have occurred be met. She must say so, moreover, without invoking once more the problematic notions of agency and action. Intuitively, one might want to say of Davidson's climber that what goes wrong is that although his beliefs and desires cause a bodily movement, they do not do so by way of the agent's *action*. But if *that* is the best that can be done for the causal theorist, clearly she has got nowhere. Agents and their actions need to disappear from the causal story altogether if the causal theory is to do the work required of it.

Sometimes, the problem of deviant causal chains is treated in the literature as though it were merely a funny little philosophical parlour game: its intrinsic relationship to important philosophical problems is left rather obscure. But I hope it may already be clear that the problem is actually of quite momentous importance. I am in agreement with John Bishop when he says that 'dealing with causal deviance is actually at the cutting edge of the attempt to rebut a historically and currently influential source of skepticism about the place of persons in nature'.[8] The question whether actions really can be accommodated within a deterministic picture of the universe is, at the very least, closely related to the question whether the problem of deviant causal chains can be satisfactorily solved. If it cannot be, then one very obvious strategy for the reconciliation of agency and determinism will have been blocked. Perhaps others are possible, but it is at least not immediately easy to see what they might be.

The challenge of solving the problem of deviant causal chains has, of course, been vigorously pursued by quite a large number of philosophers, and there is not space here to do proper justice to the range of ingenious proposals that have been presented over the last forty years or so. Rather than attempt an exhaustive assessment of the range of

---

[8] Bishop (1989: 7).

proposals currently on the table, therefore, what I shall try to do is to describe a *tendency* that I think it is possible to discern in the literature on the question. I shall try to explain why I think the tendency has arisen and why I am inclined to deep scepticism about whether any strategy that constitutes an instance of this tendency is likely ever truly to succeed.

Many approaches to the problem of deviant causal chains have begun from the not unattractive idea that what is missing in the deviant cases is a certain kind of *control*. Davidson's nervous agent clearly does not control the release of his grip. But what exactly is control? One natural suggestion likely to be amenable to the compatibilist is that control is not just a matter of the causation of movement by an agent's mental states; it requires also a certain kind of *sensitivity* to changing circumstances. In a case in which a genuine action occurs, the thought goes, it ought to be true that had the agent had slightly different reasons or slightly different intentions from those she in fact had on the occasion in question, a movement of an appropriately different kind would have occurred. But in a deviant case this will not in general be true. Suppose, for instance, that Davidson's climber believed, not that he could *right now* rid himself of the weight and danger of supporting his partner by simply unloosing his grip, but rather that he would be able to do so in, say, about ten seconds' time, perhaps because he believed that his partner would, at that point, himself let go of a second cable by means of which he was attached to the first climber's belt. If the original thought was unnerving, the thought goes, then surely this only very slightly different thought might be unnerving too and there is no reason, therefore, to suppose that it would not have produced the same nervous unloosening of the grip as occurred in the original situation. But had the original movement been the result of a true *action* it would be implausible to suppose that it would have occurred even under these changed circumstances. For the climber under these altered circumstances would have had no reason to release his grip on the rope at the very time at which he did in fact let go; that would have been ineffectual in attaining his intended end since his partner would have continued to remain attached to him by means of the second cable. The hope is, then, that some condition of counterfactual sensitivity to reasons might serve to distinguish deviant from non-deviant cases.

The trouble with most versions of this idea, though, is that counterfactual sensitivity to reasons, intentions, and the like may be present in a situation in which, intuitively, the agent still fails to act. Omnipotent and beneficent agents capable of ensuring that one's bodily movements always correspond beautifully to changes in one's belief and desire (or intention) states are the usual means by which this is demonstrated. One can imagine, for instance, a knowledgeable neurophysiologist who disables an agent's normal capacity to effect motor control, but who then goes on to intervene in such a way as constantly to produce motor impulses in that agent that are designed to effect the very motions needed to fulfil completely appropriately what he knows to be the agent's intentions. In such a case as this, it is very counterintuitive to suppose that what occurs under these conditions is ever an instance of action on the agent's part. But counterfactual sensitivity to reasons appears to be perfectly present. There must, then, it is inferred, be something more to agent control than mere counterfactual sensitivity.

It might be tempting to think that perhaps we merely need to add to the sensitivity condition a further condition specifying that the causal chain from mental states to bodily movements 'may not run through the intentions of another person',[9] as Peacocke puts it. One finds this combination—of some variety of sensitivity condition and a stipulation which is in one way or another designed to preclude cases of intervention by other agents from counting as action—in the suggestions made by a very large number of those philosophers who have reflected on the problem of how to specify the type of causal chain or mechanism that might constitute a true action. I shall call accounts of this sort, accounts of the *classic bipartite* type.[10] It is distinctive of classic bipartite accounts that the necessary and sufficient conditions for action that they seek to offer supplement the basic causal theory with requirements of two sorts: some kind of sensitivity requirement and an extra clause designed to rule out cases of manipulation in which a sensitive causal link between mental states and action is maintained somehow by the intervention of another agent. There are, however, a number of difficulties with accounts of the classic bipartite sort.

One immediate problem is that it is not obvious that there could not be cases in which the chains productive of bodily movement do run through the intentions of other agents, but where those chains seem intuitively still to be constitutive of actions. John Bishop imagines, for instance, a person fitted with a successful prosthetic neural replacement that one day breaks down. It is briefly repaired by having a second agent intentionally hold the broken wires together until they can be properly resoldered. There seems no reason to think, in a case like this, that the first agent does not remain in direct control of his or her bodily movements, despite the fact that the causal chain from her intention to her bodily movement is dependent upon the (in this case, benevolent) intentions of a second agent.

It might be responded that dependency upon the intentions of a second agent is not the same thing as the causal route from intention to bodily movement going *through* the intentions of a second agent. As Magill remarks, of Bishop's imaginary case, 'the causal route does not pass through the second agent's intentions: it passes through the wires'.[11] But it is surely possible to alter Bishop's imaginary case slightly so that the second agent is required to do more than merely hold the wires together. He might, for example, as David Hillel-Ruben suggests, need somehow to take account of the first agent's movements and adjust the level at which he must hold the nerve ends.[12] Here, the second agent's intentions would seem temporarily to have become part of the system by

---

[9] Peacocke (1979: 88).

[10] Despite important differences amongst them, I think the theories of all of the following deserve to count as instances of the classic bipartite type: Pears (1975), Peacocke (1979), Bishop (1989), Fischer and Ravizza (1998).

[11] See Magill (1998).   [12] Hillel-Ruben (1991).

means of which the correct type of neural connection is maintained for the first agent. It is hard to see, therefore, how they could avoid constituting an essential part of the causal chain leading ultimately from the first agent's intention to action. And yet intuitively it still feels as though this should count as a case in which the first agent acts; the second agent is a mere cog in the machine that constitutes the first agent's means of acting, not a true controller of his movements.

It is for reasons such as this that Bishop himself concludes that no account that merely rules out what he calls 'heteromesial' cases *tout court* is likely to be satisfactory. However, Hillel-Ruben's example also seems to be a counterexample to Bishop's own slightly different suggestion as to what one might need to add to the sensitivity condition in order to obtain necessary and sufficient conditions for action. Bishop suggests the following:

M performs the basic intentional action of a-ing if and only if:

- M has a (basic) intention to do a and
- M's having this basic intention causes M to produce behaviour b, which instantiates the types of state or event intrinsic to the action of a-ing, where
  i) the causal mechanism from M's basic intention to b satisfies the sensitivity condition and
  ii) if this causal mechanism involves feedback, then the feedback signal is routed back to M's central mental processes if to anyone's.

But in Hillel-Ruben's imaginary example, feedback needs to reach the second agent's central mental processes, and not only those of the first, if the neural connection is to work properly. Once again, then, the condition we have added to the sensitivity condition appears to rule out good cases along with bad.

It might be said, though, that even if conditions such as those offered by Bishop turned out not to be *necessary* for agency, they might still be sufficient, and that this is all that needs to be shown to demonstrate that agency would be perfectly possible in a deterministic world. But the question is whether these purportedly sufficient conditions can genuinely be regarded as themselves properly free of the idea of agency itself. For as Bishop himself notes in discussing how to prevent the correct subset of heteromesial cases from counting as instances of agency, it will not do simply to say that we must exclude those heteromesial cases *that block the agent's control*. That might indeed supply conditions that were sufficient for an instance of agency, but conditions formulated in this way could scarcely do duty as a purely event-causal analysis of that notion. And there must be room for doubt about whether condition (ii)—the condition which specifies that feedback must be to central processes which are 'the subject's own'—is illegitimate in the same sort of way. For we need to ask what reason there is for thinking that it will be possible to spell out what makes a 'central process' count as the subject's own, without already relying on the idea of agency. Spatial positioning inside the agent's skull or even inside her brain will surely turn out to be insufficient for a central process to belong to the agent, for there would seem to be no reason in principle why an omniscient and beneficent controller should not have her thought processes housed within the same skull, or even some part of the same brain, as that of the agent herself. And even supposing feedback were to those 'central processes' normally involved in the production of action by a given agent, what is to prevent an omniscient agent of the sort originally introduced so as to make trouble for the pure sensitivity condition reading off the relevant feedback information and adjusting the agent's movements accordingly, so that it remains another agent who produces and controls the action? What seems needed is not the specification that feedback reach the original agent's central processes, but that it *not* reach those of another in such a way as to enable that other to usurp the original agent's control. But now we seem to be back with the general idea that feedback to other agents *of a sort which is then utilized in such a way as to block the original agent's control* is not allowed.

In general, indeed, I think our suspicions ought to be raised by any purportedly event-causal account of agency in which it is specified that some crucial process, mechanism, etc. must 'belong' to a given agent.[13] For this idea that a process can 'belong' in a distinctive way to a particular subject such that that subject initiates and controls the way that process develops, is, in a way, the idea which is at the heart of the concept of agency. It is no help in analysing or understanding that distinctive notion, therefore, if the analysis produced retains the notion of a process or mechanism's 'belonging' to the agent, unless the relevant notion of ownership is properly unpacked in such a way as clearly to reveal that it does not smuggle in surreptitiously the very notion we are attempting to analyse. My suspicion is that Bishop's account (and others that are similar) simply replaces the difficult idea of a bodily movement being produced and controlled by an agent with the equally difficult idea of a central process being produced and controlled by an agent, which merely pushes the problem back inside the body without solving it.

Moreover, one might think that the very idea of attempting simply to supplement the sensitivity condition with a ban of some kind on causal routes that go through other agents is objectionably ad hoc. For even if such an account could be defended against counterexamples, it does not properly help us to see what exactly would be *wrong* with those routes, except that we are going to need to exclude them if our account in terms of sensitivity is not to founder on counterexamples. Whereas, it seems to me, a truly satisfactory account of action would deliver conditions that were not only de facto sufficient for action but which also managed to *illuminate* the question what it is for an agent to act. An account based purely on a sensitivity condition might have seemed to hold out the promise of providing such illumination. But if such an account is found

---

[13]   Thus, for example, Fischer and Ravizza's (1998) claim that the 'reasons-responsive mechanism' neces-sarily engaged in any instance of morally responsible action must be 'the agent's own' if we are to have conditions sufficient for morally responsible action is vulnerable to the same sort of worry.

wanting because of the possibility of cases of manipulation by another agent, then it will not do simply to attempt to tack on an extra condition so as to exclude cases of manipulation by fiat. We might thereby arrive at sufficient conditions for action, but they would hardly be illuminating ones. What is really needed from the causal theorist is a set of *positive* conditions that are such that, given that they are satisfied, manipulation would be *already* ruled out because they are precisely conditions in which the agent *herself* directly controls what happens to her body.[14]

It might perhaps be wondered whether scepticism about the possibility of a satisfactory resolution to the problem of deviant causal chains amounts to scepticism about the very possibility of a naturalistic account of agency. For it might be said that there must surely be *something* to be said, even by the incompatibilist, about why the bodily movement produced by the nervousness of Davidson's climber does not count as the result of an action on the part of the agent. If nothing further can be said than simply that it is *not* such a result, are we not left with an unreduced, inexplicable, and utterly mysterious conception of agency? I agree that more must be said, and the account of agency I shall be developing in subsequent chapters will say more. But it cannot be assumed from the outset, as I believe the causal theorist assumes, that the causal role of specifically *mental* states is bound to be central to the answer to this question. Indeed, I shall be arguing that we are unlikely to make progress until we firmly drop the assumption that mental states have to figure in the production of actions. Certain of the conditions that the causal theory tends to suppose are necessary for the occurrence of actions, I shall try to suggest, are not, in fact, necessary for it. And even if we restrict our attention to the kinds of deliberated action likely to be central to the causal theorist's view, it still cannot be assumed that an entirely deterministic picture of the causality that is indisputably involved in the phenomenon of action will be adequate to account for it. In a sense, of course, there is nothing for me to object to in the claim that in order for me to settle the question whether I shall φ at t, it is sufficient for my body to perform, at t, movements of a sort that may count as intrinsic to φ-ing, and for those movements to be caused in the right sort of way by something like an intention of mine. That is indeed quite sufficient. But the naturalistic incompatibilist will want to insist that once we have successfully spelled out what it takes, exactly, for the causation to be of the right sort, we will in effect have spelled out a conception of the *indeterministic* phenomenon philosophers have traditionally called 'the will'.

---

[14] Cf the remarks made by Paul Snowdon (1998: 304–5) on the explicit exclusion of 'capricious wills' from the chains of causality that generate true *perceptions:*

'We need to ask how we, each of us, realized that capricious will causation was an excluded possibility. Clearly, it is not a condition we were introduced to, instructed about. It seems, then, that we must count recognition of it as flowing from whatever more general instruction or explanation we received. But this seems to mean that it cannot be a condition that figures as an independent clause in the analysis'.

3.5 The disappearance of the agent

In order to introduce a second concern about the Causal Theory of Action, it will be useful to begin from an influential article by J. David Velleman (1992). Velleman characterizes what he calls 'the standard story of human action' as follows:

There is something that the agent wants, and there is an action that he believes conducive to its attainment. His desire for the end, and his belief in the action as a means, justify taking the action, and they jointly cause an intention to take it, which in turn causes the corresponding movements of the agent's body. Provided that these causal processes take their normal course, the agent's movements consummate an action, and his motivating desire and belief constitute his reasons for acting.[15]

However, Velleman finds the standard story of action wanting. The reason, he says, is that the story 'fails to include an agent or, more precisely, fails to cast the agent in his proper role. In this story, reasons cause an intention and an intention causes bodily movement, but nobody—that is, no person—*does* anything'.[16]

It will be objected, of course, by the proponent of the standard story that the events described in it and the causal relations amongst them together *amount to* an agent acting. Velleman considers the suggestion that demanding that the agent appear in the story would therefore be like demanding that a cake appear in its own recipe, an illegitimate demand based on a failure to understand what the relationship between the story and the phenomenon it is supposed to explain is meant to be. But Velleman denies that the events recounted by the standard story could constitute an agent's activity in this way. His reason is that:

...various roles that are actually played by the agent himself in the history of a full-blooded action are not played by anything in the story or are played by psychological elements whose participation is not equivalent to his. In a full-blooded action, an intention is formed by the agent himself, not by his reasons for acting. Reasons affect his intention by influencing him to form it, but they thus affect his intention by affecting him first. And the agent then moves his limbs in execution of his intention; his intention doesn't move his limbs by itself. The agent thus has at least two roles to play: he forms an intention under the influence of reasons for acting, and he produces behaviour pursuant to that intention.[17]

Velleman himself has nothing against the reductive ambition to account for human action entirely in terms of the occurrence of certain sorts of psychological states and events and the existence of particular kinds of causal relation between them. But the standard story, he insists, cannot be right because roles that we normally want to accord to *the agent* (such as that of moving his limbs in execution of his intention) are just missed out of the standard story altogether. In the standard story, the intention directly causes the bodily movement and there is nothing left for the agent (or any psychological events

---

[15] Velleman (1992: 188).   [16] Velleman (1992: 189).   [17] Velleman (1992: 189–90).

and states which we might, if we have reductionist ambitions, hope to have perform his role) to do.

How can I tell that the involvement of these mental states and events is not equivalent to the agent's? I can tell because, as I have already suggested, the agent's involvement is defined in terms of his interactions with these very states and events, and the agent's interactions with them are such as they couldn't have with themselves. His role is to intervene between reasons and intention and between intention and bodily movements, in each case guided by the one to produce the other. And intervening between these items is not something that the items themselves can do. When reasons are described as directly causing an intention and the intention as directly causing movements, not only has the agent been cut out of the story but so has any psychological item that might play his role.[18]

Velleman has his own suggestions, of course, as to how the reductionist's story might be amended so as to allow for something that genuinely could perform the agent's role and take its place in the account. But for now I wish merely to concentrate on the intuition that the standard story must be wanting, for the standard story (or at least some variant of it) is precisely what the determinist wishes to offer us as an account of agential settling. If the standard story is problematic, therefore, the determinist's account of agential settling will likewise be flawed.

What exactly is it that Velleman finds unsatisfactory about the standard story? The suggestion seems to be that the psychological states and events that appear in it are psychological states and events, to which commonsense psychology generally conceives of the agent as related in various ways. In particular, she is often related to these things by way of various varieties of *activity*. In what Velleman calls a 'full-blooded' action, for example, the agent *considers* certain reasons, *forms* an intention, *acts* on that intention. And the considering, forming, and acting that is done by the agent is therefore simply missed out of the story when we are invited to imagine that reasons by themselves causally produce intentions or that intentions by themselves causally produce bodily movements. Rather than providing a story that shows how the agent's role is played by various events and states, therefore, the standard story merely fails to recognize central aspects of the agent's role by simply leaving them out. The standard story, therefore, Velleman concludes, cannot be correct.

Here is another way of making what I think is ultimately the same point. The concepts in terms of which the states and events that figure in the standard story are described—concepts like *belief, desire, intention,* etc.—are personal-level concepts designed to appear in explanations of why human beings *do what they do* (not, in the first instance anyhow, in explanations of why their bodies move as they do). If we are intent on converting these explanations (which usually do not mention beliefs and desires at all, but rather utilize a sentential construction 'because I believed...', 'because

---

[18] Velleman (1992: 190).

I wanted...', etc.) into a causal story featuring certain causally efficacious *items*, items such as beliefs, desires, etc., we will have to be sure that the items that constitute the *effects* in the story, as well as those that we deem to be the causes, are of the right kind. And that means, given that the explanations from which the causal story is derived are explanations of why people *did* certain things intentionally, that the effects that are caused by the beliefs, desires, intentions, etc., are going to have to be *actions*. It is people's intentional *doings* that get explained by appeal to what was wished for, hoped for, intended, and the like. No doubt, when people do things their bodies must usually move, so that an explanation of why they did those things can at the same time become an explanation also of why their bodies moved (in consequence of their doings, as it were). But the doing itself—the moving of those bodies by the agents concerned—is, on the folk-psychological way of seeing things that gives concepts like belief, desire, and the rest their place in the system, utterly essential to the production of the movements, and the movements cannot take place without this role being played by the agent. The action cannot simply be missed out of the causal chain as though intentions could take one directly to movements without the agent having to *do* anything to make this happen. The exertion, the execution, which is characteristic of action, must occur before any part of the body can be in voluntarily produced motion.

None of this implies yet that one cannot give a pure event-causal story about what happens when someone acts. But it does imply, so it seems to me, that one cannot give a pure event-causal story in which the antecedent causes of bodily movements are said to be things like beliefs, desires, and intentions. These concepts are part and parcel of a way of thinking about action from which the agent and her doings cannot simply be banished, for the way of thinking is designed in the first place to be a story in which the agent and her acting essentially features. If there *is* a pure event-causal story to be told about action (and I do not at this stage want to rule this out as a possibility), it has to be told at a quite different ontological level from this, one involving, say, neural firings and muscle contractions. It cannot be a story in which the role we normally suppose action to have in the production of voluntary movement is simply taken over by states like intentions, even what have come to be known as 'immediately executive' intentions.[19] Even an immediately executive intention has to be executed.

How does the failure of what Velleman calls the standard story bear on the question with which we began of whether an agent's settling something can be constituted by her decisions, choices, intentions, or whatever, causing her bodily movements? The difficulty may perhaps best be seen diagrammatically. The determinist wants to present Figure 3.1 (or something very like it) to explain what it means for an agent to settle the question whether her body will move.

---

[19] See O'Connor (2000: 72), for the notion of an immediately executive intention.

S's settling whether her arm will move

is constituted by

S's belief + S's desire

causing

S's intention to raise her arm

causing

S's arm-rising

Figure 3.1 A causal theorist's picture of action.

But we have seen that this picture cannot be satisfactory. Intentions do not cause arm-risings except by way of causing agents to raise their arms. This diagram is therefore going to have to be replaced by Figure 3.2.

S's belief + S's desire

causes

S's intention

causes

S's action (= S's raising her arm, = S's settling whether her arm will go up)

causes (or better, is a causing of)

S's bodily movement

Figure 3.2 The inevitable reintroduction of action into its own causal analysis.

Now, however, we have been forced to reintroduce the analysandum as a *part* of the structure in terms of which we had hoped to analyse away the idea of a agent's settling a matter. The lesson, I think, is that one cannot hope to analyse what it is for an agent to act in terms merely of the causation of her bodily movements by various of her mental states, because her action has to be a *part* of this story, the part that connects those non-active mental antecedents to her bodily movements. It is the *agent* who has to settle the question whether those mental antecedents will result in a movement or not. That is the way commonsense psychology tells the story of action, and it cannot be retold at this level of ontology without her participation. If there *is* a story about the agential causation of bodily movement from which she and her actions are absent, it cannot be one in which her desires, beliefs, and intentions are asked simply to *take over* her role as a producer of movement. It must rather be a story whose participants are at a different ontological level altogether.

3.6 Settling and the antecedents of action

The objection with which I am currently attempting to deal, recall, alleges that it is possible to concede that agents are settlers of matters without invoking the robust conception of settling that demands an open future. For an agent to settle a matter, it is said, is simply for certain of her mental states to cause certain bodily movements. The occurrence of these bodily movements will then either constitute that matter's coming to be settled (e.g. the agent settles whether her arm goes up at *t*) or will cause further events that settle the matter (e.g. the agent's arm going up causes a ball to be prevented from entering the goal net and so settles the matter of whether or not a goal will be scored at *t* + 1). But none of this requires indeterminism. It is all totally consistent with a purely deterministic causal story.

But this story, I would like to suggest, has always faced a particular sort of embarrassment. The embarrassment is that a great deal of our purposive activity does not really seem to be preceded at all by the sorts of mental events and states that figure in the story. Often, I just seem to *act*, without any prior deliberation, without first deciding or choosing to do anything, and without at any stage consciously forming an intention to act in the way that I do, or being conscious of the existence of such a prior intention. I have already mentioned the existence of the sub-intentional act, and these phenomena—the scratchings, shufflings, twiddlings, and jigglings that together constitute quite a large sub-class of our bodily movings—present the most obvious counterexamples to the claim that to act is to have a bodily movement caused by something like a prior intention, decision, or choice. But even if we restrict ourselves to the realm of the clearly purposive and intentional, it is not always completely obvious how exactly the causal story whereby mentality gives rise to bodily movement is supposed to go. For example, I am now typing. As part of this clearly purposive activity, let us say I type the letter 'v'. Presumably, I did so intentionally, for I definitely meant to type that letter and not some other, given that I was trying to type the word 'activity'. There is certainly a reason-giving explanation of why I typed a 'v'. But did I, just prior to my typing it, 'form an intention' so to type it? Did I decide or choose to do so? What is the reason for saying that I did? I was certainly not aware of any such intention (or decision or choice). One could of course try to say that the intention involved was a more *general* one that it might be more plausible to suppose really *did* precede my activity, such as intending to type a particular sentence, perhaps to express a particular thought, or even just the general intention to type a bit more of this chapter this morning. But if the relevant intentions are just these general ones, how exactly do they manage to explain each of the different sub-actions that constitute the actions necessary for the fulfilment of the general intention? Aren't they too general to do that? Or, alternatively, one might try appealing to the fact that not all mental phenomena

ACTION AS SETTLING 67

need be conscious. Perhaps then there was an unconscious intention to type a 'v' the existence of which, prior to my action, can somehow be inferred from what occurs. Certainly my body must somehow get ready to type the wanted letter: there have to be cognitive processes that ensure that my finger eventually ends up over the right key, so *something* has to happen in advance of the bodily movement itself. But what makes it appropriate to describe this prior processing as the formation of an intention specifically to type a 'v'? Why is it not just what we have said it is: processing that enables me to carry out an action of a type that I really *did* form an intention to perform (e.g., expressing a particular thought)?

I do not mean to suggest that there is nowhere for the causal theorist to turn in order to attempt to answer such questions. There are of course all sorts of strategems open to such a theorist at this point, all sorts of things she could say in order to try to preserve the general idea that agency, roughly speaking, is always about something in the realm of the mind (something like an intention) causing something in the realm of the world (something like a bodily movement). But before engaging in what I think is likely to be a rather tortuous attempt to defend the idea that actions always *are* preceded by such mentalistic episodes or conditions, ought we not to ask what exactly is the reason for insisting upon preserving it? We have already assembled a number of powerful reasons for doubting that this picture captures the essential features of agency, not the least of which is the undoubted existence of sub-intentional acts whose antecedents do not seem to feature in consciousness (or indeed in the realm of the intentional or the rational) at all. And surely it must be a reason for suspicion that the compatibilist's model of agential settling here is basically Cartesian. The agent is identified with certain of her mental states and events, and *her* settling how her body will move is then thought of as *their* settling how her body will move; that is to say, in what looks from this point of view as though it ought to be the best case, as their deterministically causing the wanted bodily movements. But we human agents are not purely mental beings, we are embodied ones. A proper recognition of what it means for this to be true may make it possible to see that the settling of things by us is not necessarily the same thing as the settling of things by what is normally thought of as the paradigmatically mental aspect of our natures. If active settling (that is, agency) were instead to be thought of as an intrinsically psychophysical business that simply refuses breakdown into a mental antecedent and a physical effect, then perhaps we would not need any longer to defend the thought that if we are genuinely to do things, we must ensure that what we no doubt think of as our top-level capacities must always somehow be actively engaged.

I have not offered utterly conclusive reasons for thinking that there are bodily movements caused when we act, which are definitely *not* brought about by any prior mental states. There are too many possible ways for the compatibilist to stretch and extend the concept of a mental state in order to accommodate apparent counter-examples for it to be sensible for me to attempt to provide such conclusive reasons. But it does seem to me that the conception of what it is for an agent to move her body, which I have attempted to delineate in Section 2.4, offers a much more natural and unforced account of the phenomenon of bodily action, one which does proper justice to the huge extent to which the detailed execution by us of our activities is orchestrated by processes that are non-conscious and that occur well below the threshold of our attention. I conclude, then, that the settling of matters by agents that occurs when they act, is not, for this, as well as for the other reasons I have considered, well understood in terms of the purely causal necessitation of those same matters by mental events and states.

Perhaps the compatibilist might be inclined to suppose, at this stage, that this point could be safely conceded, without detriment to the general strategy he is hoping to pursue. He might, that is, suppose that even if it is conceded that our bodily movements do not need to be caused by mental events or states, in order for us to count as having acted, they certainly have to be caused by something: by the operations of various bodily systems of motor control that are under the general supervision of the conscious parts of the mind. It is the operation of these systems, he may now say, that constitutes the settling by agents of how their bodies shall move. And there is no reason for supposing, he will add, that these systems do not operate deterministically. Indeed, it is not clear how their operating indeterministically could introduce a true possibility for action that would not have been there without the indeterminism.

This is indeed a tempting riposte, but it is important to see that in making it, the compatibilist has shifted ground. The compatibilistic suggestion we have been considering, recall, is that, although it is true that actions are settlings of certain bodily matters by agents, we can understand what might be *meant* here by talking of an agent's 'settling' of things by way of the suggestion that when we speak of someone's having settled some matter, we really mean that some decision or choice of theirs (or perhaps some other sort of mental event or state of theirs) caused an outcome that either constitutively or causally settled that matter. The new proposal is different. It is not any longer a proposal about how to *understand* talk of agents and their settlings of matters in terms that do not involve any irreducible commitment to agents and their actions. Rather, it is a proposal about what the settling of thing by agents might in the end be found actually to *consist in*. Such a compatibilist might perhaps be inclined to concede the point, argued for in various ways in this chapter, that the conceptual framework in terms of which we characterize and explain actions is one from which agents and their settlings of things cannot simply be banished without irreparable damage to the framework. This compatibilist might even concede that actions represent, conceptually speaking, a form of causation that is necessarily indeterministic. Nevertheless, she will insist, the reality underlying the causation of the movements that we think of as agent-caused may, for all that, be a deterministic one.[20]

---

[20] Something akin to this view is argued for by John Bishop in his (1989).

One question is whether such a position as this really counts as compatibilism. For if it is conceded that it is a central part of our concept of action that agents settle things that were not previously settled, we must ask whether there are really agents who really act, according to this compatibilist. If there are and they do, then doesn't that mean that an indeterministic conceptual framework is in fact instantiated, and therefore that universal determinism is false? But if there aren't and they don't, then the position is surely eliminativist about agency rather than compatibilist. Agency is thought of merely as an illusion to which we are perhaps inevitably inclined to succumb but the basic features of which are not really present anywhere in the universe.[21]

In subsequent chapters, I shall devote some attention to the question whether some plausible version of compatibilism might be constructed based on this form of metaphysical (as opposed to conceptual) reductionism about agency. But I hope that the current chapter has responded to the main objections likely to be raised in respect of my claim that (i) if there are actions then there are settlings of matters by agents, and that (ii) the settling of matters by agents cannot be regarded, as the compatibilist supposes, as conceptually equivalent to the causation of bodily movements by those agents' mental states. It may be said that my characterization of agency as a concept that essentially involves the phenomenon I have called 'settling' might in the end have to be given up if it proves impossible to show how such a phenomenon might be naturalistically instantiated. In the next chapter, though, I shall try to argue that this conception goes very deep indeed and that it may be nigh on impossible for us simply to relinquish it. I shall also be attempting to argue that this same deeply rooted indeterministic conception of agency is thought of by us, from an early age, as applicable to many animals, no less than to human beings. Settling, I shall try to suggest, is a phenomenon that is naturally thought of as a widely possessed capacity of animals and so that no account of our own agency that gives it an entirely separate treatment from that accorded to the agency of other animals is likely to be satisfactory.

---

[21] Might it be suggested that even though the aspect of the concept of agency that concerns indeterministic settling is not truly instantiated anywhere in the universe, a sufficient number of *other* features of the concept are indeed instantiated to make it reasonable to say that there is agency? Such a view might perhaps be thought consistent with 'best deserver' analyses of the applicability of so-called 'folk' concepts. However one will find this suggestion plausible only to the extent that one regards the idea of the strong conception of settling as a relatively peripheral feature of the concept of agency, rather than (as I do) the very core. Support for the idea that it really is part of the core concept will be provided in Chapter 4.

4

Animal Agency

Do any non-human animals deserve to be called agents? This is only partly a question about animals. It is at least as much a question about agents—or rather about the *concept* of agency. I shall, accordingly, devote a large part of the current chapter to the question what exactly it might be to suppose of something that it is an agent. The term 'agent' itself, of course, will not be much help; it is a promiscuous term, with a variety of applications. One finds confirmation of this in the philosophical literature, where different writers appear to presuppose very different ranges of applicability for the term 'agent': from exceedingly narrow uses, whereby only rational, morally sensitive and reflective human adults are permitted to count as true agents, to very broad interpretations, which permit even inanimate possessors of causal powers (such as volcanoes, waves, and the like) to fall under the concept.[1] But it would be premature to conclude that the question whether animals are agents is bound to dissolve into nothing more than an empty semantic dispute, fuelled by a range of alternative definitional specifications. Perhaps the term 'agency' is indeed associated with a variety of concepts, but it does not follow that none of these concepts themselves[2] can be

---

[1] See Alvarez and Hyman (1998) for the view that inanimate substances can be capable of action and so should be regarded as agents.

[2] Here is not the place to enter into a discussion of the vexed question what concepts are. An adequate treatment of that question would demand a book in itself. But it may be appropriate to note here that I shall be assuming in what follows that certain concepts, of which there is good reason to suppose *agency* (in the sense I shall be utilizing) is one, can be regarded as having an identity that is more or less independent of that of the linguistic terms by means of which we might attempt to gesture at or refer to them, one which, indeed, does not depend even on the existence of any such linguistic terms. The grasp of a concept can be detected—even when it goes unrepresented in any lexical term or structural feature of a given language—in such phenomena as inductive projection and other forms of reasoning that reveal features of the organization of a subject's thought. Take, for instance, the young child's conception of an *animal*. Young children tend to deny that human beings are animals, thereby revealing that they associate with the linguistic term 'animal' a concept which is clearly distinguishable from the biological concept roughly corresponding to the idea of the animal *kingdom*, a concept which eventually becomes one admissible interpretation of the word *animal* for older children and adults (see Carey, 1985). Nevertheless, there is no doubt that young children *have* a concept that has the same extension as that picked out by 'animal' in the phrase 'the animal kingdom', a concept that applies to human beings as well as mammals, fish, reptiles, birds, insects, etc. What gives us the right to say this, granted that these children mostly emphatically deny that human beings are animals? The answer is: their patterns of inductive projection. These same children who deny that human beings are animals nevertheless attribute animal properties of various sorts (e.g. eating, breathing, being susceptible to pain, capacity for self-movement) only to animals (including human beings), and never to plants or inanimate objects. Animals are categorized together for the purposes of such inductions and are in this way distinguished

rendered determinate, or that we cannot elucidate any of them in such a way as to give us a reasonable purchase on the question what it might mean to ask of some species of animal whether its members can truly *act*.

I shall be attempting to argue, using evidence from developmental psychology as well as more philosophically traditional appeals to intuition and to conceptual relations, that there is a robust and distinctive *agency* concept that deserves to be recognized as a hugely powerful organizer of human thought. It is part and parcel, so I shall claim, of the 'theory of mind' or 'folk psychology' that many psychologists and philosophers have insisted must have a modular basis in the human mind. It is part of the 'matched set' of concepts that Davidson argues constitutes propositional attitude psychology;[3] indeed, it is a precondition of any non-metaphorical use of concepts like belief, desire, and intention that an agent *possessing* those beliefs, desires, and intentions be presupposed. Thus conceived, the agency concept deserves to be thought of as a distinctive conceptual possession with its own characteristic profile; its lineaments can be traced from its roots in infancy, where experimental data from developmental psychology must be our guide, to its mature form in the conceptual thinking of adults, where its basic features continue to be discernible through all the conceptual elaboration and refinements that scientific knowledge and reflective thought have grafted onto it (different elaborations and refinements having been found appealing, no doubt, by differently educated and differently predisposed individuals). I shall suggest, in what follows, that the normal development of the infantile processing of animal activity results in the eventual emergence of a mature conception of agency that has roughly[4] the following features:

(i) an agent can move the whole, or at least some parts, of something we are inclined to think of as *its* body;[5]

(ii) an agent is a centre of some form of subjectivity;

---

clearly from non-animals by young children. And so it may be argued that these children do have some version of the 'kingdom' concept, even though they do not associate it yet with the word 'animal', in the way that adults eventually learn to do. The lineaments of the relevant concept are thus determined by deep yet empirically tractable questions about which things are classed together for inductive purposes, rather than merely by dispositions to apply some word or other.

[3] Davidson (1982: 318).

[4] The word 'roughly' is not intended to indicate that these features may not be strictly necessary conditions for the existence of an agent. I believe that each *is* thus strictly necessary. However, (i)–(iv) represent necessary conditions that are of a special kind, because they are not properly independent of one another: they represent various different, related aspects of a conceptualization that comes *as a package*, and the word 'roughly' merely indicates my uncertainty about whether there might be other elements in this package that I have not noticed and which might therefore later need to be added.

[5] I am inclined to think that there are no clear, actual examples of creatures without the power of locomotion that we might nevertheless want to regard as agents, because it seems to me that the evolution of the powers constitutive of agency has in fact only been found to be necessary for creatures that move their whole bodies through the world. Nevertheless, it seems to me that an agent that could move only certain bodily *parts* is at least conceivable (or at any rate, I see no clear reason, at present, to rule it out).

(iii) an agent is something to which at least some rudimentary types of intentional state (e.g. trying, wanting, perceiving) may be properly attributed;

(iv) an agent is a settler of matters concerning certain of the movements of its own body in roughly the sense described in Chapter 2, i.e. the actions by means of which those movements are effected cannot be regarded merely as the inevitable consequences of what has gone before.

Feature (iv), of course, will turn out to be particularly crucial for me, since it is in virtue of (iv) that the *agency* concept can be seen to embody a *prima facie* commitment to indeterminism. But it is also the inclusion of (iv), I anticipate, that is likely to prove most controversial. In view of this, I shall devote quite a large portion of the chapter to the consideration of what may be said in justification of its inclusion.

I shall need, of course, in order to make the case for the view that large numbers of animals deserve to be thought of as agents, to say something about animals as well as about the concept of agency. Despite the fact that I believe (ii) really is an important part of the agency concept, I cannot here attempt directly to defend the view that many non-human animals are *conscious* (though it seems to me quite obvious that it is true), since, though important, and unquestionably relevant to the questions in which I am interested, it is too large a topic in its own right to receive adequate treatment in a book whose main concerns lie elsewhere. I shall content myself merely with commenting here that it seems to me very natural to think that the attribution of agency (and related intentional states, like desire) to an animal is closely connected with the idea that that animal possesses a subjective perspective of some kind (though perhaps one very different from any we are able easily to imagine) from which it is able to perceive a world of spatially and temporally ordered objects and events, through which it is able to move, monitor its own movements, and on which it is able, when necessary, to act with purpose, distributing its own activities across time and space according to a plan of its own design. I am inclined myself, indeed, to think that the ascription of intentional states like beliefs and desires to systems that it is *not* natural for us to think of as conscious (e.g. computers and robots) feels metaphorical; and that true thinking is hard to ascribe where a subjective viewpoint is thought of as entirely lacking.[6] If it were true, as this would suggest, that the literal ascription of thoughtful states to an organism goes hand in hand with the attribution of a subjective viewpoint to that same organism, then (ii) and (iii) would be parts of the same package of ideas and not utterly distinct conditions that might conceivably be instantiated separately from one another.

This is as much as I shall say directly in support of the attribution of consciousness to animals. It *will*, however, be important for me to rebut the suggestion that I believe has been generated by the scrupulous avoidance within certain important branches of biological science of descriptions of animals that might appear to imply the existence of

---

[6] For arguments to this effect, see also Searle (1984, 1992) and Strawson (1994a).

subjectivity, that science has simply *shown* that animal behaviour is no more than 'a set of tropisms and taxes',[7] entirely explicable by appeal to the thoughtless operation of 'instinct'. Such ideas may threaten to undermine not only the idea that animals are conscious, but also the legitimacy, in respect of their activities, of the intentional stance itself, and therefore also, on my view, the legitimacy of the view that they are agents. It may be, of course, that not all types of intentional state are sensibly attributable to all types of agent. The states we most naturally turn to in order to describe the mentality of non-human animals, indeed, are often not really *propositional* attitudes at all; they are more likely to be such things as seeing, wanting, and trying to get, none of which is associated with a verb that *needs* to take a proposition as complement, and the latter two of which positively have to be forced into the propositional attitude mould: to make verbs like 'want' and 'try' take a 'that' clause requires some effort.[8] Nevertheless, seeing, wanting, and trying to get are attitudes that fit together in much the same way as their more sophisticated and (sometimes) genuinely propositional cousins, belief, desire, and intention. Crucially, like their propositional cousins, they require at the heart of things an *agent* who sees, who wants, and who tries. I shall suggest that the stark contrast between human beings and animals of all kinds that is invited by the idea that only *our* activities genuinely merit intentional forms of description, while all else can be consigned to the realm of the thoughtless and robotic, ought not to stand the scrutiny of an age that has accepted the principle of evolutionary continuity. It should be regarded as a relic of Cartesianism, enabled to survive the nineteenth century only by the unlucky circumstance of the rise of methodological behaviourism at the start of the twentieth, which kept it in business far longer than it ever deserved.

Of course, I shall be able, in this part of my endeavour, to make common cause with many *compatibilist* writers. One finds in the philosophical literature on agency, mental causation, and free will many different versions of the idea that animals (including ourselves) can be legitimately regarded *both* as intentional agents *and* as deterministic systems. Dennett's suggestion that what he calls 'the intentional stance' provides a means of understanding the attribution of agency to complex systems that is entirely compatible with mechanistic sub-personal accounts of their behaviour is perhaps the best-known of these accounts,[9] but some forms of functionalism and many non-reductive forms of physicalism can also be regarded as falling under this head.[10] It is not surprising, indeed, that views of this compatibilist type almost exhaust the field in philosophy of mind, for they promise to permit us to combine our hazy views about what we suppose science has told us must be the truth about animals, with a continued conviction (especially in our own case) that it cannot be wrong to suppose that *thinking* (in all its forms) is very often the spring from which action flows. But despite the obvious temptations of such compatibilistic views, I shall be arguing eventually that

---

[7] See Griffin (1981: 3).   [8] See Steward (2009b).
[9] See Dennett (1971, 1973, 1987).
[10] See e.g., Fodor (1987), Dretske (1988), and Searle (1992).

they are mistaken. I have already argued in Chapter 3 against the sort of compatibilism that seeks to explicate agency in terms of causation by states and events, terms for which are derived from personal-level vocabulary ('beliefs', 'desires', 'decisions', etc.). In this chapter I shall commence my argument against the alternative suggestion that the conceptual apparatus distinctive of agency is compatible with a wholly different, *but still entirely deterministic*, way of thinking about what lies behind the movements of animals, based in the sciences of physiology and neurophysiology and the further 'lower-level' sciences such as genetics, molecular biology, and chemistry to which those disciplines in turn defer for the deeper explanation of the phenomena that they disclose.

The argument against this form of compatibilism will be begun in this chapter, but it cannot be fully completed here. My aim in Chapter 4 is to make a strong case for the view that:

(1) a concept with roughly the structure delineated by (i)–(iv) above ought to be thought of as part and parcel of folk psychology
(2) if this concept truly applies to anything at all, it should be regarded as applying to many animals, as well as to human beings.

I shall also try to say something about how we are to decide *which* animals it should be thought of as encompassing. But it is a further claim that will require much more work—work that will not be done until Chapter 8—to show that this indeterministic conception of agency that I wish to argue we undoubtedly possess really could be instantiated in the world as we know it. For this reason, I do not really expect at this stage that my arguments are going to convince the sceptical, although I hope they will at least engender doubts in the minds of some of the compatibilist faithful. In the absence of an explanation of how it is so much as *possible* that there should be creatures that are true settlers of matters, it is bound to seem easier to deny the premises of arguments against otherwise quite plausible views that deny this than to accept the consequences of those arguments. The most powerful motivation to compatibilism has always been the reflection that it is no easier to see how indeterministic processes of a physiological sort could possibly sustain agency than it is to see how deterministic ones might allow for it. It might seem to be an all-round better bet, even if one does not need to be convinced that many animals are worthy of admission to the realm of cognition within which intentional attributions make sense, to suppose that they are enabled to do so by virtue of their status as highly complex yet *deterministic* systems rather than by virtue of a necessarily indeterministic power of agency whose meta-physical possibility we have as yet been given no help with understanding. But the explanation of how there can be such a thing as settling that amounts to more merely than the occurrence of indeterministically caused events, will require a great deal of philosophical spadework. Orthodoxies concerning such things as causation, supervenience, and ontology will all need to be carefully examined and in some cases rejected, and an alternative framework based upon a workable conception of emergence and of top-down causation will need to be developed. This work I defer until later chapters and I ask dubious readers to remain patient until that spadework is done.

4.1 The concept of agency and the theory of mind

If one watches a large farm animal, such as a cow or a sheep, engaged in its normal activities, it is almost impossible, I suggest, for a normal and unprejudiced human being to avoid looking upon it as an agent. One supposes, that is, that though nature may have prescribed for it a number of essential activities (grazing, mastication, sex, drinking of water, etc.) from which it is certainly not free to forbear, *it* nevertheless determines the details of how, when, and where exactly these activities are to be carried out. If it moves suddenly from one side of the field to another, for example, we might hypothesize that that was because the grass looked better over there, or because it was shadier, or because it wants to be nearer its calf, which has wandered off in that direction. It is most unlikely that anyone not already encumbered by theoretical prejudices would suppose it had been caused to make its trek across the field by a strictly reflex action or a simple stimulus–response mechanism. The activity of a cow or a sheep, I suggest, simply does not *look* as though it could be explained by such means. It looks as though it involves such things as desires and perceptions and decisions on the part of the animal itself, and we have not the faintest idea how to explain the origination of its movements without invoking such mentalistic concepts. Our natural inclination is to think of such an animal as a creature that can, within limits, direct its own activities and that has certain choices about the details of those activities. To invoke the terminology of Chapter 2, it is natural to think of such animals as the *settlers* of various matters that concern the movement through time and space of their own bodies. I submit that it goes deeply against the grain to suppose that each exact detail of each movement orchestrated by an animal was settled at any point prior to a period broadly concurrent with what we think of as the period of the animal's action.

Research in developmental psychology strongly suggests that this prejudice may be the inevitable result of cognitive systems designed from the outset to facilitate the application of mental concepts to certain of the entities we meet with in experience. That there are such 'domain-specific' cognitive systems specifically designed to aid and abet the development of particular concepts and categories is now psychology's favoured answer to the difficult questions it has always faced about:

(i) how it is possible for young children to learn so much so fast;

(ii) how they know which of the perceptual features they meet with in experience to attend to and to utilize as the basis of their rudimentary classifications and inductive projections, and which to neglect as irrelevant;

(iii) how they can so reliably generate the concepts they require to learn a human language;

(iv) more generally, how it comes about that most children learn to think in a distinctively human way, despite the fact that many other ways of thinking (categorizing, conceptualizing) would appear to be in principle possible.

It is now very widely accepted that a child reliant only on general forms of processing, constrained by nothing more than, say, the principles of logic and the raw, unconceptualized evidence of perceptual experience, would never be able to generate the rich conceptual structures that children in fact manage to acquire with ease, and which form the basis of all subsequent learning, scrutiny, and reflective thought. And quite apart from such general considerations, there is now a substantial amount of specific empirical evidence for the view that certain areas of human cognition (e.g. language) are subserved by specialized cognitive systems that impose their own constraints upon the forms that intellectual development may possibly take in those areas.[11] It has, for these reasons, become more or less orthodox in psychology to suppose that the child must benefit quite extensively from a range of innately provided 'domain-specific' processing modules that give its development a 'leg up', so to speak, helping it to sort properties that matter from those that do not and to categorize and conceptualize its experience along the lines that it will eventually require in order to manipulate and understand the physical world and, even more importantly, to participate in linguistic and other forms of social interchange so as to be able to co-operate and communicate with others.

The question what sorts of things might constitute the 'domains' for which evolution has found it necessary to supply us with specialized cognitive processing devices is, of course, a vexed one, to which I shall not attempt to supply any kind of general answer. It is, however, a very widely held view that one of the most promising candidates to constitute such a 'domain' is the realm of understanding that involves the attribution of mentality to certain of the things in the world. Both naturalistically inclined philosophers and developmental psychologists have argued that if infants and young children were restricted only to the sorts of reasoning and empirical evidence that philosophers have permitted themselves in attempting solutions to the so-called problem of 'other minds', it is impossible to see how they would ever manage to come by the system of interpretation by means of which the young child in fact effortlessly manages to encode certain motions as purposive actions, and treats them as revelatory of mental functioning.[12] Although there is much debate about what kind of processing, exactly, lies behind this capacity for 'mind-reading', and particularly about whether or not the knowledge imputed to the developing child should be thought of as a *theory*, there appears to be generalized agreement that at any rate, some form of specialized, domain-specific processing must be involved.

---

[11] See e.g. Chomsky (1959, 1965, 1975, 1980, 1988, 1991) and Pinker (1994).
[12] See e.g. Gordon (1986), Goldman (1989), Wellman (1990), Perner (1991), Harris (1992), Gopnik and Wellman (1994), and Nichols and Stich (2003).

I do not want to become embroiled here in the details of these debates.[13] I would like simply to express my concurrence with the general view that some form of domain-specific processing must be responsible for the emergence of the capacity in young children to treat certain entities as psychological beings and then to note what I regard as a very curious feature of most of the literature in this area. The curious feature is that the capacity to 'mind-read' is almost universally treated as though it were equivalent to the capacity to postulate propositional attitude states whose independent 'behind-the-scenes' interactions are then supposed to be used by the child to explain (whether by way of the explanatory structure of a theory, or the deliverances of a simulation module) the behaviour of the entities in whom they are thought of as residing. This is particularly clear in the literature on 'theory of mind', where the idea that children deploy such a theory has often been construed simply as the suggestion that they postulate a range of unobservable theoretical 'entities'—beliefs, desires, and the like—in order to explain the behaviour of the favoured class of minded individuals. This view no doubt encourages the conviction that whatever it is that children (and later, we adults) take to be involved in the postulation of a mind, it is something that there is no reason to suppose inconsistent with determinism. But what this crucially misses out is that the conceptual framework that children in fact acquire (and that we adults go on to continue to use for the rest of our lives) is a framework, surely, which postulates not independent mental 'states' causally interacting, but rather a minded entity that *possesses* those states, and that *acts* in the light of them. Such things as beliefs and desires, according to our folk theory, have to be *had*; beliefs require believers and desires desirers. This ownership relation, moreover, is not merely a matter of the states in question being located inside a given animal body; it is a matter of their being ascribed to something whose informational and motivational properties those states describe, and which thing is *itself* regarded by folk 'theory' as the possessor of the causal power that gets the animal body into voluntarily produced motion. The mental states are simply not thought of by our folk psychology, I maintain, as independent causally efficacious entities. They are thought of rather as features of a *substantive* entity—an agent—which must *act* if any bodily movement is to result from its desires and beliefs and whose actions are thought of as explicable by appeal to, but not as deterministically caused by, those desires and beliefs. The *agent*, and not her desires and beliefs, is thought of as retaining the ultimate power to produce, or not to produce, bodily motion.

---

[13] The most prominent of these controversies is that between simulationism and the so-called 'theory theory'. Although I aim to avoid having to take a stand on this debate, it perhaps should be said here that the tendency to talk of folk psychology as though it were a theory has probably encouraged ways of thinking about what commitment to it involves that are inimical to my views. It may perhaps have encouraged, for instance, a tendency to think of what is available to observation as raw behaviour, conceived of as a pattern of bodily movements, which 'folk theory' then explains by means of the postulation of a variety of unobservable entities (mental states such as beliefs, desires, and intentions). Whereas in fact, of course, observation comes thoroughly drenched already (and from an exceedingly early age) with the commitments of folk psychology. As I suggested above, one normally *sees* a cow as an agent. One does not *judge* that on balance, beliefs and desires provide the best explanation of its behaviour.

Where agents are present, a certain spontaneity is part and parcel of the conceptual scheme we deploy, for an agent is a controller of motion that indeed *responds* to incoming information and to the motivational effects of desire, but which does so 'at will' and therefore with a certain freedom. Agents' actions are conceived of by us, I claim, as newly initiated injections into the course of history rather than merely as the inevitable consequences of preceding chains of events. The agent is at the same time conceived of both as a possessor of its intentional states and also of its body, to which it cannot be reduced, for it is a *controller* of that body.[14] This latter point is the thought encapsulated by feature (i) of the conception of agency that I outlined above[15] and it is entirely missing from most standard accounts of what folk psychology entails. Feature (ii)—the idea that an agent is a centre of some form of subjectivity—is also largely neglected, and feature (iv) is almost never acknowledged as belonging in any way to our folk conception of mindedness.[16] It is only feature (iii) to which any attention ever appears to be paid.

I suspect that features (i) and (iv) go largely ignored for the bad reason that it is supposed that they must embody an incoherent or metaphysically impossible conception of what agency involves.[17] I say that the reason is bad not because I believe it is wrong to suppose that this conception must be incoherent. For although I do believe that it is wrong to suppose that this conception is incoherent, I am not yet in a position to show that this is so. I say that the reason is a bad reason because if what we are really interested in is the shape of our concepts, we should not allow the fact that a folk theory appears to be metaphysically problematic to distract us from our descriptive task. Our folk theory might, for all that, be as described. I suspect that philosophers and psychologists who have themselves been unable to see what might be meant by an agent's causing some event if not simply that some mental state or event *within* that agent caused that event, have been much too ready to propose that folk psychology is a system of interpretation that implicitly makes this same reduction. But this, on my view, is enormously to underestimate how very different is the scheme of causal explanation embodied in the mentalistic notions central to folk psychology from those in operation elsewhere. It is also to underestimate how utterly central to this scheme is the notion of an *action*, conceived of as an irreducible and spontaneous (though not, for all that, *inexplicable*) input into the world from the agent. Indeed, actions do not really figure at all, on my view, in the folk-psychological schemes of

---

[14] Perhaps it needs saying that there is no need whatever for this folk-psychological conceptual framework to embody any sort of Cartesian dualist metaphysics (though such a metaphysics might well come to be grafted onto it in due course). The possessor of the mental states in question can perfectly well be conceived of as a physical entity—the concept one needs, roughly, is the generalization to other animals of the Strawsonian concept of a *person*—a thing that is a bearer both of physical and of psychological predicates (Strawson 1959: Chapter 3).

[15] See p.71 above.

[16] The only exception I know of is the work of Shaun Nichols, which I shall consider later.

[17] The neglect of feature (ii), of course, has a long and distinguished history, about which I shall say a little more later in the chapter.

explanation offered by many philosophers, psychologists, and cognitive scientists as a description of our folk 'theory'. All one can discern there are bodily movements$_I$ in Hornsby's sense.[18] Bodily movements$_T$, the causings by agents of bodily movements$_I$, are simply not granted any existence of their own at all in most standard accounts of the structure of folk psychology. But they are, in my view, utterly crucial elements of the folk-psychological way of thinking about the intentional causation of animal movement. Perhaps it may be that this scheme of explanation will indeed be found, in the end, to be metaphysically incomprehensible. But we should not deny its existence from the very start just because we find it hard to understand how it could be instantiated.

Is there any way of arguing further for the view that our folk-psychological view of things embodies a commitment to something like the view of agency I have sketched above? In some ways, I confess, it seems so utterly obvious to me that folk psychology involves a commitment to the existence of agents whose exertions are required if anything is ever to be *done*, and which exertions are conceptualized by us as bearing only indeterministic relationships to their causal antecedents, so that they are spontaneous inputs into the course of nature, that I find it hard to know how to argue for it, except by repeating things I have already said. One way of bolstering the argument, though, is by appealing to the very persistence of the free will problem, and the ease with which it can be explained to the uninitiated, which might themselves be regarded as reasons for wondering whether any account of folk psychology that simply proposes that actions are events conceived of as being deterministically caused by prior mental states can really be quite right. That the free will problem is so very easy to understand and yet so very difficult to make disappear to anybody's real satisfaction is good evidence, so it seems to me, that it derives from beliefs about agents' capacities which, while they cannot be reconciled happily with the deterministic stories to which our later education predisposes us, cannot readily be given up either. The dualistic schemes of various kinds that populate the philosophy of action and of explanation (reasons vs causes; Verstehen vs Eklären, agent causation vs event causation, actions vs events) are likewise witness to the existence of a conceptualization of agency that will not readily bend to the requirements of the explanatory schemes in operation in the natural sciences. But can we do better than this? Is there any way of establishing empirically, for instance, that folk psychology really does conceive of agents in the way I have suggested it does?

In the sections that follow, I shall try to do two things. I shall begin by examining the only attempt I know to provide experimental evidence for the view that young children do indeed have a 'folk' commitment to something like the concept of agency that I have characterized. The work in question has been done by Shaun Nichols, who believes that a commitment to what he calls 'agent causation' is part of our folk

---

[18] See Section 2.2 for an explanation of the important distinction between bodily movements$_I$ and bodily movements$_T$.

psychology. He maintains, moreover, the interesting thesis that perhaps the historical recalcitrance of the free will problem is owing to the fact that there are two different cognitive systems underlying the opposing intuitions in the area.[19] The first of these systems, according to Nichols, utilizes the notion of agent causation and therefore generates an intuition of indeterminism with respect to the behaviour of at least human agents. The second is a view of human actions and motivations as related to one another by means of regular principles, and which underwrites a set of equally strong deterministic intuitions. I think this hypothesis is rather promising; indeed, the view offered in this book will, in a sense, constitute a version of it. But it is a version that differs significantly from Nichols' own view; since I regard the source of our deterministic intuitions as largely *cultural*. I believe we have them not because of any innate tendency to construe agency deterministically, but rather because of such things as the huge success of the seventeenth-century scientific revolution; the impressive results of sciences such as genetics and molecular biology, which have looked to explain properties of wholes in terms of properties of their parts; and the invention of the computer and the resulting temptations of mechanistic models of animal life. It is these developments that have made us think that a sensible naturalism requires a deterministic conception of the biological realm. What needs to be shown, then, is that this perception is mistaken.

Unfortunately, I think it unlikely that Nichols' empirical results are likely to cut any ice with those who see no reason to think that folk psychology embodies any indeterministic thinking about agency, since they are capable of multiple interpretations. They are perhaps suggestive, but no more.[20] It is, moreover, quite hard to see how compatibilist-friendly interpretations could be definitively ruled out by further empirical investigations. I shall conclude, therefore, that until the ingenuity of developmental psychologists suggests other empirical approaches, we are thrown back on the kind of appeal to the intuitions of individuals about what *their* folk psychology appears to involve that I have just attempted, and the not inconsiderable evidence that is provided by the historical persistence and recalcitrance of the free will problem.

The second thing I shall try to do is to make a case for the view that our predisposition to think in these 'agent-causationist' ways is not restricted to our folk 'theorizing' about the behaviour of *human beings*. I have already asserted at the beginning of this section that we human beings have such predispositions at least when considering the activity of large mammals such as cows and sheep. However I have not yet backed up this claim, and it will be important to do so, particularly in the light of the fact that I want to claim that thinking of something as an agent brings with it such significant metaphysical commitments. In some ways, what I conceive of as being my task here is a

---

[19] Nichols (2004). Nichols is not the only person to have made this suggestion: see also Spelke, Phillips, and Woodward (1995: 72).

[20] It is only fair to Nichols to note that he is extremely cautious and tentative in the claims he makes for his empirical data, and regards his paper as 'exploratory and programmatic' (Nichols 2004: 474).

curious one: what I would like to try to do is to persuade those who might be inclined to *accept* that they have (what they regard as quite possibly incoherent) agent-causationist intuitions about the actions of human beings, but are nevertheless inclined to *deny* that they possess any such intuitions in respect of animal behaviour, that in fact they do possess such intuitions. And persuading people that they do in fact have intuitions that they firmly claim they do not have is a funny business to be in. But experience of discussing my views convinces me that there are quite a lot of people in this category. Their insistence that they are completely happy to regard all non-human animals as deterministic automata needs to be addressed. I shall not insist here that these people must be *wrong* to suppose that animals are deterministic systems—that is the task of the rest of this book. I shall only try to show for the moment that, in saying so, they are insisting upon drawing a line where the systems with which evolution has endowed us for dealing with the various forms of causally efficacious entity we encounter in the world did not decide to draw one, and are thereby denying, no doubt for what they think of as good reasons, the untutored verdicts of more primitive cognitive systems. Of course, evolution may not have drawn lines in what, on reflection, we come to think are the right places. But in this particular case, I shall argue, there are grounds for distrusting the conceptual redrawing that there is reason to think these individuals must at some point have undertaken.

4.2 Nichols on our folk-psychological commitment to agent causation

Disappointingly, there does not seem to have been a great deal of empirical developmental work on children's conceptions of those powers of agents that might be thought to reveal commitment to a view of agents as indeterministic settlers of matters. Shaun Nichols, however, has undertaken at least some limited empirical work in this area, which, he argues, does provide a certain amount of support for the idea that young children deploy a notion of what he calls 'agent causation', a notion that might perhaps be thought to be closely related to the concept of agency as I construe it. In this section, I shall briefly summarize and discuss some of Nichols' results. However, the theoretical framework in terms of which Nichols understands the belief in agent causation is, I believe, rather problematic. Moreover, I am not convinced that the experimental data obtained by Nichols can really be used to support our shared view that commitment to a distinctive agency concept is a developmental norm. Rather regretfully, then, I shall have to conclude, in the end, that proper empirical support for this conclusion, beyond what is available from earnest appeals to adult intuition, must await the results of further study.

Nichols defines possession of the notion of 'agent causation' in terms of two beliefs: (i) that actions are caused by agents and (ii) that for a given action, an agent could have done otherwise. In order to show that young children do indeed believe the first of these claims, Nichols first argues on the basis of existing developmental data that they believe something he calls the 'Correlation Principle', which is the principle that if there is an action there is an agent. He then follows this up with an argument to show that given that they accept this, it is plausible also to suppose that they accept what he calls 'the Causal Principle': that an agent is a causal factor in the production of an action. But it is not clear what conception of an 'action' it is that Nichols is utilizing here. On the view that I urged in Chapter 2, on which actions are settlings of things by agents, the existence of actions is simply *logically* related to the existence of agents, so there cannot be an action that does not have an agent. On this view, there is no need to show that children believe that there are *correlations* between actions and agents, because to discern the one *just is* to discern the other. Actions and agents on this view are just part and parcel of the very same interpretive framework. Moreover, there are strong reasons for thinking that the view that actions are caused by agents is rather straightforwardly incoherent (see Section 2.3), and though (as I have in effect already remarked) the fact that a view is incoherent does not mean that we might not be predisposed to hold it, it might surely be a reason to check that there are not other, less problematic ways of formulating what it is we are proposing the child might believe. And there *are* less problematic ways of formulating the intuitions that are at the heart of agent causationism, as recent proponents of the agent-causationist view have frequently urged.[21] We can say that it is movements (and not actions) that are thought of by the agent causationist as being caused by agents and that actions themselves are the causings by agents of those movements. Thereby we would avoid at least some of the more obvious difficulties often alleged to beset agent causationism, in particular the dilemma that it is alleged to face by Davidson.[22] For these reasons, therefore, I do not accept Nichols' suggestion that (i) should be regarded as an essential part of an implicit commitment to agent causation. Moreover, I shall in any case come on to discuss in Section 4.4 some of the developmental results that Nichols (mistakenly, in my view) takes to indicate the child's acceptance of (i). I shall therefore largely ignore the claims Nichols makes on behalf of (i), and proceed to focus on what he has to say in support of (ii).

Nichols offers the results of two experiments in support of his claim that children regard agents as having an (indeterministically conceived) capacity to do otherwise. In the first experiment, children aged between 3½ and 6½ were asked of an agent whom they observed 'exhibiting some motor behaviour'[23] whether that agent could have done otherwise, and also asked of an inanimate object whether it could have done other than it did. For instance, in one of the agent cases, children were shown a closed box with a sliding lid. The experimenter said, 'See, the lid is closed and nothing can get in. I'm going to open the lid'. At this point, the experimenter slid the lid open and touched the bottom of the box. Then the child was asked: 'After the lid was open, did I have to touch the bottom, or could I have done something else instead?' In the

---

[21] See e.g. the references provided above, Chapter 2 note 26.   [22] See Davidson (1971: 52).
[23] See this chapter, note 40 below for an explanation of the scare quotes.

parallel inanimate object case, the children were shown the same box with a ball resting on the lid. The lid was then opened and the ball fell to the bottom. The children were asked 'After the lid was opened, did the ball have to touch the bottom, or could it have done something else instead?' In a second task, designed to help rule out one kind of deflationary interpretation of the results of the first, children were asked whether agents *chose* not to undertake a task that the children (but not, so far as the children knew, the agents) knew was actually impossible to carry out (e.g. to remove money from a table to which the money was glued) in the case (i) where the agent tries and fails the task and (ii) does not try at all.

Nichols' results in the main part of this experiment suggest very strongly that children do maintain that human agents, but not inanimate objects, could have done other than they actually did. Every child tested on the first task maintained that the experimenter could have done something else, and all but one said that the inanimate object had to do what it did. Nichols also maintains that the results obtained on the second task suggest that children are not merely operating with a notion of ability to do otherwise that is simply equivalent to the idea that external constraint is absent, since they tended to think that an agent made a choice even where she was in fact externally constrained. In addition, Nichols reports the results of a second experiment in which children were asked whether (i) an agent could have done other than she did, even in a case in which it is specified that everything in the world is the same right up until the moment of choice, and (ii) whether an inanimate object could have done something other than it did, even in a case in which it is specified that everything in the world is the same right up until the moment at which it does what it does.

For example, children were given a case in which Joan is in an ice-cream store and chooses to have vanilla. They are then asked to imagine that everything is exactly the same up until the moment at which she chose vanilla, and are asked whether, in that case, she had to choose vanilla. In a second case, they are told about a pot that is put on a stove to boil and are asked again whether, if everything in the world right up until the moment at which the pot boiled had been exactly the same, the water would have had to boil. And in a third type of case, designed to probe a suggestion of Nichols that the development of moral concepts may be connected with the formation of the notion of agent causation, children were asked also about a case in which an agent steals a candy bar. Once again, the question they are asked is whether, in an imagined world in which everything in the world right up until the moment at which the agent chose to steal the candy bar had been the same as in the actual world, the agent would have had to choose to steal it or whether she could have chosen differently. Nichols' results for this second experiment showed a significant difference in responses between the physical and the moral cases, participants being more likely to say that the outcome had to happen for the physical cases. They were also more likely (but not quite so much more likely) to say that the outcome had to happen for the physical cases than for the spontaneous-choice cases (though two respondents interestingly gave deterministic responses in all cases).

What are we to make of Nichols' results? The difficulty is that it is hard to maintain (as Nichols himself admits) that they unquestionably reveal a commitment on the part of the children in question specifically to an *indeterministically conceived* capacity to do otherwise on the part of the agent. No compatibilist is likely to deny that children (or adults) think that an agent who performs a given action could generally have done otherwise, in a way that, say, a billiard ball could not have diverged from its existing path. She will simply insist that there is nothing in this commitment that either actually does imply, or need be thought by the child in any way to imply, the falsity of determinism. And since that is so, the results of the first experiment seem almost beside the point. The second experiment is, of course, intended to provide some evidence for the view that children are indeed inclined to think of the capacity to do otherwise in an indeterministic way, because of the stipulation that, in considering the question whether a given agent could have chosen differently, they are to imagine that nothing is altered right up until the moment of choice. But of course it is very unclear how the children in question might have been inclined to interpret that stipulation. In particular, it surely cannot be ruled out that they interpreted the instruction in such a way as entirely to ignore the way things were *with the agent*, for example that they did not understand that they were to maintain the relative strength of the agents' desires constant, as well as everything else. And unless this possibility is ruled out, the compatibilist will have a perfectly coherent story to tell about why Nichols obtained the results that he did.

Unfortunately, then, it does not seem to me as though Nichols provides any very convincing empirical support for the view that children are implicit operators of an indeterministic agent-causationist metaphysics. Until further experiments are done, therefore, the case for the claim that agent causationism is part and parcel of folk psychology must rest on more traditional philosophical appeals: firstly to extant adult intuitions about what is involved in the postulation of minded entities with the capacity to act, and also to the powerful circumstantial evidence that is provided by the tenacious hold on the human imagination of the free will problem. Let me be clear that I do not think the case, thus supported, is weak. The philosophical literature is simply full of evidence of the existence of the intuitions I have attempted to elicit: that it is agents and not their states that make things happen, that an agent who does something intentionally could always have refrained from doing that something at the very moment of action, that actions are 'up to' their agents, that actions are spontaneous injections into the course of nature and not merely the inevitable consequences of what has gone before, and that reasons 'incline without necessitating'.[24] But it is also full of the writings of those who believe these intuitions to be not the promptings of cognitive systems whose verdicts deserve to be heard, but mere primitive confusions that a little science and a little philosophy should soon clear up. Much of the rest of this

---

[24] Leibniz, (1956 [1707]: 57).

book will be taken up with the attempt to show that, on the contrary our 'agent-causationist' intuitions are there for the very good reason that they are the product of cognitive systems that help us discern (though not infallibly, of course) the many genuine instances of agency that there are in the world around us.

Before proceeding to undertake that task, though, I want to try to say something in defence of my view about where exactly we ought to think of those agent-causationist intuitions as leading us. In particular, I want to try to argue that the conception of agency with which I have tried to suggest we end up (that characterized by (i)–(iv)), is one which, if it applies to anything in the world at all, applies not only to human beings but also to a wide variety of animals. And to begin that task, I want to consider the strong evidence for the view that the concept of agency is an outgrowth of the concept of *animacy*. That this is so, of course, does not show that all animals are agents, according to the concept of agency that is part of folk psychology (something I explicitly deny), nor that all agents are necessarily animals (something I deny also). For the concept of agency is indeed a *concept*, which means that the normative question whether it does indeed truly apply to an entity can always be raised, even if that entity was something of a kind that the concept was evolved in order to deal with. But it does suggest that the evolutionary *point* of the concept of agency (and relatedly, of course, the concept of mind) has something important to do with the need to conceptualize animal activity differently from the activity of other things. Substantial portions of folk psychology, I shall suggest, are meant to be for animals, too. And that means, I think, that there is something likely to be wrong with the insistence that in so far as we have indeterministic intuitions about agency, we have them only in respect of human beings. Those who claim not to have them in respect of non-human animals, I want to suggest, have allowed a certain conception of what the truth about animals must be to cloud a natural and more basic predisposition to believe that the truth, in fact, is something quite other.

4.3 Folk psychology and the animate–inanimate distinction

The capacity to attribute fully-fledged propositional attitudes to agents is an impressive and complex ability that most psychologists believe does not begin to emerge until at least halfway through the second year of life, and which takes several years to come to full fruition. The capacity to distinguish animates from inanimates, by contrast, develops much earlier, as does what seems likely to be a related sensitivity to goal-directed actions. It is now more or less uncontroversial amongst psychologists that domain-specific processing of some kind is responsible for the infantile conceptualization of animate movement and change. There is, however, still plenty of controversy about how the relevant processes are organized, which features they respond to, and how they are best to be described. There is very strong evidence that from early infancy, human beings process information about the movements of animate entities quite differently from the movements of inanimate ones, and that they bring to bear on these movements explanatory principles never normally looked for in the explanation of purely mechanical interactions.[25] Infants as young as 7 months appear to make distinctions between things that can move themselves and things that require an external source of energy (e.g. a push or a pull from some other object) to make them move.[26] Spelke, Phillips, and Woodward (1995), for example, report an experiment that appears to show that 7-month-old infants do not apply the contact principle—the idea that objects act upon each other if and only if they touch—to human beings, though there is a wealth of evidence to suggest that they reason in accordance with the principle where inanimate objects are concerned.[27] Infants' interest (as measured by looking times) in a videotaped display in which one large, brightly coloured object with a 'meaningless' shape moved towards a second, stopping a little way short of the second, to be followed by movement in the second object, was reliably greater than in an event in which contact occurred. This suggests that infants were surprised, in this case, by the violation of the contact principle. However, no such effect was remarked when the same patterns of motion were presented but where the objects in question were human beings. Here there seems to be no expectation that the objects will conform to the contact principle. Even at this early age, then, it appears that different causal principles are applied on the one hand to the motions of inanimate objects, and to human agents on the other.

Other evidence suggests, though, that it is not only human agents whose motions are differently coded and conceptualized by the developing infant. Gelman (1990) proposes that an early *general* distinction is made between animates and inanimates. which is shaped and facilitated by two important 'skeletal causal principles', which she calls *the innards principle* and the *external agent principle*, respectively. Processing governed by the innards principle, she argues, treats certain natural objects—the ones we call 'animate'—as though they have something 'inside' them that explains their movement and change. Processing governed by the external agent principle, on the other hand, is constrained by the expectation that movement in a given object requires the imparting of some sort of external impetus or force.[28] These skeletal principles, Gelman proposes, work together with complementary perceptual processes that focus attention on features either innately known or swiftly learned to be relevant to the categorization of objects as animate or inanimate (such as presence of faces, biomechanical patterns of movement, surface cues indicating the nature of the 'stuff' of which a thing is made), in

[25] See e.g. Premack (1990), Gelman (1990), Leslie (1994), Gelman, Durgin, and Kaufman (1995), and Spelke, Phillips, and Woodward (1995).

[26] See Premack (1990) and Leslie (1994).

[27] See Leslie (1982, 1984), Leslie and Keeble (1987), and Spelke and Van de Walle (1993).

[28] See also Leslie's (1994) account of the module he called 'ToBY' (Theory of Body), which amongst other things assigns a source of energy to any given motion according to the answer to the question whether it was made to move by something else, or alternatively, has an internal source of energy.

order to aid in the rapid accumulation of knowledge about the animate–inanimate distinction. A study by Massey and Gelman asked 3- and 4-year-old children whether each of a range of novel items pictured in a range of photographs could move itself up and down a hill or not.[29] The photographs included four different exemplars from each of the following five categories: (i) mammals, (ii) non-mammalian animals, (iii) rigid complex objects, (iv) wheeled objects, and (v) statues that had familiar animal-like forms and parts. None of the children could name or identify any of the objects and yet the children reliably answered of all the animals—mammalian and non-mammalian— that they could go up and down the hill by themselves. They denied that this was so in the case of the statues. Apparently, then, these children were already highly sensitive to the cues for animacy and inanimacy present in these photographs and were able to utilize this knowledge, together with the general rule that all animals can move themselves and all inanimate objects required an external agent in order to move, to predict correctly whether or not the item in the photograph would be able to move up and down the hill on its own.

It appears, though, that the presence of these extra perceptual features is by no means required in order to cue the type of processing associated with the discernment of goal-directed action.[30] Research carried out by Gergely et al. (1995) appears to demonstrate that infants as young as 12 months old interpret computer animations in which a small circle approached and contacted a large circle by jumping over an intervening obstacle, in a way that reveals that they apply what Gergely and Csibra (2003) have called 'the teleological stance' in such cases. The teleological stance, as characterized by Gergely and Csibra, is non-mentalistic in that it does not involve the attribution of true intentional states to the agents involved. Rather, the stance is based on relationships between three crucial representational elements: the action itself, a possible future state (the goal), and the relevant situational constraints. Given information about two of these three elements, infants are able to make an inference about the third, based on what Gergely and Csibra call 'the rationality principle'. This principle supposes that agents will in general take the most efficient action for achieving their goals given the situational constraints *as these are perceived by the infant herself.* For example, in one of the violation-of-expectation studies conducted by Gergely et al. (2005), infants who had been habituated to the computer animation described above were then tested to see what happened if the 'situational constraint' (the intervening obstacle) was removed. Infants were shown two test displays: the same jumping goal-approach as they had seen during the habituation phase (only now without the obstacle) or a novel straight-line approach. Infants looked longer

---

[29] See Massey and Gelman (1988).

[30] Though the matter remains controversial. See Woodward (1998) for a view opposed to that outlined in what follows. It should be noted, though, that this controversy is orthogonal to the main concerns of the present chapter; for both camps agree that the development of the agency concept is early, and precedes by many months the establishment of any facility with true propositional attitude attribution.

(indicating violation of expectation) at the jumping action, arguably because, in the absence of the obstacle, they regard this as an inefficient means to the goal. But crucially, no attribution of intentional states to others is required in order to apply the teleological stance. All that is required is the simple postulation of an action with a goal. It is thus a simpler stance than the intentional stance proper and does not require any understanding of such things as pretence or false belief.

It seems very plausible that the basic distinction between things that move them-selves (as the objects in the animated display at least appeared to) and things that require some kind of external impetus in order to move provides the initial criterion of selection (or at any rate, one of the most important criteria) by means of which objects are or are not treated as potential candidates for inputting into the further module or modules that embody the infant's nascent conceptualization of mind. This is the view both of Premack and of Leslie, although their accounts of the structure of the mind module differ in various respects.[31] According to Premack's theory, the infant divides the world into two kinds of object: those that are and those that are not self-propelled. This then becomes the basis of further differentiated interpretations of the movements in question:

...first, the infant perceives certain properties, for example, one object is moved by the other under conditions of temporal and spatial contiguity, versus the object is self-propelled...second, the infant not only perceives, but also interprets, that is, the infant's perception is the input to a slightly higher-order device that has interpretation as its output. The interpretations in the two cases in question are causality and intention respectively.[32]

Leslie's early view is somewhat similar, in that he too supposes that infants are innately predisposed to pay particular attention to the question whether a object is or is not made to move by something else, and that this distinction then serves as a means of selecting inputs to a higher level subsystem that he calls ToMM (Theory of Mind Mechanism). For Leslie, though, there are reasons for dividing ToMM into two parts: one concerned with agents and the goal-directed actions they produce, the other, more sophisticated module with propositional attitude ascriptions. According to Leslie, what he calls ToMM system$_1$ begins to develop at an age of around 6–8 months, one of the first signs of its development being the following of eye gaze. System$_1$ can represent an agent as acting to bring about a state of affairs and thus recognizes the basic notion of a creature's having a goal or end. Other indications of the emergence of system$_1$ include the fact that infants begin, during the second half of the first year, to acquiesce and help in achieving the recognized goals of others, for example in positioning to be picked up or to have a nappy changed—and also begin requesting behaviours, for example handing an object to its mother as a request to operate it. But Leslie argues that this concept of goal-directedness is not yet a propositional attitude notion because 'acting to bring about...' does not describe an attitude to a proposition, but rather an

---

[31] See Premack (1990) and Leslie (1994).   [32] Premack (1990: 3).

endeavour to change physical circumstances.[33] Propositional attitudes proper are the preserve of what he calls ToMM system$_2$, which does not begin to develop until during the second year and which involves the attribution of full-blown representational states, such as beliefs, to others. According to Leslie, the most obvious early sign of the emergence of this system is the ability to pretend and to understand pretence in others. This normally happens at between 18 and 24 months of age. Eventually, ToMM system$_2$ presumably develops into what underwrites the normal capacity to apply the intentional stance, a perspective from which behaviour is explained and predicted by means of the attribution of such things as beliefs, desires, and intentions to agents.

Suppose some story of this kind were correct in broad outline. If it were, it would follow that non-self-movers, on the whole, would not be considered to be contenders for possession of mind at all.[34] Self-movers, though, would go forward, to be inputted experimentally into the developing mind module(s), which then attempts to assign such things as goals and intentions to the candidate agent. Not every self-mover may be able plausibly to sustain its candidacy for very long, of course. Gelman, Durgin, and Kaufman note that machines represent an interesting hybrid category since although they appear to move on their own they are made of inanimate material, do not exhibit typical biomechanical motions, and do not adjust well to local environmental problems:

Robots are not particularly good at adjusting their motions to local perturbations in the environment; in contrast, so predictable is the animate world's ability to deal with unanticipated holes, bodies of water, oil slicks, branches that come below the head, sun in the eyes, weather changes, etc., that we almost forget how remarkable are the action abilities of the animate world. This reflects the fact that machines do not exhibit the kind of action that is controlled by biological mechanisms...—action patterns that are noted by infants...and used as cues for animacy. Additionally, machines are made of the wrong stuff.[35]

---

[33] For similar views, see Golinkoff (1981) and Poulin-Dubois and Schultz (1988).

[34] What about dolls, teddy bears, and the like? While the tendency of young children to attribute mental states to their toys may be testament to the power of *facial features* to serve as a preliminary guide in the sorting of objects into those which are and those which are not potential candidates for application of theory of mind (and see Johnson (2000) for further evidence), it seems fairly clear that children are aware from a pretty early age that dolls and the like are only 'pretend' subjects. In the Massey and Gelman study mentioned above, for instance, children were clear that figurines, statues, and the like could not move themselves up or down the hill, and justified this claim when asked by appeal to the fact that these things were (i) not real or (ii) made of the wrong 'stuff'. There is also evidence that much younger children than these are sensitive to information that distinguishes between realistic three-dimensional replicas of animals and non-animals (Smith 1989). Though faces matter, then, and though Leslie is surely right when he speculates that 'it seems highly likely that such low-level mechanisms have inputs into ToMM' (1994: 145–6), it seems likely also that ToMM quickly learns to override the *prima facie* evidence of mindedness that is supplied by a face. Children swiftly learn, in other words, that a face is not a sure sign of a self-moving animal, nor, therefore, a sure sign of a mind.

[35] Gelman, Durgin, and Kaufman (1995).

These authors are admittedly primarily interested in the child's conception of *animacy*, not agency, but it is not implausible that the problems robots generally swiftly encounter in dealing with obstacles renders them unsuitable candidates for genuine agency too. Initially-formed hypotheses about purposiveness, for instance, might be hard to maintain in the face of a robot's very limited abilities to keep itself on course despite deflections and obstacles: one cannot readily tell what might be the aims of something that cannot devise ways to overcome quite simple problems in order to achieve them. ToMM system$_1$, it is reasonable to suppose, can only really get going properly where the objects with which it is confronted are good at attaining their goals, and robots, even when such 'goals' are programmed in, are not terribly good at it, except in extraordinarily artificially constrained environments. Added to the fact that robots do not move in the ways typical of the animal agents in response to which ToMM must originally have evolved, and are generally made of a very different kind of material, it would perhaps not be surprising if, as Gelman, Durgin, and Kaufman speculate, they are eventually assigned to a category of their own: self-movers, perhaps, but not necessarily ones to which coherent goals can readily or profitably be ascribed, and almost certainly not ones that deserve the further attentions of ToMM system$_2$. This initial prejudice, presumably, might later come to be confirmed when, as older, more mature operators of the 'innards principle', we come to recognize that although there is indeed something inside a robot that guides and controls its behaviour, that something is a very different sort of something from whatever it is that is inside an animal, a 'something' which, we are inclined to suppose, requires no subjective perspective, no intentional states, and certainly nothing amounting to spontaneous injections into the course of nature on the part of a robot-self.

This sort of account fits well with more recent proposals by Biro and Leslie (2007), who offer what they call a 'cue-based bootstrapping model' of infant development. In this model, an initial sensitivity to certain behavioural cues for goal-directed action leads to learning about further cues, which in turn feed back to force revisions, modifications, and developments of the original cue-based system. On this view, the infant begins with a core notion of a goal-directed agent that is triggered by a certain range of cues (for example, self-propelled motion, equifinality,[36] and an action-effect). Infants then gradually begin to calculate the statistical associations between these cues, and between these and other properties of the events they witness, such as the general appearance of things likely to exhibit the cues. Once such associations have been learned, infants can anticipate goal-directed actions without direct benefit of the cues and can also reject certain candidacies, despite the superficial evidence provided by the cues. In this way, we might conjecture, children eventually become able to discern an

---

[36] 'Equifinality' is a property possessed by an act-type when it may be accomplished by any one of a number of different means. It may be emphasized experimentally by ensuring that e.g. a touched object is touched successively from a number of different angles, or that a pursuing object takes more than one route to its quarry on different occasions.

action even in the absence of any type of motion at all (e.g. when someone is deliberately keeping still for the purposes of a game of musical statues), and also to decide that what they have witnessed is not an action, despite the presence of the cues (as for example with a computer animation in which one circle 'pursues' another). The cues are thus not *criteria* for the application of the developed concept, they are rather clues utilized by the mind module en route to the establishment of a more mature conceptual capacity.

For this reason, the fact that the concept of agency is an outgrowth from the concept of animacy does not imply that nothing made of inanimate matter could ever conceivably constitute an agent, according to the conception of agency that develops out of the categories whose general lines are established by this early processing. Being made of the right kind of stuff and moving in characteristically biomechanical ways are doubtless important *cues* for the attempted application of the agent concept, but it does not seem likely that they are *criteria* for the application of the developed concept. The test for this can only really be what people are inclined to think when asked. My own experience with generations of students suggests that on the whole, people are inclined to agree that what a thing is made of and what it looks like can in the end not be allowed to count definitively for or against its agency or mindedness, conceptually speaking. Most agree that there is no a priori reason why an artificial system that could display sufficient flexibility and intelligence in its responses to its environment might not eventually demand interpretation as a conscious and thoughtful wielder of agency. There may in fact be empirical reasons, of course, why only certain sorts of matter can support the phenomena associated with consciousness, subjectivity, and the capacity to settle things. Indeed, it seems to me quite likely, as John Searle has argued, that consciousness will turn out to be essentially a biological phenomenon, as will agency, in my robust sense of that term. But we are not yet in a position to be able to be sure that this is so. And there is nothing in the *concept* of agency itself, I believe, that rules out the possibility of its instantiation in artificially created, non-biological matter. If this is an impossibility, it is an empirical, not a conceptual one.

Neither is it the case that the agency concept is applicable to all animals, despite its deep connections with the animate/inanimate distinction. It does not follow from the fact that the agency concept develops out of information processing systems designed to conceptualize the movements of animal entities in a special way that we cannot, as more mature wielders of the concept thus formed, then ask the *normative* question whether the concept truly applies to creatures of a given sort. The concept, once formed, has its own integrity, for it is indeed a *concept* that has been formed and not a mere disposition. It is perfectly possible, therefore, after reflection or empirical investigation, to decide that a given type of animal does not meet the conceptual criteria for agenthood because it has been discovered in the case of that animal that what perhaps to a first view *looked* a bit like a case of agency, in fact does not qualify. A paramecium, for instance, might move in such a way as initially to suggest the applicability of the agent concept and to cue its application in young children (or even in adults) watching the movements through a microscope, say (just as the kinds of animated computer displays described above cue the attempted application of the scheme, in ways that leave a distinctive phenomenological trace when one perceives such displays, despite the fact that as an adult one knows perfectly well that the little circle is not really trying to contact the larger one). But once we find out that a few simple equations govern its movement through the water, there is no reason to suppose that there is any role left for a paramecium-self to play in the control of the paramecium body. There is, in fact, only the body, actuated by a range of forces. And this means that the paramecium cannot be an agent, according to the agent concept described by (i)–(iv). None of its interactions with the environment need be mediated by anything thought-like, and none need involve anything like choice or decision on the part of the paramecium. Everything can be arranged by means of simple chemical processes, and the postulation of mentality under these circumstances is surely *de trop*.

What the paramecium case shows, though, is the vulnerability of the untutored perceptually based intuitions that select potential inputs for the mind module, to the results of subsequent reflection and enquiry. The paramecium looked as though it might have had a mind; but it turned out that it did not. And having made this concession, of course, it might seem as though we are at the top of a slippery slope. Might we not also need to revise untutored views of animals rather more complex than the paramecium? Might not such things as worms and insects, say, succumb to a similar treatment? Indeed, why stop there? Perhaps even the agency of cows and sheep will turn out to be comprehensible without any essential invocation of thought or mentality of any sort. And what about our own agency? We too are actuated by chemical processes and neural mechanisms. Once we have given up on the paramecium mind, is there anything to stop the whole of folk psychology collapsing like a giant house of cards, as eliminativists have always suggested it will, in the face of the advancing neurobiological sciences?

It is such thinking as this, I think (aided by other forces that I shall shortly discuss) that has given rise to the huge distrust that now attaches (across large areas of philosophy, cognitive science, psychology, and biology) to the spontaneous codings of the mind module, and which has led, indeed, to a failure even to recognize what its spontaneous codings *are*. For that is what I take the frequently declared absence of the intuition that animals are agents to be. The available evidence suggests that the mind module is primarily designed to take as its inputs those entities initially coded by lower-level modules as animate. Animals, I maintain, tend to be thought of and perceived by us initially as *agents*, and this entails, I suggest, that we think of them and perceive them as (i) possessors of bodies that they control; (ii) centres of subjectivity; (iii) possessors of some varieties of intentional states; and (iv) settlers of matters that concern the movements of their own bodies. As I have stressed, the concept of agency is not itself a biological concept: we are prepared to consider the attribution of agenthood to non-animate systems and also prepared to deny it, on reflection, to animate ones. The agent/non agent distinction is not the same as the animate/inanimate distinction. But we ought not to allow the fact that there is room for reflective input into the precise boundaries of the *agent* category to distract us from the central and important truth that many, many animals are placed inside it by the more unreflective systems with which nature has endowed us for dividing up the world, and moreover that animals appear to constitute the main candidates for conceptualization according to that scheme, so far as nature is concerned. Perhaps no non-human animal could truly *be* an agent in the sense implied by (i)–(iv) above; perhaps not even any *human* animal could be one. These are issues yet to be addressed. But my concern at present is not to show that animals are agents, but merely to insist that some part of us finds it almost impossible not to categorize them as such and to plead that this intuition deserves not to be lost underneath the mountain of epistemological scrupulousness, religious and cultural anthropocentrism, Cartesian dualism, and behaviourist scientific methodology that has, I believe, been deposited on top of it by recent, and indeed by some not so recent, intellectual currents. It seems to me that the results of this primitive and unreflective categorization are phenomenologically tangible to those open to its influence: watching a bird pecking around for food or a cat stalking a mouse is just utterly unlike watching, say, trees blow in the wind or a car drive down a road. To watch a creature engaged in such goal-directed activity is, I maintain, to think of it as a moment-to-moment controller of its own body, a centre of subjectivity, a possessor of some representational and some motivational states (whether or not we are prepared to call these 'beliefs' and 'desires'), and a settler of matters that concern its own bodily movements. This way of thinking is, moreover, at the same time a way of *seeing*.[37] These intuitions undoubtedly become less powerful as the animals in question become less easy to categorize as animate to begin with (e.g. where facial features are absent or difficult to perceive) or where many of a given creature's movements cannot easily be interpreted as the results of intentional, goal-directed actions (e.g. where it is obvious that some 'tropism' or other is really responsible for some movement or other, as when a moth flies repeatedly into a light) or where it is just more difficult, owing to factors to do with size, speed, and habitat, for us to watch a creature's activity over the period of time that might be necessary to reveal the goal-oriented patterns in its behaviour. The concern that the truth is perhaps that the strength of the intuitions diminish as a creature becomes less like a human being and that this might not really constitute an adequate basis on which to make or deny ascriptions of mindedness is, of course, a legitimate one. But before we embark on the task of interrogating our intuitions, we should at first allow them to register with us, for perhaps it may be that they make distinctions in the places they do for reasons not altogether unconnected with the fact that there are indeed distinctions in those places that need to be discerned.[38]

---

[37] Cf Wittgenstein: 'We say: "The cock calls the hens by crowing"…Isn't the aspect quite altered if we imagine the crowing to set the hens in motion by some kind of physical causation?' (1953: §493).

[38] Though these distinctions need not, of course, be *sharp*. There is a distinction between red and pink even if there is no fact of the matter as to how certain intermediate shades are to be classified. I return in the

In Sections 4.5 and 4.6, I want to turn to examine some of the forces that I think have militated against recognition and acceptance of what I maintain is the reading of animal behaviour as agency to which our cognitive systems naturally incline us. There are a great many of these forces but some are less in need of my attention than others, being systems of ideas whose star is already well on the wane (such as Cartesian dualism, for instance). I shall focus here on two culprits:

(i) the *language* used in several branches of science important to our developed thinking about animals, a language which, in its concern to avoid any undue intimations of animal mindedness or agency in its descriptions of animal behaviour, has, I believe, encouraged the idea that there can be no place for animal mindedness or agency in a scientific view;

(ii) the philosophical thought that if there is to be a logical stopping point on the 'slippery slope' mentioned above, the logical place to stop is at human beings, because of the unique epistemological perspective offered us, by self-consciousness on the one hand and language on the other, on the facts constitutive of our own mindedness.

Then, in Sections 4.7 and 4.8, I shall turn to a line of thinking more amenable to my suggestion that there is no huge and unbridgeable divide between the agency of humans and that found in a large range of simpler creatures. This is provided by Daniel Dennett's conception of the intentional stance. Dennett's ideas lend support to the claim, on which I also wish to insist, that many animals ought to count unequivocally as agents. I shall suggest that Dennett's views are also the best place to begin thinking about the question how to decide *which* animals merit the application of the relevant scheme of explanation. But I shall not accept two crucial features of Dennett's view, and it is this that will permit the room for manoeuvre in which I shall attempt to stake out my own incompatibilist theory of agency, in contradistinction from Dennett's resolutely compatibilist stance. Firstly, I shall insist that the scheme of explanation in question should be thought of as involving not only (and indeed, not always) beliefs, desires, and intentions but also the concept of an *action*, a concept that is completely missing from Dennett's picture of what it is to adopt the intentional stance with respect to a given system. Secondly, I shall not accept the view that the mere *availability* of appeal to the intentional or teleological stance for explanation and prediction is a sufficient criterion of agenthood: I shall suggest, as others have done, that one can fruitfully treat as agents many things that clearly are not agents. Rather, one needs the idea that there are certain creatures whose role in the world and its happenings cannot be correctly understood *at all* without adopting at least the teleological stance, creatures whose workings one would misunderstand entirely were one to fail, for some reason,

---

final section of this chapter to the important question of what we are to say about the boundaries between the minded and the non-minded, and will defend the view that there are bound to be creatures with respect to which there is no clear fact of the matter about whether or not they are agents or have minds.

to characterize them as agents. Then I shall turn to consider the claims of two kinds of intuitively fairly lowly animals to be accounted agents in the light of the emerging account of agency; I will defend my view against the accusation that it must presuppose sharp boundaries where it is not plausible to suppose there are any.

4.4 Scientific language and conceptions of animals

Concern about the imputation of a kind of mental life to animals that is more luxuriant than might strictly be warranted by the available evidence was widespread across many branches of the sciences that bear on animal behaviour during the twentieth century. Anthropomorphism, as Eileen Crist remarks, is 'presumed to be a naïve view, an illusion generated through superficial analogies between human and animal behaviour, a deluded projection of the wealth of human experience onto a world that is putatively less rich'.[39] Many scientists have explicitly declared their allegiance to methodologies that it is hoped do not go beyond what is strictly observable in their descriptions of animal activities. Many more have at least implicitly adopted those methodologies in their adherence to certain of the reporting conventions that now govern many scientific accounts of animal behaviour. A technical language that attempts to avoid wherever possible the imputation of mental lives to animals has been developed in a number of scientific areas. This language replaces talk of animal agents and such things as their actions, emotions, and desires with reference to mechanistic processes such as 'stimulus–response patterns', 'innate releasing mechanisms', 'motor sequences', etc.[40] Crist, whose excellent book on this subject cannot really be recommended highly enough, quotes Barnett's dismissive comments on Darwin's use of emotion terms to describe the behaviour and demeanour of animals as representative of the views of explicit advocates of this approach to animal behaviour:

Darwin…took it for granted that terms like *love, fear* and *desire* can usefully be employed to describe the behaviour of animals…Since his time it has gradually been found more convenient to describe animal behaviour, not in terms of feelings of which we are directly aware only in ourselves, but in terms of the activities that can be seen and recorded by any observer; we may also try to describe the internal processes that bring these activities about. Thus today it is unusual for ethologists to speak of emotions…If the word emotion were to be used in the scientific study of animal behaviour, its meaning would have to be shifted from the familiar subjective one; it would have to be used to refer, not to feelings, but to internal changes that could be studied physiologically.[41]

Darwin, on the other hand, serves, for Crist, as the representative of an older, less methodologically encumbered tradition of scientific investigation of animal behaviour,

---

[39] Crist (1999: 152).

[40] See p. 82 above for a minor example of this tendency to replace natural vernacular description even of human action with quasi-technical vocabulary, in the work of Nichols. Hence, the scare quotes.

[41] Barnett (1958: 210), quoted by Crist (1999: 22).

one that does not doubt the evolutionary continuity between humans and animals, and that does not doubt either the appropriateness of descriptions that accord meaning to animal activities and authorship to their actions. The contrast Crist draws between Darwin's rich evocation of 'a cat in an affectionate frame of mind' ('She now stands upright, with slightly arched back, tail perpendicularly raised, and ears erected; and she rubs her cheeks and flanks against her master or mistress. The desire to rub something is so strong in cats under this state of mind that they may often be seen rubbing themselves against the legs of chairs or tables, or against door posts')[42] and Barnett's contemptuous observation that 'today, this behaviour might be described in terms of "cutaneous stimulation"'[43] demonstrates very clearly the impact that technical redescription can have on our understanding of animal life. A cat whose behaviour is described merely as the more or less automatically produced effect of 'cutaneous stimulation' is imaginatively conceived of in a very different way from one whose description is allowed to benefit, as Darwin's does, from the vocabulary of affection, desire, and action. As Crist observes, 'What in Darwin's hands are expressive gestures become, in Barnett's description, nonsignifying movements; from an experiencing subject, the cat is transformed into a vacant object'.[44]

The formative role played by this technical language in our conceptions of the animals thereby depicted is a central theme of Crist's book. Crist points out that it is a fantasy to suppose that this technical vocabulary, which is introduced so as to avoid any unwarranted mentalistic attributions to animals, is a mere neutral medium in which their behaviour can be dispassionately and objectively recounted. There simply is no such neutral medium. She notes that such language does not merely avoid the imputation of mentality to animals, but effectively denies the relevance to the understanding of animal behaviour of the experiential, subjective perspective of the animals in question. The animal as subject and agent effectively disappears from the scene altogether, to be replaced with a mere body, an object unenlivened by any perspective or viewpoint on events, which is portrayed as a simple locus for the meeting of various interacting forces. What begins as epistemologically motivated caution ends as a metaphysical commitment to the placing of animals on the other side of a crucial divide between we humans and the rest of nature.

Consider, for instance, the contrast drawn by Crist between Darwin's description of the mating behaviour of the male stickleback and Nikolaas Tinbergen's description of the same behaviour. Tinbergen was one of the chief founders of classical ethology, a tradition that Crist considers to be one of the mot important inaugurators of the technical descriptive conventions whose pretensions to neutrality she seeks to undermine. Darwin describes the courtship in terms of goal-directed activity on the part of the stickleback, aimed at encouraging the female into a nest he has built for her:

---

[42] Darwin (1965 [1872]: 126–7), quoted by Crist (1999: 28).
[43] Barnett (1958: 225), quoted by Crist (1999: 28).   [44] Crist (1999: 28).

The male stickleback (*Gasteroosteus leiurus*) has been described as 'mad with delight' when the female comes out of her hiding place and surveys the nest that he has made for her.[45]

He then continues with a quote from the naturalist Warington:

He darts around her in every direction, then to his accumulated materials for the nest, then back again in an instant; and as she does not advance, he endeavours to push her with his snout, and then tries to pull her by the tail and side-spine to the nest.[46]

In Darwin's description, the stickleback's behaviour is described in a way that imports urgency and an almost comic hopefulness to what are unmistakeably conceived of his actions. Tinbergen, by contrast, replaces action with mechanism:

One of the most complex analyses of chain reactions…has been carried out with the mating behaviour of the three-spined stickleback. Each reaction of either male or female is released by the preceding reaction of the partner…The male's first reaction, the zigzag dance, is dependent on a visual stimulus from the female, in which the sign stimuli 'swollen abdomen' and the special movements play a part. The female reacts to the red color of the male and to his zigzag dance by swimming right towards him. This movement induces the male to turn round and to swim rapidly to the nest. This in turn induces the female to follow him, thereby stimulating the male to point his head into the entrance. His behaviour now releases the female's reaction; she enters the nest…This again releases the quivering reaction in the male that induces spawning. The presence of fresh eggs in the nest makes the male fertilise them.[47]

In Tinbergen's description, the goal-directed sequence of emotionally charged activities undertaken by the stickleback, which is described by Darwin and Warington, has been replaced by a 'chain reaction' in which each link of the chain is conceived of as 'released' by some preceding event. The stickleback, indeed, does not really figure in Tinbergen's account as an agent at all: he is portrayed, in essence, merely as a *place* in which a series of automatic responses occurs.

Note that I am not here intending to insist that it is Darwin rather than Tinbergen who gets things right with respect to the stickleback. The present point is merely that Tinbergen is mistaken if he supposes that his description of the stickleback's behaviour is innocent of its own commitment to a metaphysical picture. Technical languages convey their own connotative and imagistic effects and the result, as Crist notes, may be a *mechanomorphic* conception of animals that cannot be regarded as any better justified than its anthropomorphic rival. Besides, even if it can be allowed that naivety may sometimes be involved in the interpretation of very simple animals as possessors of subjectivity and wielders of agency, there is certainly a naivety also in the epistemological impulses that generate the flight into technical terminology in the first place. For they are born, as Crist also notes, of a conception of the mind as essentially 'inner', a

---

[45] Darwin (1981 [1871]: vol.2, 2), quoted in Crist (1999: 168).
[46] Warington, R. (1855: 279) quoted by Darwin (1981 [1871]: Vol. 2, 2).
[47] Tinbergen (1989: 47–8), quoted in Crist (1999: 168–9).

secret, private pocket of consciousness within, about which nothing can be objectively known and with respect to which science ought not therefore to presume to have opinions. But we need not think of what it is to have a mind in this way at all. The mindedness of Darwin's cat, for instance—its affectionate mood—is represented by him as a fact of the matter that is entirely open to a responsive view such as humans are happily granted by nature. We can just *see*, he suggests, in the way it purrs and rubs its head against its owner that that is how things are, just as we know in the same sort of immediate way what a human smile or the growling of a dog mean. And the idea that our attribution of mindedness to others—whether humans or animals—is rather a matter of directly reporting how things seem to an unprejudiced eye than of shakily inferring a hypothesis about the secret interior of another being of which we are in contact only with the external shell, has a very great deal to recommend it, not least because we no longer have to wonder why on earth the shaky hypothesis would ever have so much as occurred to us in the first place.

Might it not be argued, though, that there is empirical evidence in favour of taking a mechanomorphic view of some creatures? Animals will react, often very vigorously, to artificial representations of the animals to which they normally respond, and this fact is often offered in support of the mechanomorphic conception. A male stickleback, for instance, will react with aggression to a mere oval shape bearing the red splodge characteristic of other males in mating season; a male robin can be induced to respond in a similarly aggressive manner to a tuft of red feathers. Does this not reveal clearly that what we might naively take to be goal-directed behaviour when another stickleback or robin is the target, is in fact merely an automatic reaction to a given stimulus?

The question is, though, why these reactions should be thought to reveal any such thing. Humans can be induced to respond sexually to pictures in pornographic magazines, but this hardly justifies the conclusion that the entirety of their activity when they engage in real sexual intercourse with one another can be understood merely as the automatic operation of a stimulus–response mechanism. All one can safely conclude is that in certain areas of animal activity involuntary responses are bound up in complex ways with the activity in question and that these involuntary responses can be produced even in the absence of their normal triggers. But it does not follow that nothing is ever going on when that activity occurs in its normal environmental context, apart from the automatic triggering of involuntary responses. Nor, indeed, does it even follow that the animal must be unaware that there is any difference between the natural and the artificial situation. I conclude, then, that the fact that animals can be induced to respond to artificial models that copy some features of the animals that usually trigger these responses is insufficient evidence for the claim that simple stimulus–response accounts of the entirety of the associated natural behaviour must be correct.

The trouble with the technical language in terms of which many scientists have been encouraged to write about animals is that it has, whether knowingly or not, advanced the idea that a mechanomorphic conception of animals is somehow more scientifically respectable than the picture of animals as agents that, so I claim, is the usual product of the cognitive systems with which we come naturally endowed. Scientists know, we may inadvertently infer from their use of this language, that animals are in fact mere automata, whose behaviour is entirely explicable by means of what Griffin has called 'compounded layers of stimulus-response formulations'.[48] But of course no scientist knows any such thing about any animal of any appreciable degree of complexity. The field remains wide open then, I suggest, for the alternative conception of animals as agents, i.e. possessors of bodies, centres of consciousness, subjects of at least rudimentary sorts of mental state, and settlers of matters that concern the movements of their own bodies. There is no reason to suppose that we must be engaging in infantile anthropomorphizing when we take them to be agents. Indeed, there are many reasons for supposing that unless we do so, we gravely mistake their natures.

4.5 A 'logical' stopping place?

One sometimes finds the argument, especially in the scientific, rather than the philosophical literature on animal behaviour, that we are secure in the knowledge that we human beings have consciousness, feelings, desires, and the rest; and that it is only with respect to other animals that we must exercise caution. Barnett, for example, whom I quoted above, notes that 'we are aware only in ourselves' of the feelings that we sometimes nevertheless carelessly impute to animals. But of course, if to be aware of a feeling is to *feel* it, an individual human being can be aware only of his or her *own* feelings. Some justification would seem to be needed, if this is my starting point, even for the assumption that other human beings are subjects of experience. And what might the justification be? Other human beings can *tell* me that they have experiences, of course, but what would be the reason for thinking that these displays of 'linguistic behaviour' are any more safely revelatory of inner life than behaviour of any other sorts? If one's epistemological starting position is that of the isolated human subject confronted merely by the outward behaviour of other creatures from which she must attempt to reason towards the existence of a conscious interior, the position is surely hopeless, whether those other creatures are human beings or non-human animals.

One might object that it is not stupid for me to believe that my conspecifics are more likely to be like me in various important ways than are creatures belonging to other species. And it is certainly true that if I am allowed the resources provided by inductive projection, I might indeed have somewhat stronger evidence for the view that other human beings are mentally like me than that non-human animals are. But this point of view could scarcely justify a position according to which *only* my conspecifics are regarded as likely to be minded agents at all. For animals of other

---

[48] Griffin (1981: 107).

species are rather like me too: many of them have brains and engage in activities not altogether unlike those in which I sometimes engage. So once induction is allowed on the scene, it is hard to see how it is to be prevented from justifying at least *some* inferences to the mental states and to the agency of other animals.

I see no real reason whatever, therefore, for supposing that our slide down the 'slippery slope' to which I alluded earlier ought 'logically' to be stopped only at the point at which human beings are encountered upon it. On the contrary, this is an entirely illogical stopping point, whatever one's epistemological framework. If one insists upon a point of view according to which one only knows about subjectivity and mindedness when one *is* the relevant subject, then the mindedness of other human beings is no less problematic than is the mindedness of non-human animals. If, on the other hand, one forsakes this position in order to help oneself to the plausible claim that ones conspecifics are more likely to be like oneself in various ways than are other animals, one has already conceded, in effect, the claim that other animals are nevertheless still *quite* likely to be like oneself in various respects: they are animals, after all. And this is to open the door to the perspective I would like to recommend: an evolutionary perspective that acknowledges the continuity that exists amongst animals, not only in physiological and morphological respects, but also in respect of their cognitive and emotional lives and, in particular, in respect of their qualifications to be accounted agents.

I have already conceded, though, that there may be animals too lowly to be regarded as having a cognitive life, and too lowly therefore to be regarded as agents, according to the conception of agency captured by (i)–(iv). It might be asked, then, if we are to permit some but not all animals to partake of mentality, how we are to decide which are which? In the final sections of this chapter, therefore, I want to turn to examine Dennett's work on the intentional stance, which I believe offers a very helpful approach to thinking about the mindedness of animals, and then to attempt to apply an amended version of a somewhat Dennettian approach to a couple of concrete cases. I shall not agree with Dennett's position in every respect. In particular, what he conceives of as a 'stance', I conceive of rather as an unavoidable cognitive imposition on the human conceptualization of reality; and what he sometimes seems to think of as merely a *practically* indispensable way of explaining and predicting the behaviour of agents, I claim is a genuinely *metaphysically* indispensable way of explaining and predicting that behaviour. But Dennett, at least, believes wholeheartedly in the principle of evolutionary continuity and is anxious not to erect absurd barriers between humanity and the rest of nature. I shall begin, then, by explaining what I take his position to be and how I hope to utilize it in order to answer the question of how we are to decide where agency ends and mechanism begins. I shall then go on to indicate the ways in which I intend to depart from Dennett's views in order to develop my own conception of how the phenomenon of agency is to be fitted into causal reality.

4.6 Dennett on the 'intentional stance'

Dennett's work is rarely explicitly addressed to the concept of agency. His main concern in writing about the intentional stance is generally with the attribution to individuals of intentional psychological concepts like 'desire', 'intention', and in particular 'belief'. However, the concept of agency evidently goes hand in hand with the attribution of at least some forms of intentional state for one who subscribes to anything like the model of agency that (i)–(iv) suggests. Indeed, if there are conceptual connections between (i), (ii), (iii), and (iv) of the kind I have suggested there might be, a creature that counts as a *genuine* possessor of mental states is bound, at the same time, to qualify as some kind of agent. It may well be fruitful, therefore, to examine Dennett's influential approach to the question what it is to be a bearer of intentional states in case it casts light on our related question how we are to decide which animals are agents.

When is it right to think of a system or creature as a possessor of intentional states? Dennett both explicitly answers this question and also, in a sense, refuses to accept that it *can* be answered with all the precision and exactitude that we might wish. His explicit answer is that what it is to be a true possessor of intentional states is to be an *intentional system*—a system whose behaviour is 'reliably and voluminously predictable via the intentional strategy'.[49] For Dennett, the intentional strategy is a way of treating an object as though it were a rational agent with such things as beliefs, desires, and other intentional states. By deciding which beliefs and desires such an agent *ought* to have, given its position in the world and its general goals, one comes to form a view about which it *does* have. One can then form a prediction about what it will do based on the idea that a rational agent acts to further its goals in the light of its beliefs. Dennett believes that if it is fruitful, for explanatory and predictive purposes, to treat an object in this way then the object counts as an intentional system.

How fruitful must the strategy be before the object in question can be said to be an intentional system? This question needs serious consideration because, as Dennett recognizes, one can apply the intentional strategy to almost anything. The behaviour of a thermostat, for instance, can be predicted by attributing it the belief that the room is at 19°C (a belief it ought to have, since the room is indeed at that temperature) and the desire that the room be at 20°C. The behaviour of lightning can be explained by attributing it the desire to get to the ground as quickly as possible and the belief that the lightning conductor is the best way to get there. Even the (non-) behaviour of a lectern can be explained as the result of its powerful desire to remain at the centre of the civilized world, and its belief that that is where it is indeed currently located.[50] And yet we do not generally tend to think of such entities as thermostats, lightning, and lecterns as possessors of intentional states. Is there no principled way to distinguish the impostors from the real thing?

---

[49] Dennett (1981: 15).   [50] See Dennett (1981: 22–3) for these examples.

Dennett does not deny that thermostats, lightning, and particularly lecterns, are poor candidates for the application of the intentional strategy. In the case of the lectern, he notes that we get no predictive power from the intentional strategy that we did not antecedently have: 'we already knew what it was going to do—namely nothing—and tailored the beliefs and desires to fit in a quite unprincipled way'.[51] Similar things could be said of the lightning and the thermostat: one can only use the intentional strategy for prediction in their case once one has already figured out how it is that they behave in general; one already needs to have observed, for example, that the thermostat switches the boiler on when and only when the room dips below 20°C before one can explain (or predict) by reference to its desire to keep the room at 20°C a future switching on of the boiler. But then one has no *further* need of a specifically intentional approach. One can just use the regularities by themselves. However, Dennett also refuses to accept that there is anything but a (huge) difference of degree between these degenerate intentional systems and the animals, computers, and persons with respect to which (in Dennett's view) the intentional strategy gets the kind of proper grip that makes us feel that in these cases we are dealing with the genuine article. He is insistent that there would be something wrongheaded about the attempt to sort the 'real' believers from the rest: it would be 'a Sisyphean labor, or else would be terminated by fiat'.[52] The dividing lines here are not sharp, according to Dennett. What there is, is a continuum. There are places on this continuum where we are confident that the phenomena do not justify the attribution of belief and other mental states, and places on it (at the other end) where we are confident that they do justify such attributions. And in the middle, there are a range of cases about which we are not sure what to say, and never will be because there are simply no facts of the matter that could decide the question. For the only question to be asked is whether the intentional stance 'reliably and voluminously' predicts the behaviour of the system; just how reliable and voluminous the predictions have to be in order to satisfy this is a question that simply has no definite answer.

There is much to be said for Dennett's position. Its gradualism, often regarded as problematic by those convinced that there must be sharp lines to draw between the true believers and the rest, can be regarded in many ways a strength, at least when one is thinking about animals, for it seems implausible to suppose that there is any *definite* place where, as one descends the hierarchy of neurophysiological complexity, one switches over from the intentional agents to the mere mechanisms. It seems much more likely that there is a fairly large grey area where we are not sure what to say. It is also likely that in at least some of these cases, there may simply be no way of resolving the question except, as Dennett himself suggests, by fiat. Epistemologically, too, the view is appealing, since the question whether or not something has beliefs and desires ceases to be a question pertaining to the inaccessible and private contents of a creature's consciousness or even to the (for all practical purposes) equally inaccessible recesses of a

[51] Dennett (1981: 23).   [52] Dennett (1981: 22).

brain or other hardware. It becomes a question to which everything that could possibly be relevant is readily available to the well-positioned observer; all we need to do to answer the question is to try out the intentional strategy and see how well it works. And even though there may be no definite answer to the question how well is well enough, it is not as though the question is ultimately to be settled by means of facts that are hidden from us. Where the thoughtful, perceptive, and persistent operator of the intentional strategy cannot decide whether a system has beliefs or not, we should conclude that there simply is no fact of the matter. Moreover, the holistic nature of intentional attributions is well captured by Dennett's picture, as is the deep connection between the richest versions of the intentional scheme of explanation (those involving reference to true propositional attitudes, such as beliefs) and the ideal of rationality. And despite what sometimes seems to be his reluctance to give definitive answers to the question whether a particular kind of creature or system is or is not a rich enough intentional system to count as a real believer or desirer, Dennett unquestionably has the resources to justify many of our intuitive judgements. In particular, it seems to me that he need not court the opprobrium he has sometimes faced for refusing simply to *deny* that such things as simple thermostats and lightning have beliefs and other intentional states. He should say that it is just absolutely clear that these things are *not* versatile and impressive enough to qualify. The wish to preserve the thought that there will be cases that we cannot resolve, even in principle, does not justify the insistence that there are *no* clear cases whatever. Thus understood, Dennett's view then also provides a sensible justification for the view that inanimate possessors of causal power such as waves and the sun do not count as intentional agents because there is simply nothing to be gained in the way of explanatory or predictive power by adopting the intentional stance in respect of their activities.

There are, however, aspects of Dennett's view that are apt to feel uncomfortable and unintuitive, a fact that is reflected in the now vast literature that has been produced in response to his work. One potential sticking point is that no important connection between intentional attributions and *consciousness* is allowed for by Dennett's view; at any rate on the assumption that we do not want to attribute consciousness to computers. Dennett is happy to propose that the intentional strategy works really rather well to predict, for instance, the next move a chess computer might make. Some philosophers have been inclined to think that this must be to underestimate the role we normally give to the assumption that a system is conscious when ascribing it states such as belief and desire. Many have also felt unhappy with the extent of Dennett's implied instrumentalism; the suggestion that whether or not a creature has mental states is a matter of whether it turns out to be useful to think that it does has been hard for many to swallow. And though it is less often mentioned, it should also be said that Dennett more or less neglects altogether the connection between the concept of *action* and the possession of mental states. Dennett recognizes no category of action distinct from the concept of a bodily movement produced by various sorts of intentional state, so it is not surprising that he allocates it no role in his theory. But as I have endeavoured to argue, the concept of an action—a causing by an agent—has a crucial role to play in our *folk* 'theory'. And perhaps it is not implausible that our reluctance to suppose that a computer could *really* believe anything has as much to do with our assumption that it cannot truly *act*[53] as it does with the assumption that it has no conscious life. Indeed, it seems very plausible that these two assumptions are rather intimately connected.

Is there any way of remedying these deficiencies? Perhaps not without abandoning some of what is truly distinctive and indeed some of what is truly appealing about Dennett's approach. But what I would like to suggest is that it might be possible at least to harness some of the power of Dennett's suggestion as to how we might go about deciding whether or not a system should be attributed intentional states, while at the same time embedding his ideas in the somewhat different context offered by the view of agency represented by conditions (i)–(iv). This, I shall argue, permits us to ameliorate the extent of the instrumentalism implicit in Dennett's views and at the same time enables space to be made for the possible relevance of considerations to do with consciousness and will to the question whether a system *is* an intentional agent without sacrificing the gradualism and epistemological transparency that make Dennett's view of the attribution of intentional states so very appealing.

The concept of an agent that I have been trying to develop during the course of this chapter is unquestionably a much richer concept than Dennett's conception of an intentional system. Agents must satisfy conditions (i), (ii), and (iv), as well as (iii). Indeed, according to me, they *cannot* properly satisfy (iii) unless they can satisfy (i), (ii), and (iv) as well. But what one may concede to Dennett is that there is, of course, no *independent* way of telling whether an entity satisfies any of these conditions. There is no special means by which one can tell whether a creature is a true possessor of its body, for instance, or whether it is a subject of experience. Rather, on the view for which I have been arguing, we are inclined to ascribe the properties implicit in (i)–(iv) all together, as a unified package, to entities that suggest themselves to the mind module as appropriate candidates.[54] But which things are the appropriate candidates? It might

---

[53] Note that this is so even if there are indeterministic processes within the computer. For it is still those processes that settle matters: the computer is nothing more that a locus for their (in this case indeterministic) unfolding.

[54] Dennett simply supposes that the different aspects of mindedness represented by (i)–(iv) can be readily separated out, one from another, and treats the possession of intentional states as though it were something that could be readily understood without reference to anything murky such as consciousness, selfhood, or will. This, indeed, is the default position across a wide range of literature in philosophy of mind, where intentionality, consciousness, the self, and action are dealt with, by and large, as four almost entirely separate topics. But this undoubtedly underestimates the importance of the *connections* that exist between the various parts of the idea of mindedness, connections which are fully present in the concept of agency that, I claim, emerges as a unified classifying device from the mind module, connections that can be easily lost in our philosophical attempts to separate the strands analytically from one another. The failure to recognize the importance and distinctiveness of the concept of an *action* (and, correlatively, the importance of the *agent*) in the folk-psychological scheme has, I believe, made it seem easier than it really is to perform such an analytical separation: if the causal role of an intentional state is limited to its interacting with other such states in order to produce bodily movements, then there is no obvious reason why a non-conscious and non-spontaneous entity, such as we generally suppose computers and robots to be, might not be thought to possess such a thing.

seem philosophically unsatisfactory to leave things entirely up to the unbidden promptings of the mind module, and in any case I have already conceded that there are cases in which those unbidden promptings might need revision in the light of scientific investigation. What, then, is to be our guide to classification and categorization?

It is here, I believe, that Dennett's approach (somewhat modified) can help us. We can decide whether or not something is an agent by deciding whether or not it is a creature or system with respect to which it is *necessary*, if we are to explain its behaviour, to utilize at least the teleological stance. This suggestion differs from Dennett's own in two main respects. The first is the focus on the *necessity* to take the stance in question. Dennett does indeed believe that the intentional stance is necessary if we are to explain the behaviour of complex creatures (including ourselves), but he is also prepared to regard as intentional systems (albeit of a rather degenerate kind) things to which it is perfectly possible and in many ways preferable to take other 'stances', such as thermostats. On my view, though, thermostats would be *definitively* ruled out: we just do not need the intentional or even the teleological stance in order to understand why they do what they do when they do. Paramecia would also fail the test, given that we are able precisely to explain their movements by way of equations relating the speed and direction of their motion to such things as water temperature, pH, and light. But more controversially, computers and robots, too (at any rate, of the sort we so far know about) would not pass this test for agency. For even if we are ignorant of the details, we are sure that an explanatory account can be given of every change a computer undergoes without any essential appeal to the notion of an agent or an action. And this, ultimately, I claim, is what disqualifies it from *being* an agent. If we like, we can make some limited use of propositional attitude ascription to help us think about what a computer might do under different conditions. But even if we do not know precisely what they are, we are sure that there are other, non-intentional ways to think about the happenings in a computer, ways that would reveal each change within it to be explicable in terms of preceding states and events or else the result of a genuinely random occurrence. Folk psychology is not a metaphysical necessity for the explanation of the changes that occur within any artificial system of this sort that has so far been invented.

Now, it will be said that this test for agency simply cannot be satisfactory, since there is a sense in which a teleological or intentional stance is never strictly necessary 'in principle', even for higher animals or even for us. It will be objected that there is always a perspective—the physical stance—from which all animal movement, however

But if intentional states are thought of instead as special relations between an *agent* and its environment, relations that help explain a special variety of causal input into reality that is called an *action*, and which essentially involves the postulation of both subjectivity and spontaneity to the individual that is the source of that causal input, it becomes much less clear that a computer or robot could truly possess an intentional state. It will just not be the right sort of thing to be a *possessor* of them once possession is thought of as something different from *housing*.

complex the animal, could be safely predicted and explained if we could only get a proper grip on the enormously complicated 'initial conditions' we would have to specify in order to make the wanted deductions from physical law. But this I dispute. It is a mere dogma that, I shall argue in subsequent chapters, there is simply no good reason to believe. I dispute it because I believe that these higher animals are agents, that agents are settlers of matters that concern the movements of their own bodies, according to the agency concept with which we are supplied by the mind module, and that something that is a settler of matters concerning movements of its own body simply cannot at the same time be a thing the precise details of whose movements are predictable or explicable by derivation from any deterministic theory. If there truly *are* agents, I insist, then they cannot be things whose movements are predictable from a purely physical stance. That would render the distinctive perspective afforded by the teleogical and intentional stances utterly null and void from a metaphysical perspective (though it might of course still be of pragmatic value). As argued in the previous chapter, either there are no agents or determinism is false.

The second respect in which my view differs from Dennett's is that the adoption of the teleological or intentional stance, for me, involves more than merely the attempt to treat a system as an instantiator of certain states. It involves also the supposition that the entity in question meets conditions (i)–(iv). But we can only decide whether or not a creature does indeed satisfy those conditions by seeing whether or not there are perfectly satisfactory ways *other* than those provided by folk psychology, i.e. the agency scheme, by means of which to causally explain its activities. If there are such alternative ways, we should decide that the appeal to agency is really no more than (at best) a useful heuristic device that adds nothing that is truly of deep *metaphysical* significance to the causal workings of the entity in question, however crucial it may be to our ability to offer ourselves explanations we find manageable and satisfying. However, if there are no such alternatives, we must continue to use the folk-psychological scheme in which the creature's movements are thought of as productions *of* that creature, explicable by appeal to what it wants and what it knows about the world around it. Where we cannot do without folk psychology, I wish to argue, there is a *reason*, rooted in the mode of functioning of the entity in question, why we cannot do without it.[55] The need for folk psychology, I shall insist, arises out of the fact that the settling of matters by animals genuinely is a very special form of causation indeed, so that it is not at all surprising that evolution has endowed us with specialized cognitive systems for its discernment. The teleological and intentional stances work, I shall argue, because they enable us to recognize the very real causal role that is played by the *organism* and its assessment of its options in the light of its knowledge, experience, and desires in the generation of its own behaviour. This role, crucially, cannot be properly represented by any purely deterministic story about the causation of that behaviour, since the

---

[55] The intentional stance can still be useful, of course, even where there is no such reason.

emergence as part of biological reality of creatures that can act constitutes a real source of indeterminism in the world. My anti-Dennettian suggestion, then, will be that we have to treat certain things as agents, roughly speaking, because that is what they are, and not the other way around.

The suggestion that Dennett misidentifies the correct direction of explanation in this area is by no means a new idea; many philosophers have found unpalatable what they sometimes call Dennett's 'instrumentalism' about mental states,[56] by which they generally seem to mean the idea that *all there is* to being a believer (or desirer or intender, or whatever) is being a system whose behaviour is fruitfully predicted and explained from the perspective provided by the intentional stance. Desires, beliefs, intentions, and the like, it is insisted by these objectors, are *real*, and it is complained that it goes against this strong intuition to regard their possession by an agent as merely a matter of explanatory convenience.[57] I agree with those who find some aspects of Dennett's instrumentalism unsatisfactory. But at the same time, the resort of Dennett's 'realist' opponents is all too often a variety of 'token physicalism' whose appeal to relations of identity, constitution, realization, and efficacy amongst so-called 'token states' is of dubious philosophical coherence, and whose empirical commitments to the instantiation of particular types of causal structure in the brain is an *a prioristic* encumbrance of which we ought, I think, to be pleased to be relieved. The focus of these philosophers has tended to be on the intentional *states* themselves, rather than on the powers available to the possessors of them—a focus that seems to me to be a mistake.[58] I hope, by developing the concept of a creature (or system) that is a true settler of outcomes, to find a different, and, to my mind, more plausible way of making sense of the intuition that there is a real distinction of kind to be made (though again, not necessarily a *sharp* one) between something that is a true agent and a whole variety of other systems and creatures that are sometimes used to test our intuitions about where mechanisms end and agency begins, including simple feedback systems such as thermostats, the impressively more complex productions of human designers such as chess-playing computers, and the humble paramecium.

4.7 Which animals?

Which animals, it might be asked pass the crucial test? Where *does* agency end and mechanism begin? I would like, in this section, to consider two specific examples in order to explain how I propose that this question ought to be approached in the light of what I have said so far, and also to attempt to rebut the accusation (which I anticipate) that my view must be committed to the existence of implausibly sharp lines between

---

[56] Though Dennett himself is not always content with this label; he sometimes insists that he ought to be accounted a kind of 'realist'. See in particular Dennett (1987: 39–40).

[57] For views of this sort, see e.g. Pylyshyn (1984), Fodor (1987), and Lycan (1988).

[58] For my worries about the concept of a token state, see Steward (1997).

the agents and nonagents. I begin with the case of the jumping spider, *Portia*, some of whose impressively intelligent behaviour is described in an interesting paper by Stim Wilcox and Robert Jackson.[59]

The jumping spider, *Portia*, preys on other spiders. Wilcox and Jackson report the following set of observations of one particular spider in the rainforest of northeastern Australia. The spider begins by stepping carefully out onto the edge of the web in which its target spider is sitting. *Portia* begins to try to tempt the prey spider out of the centre of its own web by plucking at the web with its legs, making signals that mimic the struggles of a trapped insect. When this technique produces no movement on the part of the resident spider, it varies the speed and rhythm of its signals, producing a kind of random array of signals, until eventually the prey spider swivels around towards *Portia*. *Portia* now repeats the signal again and again, but elicits no further response, at which point she reverts to the random array. When the prey spider still makes no further movement *Portia* adopts a second plan. She walks slowly and carefully across the web, intermittently making a variety of signals, taking advantage of the cover provided by the wind to move more swiftly during periods when the web is being rustled. Unfortunately, though, as she approaches, the resident spider moves swiftly and aggressively towards her, and she retreats back to the edge of the web once again. Now *Portia* changes strategy more radically. She undertakes a lengthy detour, first moving away from her prey and around a large projection on the rock surface, losing sight of her prey along the way. About an hour later, she appears again, positioned now above the web on a small overhanging piece of rock. She now lowers herself down through the air, arrives level with the resident spider, and suddenly swings in to grab it, sinking her poison-injecting fangs into the victim.

It seems impossible to understand what has gone on here, I suggest, without making use of the idea of the spider as an agent. *Portia*'s long detour is particularly impressive, showing a capacity for the flexible planning of strategy, an appreciation of spatial relations, and a capacity to retain an intention over a period of time that cries out for the sort of conceptualization that folk psychology offers. *Portia* wants to eat the resident spider, conceives of various plans for doing so—some remarkably sophisticated—and then enacts them, responding flexibly as she goes to the possibilities afforded by contingent circumstances (e.g. the rustling of the wind). No doubt much of *Portia*'s behaviour is dictated by instinct, for example the mimicry technique. But there is also judgement here and what seems unquestionably to be a form of thinking. The spider's behaviour is too variable, flexible, well-adapted to the peculiarities of circumstance and revelatory of a capacity to monitor its own progress through space and time to be understood in any other terms. There is evidence of a moment-to-moment control in the face of evolving environmental circumstances that cannot be understood except in terms of a form of agency. The mind module is in business.

---

[59]   Wilcox and Jackson (2002).

Is it possible that empirical investigation might provide an explanation of the spider's behaviour that might entirely usurp the one that folk psychology is inclined to give? Perhaps it cannot be ruled out completely. But there are reasons, I think, for regarding it as extremely unlikely. We could of course find out more—lots more—about the systems that underpinned the spider's perceptions and its motor co-ordination, and lots more too about the intervening cognitive processes. But I would maintain that nothing we could find out would be likely to deliver a causal explanation of why the movements that constituted its detour occurred that did not appeal to a teleological idiom. Dennett, note, might think he could say the same: he is insistent that there are 'real patterns' that can be discerned only from the intentional stance and so that there are true explanations that would simply be unavailable to a Laplacean super-physicist, attempting to predict each momentary state of the universe from the preceding one. But Dennett *also* seems to think that it is compatible with this insistence to suppose that the Laplacean super-physicist would still be able to say, at the time t_1 when the spider was attempting its first strategy, that at t_2, an hour and a half later, say, it would be making the motions constitutive of its swinging into the web to eat its prey. And that is what I do not accept. For that is to deny that nothing of the sort was settled until the spider settled it, by enacting its plan of action in precisely the way that it did.

If spiders can be agents, though, how much further down the scale of complexity must we go before agency is lost? To consider the issues that might be involved in trying to decide, I want now to turn to what I regard as a less clear-cut case: the earthworm.

In what was to be his last work, Darwin (1881) undertook an investigation of the habits of earthworms and of their impact on the natural environment. The bulk of the work is concerned with the role played by worms in the production of what Darwin called 'vegetable mould', by means of the digestion of leaves and other vegetable matter. However, Darwin also devoted some attention to worm behaviour, wishing 'to learn how far they acted consciously and how much mental power they displayed'.[60] Darwin was clearly struck by a number of observations that appeared to him to suggest a certain degree of intelligence and other mental powers in the worms. He noted that sometimes, when a worm was illuminated, it would dash suddenly into its burrow, which, he says, might naturally lead one to suppose that the action was merely a reflex one.[61] But this simple idea was contradicted by the fact that light appeared to produce a different effect on the worms on different occasions. In particular, Darwin noted that 'a worm when in any way employed, and in the intervals of such employment, is often regardless of light'[62] and reflected that 'with the higher animals, when close attention to some object leads to the disregard of the impressions

---

[60] Darwin (1881: 1).
[61] Though earthworms have no eyes, they have some sensitivity to light.
[62] Darwin (1881: 9).

that other objects must be producing on them, we attribute this to their attention being absorbed; and attention implies the presence of a mind'.[63]

A second set of much more detailed observations related to the worms' habit of plugging up their burrows with leaves, an activity which Darwin surmised might serve a number of purposes: keeping the burrows free of dirt and water, excluding draughts, and providing some protection from predators. Darwin began from a supposition about what would be likely to be the optimal way of pushing or pulling the leaves into the burrow:

> If a man had to plug up a small cylindrical hole, with such objects as leaves, petioles or twigs, he would drag or push them in by their pointed ends; but if these objects were very thin relatively to the size of the hole, he would probably insert some by their thicker or broader ends. The guide in his case would be intelligence.[64]

Darwin wished, therefore, to see whether the worms drew leaves into their burrows by their tips or by their bases, and in particular to see how they would handle leaves from non-native plants, in respect of which instincts could not have been directly formed by evolution. He first examined 227 mostly English leaves pulled out of worm burrows to see how they had been drawn into the burrows. His results were as follows:

- 80% by tip
- 9% by base
- 11% transversely.

This, he suggested was 'almost sufficient to show that chance does not determine the manner in which the leaves are dragged into the burrows' (1881: 26). Of these 227 leaves, 70 were leaves of the common lime, 'almost certainly not a native of England', and having a particularly broad base; in the case of these leaves, which would have been more difficult to draw in by the base, only 4% had been drawn in by that means. Darwin then searched for the leaves of a foreign plant that were more symmetrically proportioned, so that the advantage of drawing them in by the tip would be less significant. In the case of these (laburnum) leaves, 27%, a much greater proportion, were drawn in by the base. Darwin surmised that the worms might have developed a general habit of avoiding the footstalk, and that this might account for the fact that a still greater proportion of the laburnum leaves had not been drawn in by the base. But he also noted that the worms were sometimes able to break their habit of avoiding the footstalk in cases where this part of the leaf offered the best means of drawing the leaf into the burrow. In the case of rhododendron leaves, which often curl up while drying in such a way as to render the base sometimes narrower than the tip, 66% had been drawn in by the base or footstalk. Darwin concluded that 'In this case, therefore, the worms judged with a considerable degree of correctness how best to draw the withered

---

[63] Darwin (1881: 9).   [64] Darwin (1881: 25).

leaves of this foreign plant into their burrows; notwithstanding that they had to depart from their usual habit of avoiding the footstalk' (1881: 27).

Another set of observations concerned the worms' habit of lining the mouths of their burrows with leaves, a behaviour which, Darwin explained, was distinct from that of plugging them up, and might perhaps be done for comfort's sake, to keep the bodies of the worms from coming into contact with the cold, damp earth. Darwin kept worms in pots and provided them over a number of weeks with leaves from the Scotch pine tree (not a native of the district), leaves that consist of two needles joined to a common base. The pine leaves had all been drawn in by their bases, and the sharp points of the needles had all been carefully pressed into the voided earth with which worm burrows are usually lined. Darwin noted that had this not been done, the sharp points of the needles would have prevented the worms moving easily down the burrow and would have 'resembled traps with converging points of wire' (1881: 43). The behaviour, therefore, made evident sense. However, since the Scotch pine was not native to the area, it seemed impossible to Darwin that this behaviour should constitute an instinct produced directly by a process of natural selection.

Darwin's own conclusion appears to be that though the general *types* of purposive behaviour he examined were undoubtedly instinctive in the earthworms, the precise manner of execution of the various tasks they undertook was too variable to be strictly instinctive. He ultimately seems to have decided, indeed, that their behaviour in respect of hole-plugging is best regarded as a type of behaviour governed by *judgement*. He directly observed the worms feeling the shape of leaves before grasping them, and concluded that they must, on the basis of this preliminary investigation, make some kind of assessment of the best means of drawing them in. The conclusion that worms possess some degree of intelligence seemed to Darwin inescapable. Our immediate interest though, is not in intelligence, but in agency. Is it possible to draw any conclusions concerning the question whether earthworms might be agents from the sorts of observations of their behaviour that were made by Darwin?

Darwin's observations of the worms certainly seem to show that the principles of worm movement cannot be straightforwardly thought of as a collection of tropisms, reflexes, taxes, and the like, whereby a stimulus of a given sort produces a given automatic response. The behaviour is too flexible and variable for that to be a plausible account. Darwin also suggests that there are limits to the extent to which simple 'instinct' can explain the worms' activities, appealing, as I did in Chapter 1, to the distinction between the explanation of a *type* of behaviour (e.g. 'hole-plugging', 'light-avoidance') and the explanation of the precise manner of its execution on a particular occasion, in order to distinguish between what he regarded as inborn proclivities in the worms to indulge in particular sorts of activity and their intelligent guidance of the execution of these instinctive activities at the time of action. But of course even if we are tempted to regard the worms' behaviour as 'intelligent', that does not, in and of itself, reveal that the production of the worms' various behaviours is not an entirely deterministic matter. A complex algorithm, for instance, might govern the worm's decision about how best to draw in the leaf—by the tip, by the base, or laterally—and a similarly deterministic formula might govern the question whether a worm will or will not decide to rush into its burrow once illuminated by a bright light. It might, for instance, instantiate a 'program' such that if it were eating and could feel no vibrations of the kind that might suggest predators were in the vicinity, it would ignore bright light, but respond by rushing into its burrow if not currently engaged in the all-important process of ingesting food. This broadly functionalist account of the complex behaviours shown by animals will be the natural recourse of the determinist. The explanation of the worms' care in pressing the needle-tips of pine leaves into the voided earth linings of their burrows seems more difficult, given that they could not have benefited evolutionarily from their progenitors' experience with similar leaves. But perhaps it is not impossible that some similar mechanistic algorithmic explanation might be discovered.

Of course, algorithms and functionalist programs can potentially be fiddled with forever: we might try to respond to every bit of worm behaviour that did not fit the originally hypothesized program with a new and more complex algorithm or program that did. But there would come a point where there would be no explanatory value whatever in the algorithm, and little plausibility in the thought that the algorithm or program was in any way reflective of the mode of functioning of the worm. At that point, I suggest, it would be natural to have recourse to the idea that instead of a simple program-instantiating machine we had a different kind of system in our sights: an agent with a (in this case) fairly lowly form of consciousness, making moment-to-moment decisions about what to do, guided no doubt by instinct, sometimes pre-empted in its operations by mere reflexes, tropisms, and other involuntary responses, but neverthe-less deserving to be thought of as a low-level, conscious controller of a body, respond-ing to environmental factors in ways whose general *type* is predictable enough, but the specifics of which, as with the spider, are simply not open to exact prediction. There is reason to believe, I shall come on to argue, that provision of the sort of massive flexibility in such things as the ordering of tasks, the various possible means of carrying them out, the times at which they are to be carried out, etc., which might turn out to be hugely advantageous to a creature living in an unpredictable environment and, crucially, able to move around within it, is sometimes best served by a system that is not simply a functionalist machine, but is one involving some form of consciousness and the capacity to make the spontaneous and yet reasoned injections into the course of nature that we call actions.

I do not want to pre-empt what is ultimately the empirical question of whether the algorithmic type of approach to what looked at first sight to be flexible behaviours in the earthworm (nor indeed in any other creature) might succeed. If it did, and if it succeeded in respect of *all* the creature's behaviours, then I suggest we would have no reason to continue to maintain the view of that creature as an agent; that hypothesis would have gone the same way it went in the case of the paramecium. If it did not, then the folk-psychological interpretation would have been saved. But what counts as 'success'? It is the vagueness that attaches to this question that gives me the scope to maintain, with Dennett, that there are bound to be some creatures with respect to which there is simply no definite fact of the matter whether or not they are agents. Would the various possible mechanistic approaches to its movements have to become too complex, too overburdened by numbers of variables, too bogged down with exception clauses, in order to accommodate all the data concerning its behaviour? What is 'too complex' to count as a version of success? There can be no precise answer to this question and so, despite the fact that we can say with a good deal of assurance of many things that they definitely are agents and of a great many others that they definitely are not, there will be a number of things—and perhaps earthworms will turn out to be amongst them—about which a definite answer cannot be given. The boundary between agents and non-agents, as Dennett insists, is indeed not sharp—consciousness fades imperceptibly into unconsciousness, mindedness into mechanism—and there is no saying *precisely* which things fall on each side of the conceptual divide, though of course it does not follow that there are not things of which we can say very definitely that they fall on one side or the other.

Of course, to think of an animal as an agent is to think of it in a very different way indeed from thinking of it as a mere mechanism. It may be this fact that lies behind the very strong tendency to suppose that there just must be a clear answer to the question, asked of some creature or other, whether the light of consciousness is 'on' or 'off' inside it: whether it has a mind or not. But a sharp distinction between conceptual frameworks does not imply the existence of a sharp dividing line between the things to which we attempt to apply those frameworks. It may just be unclear how complex an algorithmic explanation or a program has to be before it is too complex to accept as a reasonable explanation of the behaviour of a system, and given the criterion of agency I have suggested above, therefore, it may be unclear, too, whether folk psychology is indeed *necessary* in order to understand it. I believe, therefore, that despite my insistence that the *concept* of agency is the robust, distinctive, indeterministic, and metaphysically committed concept that I have been maintaining it is, I can also subscribe, with Dennett, to a plausible gradualism about agency in the animal kingdom. With respect to some sorts of creature, there may just be no saying whether they are conscious possessors of their own bodies, capable of settling matters that concern certain of the movements of those bodies: the question whether this is so, I have argued, is the question whether the folk-psychological stance is truly necessary for the explanation of their behaviour, which in turn is the question whether wholly non-intentional varieties of explanation are good enough. And the answer to the question whether this is so may be vague.

It might be objected that I am not entitled to help myself to Dennettian gradualism having made the kinds of claims I have been making about agents being settlers of matters. It might be said that a thing either is or is not a true settler of matters concerning movements and changes in its own body, and that it cannot really be metaphysically indeterminate whether a given creature is endowed with the power to settle aspects of the future.[65] But what can be metaphysically indeterminate, it seems to me, is whether a thing is such as to justify the self–body distinction on which the attribution of such a power to the animal *itself* (as opposed merely to processes contained within it, say) depends. For that, I shall argue later, is the question to what extent different subordinate processes are brought into relation and harmonization—integrated into complex plans of action—in ways that demand interpretation as the influence of the whole animal on its own parts, rather than being comprehensible by means of an understanding of relationships between processes all of which are clearly sub-animalian. There seems no reason why *this* might not be a matter of degree.

From Chapter 6 onwards, I shall begin to tackle the difficult question of how we might hope to make space for a kind of agency answering to the specifications I have provided, within a naturalistic conception of causal reality. Without doubt, it is the conviction that no such space exists that motivates many compatibilists and which causes even incompatibilists what are perhaps their greatest moments of uncertainty and occasionally despair. But in my view, we ought to be more certain that we (and other creatures) are often settlers of matters than we are of the so-called 'naturalistic' conceptions of reality that threaten to make it seem impossible that we should play such a role in the world. It is more likely, I submit, that we are wrong in our philosophical preconceptions about what naturalism really entails, than that we are mistaken in our basic conviction that by acting we (and many other creatures) can settle at the time of our action that certain possible futures are to be or are not to be made actual. What is needed, I shall argue, in order to open up the proper metaphysical space for action conceived of as settling, is a robust defence of the existence, in biological systems of all kinds, of a variety of 'top-down' causation whereby the whole of an organized and integrated living system is able to affect the intuitively lower-level processes that go on in its parts. I shall try to show, in Chapter 8, that there is reason to believe that such a form of top-down influence permeates the whole biological realm. After attempting to meet the various philosophical objections, based on ideas about supervenience, causation, and the basicness of the physical with which I am confident that these suggestions will be sceptically met, I shall then try to suggest that agency is merely the most impressive form of this top-down influence.

Before proceeding with that task, though, it will be necessary, in Chapter 5, to deal with a significant objection to the main philosophical premise on which this book is based, namely that the existence of agency gives us reason to suppose that determinism must be false. The objection stems from an argument that I call the 'Epistemological Argument', and I believe it has been a major obstacle to the acceptance of views of the relation between agency and determinism such as my own. In the next chapter, therefore, I shall attempt to show how I believe the objection ought to be met.

---

[65] Thanks to an anonymous referee for raising this worry.

5

The Epistemological Argument

'The air is cold and thin up there on Incompatibilist Mountain, and if one stays up there for any length of time without getting down the other side, one's mind becomes clouded in mist, and is visited by visions of noumenal selves, nonoccurrent causes, transempirical egos and other fantasies.'

(Kane 1996: 14)

In his (1996), Robert Kane argues that four questions lie at the heart of debates about free will.[1] The questions are as follows:

1. The Compatibility Question. Is free will compatible with determinism?
2. The Significance Question. Why do we, or should we, want to possess a free will that is incompatible with determinism? Is it a kind of freedom 'worth wanting' (to use Dennett's useful phrase), and, if so, why?
3. The Intelligibility Question. Can we make sense of a freedom or free will that is incompatible with determinism? Is such a freedom coherent or intelligible? Or is it, as many critics claim, essentially mysterious and terminally obscure?
4. The Existence Question. Does such a freedom actually exist in the natural order, and if so, where?

As Kane conceives of it, the defender of a traditional libertarian position has to climb to the top of a metaphorical mountain and then make it safely back down the other side. The 'ascent' involves answering the Compatibility and Significance questions; a successful 'descent' would be constituted by the provision of satisfactory answers to the Intelligibility and Existence questions. Thus far, I have argued for what may be regarded as a negative answer to the Compatibility Question, based on the idea that:

(i) it is essential to the concept of an action that it be the settling of certain matters by an agent at the time of action;
(ii) there could be no settling of matters by agents at the time of action, if determinism were true; and hence
(iii) there could be no agents or actions at all in a deterministic world.

Although agency rather than free will has been my central concept, it should be obvious that if agency itself is incompatible with determinism there can be little

---

[1] Kane (1996: 13).

hope for free will, however one decides to define that elusive term. Whether free will involves acting for reasons or being the ultimate creator of one's own ends and purposes, or merely being able to do as one pleases, it surely involves agency. And this same point provides also my answer to the Significance Question. There are no kinds of freedom worth wanting if determinism is true, for in deterministic worlds, on my view, there are no kinds of freedom at all, since there are no actions. Since agency is the basis of all freedoms, its impossibility under determinism would ensure the impossibility also of any freedom worth wanting.

In terms of Kane's metaphor, then, I have now made my way up onto the top of Incompatibilist Mountain, albeit by means of what I regard as an undeservedly neglected (and, I confess, unnervingly lonely) path. It is now almost time to begin looking for the route down the other side. In Chapters 6 and 7 I shall tackle the Intelligibility Question; in Chapter 8 I shall do my best to try to explain what kind of natural phenomenon it is necessary to suppose agency to be if it is to have all the features I have argued it must possess, thereby providing my answer to the Existence Question. But before I embark on either task, it will be necessary first to respond to a powerful objection to my choice of a route of *ascent* for Incompatibilist Mountain: the objection, indeed, which I believe most significantly accounts for the fact that the view for which I have argued seems to be located in what is currently a very underpopulated region of logical space. The powerful objection is this: the question whether or not determinism is true is ultimately a question to which *physics* must supply the answer. And though physics appears currently to be (in the main) of the opinion that determinism is *not* universally true, we cannot be sure that physicists are definitely right about this. Perhaps at some point, empirical or theoretical considerations will compel a rethink, and it will be decided that in fact the physical laws are deterministic after all. But surely if this were to happen, we would not wish to draw the conclusion that there had never been any such thing as agency, nor any such events as actions. Surely, that there are *agents* and that they have performed *actions*, is one of the things we *know* (or at least, it is as good a candidate to be one of the things we know as anything is). It cannot be, then, that this claim is dependent for its truth on the falsity of determinism, for the falsity of determinism is *not* yet one of the things we know; it is rather a claim about the nature of physical laws that has yet to be conclusively established by physics. Perhaps if determinism turned out to be false we would have reluctantly to conclude that we had been offered reasons for concluding that we were not *free* agents or that we could not truly be *morally responsible* ones. These consequences might be unwelcome and radical but perhaps it is not inconceivable that the truth of determinism would require a reassessment of our claims to be free and morally responsible. It *is* inconceivable, though, that the discovery of the truth of determinism would lead us to reassess the idea that agents and actions *exist*. So it cannot be the case that determinism is inconsistent simply with mere agency. I call this argument the 'Epistemological Argument', because it is based on premises concerning our knowledge, or lack of knowledge, of various things (the fact that there are actions, the truth of determinism). My task in the current chapter will be to respond to it.

5.1 Determinism and physics: two claims

In order properly to evaluate the Epistemological Argument, it is essential to distinguish clearly between the following two claims:

P1: The question whether determinism is true is a question that can only be answered by physics.

P2: The question whether determinism is true is a question that may (one day) be settled by physics.

Clearly, these two claims are distinct. P1 conceives of the question whether determinism is true as essentially a physicist's question and as one, therefore, to which only the discipline of physics could possibly supply an answer. P2, on the other hand, admits only that it is conceivable that physicists will one day tell us something that implies that determinism is true (or that it is false). Unlike P1 though, P2 does not rule out the possibility that evidence or argumentation relevant to the question, or even sufficient to settle it, might equally come from elsewhere. In particular, it does not rule out the possibility that *philosophical* argument might be brought to bear on the issue. I shall contend that if P1 were true, the Epistemological Argument might indeed be worrying, but that to assert P1 is in effect simply to beg the question against the version of incompatibilism for which I wish to argue. The milder P2, on the other hand, even if we concede it, is insufficiently powerful to sustain the Epistemological Argument. I begin with a consideration of P1.

The idea that the question whether determinism is true is simply not an issue that philosophers should attempt to debate, being a purely scientific matter, is quite widely endorsed in the free will literature. Mele, for example, asserts that 'showing that determinism is true is not a philosophical task'.[2] He does not say to whom the task should fall instead, but I assume his view is likely to be the fairly orthodox one that the question whether or not determinism is true is a question for physicists to answer. Fischer also supposes that the question of whether or not determinism is true is not one that philosophy can settle. He confesses, indeed, that his primary motivation for the theory he calls 'semi-compatibilism' is his conviction that the reality of moral responsibility ought not to depend on the falsity of a doctrine that falls straightforwardly, in his view, within the purview of physics. As he puts it, 'Our fundamental nature as free, morally responsible agents should not depend on whether the pertinent regularities identified by the physicists have associated with them (objective) probabilities of 100%

---

[2] Mele (2006: 163). Presumably he also believes that showing that determinism is false is not a philosophical task either.

(causal determinism) or, say, 98% (causal indeterminism)'.[3] But are Mele and Fischer right to suppose that the question of determinism is a question to which only physics could possibly supply the answer?

If we are going to decide who might have the right to tell us whether the doctrine of determinism is true or not, we are going to have to know what that doctrine asserts. I have so far avoided attempting to define determinism, in part because there are so many different definitions on offer and it is not always easy to decide what the relationships of entailment, equivalence, etc., are amongst these different definitions. I have also been inclined to think that nothing I have said so far really depends crucially upon the specifics of any particular definition, determinism being better thought of, in my view, as a general picture or image of the nature of reality, rather than a readily formulable thesis. But a point has been reached, I think, where it would be useful to have some particular formulations in mind. For fairness's sake, and in an attempt to make it more plausible that nothing I shall say ultimately depends on the specifics of my choice of definition, I shall consider two rather different suggestions. The first is offered by Fischer, who, after conceding that it is difficult to give a straightforward account of the doctrine of determinism, writes that:

...for my purposes, I take it that the essence of the doctrine is that the total set of facts about the past, together with the natural laws, entail all the facts about what happens in the present and future. (Slightly) more carefully, the doctrine of causal determinism entails (whatever else it entails) that, for any given time, a complete statement of the (temporally genuine or nonrelational) facts about that time, together with a complete statement of the laws of nature, entails every truth as to what happens after that time.[4]

The second is Van Inwagen's snappier definition, which we have already met in Chapter 1—that there is at any instant exactly one physically possible future.[5] I shall now attempt to argue that whichever of these definitions of determinism is used, it cannot be assumed, without a great deal more in the way of justification than is generally given, that the truth or falsity of the doctrine is a matter that must fall to physics to determine. I shall further contend that to make that unjustified assumption in the present context is precisely to beg the question against the position for which I wish to argue.

5.2   Determinism: Fischer

Let us begin with Fischer's definition. Is it up to physicists to tell us whether, for any given time, a complete statement of the 'temporally genuine' facts about that time, together with a complete statement of the laws of nature, entails every truth as to what

---

[3]   Fischer (2006: 5). See also Neil Levy (2005: 52): 'The existence question, I take it, is largely (though not exclusively) the province of physicists, neuroscientists, and workers in allied fields'.

[4]   Fischer (2006: 5).   [5]   Van Inwagen (1983: 5).

happens after that time? It is not *immediately* obvious why it should be. On the face of it, there seems no reason why, amongst the 'temporally genuine facts' we might not find included (for example) certain biological, psychological, sociological, and economic facts, about which physicists can claim to have no particular expertise, not to mention a whole pile of utterly mundane particularities that belong neither to any scientific nor indeed to any other domain of enquiry, such as that there is currently a globe on my desk, that my printer is out of ink, that there are no elephants in this room, and that my favourite colour is green. Neither have we been told why the 'laws of nature' are to be regarded as entirely the preserve of the physicist; it is not immediately obvious (again, without further argument) why some of them might not belong to geology or chemistry or biology, or even to psychology or economics or sociology. *As stated*, then, there is no immediate connection between the thesis of determinism, as defined by Fischer, and physics; that connection is going to have to be *forged*.

It is not difficult, though, to see how it is that the thought arises that physics might be the science uniquely well-placed to judge the question whether determinism is true. For the thesis of determinism, as Fischer describes it, is dependent for its very coherence on our being able to make sense of the suggestion that there might be such a thing as the 'complete statement' of the 'temporally genuine' facts about any given time. I shall set aside, for the sake of argument, the question whether it is really as easy as Fischer appears to assume to distinguish the 'temporally genuine' facts from the relational ones. Let us simply accept that some workable distinction of this kind can be drawn. For present purposes, I want to focus on the other controversial idea enshrined in Fischer's definition: the idea that there could be a 'complete statement' of the 'temporally genuine' facts about any given time. If this is not to be an idea of whose undermining we are going to be able to make extremely short philosophical work, it would seem to be required that there be a satisfactory way of *constraining* those facts, so that, for example, the fact that there are fewer than 9065 discrete objects with a mass greater than 1 g on my desk at present does not count as one of the facts in question (for if *that* counted, then presumably, the fact that there are fewer than 9066 such objects, and fewer than 9067... and so on, would also have to count, and we would be faced with an infinite number of facts, which seems difficult to square with the idea that there might be such a thing as a 'complete statement' of them). Moreover, and perhaps more pertinently as regards the issue about physics that we are currently considering, the *concepts* in terms of which reality may be described seem also to present us with infinite possibilities of description, there being no obvious end to the *types* of thing of which reality is made up. How, then, might we hope to make coherent the idea of a 'complete statement' of the temporally genuine facts about a given time? It is a reflection on how we might attempt to deal with such difficulties as this that ultimately generates the thought that it is physics that must, in the end, answer the question whether or not determinism is true. For the idea to which we are going to have recourse, presumably, will be the thought that there is a finite set of *basic* facts (perhaps facts, for instance, about the nature and distribution of fundamental physical particles or of types of energy) from which all further facts, no matter what the concepts involved, might be simply inferred, so that we need only mention these basic facts in our 'complete statement', leaving the others to follow inexorably. It is *this* idea that must motivate the thought that physicists, in particular, might have some particular expertise to bring to bear on the question whether determinism is true. If all the facts, however complex, depend ultimately on the properties of basic physical particles and the laws that they follow, then it might seem that we have to defer to physicists when considering the question how the world might conceivably unfold. It is they who will tell us whether or not determinism is true, for it is they who will tell us whether the laws governing these basic physical particles are deterministic or whether they are probabilistic only, leaving scope for multiple unfoldings.

But the question is, of course, whether everything, at every level, really *does* depend in the way envisaged by this picture on the properties of basic physical particles and the laws that they follow. Philosophers are often encouraged to think that believing in the 'supervenience' of higher-level facts on basic physical ones is a minimum requirement for naturalistic sanity in metaphysics. But it is not obvious that supervenience, as generally characterized, entails that the evolution of reality over time depends (in so far as it depends on anything) only on physical laws. What supervenience on the physical is usually said to dictate is that no two worlds that were identical in all basic physical respects at a given time t could differ in any supervenient respect at that same time t. And one might conceivably concede *that*, I think, while still refusing to accept that the question what makes reality evolve as it does *over time* is a matter only for physicists. Even if one adds to the characterization of supervenience the more dia-chronically focused suggestion that there may not be a *change* in any supervenient property without a change in the 'base' properties on which it supervenes, we have not yet arrived at the idea that any given supervenient change must *depend for its explanation* upon the subvening one that (if we concede the supervenience of a wide range of higher-level properties and changes on physical properties and changes) must always accompany it. The direction of explanation might (in some instances) rather be the other way about. So far as I can see, it seems to be perfectly consistent with the supervenience of the 'temporally genuine' higher-level facts on the lower-level physi-cal ones, that physical laws are not (even in principle) sufficient to determine the state of the world at t_2 given its state at t_1—and not just for the standardly-touted reason that perhaps some of those physical laws will ultimately be confirmed by physicists to be probabilistic. One might just think (as does Nancy Cartwright, for example)[6] that such physical laws as there are, are narrow in their scope, strictly applicable only to the relatively small number of situations that correspond closely to the physical models that supply those laws with their concrete interpretations, and applying only *ceteris paribus*, even where they do apply. Indeed, if I may be permitted a short rhetorical excursus,

---

[6] See Cartwright (1999).

I would like to suggest that the idea that the evolution of reality over time might depend solely on 'initial conditions' together with purely *physical* laws, is a really quite extraordinary one. And I do not mean, in saying this, to imply merely that it is extraordinary to believe that the physical laws are deterministic rather than that they are indeterministic. I mean that it is extraordinary to believe *either* that laws at the lower level entirely *determine* (as opposed to *constrain*) the development of reality *or* that these laws 'fix the probabilities' concerning how reality will evolve, leaving some limited scope for chance. After all, the evolution of reality is profoundly influenced (we tend to think) on a large scale by such things as wars, stock market crashes, global warming, revolutions, industrialization, etc., as well as (on a small scale) by the myriad small decisions each of us makes on a daily basis. To suppose that the occurrence of any of these sorts of things is no more than the high-level manifestation of the inevitable workings-out of the consequences of the initial conditions at the start of the universe (deterministic version)—or else of those initial conditions and merely probabilistic laws, together with nothing more than what may perhaps notionally be thought of as the contribution of mere chance (indeterministic version)—is perhaps one of the most astounding things that has ever managed to obtain the status of philosophical ortho-doxy (although it must be conceded that there is strong competition for this title). To believe this would seem to be to consign all sorts of factors that it is natural to regard as causally crucial to the realms of the utterly epiphenomenal. Nothing really matters it would appear, in anything other than an extremely attenuated sense of 'matters', to the unfolding of the world, except the way physical reality was in the beginning, the physical laws, and (perhaps) whatever vagaries are allowed for by the existence of chance. How are we to make room, given this picture, for our basic conviction that *we* matter to that unfolding, both individually through our actions, and as a species through the phenomena to which our activities have given rise: societies, governments, armies, businesses, religions, technologies, art, literature, science?

The reason this only counts as rhetoric is that there are, of course, many attempts to show that our mattering in all these ways is perfectly *compatible* with everything's nevertheless being fixed by what goes on at the level of the smallest constituents of reality. I shall say more of a less rhetorical sort in Chapter 8 about why I regard views of this sort as inadequate; and I shall say more too to describe the alternative picture with which I believe it is imperative to replace this deeply non-commonsensical orthodoxy. My aim in this section, though, is not to establish the alternative picture, but rather only to show that there is dialectical space for me to *concede* Fischer's point that it is unacceptable to suppose that the question whether any of us is really morally responsi-ble for anything (or, more pertinently for my purposes, whether there are any agents or any actions) is a matter that physicists will ultimately have to settle. But this does not imply that we must immediately scurry to look for compatibilist solutions to the free will problem. For I claim only that *determinism* is incompatible with agency. I need not (and do not) agree with Fischer that whether or not determinism is true is a question merely about the nature of the basic physical laws. *That* only follows if one accepts a certain picture of the relationship between the various 'levels' of ontology, explanation, and causality: a 'bottom up' picture whereby the evolution of reality over time is conceded to be asymmetrically dependent entirely and only on the evolution of *physical* reality over time. My suggestion is that *this* is where the incompatibilist should demur. She should insist that there is more than one way in which we can conceive of determinism's being false. It might be false (as Fischer, for instance, imagines) because, although it is true that (i) the evolution of reality over time depends entirely and only on the evolution of *physical* reality over time, as dictated by purely physical laws, nevertheless (ii) those physical laws are indeterministic. But it might also be false because (i) it is *not* true that the evolution of reality over time depends entirely and only on the evolution of physical reality over time, as dictated by purely physical laws and (ii) there is, moreover, no *other* set of laws of nature that, together with the facts at a given time t, might be thought to entail the facts at $t + 1$. And the availability of this second means of arguing for the falsity of determinism shows that the question whether or not it is true is not necessarily a physicist's question. It only turns into a physicist's question once we decide to return a certain answer to the prior *metaphysician's* question how we are to conceive the relation between what we are used to thinking of, metaphorically, as the *levels* of reality. The incompatibilist, I suggest, ought not to return the answer that delivers the question to the physicists to settle.

It is not, after all, as though the belief that physical laws neither entirely determine the future, nor completely fix the chances that it will evolve globally in any given way, would be an ad hoc resource for an incompatibilist to exploit. For what is at the heart of the typical incompatibilist's thinking, of course, is the idea that on occasion, an *agent* can determine how the future will be in certain respects. That thought sits ill with the idea that physical laws, together with initial conditions at the start of the universe, determine the entire future of that universe (which is, of course, what gives the incompatibilist the basic motivation for her incompatibilism). But, as compatibilists never tire of pointing out, that thought *also* sits ill with the idea that physical laws *fix the chances* that a certain future will evolve. What the incompatibilist appears to need is a view that releases us from enslavement either to deterministic *or* to indeterministic laws of physics. And that, I suggest, is not going to be had on the metaphysical cheap. It requires no less than a re-examination of various doctrines concerning the basicness of the physical and the universal grip of physical law that we have grown used to thinking of as non-negotiable. That is what I shall try to provide in Chapter 8.

5.3 Determinism: Van Inwagen

What about the alternative definition of determinism that is provided by Van Inwagen? Recall that, according to that definition, determinism is the thesis that there is only a single physically possible future. And surely, it might be thought, it must be to physicists that we shall have to look if we are to know how many physically possible futures there are! For 'physically possible' presumably means 'possible, holding fixed the laws of physics'. And it is physicists who know about those laws.

But it does not follow that the question how many physically possible futures there might be is a question that only a physicist might presume to tackle. On the contrary, one might think that philosophical reflection, say, could perfectly well give one reason for supposing that more than one future must be physically possible (because, for instance, unless that were so, agency would be impossible), and therefore for supposing that physics is certainly *not* going to produce the contrary verdict. Belief in super-venience is a double-edged sword. If it holds, it is of course true that facts at 'higher' levels are constrained, since they cannot unfold from the present moment in ways that physics could not allow. But it also follows from supervenience that the physical facts and the physical laws must be such as to permit the existence of those higher level phenomena we know to be real. Since supervenience is true, we might maintain, and since we know that agency occurs and demands the metaphysical possibility of alternative futures, we know that the physical laws (whatever they are) are not such as to preclude the existence of such alternatives. This does not mean, of course, that there is a philosophical route by means of which we could show (for example) that the orthodox (indeterministic) interpretation of quantum mechanics was true. It means only that there is a philosophical route by means of which we could argue forcefully that *determinism* is false. This, as I have already tried to suggest, is quite a different matter.

5.4 Conclusion

I contend, then, that to press the Epistemological Argument against my position is to beg the question against it. In assuming P1, it assumes the very point that is at issue: whether it really is the case that everything that happens (including the happenings that are actions) is either entailed by purely deterministic physical laws and prior conditions, or else is subsumable, at least, under probabilistic physical laws. A much more pluralistic and multi-layered conception of causal reality is possible, or so I shall argue in Chapter 8, and so the assumption that no such view is available cannot simply be presupposed at the outset and then used as a premise in the Epistemological Argument. Without further justification, moreover, a pluralistic conception of causal reality cannot be written off as a hopelessly non-naturalistic view; all that is clear is that it is a non-*physicalistic* one (and that only on quite a strong understanding of what it is for a view to be a 'physicalist' one; for as I have intimated above, and will attempt to show in Chapter 8, I believe that pluralism and *supervenience*, as normally characterized, are consistent). The pluralistic conception is a view about the relationship between our different ways of describing the world, one that refuses to restrict true causal efficacy only to entities and properties that are part of an ontology proper to physics. To insist on the prerogative of physics to settle the question whether determinism is true is therefore to deny a claim that is at the heart of my position. It is thus an insistence that requires an argument. It is insufficient merely to *assert*, as the Epistemological Argument does, that no view according to which agency and determinism are incompatible could possibly be correct, on the grounds that the truth (or otherwise) of determinism is a yet-to-be-settled question of physics.

One might press the question, though: isn't it possible that physicists might somehow discover one day that there is only one physically possible *physical* future?—only one physically possible course of movement and change that the particles from which everything else is composed might follow? Given supervenience, it would follow that there was only one physically possible route through reality that *anything* could take, and hence that there was only a single physically possible future, *tout court*. Surely, in that case, physics would have confirmed the truth of determinism, so that anything we had argued to be incompatible with determinism would have, at that point to be given up?

I think we must concede that this *is* (epistemically) possible. But note that what we have conceded, in conceding this, is only P2. We have conceded only that it is *conceivable* that physicists might one day discover something that entails determinism. And at that point, no doubt, if I did not want to give up the claim that there are agents, I would have to look anew at my arguments for the incompatibility of agency and determinism to see whether they might be less strong than I had thought at first.[7] But the bare possibility that physics might one day come up with a surprising finding that might make one wonder about one's incompatibilist arguments is hardly a reason for deciding *now* that those arguments for incompatibilism could not possibly be sound. A convincing Epistemological Argument cannot be run on the basis merely of P2: to say that it is conceivable that physics might one day prove indeterminism wrong is to say no more, in effect, than is said when it is noted that of course more or less any view is potentially reviseable in the light of new findings. A *convincing* Epistemological Argument requires P1: it requires that determinism be thought of as a thesis that physics has exclusive rights to confirm or disconfirm, and on which neither philosophy nor any other discipline has any bearing. But to view determinism in that way is, as I have argued, to beg the question against the view that sustains my position: that determinism is best regarded as a *metaphysical* view, which is generally underwritten by a mistaken vision of the relationship between the levels of reality. I have not here attempted properly to justify my view that that vision is mistaken; I shall say more in Chapter 8. My aim here has only been to insist that I cannot be immediately sent back down Incompatibilist Mountain the way I came and forced to start again by the Epistemological Argument. The view of physics on which the Epistemological Argument is based is not compulsory, and since I shall be arguing in Chapter 8 that that view must be rejected, I should now like to plant my flag firmly on the summit of Incompatibilist Mountain, and begin looking for a good way down.

---

[7] Cf. Van Inwagen (1983: 223): '...it is conceivable that science will one day present us with compelling reasons for believing in determinism. Then, and only then, I think, should we become compatibilists, for, in the case imagined, science has *ex hypothesi* shown that something I have argued for is false...'

6

Indeterminism and Intelligibility

6.1 Beginning the descent: the Intelligibility Question

The Intelligibility Question, recall, asks whether we can make sense of a freedom that is incompatible with determinism. In this chapter, I shall begin my attempt to argue that the answer to this is 'yes'. For I believe, of course, that agency itself is incompatible with determinism (this is the view I have been calling 'Agency Incompatibilism'), that agency is itself both a type of freedom (albeit a lowly type) and moreover a necessary condition of any other types of freedom there might be, and that we 'make sense' of agency on a daily basis when we utilize the conceptual scheme of agent and action and employ the psychology that goes with that scheme—the intentional psychology of belief, desire, intention, etc., or its more primitive cousin, the psychology of seeing, wanting and trying to get—a scheme of which, in my view, the idea of an agent with a range of real metaphysical possibilities for action before her is an ineliminable part. But of course it will not suffice merely to say this and stop there. There are powerful arguments for the claim that libertarian freedom—freedom of a sort that involves such real metaphysical possibilities for action as these—simply *cannot* be made sense of, so that libertarianism is destined to be a position that is, as Kane puts it, 'essentially mysterious and terminally obscure'.[1] It might be thought that Agency Incompatibilism, despite its differences from some more traditional libertarian views, is bound to face similar criticisms. The first task, then, will be to try to get a clear sense of what these anti-libertarian arguments are, and of why it has often seemed so very hard to make *philosophical* sense of what, in my view, we mostly have no difficulty making *everyday* sense of: the essentially indeterministic phenomenon of agency.

I shall be considering two main kinds of argument for thinking that libertarian freedom is ultimately unintelligible. I shall spend Chapters 6 and 7 dealing with the first of these, which I take to be the most powerful, widely promulgated and important line of anti-libertarian reasoning. I call the argument in question the 'Challenge from Chance'. Advocates of the Challenge from Chance propose that the denial of determinism merely introduces an unhelpful randomness into the causal chains that underlie our intentional activity, and that such randomness could never help us to understand how free agency is possible. Part of my response to this challenge will consist in making

---

[1] Kane (1996: 13).

some initial concessions to it—these are the concessions to the compatibilist that were mentioned back in Chapter 1. I shall argue, for example, that the compatibilist is right to insist that nothing capable of grounding moral responsibility for an action could depend on the possibility that one might do things one does not want to do, and moreover cannot think of any conceivable reason to do. Compatibilists have often made the point that it may be in one's *power* to φ, even though (due to one's own dispositions, inclinations, motivations, reasons, etc.) there is no *chance* whatever that one *will* φ. They say moreover, and more importantly, that an insistence upon such chances cannot help to secure or improve the agent's control over the course of events. I will argue that they are quite correct in thinking so and therefore, if the libertarian thinks that having the power to φ requires the existence of some objective chance that one will φ, she is mistaken, since where what puts one's φ-ing quite out of the question is only such things as one's own wants, principles, motivations, etc. (and where there are no further *special* worries about how these wants, principles, and motivations have been arrived at) there should be no concern that an absence of possibility here amounts to a lack of freedom.

I shall also argue, however, that making this kind of concession to compatibilism does not imply that there are no robust alternative possibility requirements on action at all. What I shall try to show is that my particular brand of libertarianism, which conceives of alternate possibilities as necessary requirements of agency *in general* rather than of morally responsible forms of agency *in particular*, can make it intelligible why the existence of alternate possibilities of a rather different stripe from those that are usually thought to be wanted by the incompatibilist might be required for freedom. This, I will argue, makes it possible to justify a rather different and in many ways much more modest view of what sorts of alternate possibilities have to be available to an agent at the time of her action. Roughly speaking, my contention will be that the alternate possibilities that truly make trouble for determinism relate not to such high-level powers as the capacity to make either of the choices presented by any arbitrary moral or practical dilemma (of which powers, I suggest, it is the compatibilist who generally gives the best account) but rather to the far more basic powers that animals must possess over the movements of their bodies through space and time if they are truly to count as the sources and controllers of those movements. For each segment of activity under-taken by a given animal, I contend, it must be the case that the animal in question had the power, at the time of executing that activity, to refrain from doing so, either by doing something else at the time in question or by doing nothing. Putative activities of which this is not true, I claim, cannot count as settlings by the animal at the time of action of what is to happen to its own body, and so cannot be actions or activities of the animal at all. And *these* powers, I shall argue, cannot be understood in such a way as to be compatible with determinism; these are two-way powers that really *do* require that certain possibilities be left open by the world, for unless they are, room cannot be made for these activities to be happenings that settle certain matters that are genuinely up to the agent, as opposed to being merely the inevitable outcome of events occurring inside her body. It is this, I shall argue, that is the true source of the most powerful and plausible version of the Principle of Alternative Possibilities; and moreover, I shall contend that it makes possible, as other versions of that principle do not, a convincing response to the Challenge from Chance.

Chapter 6 will set out the challenge together with some extant libertarian responses, and I shall explain why I do not find the extant responses satisfactory, before offering the outlines of my own. Chapter 7 will then respond to a number of anticipated objections to the solution I propose.

In Chapter 8, I shall move on to consider a second sort of anti-libertarian argument. It is bound to be alleged (particularly, I think, once my response to the Challenge from Chance is on the table) that the style of libertarian view I have offered is essentially a version of 'agent causationism'. I dislike the term 'agent causationism', for reasons I shall explain in Chapter 8, and I think it is a terminology it is important to reject. However, I concede that my view belongs in the agent causationist tradition because it insists on the centrality to any view that could possibly help us solve the free will problem of a metaphysics in which agents play a crucial and irreducible causal role in the unfolding of reality through time. And for many, that will be enough already to convict me of dualistic confusions, panicky metaphysics,[2] and the intellectual sin of providing a label where what was needed was an explanation.[3] In Chapter 8, I attempt a rebuttal of these charges. The first and most important task is to defend the claim that my view does not make the causation involved in agency literally *unintelligible*. Clearly, if that were so, my proposed route down Incompatibilist Mountain would be comprehensively blocked. But it will also be necessary (in Chapter 8) to attempt an answer to what Kane calls the Existence Question: many worries about agent causationism really relate not so much to the *intelligibility* of the notion, which some compatibilist philosophers are perfectly prepared to concede, but rather to the question whether such a thing is likely to exist in the natural universe as we know and believe it to be; whether, if agency is to be the kind of phenomenon I have been insisting it must be, it can be found a respectable place in the natural world. And this is a question that belongs to the second stage of Kane's descent, the part in which the libertarian must make the case for the view that the freedom that she proposes is both desirable and coherent, actually exists in the natural order. In addition she must show us where it is to be found.

I begin, now, though, with the Challenge from Chance.

6.2 The Challenge from Chance

What I am calling the 'Challenge from Chance' has been formulated, over the years, in many different ways. The basic idea is that it is impossible to see how indeterminism could possibly provide us with anything that we might want in the way of freedom,

---

[2] C.f. P. F. Strawson (1962: 93).

[3] Nagel, for example, accuses agent causationists of 'giving a name to a mystery' (1986: 115).

anything that could really amount to control as opposed to an openness in the flow of reality that would constitute merely the injection of chance or randomness into the unfolding of the processes that underlie our activity. Let me take a relatively recent formulation of the challenge as my starting point. Mele formulates what he calls 'a problem about luck for libertarians' as follows. He notes that the typical libertarian (who, for ease of reference, I shall call 'Mele's libertarian') believes that a free decision to A, made by a given agent at a particular time *t*, could, at that very moment, have gone the other way: the agent could have decided at *t* not to A, instead.[4] In the actual world, this agent—following Mele, I shall call him Joe—decides at *t* to A. But in another world *with the very same laws of nature and the very same past*, Mele's libertarian believes, Joe decides at *t* not to A. But in that case, Mele argues, this libertarian faces the following difficulty:

If there is nothing about Joe's powers, capacities, states of mind, moral character, and the like in either world that accounts for this difference, then the difference seems to be just a matter of luck. And given that neither world diverges from the other in any respect before *t*, there is no difference at all in Joe in these two worlds to account for the difference in his decisions. To be sure, something about Joe may explain why it is *possible* for him to decide to A in the actual world and decide not to A in another world with the same laws and past. That he is an indeterministic decision-maker may explain this. That is entirely consistent with the difference in his decisions being just a matter of luck.[5]

If the difference in his decisions in these two possible worlds is just a matter of luck, Mele goes on to ask, how can it have been in any sense *up to Joe* which decision was made? How can it have been up to him which possible world became actual? Unless we can see that which decision was made was up to Joe, unless which possible world became actual was up to him, how on earth does the indeterminacy that has been posited by the libertarian contribute to his freedom and moral responsibility?

   This worry, in one form or another, is present in an enormous number of compatibilist critiques of libertarianism; it is no exaggeration, indeed, to say that it is the *main* challenge that the libertarian must meet. I shall begin by accepting the challenge as it is formulated by Mele and attempting to assemble some of the elements of my response to it. But what will gradually become clear as I assemble those elements is that I take issue with some important aspects of the way in which the libertarian position is characterized by Mele. These features are by no means unique to Mele's presentation; indeed, they have become fairly standard characteristics of many contemporary explications of what it is that a libertarian must believe. But in my view, the best version of the libertarian position looks rather different from the position characterized

---

[4] For the sake of argument, I shall not quarrel, for the time being, with the implicit assumption of Mele's libertarian that it is entirely in such mental events as decisions and choices that we should hope to locate libertarian freedom. I shall, however, argue later (Section 6.6) that this represents a serious mistake.

[5] Mele (2006: 9).

here by Mele[6] and, moreover, only this improved version has any hope of responding successfully to the Challenge from Chance. Having made my preliminary riposte, therefore, I will have to continue by explaining in some detail why I believe Mele's formulation of the libertarian position is neither unproblematic nor mandatory. In doing so, I hope to clarify in more detail the nature of the libertarianism for which I wish to argue; and to show how it makes possible a very different kind of response to the Challenge from Chance from those that are usually offered by libertarian writers.

Let us begin by trying to put some flesh on the abstract bones of Joe's situation as it is imagined by Mele. Let us suppose, first, that Joe is attempting to decide whether or not to move in with his girlfriend. Let us also imagine that he decides at *t* that he *will* move in. Let us begin by supposing further (because to make this supposition presents the Challenge from Chance in what I believe is a usefully stark form) that the case is what I shall call a *clear* case, i.e. that it is completely obvious to Joe, having briefly deliberated, what he ought to do. We can imagine, for example, that Joe loves his girlfriend very much and enjoys spending time with her; she has a lovely flat that is much nicer than his own mean bedsit, which he has always loathed, and which is also much handier for Joe's work; he dislikes his own company and solitude makes him depressed; it would be much cheaper to move in with her than to continue to pay a separate rental, separate gas and electricity bills, etc. Let us suppose, in addition, that, on reflection, immediately prior to *t* he realizes that he cannot, at the moment, think of any good reason *not* to move in with his girlfriend. And let us suppose, finally (and prescinding from the delicate question of what it might mean to say this) that Joe makes his decision *on the basis* of this rational assessment. One thing we can surely say is that in such circumstances as these, it is definitely *not* a matter of luck that Joe decides as he does, at least not in any way that might be thought to impugn such things as his agency, freedom, control, or moral responsibility.[7] His reasons are overwhelmingly good and he chose rationally on the basis of those overwhelmingly good reasons. This means, surely, that no luck of any kind we need to be concerned about had anything to do with it.

Why does Mele think that the libertarian might have difficulty explaining how this obvious truth about such clear cases is to be fitted into his picture of what happens when Joe makes his choice? The difficulty, presumably, is that as Mele conceives of it, the libertarian is committed to the view that Joe *could* have decided at *t* not to move in with his girlfriend. Moreover, on Mele's view, the libertarian is committed to *eschewing* the various rather sensible-looking ways that are available of making sense of this claim that might recommend themselves to a compatibilist. For example, on the version of

---

[6] It should be mentioned, in fairness to Mele, that he *agrees* that the best version of libertarianism looks rather different from the version that represents the view of what I am here calling 'Mele's libertarian'.

[7] The qualification is necessary because of course there is a sense in which luck is always involved in successful activity of any sort. It is always a matter of luck, in a sense, if my body and brain continue to function properly from one moment to the next in such a way that I can do such things as make decisions and act on them at all. But this sort of luck is omnipresent, and the libertarian cannot be charged with having introduced it by means of any insistence on indeterminism.

libertarianism being taken for granted by Mele, the libertarian must deny that all we mean when we say that Joe could have decided not to move in is that he could have made this decision *if he'd wanted to* or *if he had seen any good reason to do so*,[8] or that he made the decision in a perfectly ordinary way without having been subjected to, for example, hypnotic suggestion, high-pressure persuasion, blackmail, etc. All these are interpretations of what it is for Joe to have been able to do otherwise that the compatibilist will be likely happily to accept, but Mele's libertarian is understood to presuppose an interpretation of the claim that Joe could, at *t*, have decided not to move in with his girlfriend that achieves a purer focus than any of these interpretations on the moment of decision itself, and the possibilities then and there afforded by the total condition of reality. It has to be genuinely possible, according to Mele's libertarian, for the world to unfold from the moment just prior to that moment of decision *t* in such a way that instead of deciding to move in, as he actually did, Joe might instead have decided not to do so. And yet no alterations in Joe's reasons or in the train of thought immediately prior to his decision that might account for or enable us to understand this difference in the outcome are permitted to be envisaged: by hypothesis, this alternative possible world is to have exactly the same past as does the actual world, right up until time *t*, the time of the decision itself. But if this is the case, then it does indeed look as though it is bound to be a matter of luck, at least to some extent, if Joe manages to be rational and choose to move in with his girlfriend after all.

It is important, though, to be very clear exactly what the reason is for saying so, if we are not to beg the question against the libertarian. We should *not* say, in particular, that the reason is that there is nothing *about* Joe that could explain why he chooses one option in one possible world and the other in another. Mele's argument rather suggests that this is *his* concern ('if there is nothing about Joe's powers, capacities .... then the difference seems to be just a matter of luck'). However, to note the fact that there is nothing *about* an agent that could explain why he φs rather than ψs and to infer that it must therefore be a matter of luck *that* he φs rather than ψs is only permissible at best on an understanding of what it means for something to be a 'matter of luck' that need not trouble the libertarian. I shall say more about this shortly, but roughly, the basic point is this. On one understanding of what it is to be a 'matter of luck' that *p* rather than *q*, it may indeed be possible to infer from the fact that there is no explanation in terms of

---

[8] In suggesting that these are possible compatibilist analyses of the claim that Joe could have decided differently, I do not mean to commit myself to the claim that 'could have...if...' propositions of this sort ought to be regarded (even by the compatibilist) as true *conditionals*. Indeed, I believe it is clear that they are not; see my (2006b) for a detailed discussion of this matter. It is not because these claims are conditionals that they should seem to recommend themselves to the compatibilist, but rather because it can be argued that they are attributions of ability and opportunity to agents, and that it is, at any rate, not straightforwardly *obvious* that such attributions of ability and opportunity are inconsistent with determinism. Because it is the main task of this chapter to explicate and defend a version of incompatibilism, I do not go into the question what the best version of compatibilism might be. However, the clearest and most sophisticated discussion I know of what the compatibilist ought to say about these sorts of 'could have...if...' statements is that offered by Kenny (1975: Chapters VII and VIII).

any antecedent factors of why p rather than q, that it is (at least partly) a matter of luck that p rather than q.[9] However, the libertarian ought not to fear the conclusion that, on this understanding, it can indeed be said to be a matter of luck that Joe decides to move in with his girlfriend rather than not, since this is a conclusion she embraces in any case. It is a crucial part of her position, not an unforeseen disastrous consequence, that it is partly a matter of luck that Joe decides as he does in *this* sense. What is essential, though, is that she not permit a slide from this conclusion to the far more tendentious claim that if there is no explanation of why p rather than q in terms of properties possessed by the agent antecedent to the action, then it cannot be within the power of the agent to control whether p or q.[10] The assumption that the question whether an agent will or will not exercise one of her powers on a given occasion can always be answered by appealing to some antecedently existing property or properties of that agent or her circumstances, unless the occurrence is to be simply random and uncontrolled by anything, is precisely the sort of thing that a certain sort of libertarian, including Agency Incompatibilists, will certainly deny, on the grounds that agents are creatures with *two-way* powers. If there are to be creatures with two-way powers, she will insist, then there are creatures that are such that their properties do not dictate that they will act, in given circumstances, in just one possible way. If this position is not to be ruled out prematurely, then, we must be careful about what exactly our *grounds* are for agreeing with Mele that Joe's decision looks to be a matter of luck. The reason, why it does indeed seem to be a matter of luck that Joe decides as he does must not be simply that in advance of the decision he possesses no *properties* that might explain why his good reasons took effect, even though they might not have done.

What, then, *is* the reason for supposing that whether or not Joe decides to move in with his girlfriend is a matter of luck? It seems to me to be this: that the alternative future in which Joe decides *not* to move in with his girlfriend seems impossible to envisage as anything other than the occurrence of a sudden and inexplicable chance event, unrelated in any intelligible way to Joe's desires, reasons, or deliberations. It seems impossible to understand how it could have been a true *decision*, one made by Joe of his own volition, because it does not connect up properly with what we know in this case are the motivational and deliberative antecedents of what occurs. The libertarian requirement that we must make space for this alternative future, therefore, appears to amount to an insistence upon the possibility that the decision be taken right out of Joe's hands at the crucial moment.

---

[9] Only 'at least partly' because it might be argued that the mere possibility of an alternative outcome does not mean there can be no explanation of why p rather than q, since such explanations may be backed by *probabilistic* generalizations, and that this rules out its being *wholly* a 'matter of luck' that p rather than q. I shall come to this issue in Section 6.3.

[10] A similar point is made by Kane in his (2000: 161): 'one must question the intuitive connection between "indeterminism's being involved in something's happening" and "its happening merely as a matter of chance or luck". "Chance" and "luck" are terms of ordinary language that carry the connotation of "its being out of my control". So using them already begs certain questions; whereas "indeterminism" is a technical term that merely precludes *deterministic* causation'.

Indeed, it might very well be argued that the libertarian who insists that it must be genuinely possible at *t* for Joe to have made the decision not to move in with his girlfriend faces more serious problems even than the Challenge from Chance. For it is not obvious that what it appears must be his view of the situation is even coherent. The libertarian whose views we are considering insists that it must be possible at *t* for Joe to decide (inexplicably) not to move in with his girlfriend. But could a sudden and irrational chance event of the sort it appears he is insisting must be possible, bearing *no* rational relations whatever to any of Joe's reasons, desires, or prior deliberations even *be* a decision? I doubt it. It is true, of course, that we make many decisions that may be accounted irrational, for example because they do not accord with our best reasons, or with our needs, or with the account we are inclined to give ourselves of what we ought to do. But it is hard to imagine something that counts as a genuine choice of which *no* pro-attitude-involving account at all can be given, even of the 'I just suddenly felt like doing it' kind. We know that even this minimal rationality would have been lacking had Joe decided not to move in with his girlfriend, for we know that Joe did *not* suddenly 'feel like doing it'; that he did not do so is part of what has to be kept constant in the history of the decision. If it is right to think that a genuine choice has to be something with intelligible roots in such things as an agent's reasons and desires, the position of Mele's libertarian not only saddles us with the Challenge from Chance; it looks to be actually *incoherent* (if the insistence is that it has to have been possible, at the moment of decision, that the agent should have made the opposite choice from the one he in fact made, even in an utterly clear case where he has no reason or desire of any kind to make it).

Perhaps it might be said that it is too strong to insist that something that counts as a genuine choice must relate rationally to one's various reasons, pro-attitudes, and desires, that space must be made for the contrariness of human nature and for the wide variety of strange, irrational, and perverse phenomena to which the human will is subject. It might be said, for example, that we sometimes choose what we do not want in the slightest out of self-loathing or the peculiar kind of determination to which we are sometimes subject to stand in the way of our own happiness. These points are important ones, and it must be admitted, I think, that many philosophical accounts of action as they stand are probably inadequate to account for these types of motivation. It is certainly not obvious that all intentional actions that arise from such forms of motivation are describable as proceeding from anything it would be very happy to call a 'desire' or even a 'pro-attitude'. But even if it is conceded that humans are capable of making choices for which even they would accept there is nothing whatever to be said, and so that it is indeed *possible* to make a choice that does not relate in rational ways to one's beliefs, desires, and prior deliberations and which arises pathologically in some way, perhaps out of deep psychological causes, it remains very hard to see how the existence of such choices as *these* could possibly be the rock on which to found a coherent libertarianism. How could the opportunity to make decisions that bear no relation to one's reasons, motivations, or one's trains of deliberative thought be the key to freedom? On the face of it, then, I am inclined to think that even if it is not actually *incoherent* to suppose that one might make a choice that bore no rational relations to one's desires, reasons, or any prior deliberative activity, the compatibilist is right to think that the alternative possibilities that might be represented by the availability of such options can scarcely be at the heart of a plausible defence of libertarianism.

What, then, is the libertarian to say at this point? I want next to consider two common sorts of extant libertarian reply to the Challenge from Chance and to explain why I find them ultimately unsatisfactory as they stand.

6.3 Two inadequate libertarian responses

6.3.1 Contrastive explanations and probabilistic connections

The first kind of response is an attempt to defend a refusal to budge from the kind of libertarian position I have just outlined by supplementing that position with some reflections on the phenomenon of *contrastive* explanation. These are deemed to under-cut the proponent of the Challenge from Chance. This kind of respondent simply insists that it *is* always possible for a free agent who decides, at any given moment, that she will φ, to make an opposed decision at that very same moment, even in cases that are clear in the sense I have tried to characterize. It is insisted, moreover, that it is the existence of this possibility that confers freedom on those choices she *does* make in accordance with her reasons. It is then attempted to meet the accusation that under such circumstances it could only be a matter of luck that the agent makes the decision she does by means of one of two expedients. I shall not concern myself with the first of these, which is to suggest that it is a mistake for the challenger to assume, as she does, that a contrastive explanation of why an agent decides to φ rather than not to φ is necessarily required in order to avert the charge that the actual decision to φ was 'a matter of luck'; that a *non-contrastive* explanation of why the agent φ-ed may, in certain cases, be perfectly sufficient.[11] This is because this first expedient is more usually offered by the libertarian in an attempt to handle cases rather different from the one we have been considering, cases in which there are (perhaps incommensurable) reasons for and against *both* (or all) alternatives being considered, so that the case is precisely *not* clear in the sense I have tried to characterize. I shall therefore concentrate on the second of the two expedients, which is more relevant for present purposes, since in a clear case such as Joe's, we would surely hope to be able to vindicate the very plausible idea that we can give a contrastive explanation (as well, perhaps, as a non-contrastive one) of why he decides to move in with his girlfriend rather than deciding not to do so.

The exponent of the second expedient first notes what seems to be a connection between the Challenge from Chance and the question whether there is a contrastive explanation available of why the agent decided to φ rather than not to φ. The

---

[11] This first expedient is offered by O'Connor (2000: 91–3).

connection is this: it might seem at first sight to be plausible that the following general principle is true: if one is able to explain *why p* rather than *q*, it cannot be a matter of luck *that p* rather than *q*. The proponent of the second expedient then notes that in a case such as Joe's, where rational considerations and other motivational factors all point in a single direction, we clearly *are* able to explain why Joe chose to move in with his girlfriend rather than not; we explain this by citing the many reasons that favour that decision that he took into account and the fact that he could think of nothing at all to be said against it. So it would seem, if our general principle is correct, that it cannot be a matter of luck that he decided to move in with his girlfriend rather than deciding not to do so.

Now, it will be replied by the proponent of the Challenge from Chance that the proposed contrastive explanation in this case is unsatisfactory in the light of the fact that even given all these many reasons and the fact that Joe could think of nothing whatever that could be said against the decision to move in, it still remained possible, according to the libertarian, that he should decide *not* to move in. So we still need to know why Joe decided to move in rather than not, given that (according to the libertarian) both alternatives remained on the cards right up until the moment of decision. But the libertarian may insist that the challenger is proceeding here on the premise that the sheer possibility of an alternative outcome, however improbable, vitiates a contrastive explanation. And she will point out that this assumption is just mistaken. For many contrastive explanations, she may point out, are offered against a *probabilistic* background.

Consider, for example, the following case.[12] The bubonic plague bacillus will cause death in 50–90% of cases if left to develop without intervention in a human being. However, it is treatable with tetracycline, which reduces the risk to between 5 and 10%. It is possible, of course, that the processes involved in death by bubonic plague are perfectly deterministic, even given these statistics because there may be factors not yet identified, *other* than the administration of tetracycline, that help to explain the difference between the cases of bacillus infection in which death occurs and those in which death does not. But it is also possible that the processes are not deterministic. Suppose, then, for the sake of argument, that they are not; and suppose now that we want to explain why Alice, who is infected with the bacillus, survived rather than not. Could we not say that it was because she had been treated with tetracycline, even though treatment with tetracycline does not reduce the risk of death to zero? Surely we could do so. And if this seems plausible, could we not apply it equally to the case of Joe? That is, even if it is not absolutely *ruled out* that he might decide not to move in with his girlfriend, we might still judge that such a decision is terrifically *unlikely*, given that Joe is a reasonable person in possession of facts that seem to add up to an overwhelmingly powerful case, and that he is not in possession of any facts on the basis of which a case

---

[12] From Humphreys (1989: 100); discussed in Clarke (1996b) from whose discussion I have borrowed the present description of the case.

for deciding not to do so might be mounted. Given its unlikeliness, can we not insist that we are in possession here of a contrastive explanation of why Joe decided to move in with his girlfriend, rather than deciding not to move in with her, *notwithstanding* the possibility that remains open that he might nevertheless make the opposite decision? However, if we have a contrastive explanation, do we not thereby also have the means to rebut the suggestion that his having decided to move in with his girlfriend rather than deciding not to do so was a mere 'matter of luck'?

Does this constitute an adequate response to the Challenge from Chance? It is important, I think, to accept that the bubonic plague example shows that the contrastive explanation of undetermined events is perfectly possible and thus that no acceptable version of the Challenge can proceed on the mere premise that an undetermined result can never be contrastively explained. Nevertheless, it does not seem to me that the response is fully adequate to the particular case at hand because the real nub of the difficulty has still not been tackled by the mere observation that contrastive explanations continue to work perfectly well in probabilistic contexts, although that observation is correct. There are two difficulties, both pertaining to the principle on the basis of which I suggested the libertarian might hope to make her case: the principle that if it is possible to give an acceptable explanation of why p rather than q it cannot be a 'matter of luck' *that* p rather than q. One initial difficulty with this principle is that it seems too strong. For it is very tempting to continue to think that if the factors cited in the explanation of why p rather than q are not factors that strictly *rule out* q, and if we are unable to supplement those factors with additional others that, in conjunction with those originally cited *do* rule out q, that it might still remain at least *partly* a matter of luck that p rather than q. If Alice takes tetracycline and survives rather than dies, for instance, then it seems to be at least *partly* a matter of luck that she does so, at any rate unless we can give a further explanation of why *she* has survived, given that some who take tetracycline do not. Now, of course we *may* be able to do this. Perhaps, for example, (to get a little far-fetched for a moment) tetracycline works for people with a certain blood-type, but not for those without it. If Alice has this blood type we might therefore be able to maintain that it was not simply a matter of luck that tetracycline worked for her.[13] But then it is either the case that having this blood-type and taking tetracycline is sufficient for recovery, or it is not. If it is, it is not obvious why one would think the causal relationships here were ultimately indeterministic in the first place. If, as seems vastly more likely, it is not sufficient, we face the further question why some of those who have the relevant blood type and take tetracycline die and some do not. Again, perhaps there is something to say here. But the idea would be that provided we have genuine metaphysical indeterminism in the causal process rather than simply very complicated *deterministic* causal processes that we have difficulty fully

---

[13] Though of course one might think it was a matter of luck *for Alice* that she did indeed have such a blood type. But this is different from its being a matter of luck that she recovered, given that she had the blood type in question.

comprehending, there is bound to be *at some point* in this generated chain of 'why' questions a contrastive 'why' question that it is impossible to answer: two situations alike in all causally relevant respects but such that the outcome nevertheless differs. For the existence of such a situation, it might be said, is just what is implied by genuine metaphysical indeterminism. If we can stop the chain of questions with a satisfactory answer at every stage then that just shows that what we had was determinism after all. But in the indeterministic scenario, it might be said, we are bound to face at some point, a contrastive 'why' question that does not have an answer. The chain of 'why' questions is represented diagrammatically in Figure 6.1.

The idea is that if a situation is fundamentally indeterministic we will always end up ultimately on the left-hand side of a diagram such as this because there will always be a contrastive question we cannot answer; one that asks why, given total commonality in the antecedent conditions, the outcome goes one way when it could have gone another. Now, it is true that the mere fact that we can continue to generate further contrastive questions in this way does not necessarily undermine the *original* contrastive explanation we might have thought to offer. For example, our explanation of why Alice survived rather than not is not undermined by it being pointed out that we have not thereby answered the question why *she* survived whereas Bob, who also took tetracycline, did not. That is simply a different question, and it can be no objection to the claim that one has adequately answered *one* question to point out that another different question has not simultaneously been answered. Likewise, it might be said, our explanation of why Joe decided to move in with his girlfriend rather than deciding not to do so—in terms of his extremely good reasons and lack of any countervailing ones— is not undermined by it being pointed out that we have not thereby explained why his reasons took effect in this instance, as it were, rather than not doing so (given the libertarian premise that it is metaphysically possible that they should not have done). If we imagine that original explanation to be underpinned by an overwhelmingly high probability that Joe would choose to move in with his girlfriend, it might be said that that suffices to ground our explanation. But the inference from the existence of a perfectly good explanation to the claim that Joe's deciding as he did was not a 'matter of luck' *does* seem threatened. We can accede, perhaps, to the claim that his deciding as he did was not *wholly* a matter of luck. After all, we have an explanation in terms of antecedent circumstances that made the actual outcome highly probable. But there was still a chance that things would not develop in this admittedly likely fashion, so the natural thing seems to be to say that if they do not do so, then that is at least *partly* a matter of luck. We must be careful, of course, not to hypostatize luck—it is easy to fall into a way of speaking that suggests that luck is a positive causal factor in its own right, and of course it is not. It is not as though luck enters to fill the gaps left by causality; to speak of 'luck' is just

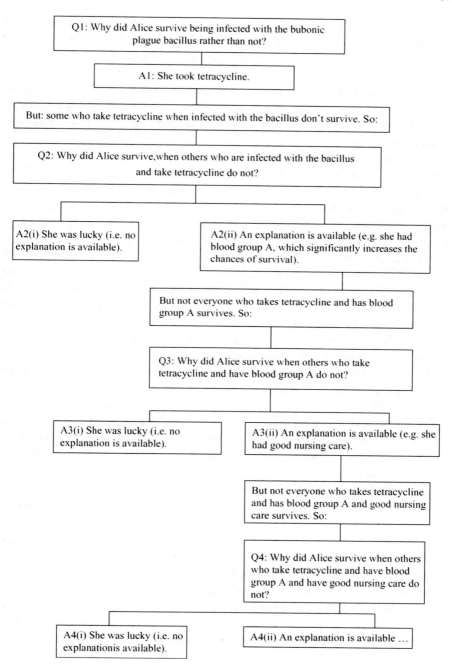

Figure 6.1 The persistence of luck.

a way of saying that *nothing* fills those gaps. To quote William James' remarks on the closely related concept of chance, it is merely to say that the outcome is 'not controlled, secured, or necessitated by other things in advance of its own actual presence'.[14] But that is something which, in the kind of case envisaged, seems to be *true*. That Joe would decide to move in with his girlfriend rather than not does seem to be an outcome that was *not* secured in advance, under the libertarian assumption currently under consideration. Some chance must remain that he would make the opposite decision at *t*.

This, though, is not the *main* problem with the envisaged libertarian response. As I argued earlier, it is not obvious why the libertarian has to *worry* about luck, thus conceived. It is the gist of the libertarian's main point, after all, that antecedent factors must not actually determine the outcome of any decision-making process if the decision is to be free. On the conception of what it is for something to be a 'matter of luck' that we are currently considering, therefore, far from being a problem for the libertarian, it would seem actually to be a wanted part of her position that Joe's decision was partly a matter of luck (if this means merely that it was not entirely guaranteed by antecedent factors). The *real* difficulty is that there is a different sense in which Joe's deciding as he did appears to have been a 'matter of luck' under the circumstances envisaged, a sense that should be much more worrying for the libertarian. The problem is not merely that there was some *chance* of Joe's not making the rational decision he did; it is that whether or not he does so in the given situation seems to be *out of his hands*: the decision Joe makes seems to be not just partly a matter of luck so far as the world in general is concerned (not guaranteed by antecedent factors) but it is also partly a matter of luck *for him*. The concept of luck, indeed (and perhaps in this respect it needs to be distinguished from the concept of chance) has its real home in the discussion of human affairs. Luck figures in our explanations when things go our way, though they might easily not have done, because of fortunate eventualities or circumstances that were not our doing. And the real problem with the current libertarian response is that it does not avert the worry that Joe's deciding as he did was at least partly a matter of luck in this rather different and (for present purposes) much more important sense. The availability of a contrastive, probabilistically-based explanation of why Joe decided as he did does nothing to allay the concern that the transition that is made from one world-state to the next when Joe makes his decision could have been subverted by an event over which Joe himself appears to have no control. Because (by hypothesis) the occurrence in question (had it occurred) would have borne no relation of any intelligible sort to Joe's motivations and desires, to his prior train of deliberative thought, to his emotional responses to the alternatives he

---

[14] See the James quote offered in Chapter 1, note 28.

is imagining, etc., we find it very hard to envisage a narrative according to which we can think of such a decision as genuinely an intervention in the world on the part of Joe. We can only make sense of it (if we can make sense of it at all) as the product of some alien sub-personal system interfering darkly with the choices Joe himself might really wish to have made, and therefore if such interference does not occur we find it natural to suppose that it must have been lucky for Joe if it did not, since it seems natural to suppose that if it *had* done so, that would not have been up to him.

It might be thought that we might, at this point, try to deny that it is merely lucky for Joe if such an event does not occur. We might try to argue, for instance, that we have some power over the probabilities that govern such matters; that it is within our power, for instance, to mould ourselves so that we become the sorts of people who tend to respond to reasons, and so in whom irrational actions bearing little or no relation to our motivations, desires, and trains of deliberation would be very unlikely to happen.[15] But even if we do indeed have such powers this does not address the main problem. Provided it is insisted there must remain *some* chance that Joe might decide to take the motivationally unintelligible course of action (as it *will* be insisted by our libertarian), we still face the difficulty that it seems to remain at least *partly* (though admittedly, now, not wholly) a matter of luck for him if he manages to choose aright. Now, if the *only* reason we were concerned about luck was the worry that an outcome's being a matter of luck makes praise unmerited and blame unwarranted, this might not matter. After all, if I can make it the case that in a given situation the chances of my succumbing to a foolish whim to damage my own happiness are minuscule (though still present), then it seems reasonable to think that I can be given credit in a situation where I make a sensible practical choice, even if it is still *partly* a matter of luck that I manage to do so. But this is *not* the only reason we are concerned about luck. Luck presents a problem not only for *moral responsibility* but also, and more directly, for *agency*. Put bluntly, agency itself seems to be inconsistent with its being even partly a matter of luck for me whether I act in this way or that:[16] the

---

[15] This suggestion is central to the position that Mele (2006) calls *Daring Soft Libertarianism*. The Daring Soft Libertarian suggests that perhaps it need not matter for freedom and moral responsibility if it is, strictly speaking, a matter of luck *at the time of action* whether the agent decides to φ or decides not to do so. Provided she is responsible for making it the case that it is very likely indeed that she would decide to φ in circumstances such as these (by, for example, working on her dispositions) she can be responsible for her φ-ing even if it *is*, in some respects, a matter of luck that she φ-ed.

[16] Of course, there can be kinds of case in which it might well be said that it was a 'matter of luck' that I acted in one way rather than another. For example, there are cases in which I just plump for an alternative which seems to me to have no real advantage over its rivals, and which turn out to be a fortunate choice, e.g. when I pick out the ticket that wins the lottery. But this is a case in which what is lucky is that my action turns out to have a property that I did not know in advance it would have—the property of being a selection of the winning ticket, in this case. This is different from what is being considered here, where the question of whether my action will occur at all is out of my control.

very fact that something is an action or decision of mine ought to mean that it is not a matter of luck *for me* that it occurs. Acting constitutes an exercise of control on our part *at the very moment at which we act*. We make our reasons take effect there and then *by acting* (or, in this case, by deciding). We cannot accede to a representation of the situation in which something that is genuinely an action or a decision of ours is represented as arising out of our reasons (or not) without so much as a by your leave, so that in effect we are reduced (at the time of action) to just waiting and seeing what results, however unlikely we may have managed to make it in advance that we will act irrationally. But this is how the alternative possibility that Joe might decide not to move in with his girlfriend is being represented by the scenario we are being invited to consider. On the one hand it is represented as a *decision* made by Joe at *t,* but on the other hand, we are given nothing at all that can help us to understand how it could have been a true decision because it does not, by hypothesis, connect with any intelligible motivation, desire, or train of deliberative thought on Joe's part. Indeed, we know that it is preceded entirely by reflection on factors that make it utterly incomprehensible. We can only then regard it as a kind of random upsurge of irrationality into Joe's psychological life. But once it is thus regarded, it just seems bewildering why anyone would want to insist on the alternative possibility in question.

Why would one want it to be possible that such random upsurges might occur? They do not seem to enhance the agent's control over anything—if anything, they would seem simply to detract from that control—because we cannot understand them as voluntary productions and they have therefore to be conceptualized as mere interferences in the normal functioning of the motivated agent. We do not (surely) want or need the possibility of deciding to do things we do not want to do *at all*, which we can see no reason to do, and which we have every reason not to do. And this is what ultimately convinces me that it is the compatibilist who has right on his side with respect to the question what sort of power to do otherwise we are really adverting to when we say that an agent such as Joe could have made the opposite decision (as we might, for example, a year later, when Joe is bemoaning the loss of his bachelor lifestyle), at any rate in a case such as this, which is clear. When we remind him that he ought to stop moaning since he *could* have decided not to move in with his girlfriend, we surely mean only to say something that is likely to be readily acceptable to the compatibilist, such as that no one forced or cajoled him to decide as he did, or that he possessed a general decision-making capacity at the time that was in perfect working order and which he could then have exercised so as to have made the opposite decision, if he had seen good reason to do so. There just seems no point at all in insisting that it is important that it is possible that Joe should have made the opposite decision at the very moment at which he made the actual one. For we cannot imagine how the opposite decision, under such circumstances, could really have amounted to a decision of Joe's at all, and so how its availability could have been at all desirable or freedom-enhancing.

I conclude, then, that this first libertarian response is unsatisfactory. Although it is perfectly true that adequate contrastive explanations of probabilistic phenomena are possible, this point is not sufficient to allay the worry that which decision Joe makes remains at least *partly* a matter of luck. Moreover, it remains partly a matter of luck not merely in the sense that the outcome is not completely determined by antecedent factors (a sense that need not trouble the libertarian), but rather in the much more troubling sense that it does not seem to be entirely *up to Joe*, at the time of the decision, which decision is made—it is a matter of luck *for him* that he makes the decision he does, not just in the sense that it turns out to be good for him to have made it but in the worrying sense that it seems to be out of his hands at *t* which decision gets made. It appears to remain possible that forces over which he has no control might intervene and prevent him from making the decision he really wants (indeed, longs) to make and, moreover, thinks it would be entirely sensible to make. And it is impossible to understand why the libertarian should want to insist on this possibility, for it is not freedom-enhancing. It is a mere obstacle to control and to the proper operation of agency.

6.3.2 The denial of libertarian freedom in the clear case

I have proceeded so far on the assumption that the libertarian will want to say of *clear* cases like Joe's, as well as of more finely balanced and difficult choices and dilemmas, that it will have to be possible, if an agent is to be free, for him to make an alternative decision from the one he actually does make, at the very time *t* at which he makes his actual decision. But a second sort of libertarian response seeks to make progress by insisting that a distinction must be drawn between cases where one's reasons make it clear what to do and cases where they do not. This second sort of libertarian *concedes* to the compatibilist that in cases such as that imagined above, where one's reasons for a certain course of action are overwhelmingly strong and it is obvious what to do, no alternative possibilities of a libertarian variety are available and so one does not act freely. On this view, it is accepted that Joe could *not* have decided not to move in with his girlfriend, his beliefs and desires being what they were, and that he was therefore *not* free (except in a sense perfectly available also to the compatibilist) to make the alternative decision. Nevertheless, it is insisted, there are many cases that are not at all like this, for example where the reasons for and against the relevant alternative courses of action do not clearly favour one course of action over another, or where a certain kind of incommensurability exists in the nature of one's reasons. In these cases at least, the libertarian alleges, it is true that the agent could have done otherwise. Van Inwagen, for example, makes a case of this sort when he argues that we have 'precious little free will' on the grounds that free will is exercised only in a sharply delimited class of cases in which moral duty or prudential considerations conflict with desire or in which our preferences for two or more competing courses of action are fairly evenly balanced.[17] However, where there is simply no need to fight temptation or to settle the outcome of a 'Buridan's Ass' type case, he suggests, there is no need to postulate the exercise of free will. Ekstrom appears to endorse a somewhat similar position, when she suggests that

Perhaps the *most* free acts derive from preferences whose probability of occurring was raised by the occurrence of previous considerations to values within a range of, say, 0.2–0.8, whereas the act would be less free when resulting from a preference at either end of the spectrum, that is, in cases where the considerations made the probability of the preference's occurrence near 0.9 or 0.1.[18]

It seems to me, however, that positions such as these are bizarre in the extreme. In some ways, indeed, they may be regarded as a kind of *reductio* of the sort of libertarianism that insists that the experience of being unsure about what to do is somehow at the heart of the free will problem. They immediately invite powerful objections of the sort raised by Wolf to what she calls 'the Autonomy View',[19] and by Dennett to the view that the ability to do otherwise is necessary for moral responsibility.[20] Surely no freedom or responsibility of any type worth wanting could be lacking to me just in virtue of the fact that I can instantly see clearly what is to be done and do not have to agonize about whether or not I should do it! Some libertarians have denied this and have toyed with the idea that although it may not be *better* not to be able to see clearly what ought to be done and to do it, one might nevertheless be *freer* under such circumstances. Ekstrom, for example, argues that 'Being pushed into deciding in a certain way by anything—whether one's grandmother, one's genetic blueprint, or overwhelmingly powerful considerations—is antithetical to free agency.'[21] But my sympathies here all lie with Wolf and Dennett. 'Powerful considerations' are just not the sorts of things that can 'push' me into deciding in a way that is antithetical to freedom because they can do nothing independently of my appreciation of them and

---

[17] Van Inwagen (1989: 405).   [18] Ekstrom (2000: 125).

[19] 'Two persons, of equal swimming ability, stand on equally uncrowded beaches. Each sees an unknown child struggling in the water in the distance. Each thinks "The child needs my help" and directly swims out to save him...We further assume that in one of these cases, the agent has the ability to do otherwise, and in the other case not. According to the Autonomy View, only the first of these agents is then responsible. But it may be that the second agent lacks the ability to do otherwise simply because her understanding of the situation is so good and her moral commitment so strong. And...this hardly seems grounds for withholding praise from the second agent while giving it to the first' (Wolf 1990: 1–2).

[20] '"Here I stand", Luther said. "I can do no other". Luther claimed that he could do no other, that his conscience made it *impossible* for him to recant...his declaration is testimony to the fact that we simply do not exempt someone from blame or praise for an act because we think he could do no other.' (Dennett, 1984: 133).

[21] Ekstrom (2000: 129).

my acceptance of them as reasons for me to act in a certain way. Reasons are just not the sorts of thing that (under normal circumstances) ought to be thought of as pushing me about, for my doing things intentionally is frequently just constituted by my acting upon them. It just seems terribly confused to suppose that just because it is highly likely that I shall φ, that this *in and of itself* reduces my freedom. Everything surely depends on *why* it is highly likely that I shall φ. And if the reason is just that, having reflected, I can see utterly clearly that φ-ing is the best thing for me to do in the circumstances, that surely has not the least tendency to suggest that I am unfree when I φ or that I could not have done otherwise in any sense that undermines any sort of freedom I should care about.

The sorts of claims I have just made are typically thought of as compatibilist property. It must be a *good* thing, the thought goes, for my best reasons to determine what I do. How could any freedom worth wanting reside in the capacity simply inexplicably to ignore what I can see to be overwhelmingly good reasons to do some particular thing? It is a powerful point, and it is one that I should hereby like to concede. There is, I agree, no value in a capacity to act utterly independently of *any* reasons, motivations, or pro-attitudes one might have, so even if we are inclined to suppose that there is perhaps *some* possibility that Joe might have made the inexplicable 'decision' at *t* not to move in with his girlfriend (because, perhaps, there is some chance that a rationally inexplicable event of this sort might have occurred at *t*), that cannot be the sort of alternative possibility on which the libertarian should insist. Moreover, if we are inclined to think it remains correct to say that Joe could at *t* have decided not to move in with his girlfriend in a sense that *does* bear on Joe's responsibility for this decision, I suggest, the right account of what it means to say so must be of the sort that is generally offered by the compatibilist. We must mean that Joe could have decided not to move in with his girlfriend *if he'd wanted to*, for instance, or that he had both the ability and the opportunity to decide not to do so, or that nothing peculiar was constraining him or compelling him to decide to do so, or perhaps we mean some quite complicated combination of all these things.[22] The compatibilist has always been quite correct in her insistence that there is no intelligible value in the possibility of making lunatic choices that bear no relation whatever to ones reasons and desires and that such a possibility cannot be the basis of any freedom we might conceivably care about.

What I next want to argue, though, is that compatibilists are apt to confuse this correct point with a different and much less plausible claim. Moreover, once the correct point is disentangled from the implausible impostor it will be seen that the traditionally 'compatibilist' point that I have conceded by no means entails compatibilism,

---

[22] Once again, I do not here attempt to make progress with the development of precisely what the right compatibilist account here should be. I merely wish to concede for the sake of argument that it seems very likely that some acceptable compatibilist account can be given.

and this will point the way to what I regard as the correct libertarian response to the Challenge from Chance.

6.4 Reasons, determination, and the 'gap'

I have conceded that, generally speaking, it is a good thing for my freedom if my best reasons determine what I do. But it is easy to slide without noticing from this entirely correct point to another claim that is by no means so uncontentious, namely that it is a good thing for my freedom if my reasons are the deterministic causes of my actions. To suppose that the first of these claims entails the second, though, is to make a number of controversial identifications: (i) of reasons with causes, (ii) of determination (in the sense used when it is said that my reasons should 'determine' what I do) with deterministic causation, and (iii) of 'what I do' with my actions. I shall now take a look at each of these identifications in turn. In a sense, the mistaken identifications are not properly separable one from another since they rely on one another for support, so there is a certain amount of artificiality involved in distinguishing them from one another in this way. However, I hope it will prove easier to explain why the slide is illegitimate by considering them one by one.

6.4.1 Reasons and causes

There is now a huge and daunting literature on the nature of reasons, the rational explanation of action, and the question whether reason-giving explanations of action may be or must be causal explanations. There is not space here to do justice to the enormous intricacy of that literature, important though it is for the free will debate,[23] and I shall not attempt here to offer a comprehensive account of reasons and the explanations in which they figure. But it is important for my purposes to distinguish between two rather different things that might be meant by the often-made claim that reasons are causes, one of which I regard as highly plausible, the other as seriously mistaken.

One thing that might be meant by the slogan that 'reasons are causes' is this: that when one explains why someone did something by giving a reason, or reasons, that motivated the relevant agent, one gives one particular sort of *causal* explanation of what they did. For example, if I explain why I took a paracetamol tablet by saying that I took it because I have a headache, I presuppose that you understand (i) that I want to get rid of my headache and (ii) that I believe that the tablet will help me get rid of it. This background being in place, you arguably now have one kind of causal story that explains why I took the tablet. Of course, whether or not one accepts the claim that the explanation is causal will depend in part on one's account of what it is to give a causal explanation. But it seems to me quite plausible that the best account we may be able to

---

[23] See my (1997) for an attempt to do it rather more justice.

give of the difficult and ubiquitous notion of causality will find that it is a concept that is sufficiently broad and unspecific to be able to accommodate the phenomenon of rational motivation quite comfortably. One might, for example, embrace Anscombe's view that the concept of cause is so utterly basic that it completely resists analysis and that in the end we are able to say little more about causality than that it 'consists in the derivativeness of an effect from its causes'.[24] Since it seems right to say that what we do often derives from our conception of what we have reason to do, one might then feel inclined to accept without further ado that reason-giving explanations are broadly causal in nature. I have no objection, therefore, to the claim that reasons are causes, if all that is meant by that claim is that explanations that work by adverting to an agent's reasons represent one important and distinctive type of causal explanation. But often, it seems to me, much more is implied by those who defend the view that reasons are causes than this relatively innocuous thesis.

What more is implied? One very commonly held view is that reasons, in so far as they are genuinely explanatory of behaviour, ought to be regarded as concrete 'states' of belief and desire, which perhaps exist somehow in the brain, and which cause (perhaps by way of intervening states of intention or events of decision-making, or both) the bodily movements that are alleged to be wholly or partly constitutive of our bodily actions.[25] However, this is a much stronger view than the mere idea that rational explanation is a form of causal explanation. For one thing, it instantly imposes a particular and controversial view of the nature of reasons, a view according to which at least some reasons ('motivating reasons') cannot be identified—as might at first have been thought natural—with the things one generally offers in answer to questions of the form 'What was your reason?'. These answers tend to be *contents* expressive of the thing believed or the end aimed at—'that I have a headache', for example, or 'so that my headache will go away'. However, such contents are abstract, whereas the view in question insists that reasons must be thought of as *concrete* entities, since only thus, it is argued, can a reason intelligibly be supposed to be a 'cause' of behaviour. There is a large literature on this question whether the reasons that motivate may be *facts* or whether they must instead be psychological states, such as so-called 'token' beliefs or desires. I cannot attempt to do justice to it all here.[26] I only note that it is not obvious that those who believe that reasons are generally such things as facts and ends rather than beliefs and desires must thereby be accounted opponents of the view that rational explanation is a form of causal explanation, and therefore that the 'reasons are mental

---

[24] Anscombe (1971: 136).

[25] Many who make this claim distinguish 'normative' from 'motivating' reasons, insisting that motivating reasons, at any rate, must be concrete psychological entities with causal power (see e.g. Smith 1994). From my point of view, though, as will shortly become clear, this distinction is otiose. It is normative reasons that motivate. I take it to be an advantage of the position argued for here that it will allow for a unified account of reasons.

[26] See e.g. Smith (1994), Dancy (1993, 1995), Stout (2004).

states' view is not forced upon us by the very idea that rational explanation is, or can be, a form of causal explanation.

A second reason why this view that beliefs and desires are concrete states of some sort must be accounted stronger than the general idea that rational explanation is causal is that it is clearly a statement of one version of the causal theory of action already considered and rejected in Chapter 3. The *agent*, note, has entirely disappeared from the picture of action we are offered, which now contains only 'states', 'events', and ensuing bodily movements. The reasons that get the agent into motion, therefore, cannot be represented on this picture as for example *considerations* to which she responded and on which she acted by taking them into account. Instead they have to figure as states with their own independent efficacy, existing inside her, and precipitating her movements without so much as a by your leave. Their efficacy, on this model, *replaces* hers rather than adding a particular sort of understanding to a causal picture that already presupposes that *she* is the basic source of those movements. Actions are present in the picture, if at all, only as things somehow constituted by the totality of what occurs in an impersonally described chain of events. They are not present as essential components connecting the agent's intentions, plans, decisions, etc., to the bodily movements₁ by means of which the agent brings about effects in the world. But this, as I have already stressed in earlier chapters, is a deeply revisionary conception of the relation between such antecedent phenomena as reasons, intentions, and decisions, on the one hand, and bodily movements on the other. For it is a crucial part of folk psychology that all the intending and deciding in the world is simply not enough to get us launched; we also have to *act*. When I wake up in the morning, for example, I sometimes decide at a particular moment to get up *right now*, and I fully intend to get up at that very moment. But sadly, I find myself still lying in bed ten seconds—and sometimes, I confess, even ten minutes—later. That this sort of weakness of will is possible shows that actually getting up requires something more than the formation of an intention. If my body is to get into voluntarily produced motion, I have to *move* it; I cannot just rely on my antecedently existing psychological states to bring about the requisite bodily motions for me. And this demands, as I argued in Chapter 3, that actions themselves have to figure in any chains that purport to connect such things as intentions to bodily movements.

It might be said at this point, though, that I have simply mischaracterized my opponent's view. The idea we are supposed to be considering, it might be said, is that reasons are causes of *actions*, not merely of bodily movements₁. The view, therefore, need not be that reasons take one to intentions and that intentions then take one straight to bodily movements₁ without any connecting action; it may rather be that intentions (perhaps in combination with other psychological states) take one to *actions*, and only to bodily movements by way of such actions. But the trouble with this view, while it successfully accommodates the crucial thought that actions are required if intentions are ever to have any effect on the world, is that it ends up misrepresenting both the nature of reasons and the nature of actions. If it is to be at all plausible that reasons are centrally involved in the *deterministic production* of actions—as is supposed to happen in the compatibilist's best-case scenario—it is not going to be sufficient to identify them with such things as states of belief and desire (though that will, no doubt, seem to be an attractive first step).[27] They are, in addition, now going to have to be thought of as things that have rather precise *strengths* and *weights*, strengths and weights that can be sensibly allocated (in principle) in advance of decision and action. For it is an incontrovertible fact that I may currently have perfectly good reasons to φ, and yet not φ or even try to φ. This being the case, what is the explanation to be of the reason's failure to precipitate an action, given the picture of reasons as deterministic causes of actions, if not that I had a *stronger* reason for doing whatever it was I did instead, including possibly doing nothing? No doubt folk psychology has a place for the rough and ready idea that some reasons are more powerful than others. But I think it must be seriously doubted whether anything still recognizable as folk psychology can tolerate the very different idea that *all* reasons may be quantitatively weighed against one another in such a way that a determinate outcome is necessitated by these in-principle antecedently attributable relative weightings.[28]

Moreover, and more crucially from the point of view of the argument being advanced in this book, if the overall constellation of one's reasons is supposed to take one *deterministically* through to the performance of a particular action or the making of a decision, it would appear that an action could not then be a settling at the time of its occurrence of any matter by an agent. This is because it would have to be already settled antecedently by the presence and relative strengths and weightings of the states in the agent's 'motivational set' (together, perhaps, with some additional non-psychological facts) that she would φ at t. We would appear to have no easy way, given this view, to respect the commonsense precept that it is frequently open to an agent *not* to act (or decide to act) in a given way, even though her most powerful reasons suggest she should do so. According to folk psychology, weakness of will is, sadly, an all-too-common phenomenon; my best reasons do not simply set my body into inexorable motion. If they did it would simply not be *possible* for me to stay in bed, even though my strongest reasons dictated that I get up; no further action on my part would be required. But we all know that this is not how things are. It is not how things are experientially speaking and it is not how things are according to the conceptual scheme in which the concepts of intention and action are essentially embedded, for as I have already stressed in Chapters 3 and 4, the *agent* herself is at the heart of that scheme and that scheme dictates that her exertions are required if anything is ever to be done on the basis of her intentions. And if these are genuinely to be actions of hers, I claim, as

---

[27] Of course, it will have to be conceded, even by those inclined towards the relevant form of psychological determinism, that reasons *by themselves* cannot deterministically produce actions. The idea, presumably, will have to be that certain reasons occurring in propitious environmental circumstances might, together with those circumstances, come to constitute a causally sufficient condition for the occurrence of an action.

[28] See Nozick (1981: 294–306) for a defence of the idea that our decisions *bestow* weightings on our various reasons, rather than being made in accordance with antecedently given weightings.

opposed merely to events occurring in and around her body, they need to be settlings of matters by her, at the time of action. That implies, I suggest, that at the time of action, the agent needs the power to refrain from the exertion in question, for that is what puts her in control of whether or not the exertion occurs and gives her true ownership of the relevant action.

Recent discussion of the free will problem has resulted in a distinction between two quite different sorts of reason for supposing that free will is incompatible with determinism. One is the traditional claim that free will requires alternate possibilities and that these are inconsistent with determinism. The other (which has perhaps become more prominent in the wake of Frankfurt's argument that alternate possibilities are not necessary for moral responsibility) stems rather from the idea that we must be the true *authors*, the real *sources* of those actions for which we are truly responsible.[29] But in my view, these two kinds of requirement are very tightly connected with one another. Indeed, I do not believe there is any alternative-possibilities requirement on free will that is independent of the sourcehood requirement. The sourcehood requirement is just what generates the alternative-possibilities requirement (or at least, the only legitimate alternative-possibilities requirement there is). Alternative possibilities are required for free action only because they are required for action;[30] and they are required for action because an action must be a *settling* of some matter or matters by an agent: this is what it is for the agent to be the *source* of the event that *is* her action. An agent cannot be a true source unless she has the power to settle what will happen.

It might be helpful here, in order to clarify the conception of action I would like to defend, to draw on some terminology that has been introduced into the literature by John Searle.[31] Searle argues that there are three 'gaps' of which any reasonable philosophy of action must take account. First, there is a gap between one's beliefs and desires and any actual decision that one makes, since one's reasons do not constitute causally sufficient conditions for one's decisions. Second, there is a gap between the decision and the action; this is what makes the space for the sort of weakness of will I described in the example above, where one decides that one will do something at a certain point in time and yet nevertheless fails to do it. Third, for actions and activities that are extended in time, there is also a gap between the initiation of the action and its continuation to completion. That is to say, having started such an activity one cannot simply sit back and allow a series of deterministic causes to unfold; one needs to continue to make a constant voluntary effort to keep going with the activity until it has been completed. I agree with Searle that these 'gaps' are a crucial part of our

---

[29] For example, Kane (1996: Chapter 3) distinguishes between the AP ('alternate possibilities') condition on free action and the UR ('ultimate responsibility') condition, which requires that, in some sense or other, the agent be an 'arché', or source, of those actions for which she is responsible; Pereboom (2001) likewise distinguishes between 'leeway incompatibilism' and 'causal history incompatibilism'.

[30] See Steward (2009a) for a detailed argument for the claim that it is the demands of *agency* and not the demands of *fairness* that generate the only legitimate alternate possibilities requirement.

[31] Searle (2001).

folk-psychological conceptual scheme and a crucial part of our ordinary way of conceptualizing actions. Without acknowledging these gaps, actions simply cannot be properly represented as the utterly distinctive phenomena they are. The deep link between action and agent is severed if one thinks of actions either as constituted merely by bodily movements caused by the right sorts of psychological states or as events intervening between psychological states and bodily movements. An agent, in this picture, becomes a mere place for the machinations of those states, and her role as a settler of matters *at the time of her action* becomes impossible to accept.

It might be said, of course, that this is all to the good. The concept of an agent, it will be said, is metaphysically problematic, and so is the concept of an action unless we can reduce it, as the causal theory attempts to do, to a series of events and states from which all reference to the agent herself has been expunged. I do not deny that the concept of action and the concept of an agent need metaphysical clarification and I will address the matter further in Chapter 8. But as I have already argued in Chapter 3, we cannot hope to get things right simply by *deleting* agents and actions from a folk-psychological explanatory framework that *presupposes* them. Reasons, for example, are used to explain, not the occurrence of certain impersonally described events, but rather why we (agents) do things; indeed, they are not even used to explain the occurrence of the events that are *actions* since they are not designed to explain *particular* occurrences at all (see Section 6.4.3 below). The result is that we cannot simply turn them into the alleged deterministic causes of particular events without travesty.

It might be thought that my continued insistence on the idea that agents have to settle matters at the time of their action simply contradicts what I have already conceded to the compatibilist. Surely, it might be said, I have already allowed that in the case of someone like Joe who can see no reason to decide not to move in with his girlfriend, it *is* already settled by his reasons (by his 'overall motivational set') that he will decide at *t* to move in with her. But it is important to realize that this is not what I have said. Even if we were to grant that it is settled at a moment immediately preceding *t* that Joe would not decide at *t* not to move in with his girlfriend (it being utterly incomprehensible why he would make such a decision, given the reasons he then has), it would not follow that it was settled at that prior moment that Joe *would* decide at *t* (as he in fact did, recall) to move in with his girlfriend. That various possibilities are utterly ruled out because of their lack of relation to any reasons or desires the agent has at the time of action does not imply that only one possibility as regards what will happen at *t* remains. On the contrary, on the view I want to espouse, any genuine agent constantly confronts a world of possibilities from which, by means of her agency, she moves ahead to forge the single path that constitutes actuality. The idea of multiple possibilities therefore remains at the heart of my position. I return in due course to explain how this point is to be defended, for it is crucial for my response to the Challenge from Chance. I turn next, though, to the next step in my critique of the compatibilist's inference from what I regard as her defensible claims to indefensible ones: the concept of 'determination'.

6.4.2 Determination

'Determine' is a relational verb that will tolerate a variety of subject-terms. A person (or other animal) can determine that something will happen. But we also often speak, especially in philosophy, of an *event* or a *state* or a *fact* determining something (usually, the occurrence of an event), or perhaps more realistically and when we are being careful, of a *collection* of such events, states, or facts doing so (in which case they might be thought, together, to constitute a 'causally sufficient condition' for the occurrence of that event). When we are thinking in this second way of the contribution made by a complex antecedent set of circumstances to the occurrence of some subsequent event, 'determine' generally means something like 'necessitate'. The idea is that a determined event *had* to happen, given its complex, causally sufficient antecedents.

It does not seem, though, as if the word 'determine' can have quite this same meaning when its subject is a person (or other animal). What could it mean to speak of a person's *necessitating* that something will happen? To say that I can necessitate something—that my arm will rise, for instance—would seem to be to suggest that I can render it *inevitable* that it will. But it does not seem to be true that I can render it inevitable that my arm will go up, even if I can raise it. I cannot ensure by the power of my will alone, as it were, that no interference will occur in the physical processes by means of which my arm is caused to rise. The power to act is not the power to render something inevitable, not even the action itself. Acting requires, for a start, the continuation in existence of the agent, and no one can render inevitable their own existence from one moment to the next, however unlikely their imminent expiration may be. And specifically bodily action, as stressed in Chapter 3, requires also the cooperation of bodily systems of motor control whose proper functioning is essential if I am to do what I am trying to do.

It might be objected that persons and other agents are, of course, in this respect no different from any other cause we are likely ever to be able to mention or label. No intuitively single cause (e.g. a given particular event) is ever, strictly speaking, a necessitator of anything, being inevitably dependent for its efficacy on the giant web of surrounding circumstances in which it is embedded. But we nevertheless speak of individual events and conditions 'determining' certain outcomes, meaning perhaps simply that the event or condition in question (whether itself determined or not by prior events and circumstances) is some crucial component of the overall necessitating mix, so that 'in the circumstances' it may be said to have necessitated the outcome. The compatibilist may suppose that in suggesting that a person might 'determine' an outcome, we are speaking loosely and mean merely to indicate that an *action* of that person is, in the same way, a crucial component of the necessitating mix, perhaps being itself necessitated by prior mental events and states (so that the agent, once again, drops out of the picture strictly speaking, her causal role being played entirely by the familiar cast of mental states and events). But this is not the only possible way of understanding what is meant by the determination of an outcome by an agent. Another possibility takes much more literally than the compatibilist suggestion just canvassed the idea that determination may be a relation between an *agent* and a state of affairs, and this suggestion is much friendlier to the libertarian. On this view, when we speak of a person's determining what will happen, the word 'determine' means something rather like what I have so far used the word 'settle' to imply. When I determine that something will happen, that is, I do not necessarily render it inevitable that it will; I do not necessarily necessitate anything (though it is true that it is good for me if my action is merely the last remaining part of a sufficient condition for the *result* at which I am aiming). But as I act, I bring a state of affairs into being that need not have been brought into being, for my action itself is something that need not have happened: it is not itself necessitated by any prior conditions. And that is what enables me to *settle* or *determine* what will occur, since in order for me to settle or determine what will occur, it is essential that the matter not be *already* settled.

It is possible, then, to distinguish two different senses of the word 'determine': to determine something can be to necessitate it (when such things as collections of events and states—or perhaps facts—are doing the determining), or, where a person or other animal is the subject, to determine something can be to settle whether and how something occurs or comes to obtain. Let us now ask what it might mean for my *reasons* to determine what I do. If one is already predisposed to think of reasons as *states* of belief and desire, one will no doubt be inclined to suppose that for my reasons to determine what I do is for those states of belief and desire to combine together (perhaps with some other states and events) to necessitate the event that is my action (perhaps by way of some intervening deciding event and/or a state of intention). The 'determination' of things by reasons would then be determination of the first sort mentioned above. But suppose one was not inclined, for the sorts of reasons mooted above in Section 6.4.1, to suppose that reasons could be readily identified with states bearing this deterministic relationship to ensuing actions. In that case, one would need a different understanding of the idea of determination by reasons. Reasons not being states of me (or my brain) in the first place, but rather essentially abstract entities— *considerations* speaking in favour of (or against) various courses of action—it would be natural to think that they could only have their influence by way of their effect on a person (or other animal) equipped with the capacity to appreciate and respond to them. *Their* determining that I will act in a certain way would then be a matter of *my* determining that I will do so, by reference only to those reasons. For my reasons to determine what I do is for me to be influenced only by those reasons in coming to a decision about what to do; it is to rule out competing explanations that advert to, for example, irrational emotional responses, reflexes, addictive or compulsive tendencies, or mad, inexplicable impulses. Their determining what I do is a matter of how it is that *I* determine (settle) what I shall do. It is *not* a matter of their constituting deterministic stative causes of the particular event that is my action. To speak of matters being determined by reasons, on this view, would be to speak of determination of the second sort mentioned above: it is to speak of how it is settled by the agent that she will do a certain sort of thing, not of the necessitation of the event of her doing that thing by antecedently existing causes.

What I am suggesting, then, is that the word 'determine' is subtly and confusingly ambiguous in a way that has caused enormous confusion in the free will literature. It may sometimes be a synonym for 'necessitate', and it is this sense of the word 'determine', of course, that is associated with the doctrine of determin*ism*. But when the term is used to relate an *agent* to an outcome it ought not to be supposed to have this same meaning. When it relates an agent to an outcome it means, in fact, something more or less synonymous with what I have previously used the word 'settle' to mean. The determination of things by agents, therefore, far from presupposing that their reasons must be deterministic, stative causes of actions, rather presupposes that they are *not*, for only thus could *the agent* be in a position to determine whether or not she will φ at *t*, by φ-ing then or not φ-ing then, as the case may be.

The confusion is easiest to see in those arguments that are sometimes found in the free will literature for the view that freedom *requires* determinism.[32] Roughly speaking, the argument is this: my freedom is at its strongest and best when what I do is determined by my reasons; so my freedom is at its strongest and best when my action is deterministically caused by my reasons. But the inference is faulty, because 'determined by' need not mean 'deterministically caused by' and in fact it does not generally mean this when its subject is an agent or an agent's reason. Moreover, 'what I do' is not an expression for which a singular term for an action may be substituted, as I shall next attempt to show.

6.4.3 'What I do' and actions

Thus far, I have suggested that the determination of 'what I do' by my reasons is not the same thing as the deterministic causation of the event that is my action by 'states' that are my reasons. If it is not to lead to confusion, this point needs to be supplemented with the recognition that 'what I do'—the thing that is explained by my reasons for doing it—is not the same thing as my action. 'What I do' is, indeed, not a phrase that refers to a *particular* event at all. The things done by us, as Hornsby has stressed, are *types* of thing: 'make my bed', 'drink a cup of tea', and 'clean my teeth', for example, are three of the things I have done this morning.[33] But none of these is an expression of the sort one might use to refer to a *particular* action. The particular actions that occurred were my making of my bed, my drinking of a cup of tea, and my cleaning of my

---

[32] See, for example, Hobart (1934).

[33] 'The phrase "do something" can mislead, because it can sound as if it reported both an event that is a *doing* and a separate event that is a *something* done. But that cannot be how it behaves. If I raise my arm at some time, raise my arm is something I do then, and my doing something then is my raising my arm then. But *what I do*—raise my arm—is not a particular event that happens at a time: the only event mentioned here is my raising of my arm.' (Hornsby, 1980: 3).

teeth.[34] But my making of my bed is not a thing I have done; one could not answer the question 'What have you done this morning?' by replying 'My making of my bed!' My making of my bed is an action of mine: not a thing I have done but rather my *doing* of a thing I have done.

To speak of the determination of *what I do* by my reasons, then, is not to speak of the determination (that is to say, the necessitation) of the particular events that are my *actions* by my reasons. What has the potential to be determined by a reason, or reasons, is rather *that the agent has φ-ed* (or is φ-ing or will φ), and these things are facts not particular events. Indeed, it is not terribly clear, I would maintain, even *what it would be* to explain a *particular action* by reference to a reason. Particular things tend in general not to be very good candidates to be the targets of explanation. It would be odd to undertake, for example, to explain a particular chair or a particular table. One could announce, of course, that one was going to explain this Queen Anne chair to one's audience, but one would have to mean that one was intending to explain, say, some particular aspects of its design or history, and of course in explaining such things one is really explaining *facts* about the chair: why it is the shape it is, for instance, or why it has scorch marks on the back. Events, granted, are very different from continuants: they occur, and so the question asked of a particular event why it occurred, can be raised. But normally, even in this case, the question in which we are usually interested is why an event of a certain *kind* occurred or why an event of that kind occurred at a given time. We are not asking for the explanation of a particular event (whatever that would mean). 'Why did that explosion happen?' I might ask, and you might tell me that it was because of a build up of methane in the room. But what I am likely really to be asking was why there was *an explosion* (in that place, at that time). I am really asking for the explanation of a general existential fact and not the explanation of a particular. Qua particular, the explosion may have many properties quite apart from the property of being an explosion. It may, for instance, have registered a certain number of decibels or it might have released a certain determinate quantity of energy. But I do not seek to explain the instantiation of all these equally. I am only interested in explaining the instantiation of the property under which I bring it in asking my question—that of *being an explosion*. This shows that it is not really the particular I seek to explain, but rather the general *fact* that an explosion occurred (in a particular place at a particular time).

There is such a thing, of course, as attributing a particular effect to a particular cause. The explosion in my kitchen yesterday (a particular event) may have been caused, for instance, by Peter's striking of the match, itself a particular event. If it was, then I can truly say that Peter's striking of the match caused the explosion in my kitchen yesterday. In saying this, I would seem to have offered a certain sort of explanation of that *particular* event. However, it is not in the least plausible that the explanations in which reasons figure are at all like this: it is not plausible that reasons are particular

---

[34] Let us suppose that for the sake of argument, I have done each of these things only once, so as to avoid complications to do with failure of unique reference.

causes. Talking of 'beliefs' and 'desires' can obscure this rather unhelpfully, as can talk of 'token states' of belief and desire. These words make it sound as though we might be dealing with particulars, but we are not. When I cite a belief in explanation of something I have done, I am citing a *fact* about what I believe that is relevant to understanding why I have done what I have done. 'Because of my belief that p' really means '…because I believed that p'. I am not mentioning a particular cause.[35]

I have argued, then, that the idea that it is a good thing if my reasons determine what I do does not imply that it is a good thing if my reasons causally necessitate my actions, for determination is not (in this case) causal necessitation and 'what I do' is not a phrase that refers to my actions. My concession to compatibilism does not, therefore, imply that it is best for freedom if my reasons causally necessitate my actions. Indeed, I have argued that if my reasons *are* to determine what I do they must *not* be states deterministically connected to the particular events that are my actions, for that would prevent me from being able to *settle* (that is to say, determine) various important matters at the time of action. Of course, I have not said yet what it could be for *me* to determine these things nor offered an explanation of the self-based metaphysics that appears to be presupposed by the very idea of an agent who is a settler. These explanations remain to be given. My aim at the present time is merely to deal with what I regard as one very powerful source of confusion that can make it seem as though determinism of a certain sort is positively required if my actions are to be properly governed by my reasons. Having explained why the requisite inference does not go through, I want next to go on to explain how the points I have thus far made enable me to meet the Challenge from Chance.

6.5 Meeting the Challenge from Chance

Recall the position of Mele's libertarian. In the actual world, we are told, an agent, Joe, decides at *t* to A. But in another world with the very same laws of nature and the very same past, Joe decides at *t* not to A. Perhaps there are a few Buridan's Ass type cases that really are like this: where Joe's decision just represents a random, last-minute plumping for one course of action or another, which simply has no antecedents of a sort that might not equally have preceded the other decision. Perhaps, for instance, after a period of uncertain dithering, Joe might choose to have chocolate rather than vanilla ice cream, simply because the shop assistant is waiting and he needs to make a choice, though he has no real preference for one flavour over the other. In such circumstances as this, perhaps it is indeed conceivable that the very same past really can give rise to either of two conflicting choices, though even here, it is hard to imagine that just prior to the moment of decision there was not some crucial event that made the decision go the way it did—the flashing into Joe's mind of an image of a bowl of chocolate ice cream, for instance, or the occurrence of the idea of some arbitrary principle according

---

[35] For extensive arguments to this effect see my (1997).

to which to make the choice, for example to use alphabetical ordering. But even if we decide that in a case such as this the libertarian would be right to maintain that Joe could, at *t*, have chosen to have vanilla, even given a past presumed to be utterly unaltered in every particular, it seems to me that the best hope for the libertarian lies in firmly denying that she believes *in general* that when an agent makes a decision at a given time *t* to A, that that agent could have decided at that very same time *t* not to A. It cannot be a general condition on free agency that a future in which an agent decides at *t* not to A could always have evolved out of a past exactly identical to the one that *in fact* evolved into the opposite decision. The compatibilist, it seems to me, is simply right to remark that this amounts, in many types of case, merely to the freedom to go mad, and that no such alternative possibility as this could possibly be the basis of a sensible libertarianism. What is essential to her view, she should insist instead, is rather this: that when an agent makes a decision at *t* to A—or indeed, whenever she acts in any way at all, for we must remember that our current focus specifically on *decisions* is one that was supplied by Mele's formulation of the Challenge from Chance and is not a focus that we need continue to insist upon, as I shall shortly explain—it is never the case that that decision-making episode or action was necessitated by prior conditions. It is (Frankfurt-examples and certain special cases aside—see below) always open to her *not* to produce that decision at *t* to A, even if it is not conceivable that a future containing the decision *not to A* will evolve immediately from a point immediately preceding *t*. Mele's negation, in other words, is in the wrong place. We do not need and should not want to have an openness in the flow of reality that consists in the possibility of our making decisions for which we can imagine no conceivable rationale. We do not therefore need the (incompatibilistically construed) power, in respect of each decision made, to have made the *opposite* decision. But we do need, if there is to be such a thing as agency at all, the general capacity to organize, order, and direct our lives in such a way that we thereby settle the particular details of what happens in those lives at the time at which we act (or decide to do something—for I take it that deciding is a *species* of acting). Moreover, I maintain, we cannot have this capacity if an action is merely the inevitable event-consequence of some set of antecedent events and states. In that case, there would then be nothing left for anyone to *do*, for there would be nothing left for anyone to settle at the time of action. Doings would become a mere part of the maelstrom of mere happenings, and agents would disappear from the world, their efficacy ceded to deterministically evolving series of events and states. Actions (including decisions) must be things, therefore, whose occurrence is always non-necessary relative to the totality of their antecedents. What this implies is that they must be exercises of a power that *need not* have been exercised at the moment or in the precise way that it was in fact exercised. The power to act, as many philosophers have remarked, is a *two-way* power: to act or to refrain from acting. That is what makes it special.[36] All sorts of objects have

---

[36] Amongst others who have embraced the idea that the power of (human) action is a two-way power, see Aristotle (1984a: 1223a 4–7), 'it is clear that all the acts of which man is the principle and controller *may either*

powers, e.g. magnesium has the power to dissolve in acid, my printer has the power to print pages of text, my heart has the power to pump blood around my body. But none of these things—magnesium, printer, heart—has, at the same time, the power *not* to exercise these other powers, once conditions for their realization are present (for this reason, indeed, it is much more natural to speak of these one-way powers being *realized* than it is to speak of them being *exercised*). Magnesium in a bowl of acid does not have the power to remain unchanged, my printer cannot avoid printing out the text it prints once I have pressed the button, my heart cannot help pumping my blood around my body provided it is working properly. In contrast, the power to act that animals possess is associated essentially and constantly, so I would insist, with a simultaneously-possessed power of *refrainment*. More will need to be said about this power of refrainment, for its precise characterization is not an easy matter.[37] In particular, it will be essential to avoid any characterization of refrainment according to which it has itself to be a deliberate act; what I shall mean by the power to refrain is something much weaker than this. And something will also need to be said to rebut the objection that the position outlined is one against which a new version of Mele's original challenge can be raised again. These questions will all be considered in Chapter 7. Now, though, having presented the bare bones of my response to the Challenge from Chance, it is time to explain why we need to break free of another of the features of the example we have so far been considering. Showing why we should break free of this second commitment will help, I believe, to explain the picture of agency that lies behind my version of incompatibilism and to increase its plausibility, for it is only when combined with the ontological modifications to the theory of agency that I shall be recommending here that the attractions of the sort of incompatibilism I wish to advocate can be properly appreciated.

6.6 Decisions, actions, and activity

Like many philosophers considering how best to formulate libertarianism (including many with more emphatically libertarian leanings than Mele himself), Mele sometimes

---

happen or not happen and that their happening or not happening...depends on him', (my italics); Reid (1858 [1788]: 523), 'Power to produce any effect implies power not to produce it'; Kant (1960 [1793]: 45) 'the act as well as its opposite must be within the power of the subject at the moment of its taking place'. It must be conceded, though, that all these philosophers have connected the two-way power of agency to the idea, specifically, of *rationality*; and though I think there *is* a connection here, in that it seems to me that the power of agency only exists at all because it may be harnessed for teleological endeavour, I believe the connection between agency and rationality to be a rather looser one than these philosophers have supposed. In particular, as argued in Chapter 2, there can, I believe, be exercises of the power of agency that are not undertaken for reasons. See Steward (2009c) for more detailed arguments.

[37] In particular, the idea that a power of refrainment is crucial to the power of action might be thought to be challenged by so-called 'Frankfurt-style' examples, which are supposed to show that there are exercises of agency in which it is nevertheless not the case that the agent could have done otherwise—and it is essential that the power of refrainment be very carefully specified if these are to be avoided. I consider Frankfurt-style examples in Section 7.2.

focuses on *decisions* as the things with respect to which, according to the libertarian, it has to be true that the agent could have done otherwise.[38] But why is this? Why is the focus in the libertarian literature not on *actions in general?* Decisions are one kind of action, no doubt—to decide to do something is to perform what may be regarded, perhaps, as a 'mental' action, and so for libertarians it certainly ought to be *true* of decisions that the agent exercises whatever freedom turns out to be characteristic of actions generally whenever she decides something. But why is libertarianism now so very often formulated as though the capacity to do otherwise that is important to freedom is one that pertains *only* to decisions and not to actions of other kinds also? The traditional form in which the Principle of Alternate Possibilities is stated speaks of agents needing to be able to *do otherwise* if their actions are to count as free. So why has the locus of alternative possibility shifted inward in so many recent formulations of what it is that the libertarian must believe? Why are libertarians now so often concerned rather with the idea that free agents might have *decided* otherwise?

The reason, I think, can be traced ultimately to the fact that many libertarians begin with the same basic ontological picture of action as their compatibilist opponents: the event-based causal chain picture that is at the heart of the causal theory of action, whereby beliefs and desires give rise to decisions, which in turn produce intentions, which subsequently generate actions. Beginning with this picture, they then conceive of it as being one of their most important tasks to uncover the particular *place* in these action-generating causal chains at which the supposition of an indeterministic nexus might help to secure some sort of freedom for the agent. And having set off from this inauspicious starting point they then quickly discover that it is rather difficult to see how the presence of indeterminacy in the nexus *between decision and action* (whether between decision and intention, or between intention and subsequent action) could possibly be helpful to a free agent. Mele makes the point by inventing a fable concerning a libertarian goddess, Diana, in an indeterministic universe, who wants to build rational, free human beings. Mele bestows upon Diana beliefs now typical of many modern libertarians, when he states that Diana 'believes that proximal decisions—typically, decisions to A straightaway—are causes of actions that execute them, and she sees no benefit in designing agents who have a chance of not even trying to A when they have decided to A straightaway, and the intention to A formed in that act of deciding persists in the absence of any biological damage'.[39] If I have decided to A straightaway, that is, and the intention I form on the basis of that decision persists (i.e. I do not change my mind), it is alleged that it can be of no conceivable help to me to build any indeterminism into the relation between decision and intention, on the

---

[38] See also Kane (1996), whose 'self-forming willings' are mostly types of choice or decision; Ekstrom (2000: 106), who believes that the alternative possibilities necessary for free agency are 'found between the agent's considerations about what to decide and her decisively formed preference for acting itself'; and Pink (2004: 92) who suggests that we allow for the possibility 'that actions can occur in uncaused form in the case of our own decisions'.

[39] Mele (2006: 7).

one hand, and action (or 'trying') on the other. For from the agent's point of view, to have chance events occurring at this point in the causal chain would only weaken her control over the course of events. It could not, it seems, conceivably contribute to her freedom of action.[40] As Ekstrom puts it, '…on the most plausible incompatibilist model of free action, it is not the presence of alternative possibilities after a decision has been made concerning what one prefers (or judges best) to do that are crucial for freedom. Rather, the crucial alternative possibilities are located further back in the causal history of the act'.[41] This is how the libertarian comes to the conclusion that it is in connection with *decisions* rather than *actions* that the agent must possess the capacity to do otherwise. Having decided what to do, the idea is, it is best for freedom if our bodies then just get on with executing the tasks we have chosen for them unless, of course, some subsequent contrary decision countermands the original order from mental HQ.

There are, however, some serious difficulties with this line of incompatibilist thinking. One problem, which is associated with a point about action already made in Chapter 3, is that it is very unclear that all or even most actions *have* the sort of causal history that Ekstrom and Mele's libertarian seem to take for granted. As Ryle noted, it will not do to suppose that all actions are preceded by decisions, since 'most ordinary actions do not issue out of conditions of indecision and are not therefore results of settlements of indecision'.[42] I have, for example, just taken a bite from a piece of toast. But as I did so my mind was firmly on other things: specifically, I was thinking about the question of what I ought to say in this paragraph. I gave no thought to the toast at all. I certainly was not conscious of a decision to take a bite before I actually did so, and the question arises what reason there could be, in the absence of any such consciousness, for supposing that some such decision must nevertheless have occurred. If it is true, as it seems to me, that there are actions like this that arise spontaneously, as it were, rather than out of prior decision-making activity, there can be no possibility of locating any alternative possibilities that might be crucial 'further back in the history of the act', for in such cases there simply *is* no suitable psychological history in which such possibilities might be located. According to the libertarian who couches his thinking in these sorts of terms, we must then either say that such actions as these are not 'free' at all and that they are merely the deterministic consequences of sub-personal processes,[43] restricting

---

[40] Cf also Kane (1996: 27): 'Incompatibilists…can live with compatibilist accounts of the relation between choice (or intention) and action. What they must insist upon is an incompatibilist account of the relation between reasons, on the one hand, and choice (or intention) on the other'; and Ekstrom (2000: 103): 'If an agent's proximal intention only indeterministically and not deterministically results in his act, then there is a chance, given the agent's intention and the reigning conditions and natural laws, that the act will not follow. But then a model requiring such indeterminism simply provides the agent with a *liability* and not the positive asset commonly thought to be secured in the possession of agential freedom').

[41] Ekstrom (2000: 105–6).

[42] Ryle (1949: 68).

[43] This line appears to be taken e.g. by O'Connor (2000: 105):

'Over the past year…in St Andrews I have formed the habit of walking along the wooded Lade Braes en route to the university. At a certain point, I have the option of remaining on the "upper path" or descending

the capacity to do otherwise only to actions that genuinely are preceded by conscious deliberative activity resulting in some kind of decisive resolution or choice, or alternatively insist that despite appearances, such actions really *are* preceded by decisions, albeit ones of which we are unconscious. But neither alternative seems to me very happy. The first option is of course at odds entirely with the approach adopted in this book, according to which all actions (and not just some privileged set, preceded by forethought and deliberation) are characterized by the capacity to do otherwise, The second just seems objectionably ad hoc; a mere inventing of psychological entities for which there is no empirical evidence for the sake of theory preservation.

As well as being based upon a phenomenologically inaccurate account of the antecedents of action, the decision-based picture seems to me also to deliver a phenomenologically inaccurate picture of action itself, at any rate on the assumption that we often *are* free agents, and so that the phenomenology of a great many of the actions we undertake under normal conditions just *is* the phenomenology of free agency. According to this picture, a maximally free agent, having decided, for good reason, to φ immediately,[44] would have no further use for the capacity to refrain from φ-ing. This is why Diana will not be inclined to insert an indeterministic nexus at this point in the causal chain. Having made a thoroughly rational decision to φ at *t*, the thought is, it is best for freedom if the action then simply follows inexorably (unless, of course the agent changes his/her mind in the interim). But leaving to one side for a minute the question whether this would indeed be best, it seems to me utterly incontrovertible that it is not in fact how things generally speaking *are*. We simply *do* (often) decide to do things—perhaps even decide to do them immediately—and then fail to do them without having changed our minds in the meantime, but just out of such all-too-human failings as laziness, ennui, inertia, lack of resolve, cowardice, etc., for example when I decide to get up *right now* and yet continue to lie in bed. It just does not feel to be a correct account of the phenomenology of action and of the various forms of executive failure to which the will is subject to assert that actions are generally brought *inevitably* in the train of decisions to undertake an action of the relevant kind, or even in the train of decisions to undertake an action of that kind *at that moment*, if indeed we ever make such decisions as these. It seems to me to be part of what it *is* to have the power of action that we are not inevitably propelled into anything—not even into acting on overwhelmingly good reasons—by such prior mental events as decisions

---

to the emerging "lower path" along the stream. For some time now, I have generally gone along the lower path on the way to the university and along the upper path on the return trip. I rarely even consider any more which of the two routes I would like to take. Usually, my attention as I approach the juncture is given over to observing the foliage and thinking about the philosophical topic with which I am currently preoccupied, daydreaming, or considering some practical matter or other. Given my preoccupied frame of mind and my fairly settled disposition to take the lower path, it is plausible to say that it is *inevitable*, on at least many of these occasions, that I will follow this route by the time I am, say, five steps from the juncture'.

[44] It should perhaps be remarked also how strange is the assumption that we make such decisions ('to φ immediately') on a regular basis.

or intentions. As I have put it often in this chapter, we also have to act, which is a further move, and what makes it a further move is precisely that we need not make it.

It might be objected that such cases as I am imagining ought to be understood as cases in which a stronger desire (e.g. the desire to remain in bed) simply comes to outweigh a weaker one (e.g. the desire to get up) at the crucial moment, thus precipitating a new decision (the decision to stay in bed after all) and hence that there is nothing that need conflict with the decision-based picture here. Rather, this is a case in which, to use Mele's phraseology, the intention to get up has *not* persisted; it has simply been replaced (at the last minute, as it were) by the intention to stay in bed, which precipitates a different decision and hence a different action. But as has often been said of such responses to the phenomenon of weakness of will, there seems to be no reason to account the desire to remain in bed 'stronger' than its competitor desire except for its *de facto* triumph, so that the explanation of what in fact happens in terms of relative desire strength looks empty. Moreover, this response once again must face the charge of phenomenological implausibility—it does not seem to me that I made a *decision* to remain in bed; I just did.

It might be said, of course, that even if I am right to insist that weakness of will of this variety does indeed exist, weakness of will is hardly paradigmatic free action. It might be insisted that it would surely be *better* if we did not have this ability to be weak-willed; that weakness of will of the sort I am speaking about is by no means freedom-enhancing, since it is often a mere obstacle to our carrying out our plans. This is, indeed, the premise of the arguments offered by Mele and Ekstrom for the view that the libertarian ought to look further back in the causal chains leading up to action for the place in which to locate any necessary indeterminism—that it could not be freedom-enhancing to have the capacity to be weak-willed. A goddess like Diana would therefore be well advised to incorporate into her well-designed agents a nexus between decision and action that is as deterministic as possible. But we need at this point, I think, to ask the question whether Diana would in fact be *able* to design something that truly counted as an agent in the strong sense explained and developed in the earlier chapters of this book, for which weakness of will was not an ever-present possibility. Mele supposes that what Diana would most like to create is a creature that could be unproblematically granted the whole panoply of intentional events and states—beliefs, desires, intentions, decisions, and the rest—and yet in which deterministic relations amongst such states would be able to do duty for the phenomenon of action. But I think it can be argued that this must be an incoherent set of desires on Diana's part. If she wants a creature that genuinely possesses intentional states, she will have to create an agent, in the strong sense of that word that I defended in Chapter 4. And if she wants an agent, she will have to have a creature that possesses throughout the time of its activity the distinctive *two-way* power to act or to refrain from acting. And if she wants a creature with this distinctive two-way power, she will not be able to avoid the possibility that when it comes to the crunch, the agent simply will not act on her prior intention to φ at t. The ever-present possibility of weakness of will, on this view, is simply the price of agency: it is the cost of ensuring that the action really does remain in the hands of the agent at the time of her action, and therefore that the agent is a settler of matters in the sense explained in Chapter 2.

From this perspective, then, there is something peculiar and wrong-headed about the starting point for the reflections of the Mele–Ekstrom variety of libertarian. Taking the notion of an agent for granted, this libertarian proceeds by trying to understand where in the causal chain constitutive of agency it would be *useful* or *valuable* to have an indeterministic nexus. And weakness of will not being useful or valuable *to an agent whose existence is already being taken for granted*, it is concluded that it is of course no good if the indeterministic nexus occurs between intention and action. No freedom worth wanting could exist in this gap. However, what this approach misses is the fact that even if weakness of will is not useful or valuable to an agent, it might nevertheless be essential to the very *existence* of such an agent. For if, as I am arguing, an agent has to be a settler of matters at the time of action, it will need to be possible for her *not* to act, at any given moment, on a previously formed intention to φ. And so one cannot safely conclude from reflections of this sort that indeterminism between intention and action is irrelevant to freedom. For if freedom depends on agency (as it surely does) and if the metaphysical possibility of weakness of will is a necessary concomitant of the power of agency, the metaphysical possibility of weakness of will will be a necessary condition of freedom, notwithstanding what is, from another point of view, its uselessness *to* the agent whose existence it makes possible.

The reasoning used by Mele, Ekstrom, Kane and others might make one wonder, perhaps: would it be better, though, if this were not so? Would it not be better if our rationally formed intentions could take us straight to bodily movements without the need for active intervention on our part (intervention that we have the freedom to undertake or not)? But the question betrays, it seems to me, a misunderstanding of the nature of intentions: to ask whether intentions might cause bodily movements but not by way of *action* is to sever intentions from the context in which talk of them makes sense. 'Intention' is a noun that derives from a verb; it is as well to remember that it is *we* who intend things. Intentions only exist in so far as sentences like 'S intends to φ' are true (not the other way around).[45] Intentions, I believe, (like beliefs and desires) are simply not *independent* causal players at all. They have their influence only in so far as our agency permits it, in so far as they are acted upon by us. One needs to ask: what would be the reason for supposing that a state that could thus deterministically bring about a bodily movement without any intervening action *was* an intention? Intentions are (essentially) things we act upon; the concept of an intention gains its significance, along with the concept of an action, from a conception of mind that applies these concepts to certain entities *together* in a kind of conceptual package. No doubt there *are* states of the brain that can deterministically bring about bodily movements without our having to do anything, but none of them could be intentions. To imagine away the

---

[45] For more detailed arguments for the view that we must take care not to reify our talk of such 'states' as beliefs, desires, and intentions, see Steward (1997).

need for the execution of the intention by the agent is, I believe, at the same time to imagine away the whole conceptual framework within which the concept of intention makes sense—to imagine ourselves away, indeed. And it is hard to see how that could be 'better' for us than a framework in which, by contrast, our presence is constantly required to supervise and oversee the direction in which our bodies will take us.

It seems to me, then, that this reason for supposing that we should look for the indeterminism wanted by the libertarian 'further back in the causal history of the act' evaporates, once it is understood why the indeterminism is really required in the first place. Of course, there will have to be indeterminism further back in the causal history of an act that is preceded by a decision *as well*, for as I have already said, decisions themselves can be regarded as a variety of action and so there will have to be indeterminacy, also, between the agent's coming to possess the beliefs, desires, etc. that are causally relevant to her decision and the decision itself. But once again, the point of this indeterminacy is not to be of 'use' to an agent conceived of as already unproblematically existing. The *point* is to allow for the agent's existence *as* an agent in the first place.

It is perfectly true, of course, that indeterminism of certain sorts at certain points in the causal processes that underlie our movings of our bodies could only be unhelpful to a free agent. Our control over our bodies certainly depends on the existence of sub-personal mechanisms, and it would indeed be a nightmare if we could not rely on those mechanisms due to the existence of chancy, indeterministic links at the level of the mechanism in question. If I need a muscle to contract, for example, it is of no conceivable help to me, for instance, if my muscle is subject from time to time to chance failures that prevent it from responding in the normal way to incoming signals from the nerves. But, firstly, this sort of thing would not be indeterminism between intention and action (which is what Mele contends would be pointless); it would be indeterminism subsequent, at any rate, to the *initiation* of the action, and interfering rather with the capacity of the *action* to deliver the bodily movement₁ that its successful completion would demand. And, secondly, such indeterministic links as are here envisaged would constitute only a low-level variety of indeterministic nexus, a nexus that could not itself provide a space into which an action might be fitted. Such low-level indeterministic links as these are, as the compatibilist has always insisted, of *no help whatever* in understanding how agency might be possible. But indeterminacy need not be thought of merely as a (lower-level) *resource* to which one can turn in order to understand how the phenomenon of agency is possible. As I shall try to show in Chapter 8, it is possible to believe rather that agency *just is* a (higher-level) indeterministic phenomenon. Mele is right that certain sorts of low-level indeterministic connections in the mechanisms on which we rely for the control of our own movement could be of no help to a free agent. But he is wrong if he supposes that the sorts of unhelpful connection he considers would truly lie at a point that is well described as being 'between intention and action'. He would also be wrong, as I shall later try to show, to suppose that we can make no sense of indeterministic connections that are utterly different from the sort he imagines as presenting obstacles to our exercises of agency. Indeterminism may come in many different shapes, sizes, and places, and the unimportance for agency of the low-level sort of disruptive, chancy effect I have just considered does not imply the insignificance of any variety of indeterminacy we could imagine.

Where, then, might be the right place to locate the wanted indeterminacy? The right answer, I think, is that it has to be present *throughout* anything that genuinely constitutes an exercise of agency. At each point in time at which something that is truly a piece of an agent's activity is going on, the agent must possess a power of refrainment with respect to that piece of activity such that she is able to cease from that activity at any time and *need not*, at any point, exert the capacity that she does in fact exert in acting. The alternative possibilities that attach to the activity of agents are not present merely at particular crucial *moments*: at the 'moment' of action, for example, or at the 'moment' of decision, moments at which subsequent deterministic chains of events are, so to speak, unleashed by the indeterministic interventions of agents. Instead they should be thought of as being more or less constantly present throughout the *whole* of any period of activity or indeed, any period of waking inactivity. At more or less any point during my waking life, I should like to insist, there are a whole range of things I might do, a whole variety of ways in which I might move my body and thereby bring about changes of various sorts in my environment, and, of course, beyond. Although, as an agent, one has of course to rely on numerous sub-personal processes, one is, as an agent, *constantly* in a position to intervene and stop those processes in their tracks, replacing them with others as the need arises (though of course there are limits on what is possible in this respect, as will be mentioned in Chapter 8). Alternative possibilities of some sort or another, I want to insist, are *always* there, and not just at something called 'the moment of decision' or 'the time of action', but at every moment of an animal agent's waking life. Every moment is potentially a moment of decision and a moment at which some new action might be initiated.

As I have already mentioned, one philosopher who has argued in what might seem to be a similar vein for the essentiality to the phenomenon of action of a series of 'gaps'—gaps between reasons and decisions, gaps between decisions and actions, and gaps between initiated actions and their completions—is John Searle. But I think, in fact, that we need to go a step further than Searle does, in order to combat the line of thinking that leads to the problematic picture that Mele and Ekstrom find themselves compelled to endorse, which pushes the locus of freedom back into the mental realm. In speaking of 'gaps', Searle, like Mele and Ekstrom, continues to work for the most part with the standard picture of an action as constituted by a causal chain of interlinked events and states, albeit a chain of events and states in which there have to be 'gaps' if the role of the agent is to be properly represented; gaps in which the self can 'operate', as Searle is inclined to put it. But I would like to suggest that it may be better not to think of agency in terms of such individual actions and individual chains of this kind *at all*—with or without the gaps. Once we are thinking in terms of these chains, it is hard to avoid the picture I am anxious to escape: that of the agent as a mysterious exerter of indeterministic influence at crucial points in an otherwise perfectly deterministic chain. That is a picture that (rightly) provokes the opprobrium of the naturalistically inclined, and which should be rejected likewise by the naturalistically inclined libertarian. I should like to suggest rather that the phenomenon of agency is normally best thought of not in terms of numerous discrete and separable 'actions' that the agent consciously initiates by intervening in the 'gap' or 'gaps', but rather in terms of a stream (or normally in fact, of course, numerous concurrent streams) of ongoing *activity*. Agency, as I have already claimed in Chapter 3, is better suited to a *process* than to an *event* ontology. This ontological shift may help us to see, I think, how we can think of the process of acting as something that is characterized by the presence *throughout its length* of alternate possibilities. An agent who is acting, I should like to suggest, has a constant and ongoing capacity throughout the period of the action to do such things as: cease from an activity in which she is currently engaged, alter the speed of some movement in which she is currently engaged, change the direction of a movement, begin new types of movement either instead of, or as well as, those already being engaged in; etc. These are constant and ongoing capacities that make it the case, with respect to any activity that in fact occurs, that the agent need not have acted in the precise way she did because she need not have moved her body in the precise way she did. Being the overall controller of the movements of that body, all these details are down to her to settle at the time of the action. She could have been quicker or slower, for example; she could have stopped halfway through; she could have changed her direction, lifted her knees higher, kept her hands by her sides, etc. And we should not say that all these 'could haves' ought to be replaced by 'could have if she'd wanted/decided/chosen to'. For we do not typically choose or decide these features of our bodily activities at all. Our agency in respect of them does not consist in a power to unleash-by-choosing-it some particular type of movement as opposed to some other. It consists rather in the simple power to move one's body in ways one need not have done: to determine or settle, though not necessarily by choosing, how our bodies will move.

Does it follow from the fact that they are not in all respects products of choice or decision that these movements are mere sub-personal phenomena, of no conceivable interest to the philosophy of action and agency? On the contrary: such movements, I insist, make up the bulk of our active lives. Such things as deliberated choices and decisions of course are an important part of what gives overall shape to those lives. They are significant factors in the determination, for example, of whether I shall be a firefighter or a farmer, a doctor or a DJ, and so of whether I shall carry out any of the sorts of activity typical of lives of that sort. They will also help to determine my political agendas, moral principles, personal commitments and ambitions, and so on. And if one is interested primarily in actions because of their importance for the topic of moral responsibility, it might well be that one would want to focus on such crucial and significant choices and decisions as these. But if one is interested in action primarily from a metaphysical point of view, one must pay attention also to the lowly feats that make up our everyday lives: to what happens when we eat, drink, amble and shuffle about, cook, clean, tidy up, smile, nod, talk, ablute, etc. These activities are not, by and large, well conceived of in terms of the causation of movements by prior choices. Our control of them is not a simple matter of mental causation. But that is not to say that we have nothing much to do with them at all, that they are mere bodily phenomena of no greater significance for our agency than mere reflexes and tropes. On the contrary, the agent maintains a constant *supervisory* role over the maelstrom of neurological activity that constitutes their enaction, integrating and orchestrating the movements that together create a life: a stream of purposive activity directed to a large variety of different goals and needing to be constantly adjusted in the light of new developments. It is important to remember that *initiation* of causal streams is only one aspect of this. The capacity to stop and the power to alter what is going on are just as important as the capacity to start. The event-based focus on 'decisions' and 'actions' has perhaps encouraged the tendency to suppose that the role that the agent has to play, if there is one, must be a kind of initiatory button-pressing, whereupon a stream of purely physical events is triggered by some peculiar intervention of the agent. But quite apart from all the usual worries that this picture generates, it is also wholly inadequate to the temporally protracted nature of the majority of our actions, which are messily diverse in temporal character. Some, like shootings, are admittedly over and done in an instant (and it is no coincidence that actions of this type are often chosen by philosophers as examples). However, others, such as going for walks or writing letters, are more protracted. Our control over them is not well thought of as a matter of deliberate initiation—either of the whole sequence in which the activity consists or of the parts into which it might be broken up. These actions are *activities*—processes, and not events—and our attempts to formulate whatever may be the modal requirements on their enactment—whatever has to be the case concerning our ability to do otherwise with respect to them—needs to respect this temporal character.

In the current chapter, then, I have attempted to outline my response to the Challenge from Chance. In many ways, of course (as promised) my response consists of concessions to the compatibilist proponent of the Challenge. I have tried to suggest that it is a mistake for the libertarian to insist quite generally that it must be true of any agent who makes a free decision at t to φ that she could, at that very same time t have instead made the decision not to φ—at any rate, if that 'could have' is construed in the way that the libertarian typically construes it, namely as involving the existence of a possible world with the very same laws of nature and the very same past but in which the opposite decision is made at the very same moment. In clear cases, it seems to me, we neither actually do have nor should wish to have the capacity to have made a decision opposed to the one we actually make, at any rate when this capacity is construed in the standard libertarian way. It is, I have suggested, questionable whether it is even coherent to suppose we might have such a capacity in a clear case, for it is not obvious on what basis we should regard the agent as having 'decided' anything in the alternative possible world, given that the so-called 'decision' by hypothesis bears no intelligible relation of any kind to any of the agent's motivations, beliefs, deliberative trains of thought, etc. But even if it is coherent, it is hard to see how the capacity could be valuable. It is rather the compatibilist, I suggest, who gives the best account of the power to have made the opposed decision that it might be coherent to wish for in such cases. What it is intelligible to hope we might have is the capacity and opportunity to have made the opposite decision *had we seen any reason to do so.*

But neither do I accept that in clear cases (or indeed in any others) decisions are deterministically produced by reasons (or by anything else), as suggested by the proponent of the second kind of libertarian response I considered in Section 6.3.2. We do not always have the (incompatibilistically construed) power genuinely to make an *opposite* decision from the one we in fact make at *t*, but we always have the power *not* to make that decision then, for a decision is a kind of action and it is essential to actions of all kinds that they are the exercises of powers that are *two-way*. Decision-making events, therefore, even in clear cases, are not necessitated by their antecedents. I have tried to show that confusion can arise about this because 'determination' is an ambiguous term, and also that although we should be pleased to have our reasons determining what we do (or decide) in the sense of *our* determining (that is to say, settling) what we shall do (or decide) by reference only to reasons, this is not the same thing at all as those reasons serving as necessitating causes of our actions (or decisions). They are not and could not be: actions must be settlings and therefore require an absence of necessitating causes.

On this basis, I have offered my own, somewhat different version of libertarianism, which continues to insist on the importance of alternative possibilities, but suggests that the important possibilities are rather different ones from those envisaged by Mele's libertarian. For a start, the alternative possibilities I demand are requirements of agency in general, not merely of so-called 'free' agency. They are requirements in simple cases of hair-brushing, teeth-cleaning, bed-making, and tea-drinking, just as much as they are requirements in the cases of moral predicament and agonized deliberation that litter the literature. I have also suggested that we should construe the capacity that we require of an agent as an *ongoing* capacity to stop or alter what she is doing in any of an almost infinite variety of ways, a capacity that is present throughout the whole of the period of activity, and not one confined to a certain point in a causal chain of interlinked events and states. I have suggested, furthermore, that once we have this picture in mind, we need not accept the restriction of alternate possibilities to the sphere of decision-making that has been common in the recent literature. We can insist that they pertain to actions in general, not merely to a 'point' on an internal, mentalistic causal chain between reasons and decision.

That, then, is the outline of my response to the Challenge from Chance. In the next chapter, I shall raise and reply to a number of natural objections to that response, and will try to defend it against the worries that I anticipate might arise.

7

Responding to the Challenge from Chance: Some Objections

In this chapter I intend to answer three objections to the various claims made in the last chapter in response to the Challenge from Chance. There may, of course, be other objections to my position that have not occurred to me, but the three I shall treat here represent the three that seem to me the most obvious, natural, and pressing for someone who wishes to defend the view outlined in Chapter 6. I shall look first, in Section 7.1, at the objection that my response to the Challenge from Chance must be hopeless since a slightly revised challenge of the very same sort that Mele presses on the libertarian can simply be raised again, in connection with my new account of the alternate possibilities possessed by the agent in the case imagined. Then, in Section 7.2, I shall turn to look at an objection I have already mentioned once or twice in passing, an objection that might be thought to arise from so-called 'Frank-furt-style examples'. This objection contends that such cases are clear counterexamples to the assertion, essential to Agency Incompatibilism, that a power of refrainment is central to agency. For such examples are supposed to be instances of cases in which it is clear that the agent acts—indeed, acts responsibly—even though she could not have done other than she did and hence even though she could not have refrained from her action. Clearly, then, an account such as mine will need to say something about these sorts of examples. Finally, in Section 7.3 I shall consider the worry that the sort of power of refrainment I have highlighted as an essential feature of anything that deserves to be called an action is just too flimsy and unimportant—not suffi-ciently *robust*—to underwrite libertarianism. At the end of this discussion I hope I shall have both refined and made out a good case for my response to the Challenge from Chance, and therefore a good preliminary case for Agency Incompatibilism, the position in which that response is embedded. It will then be time to turn to address (in Chapter 8) what I imagine will be the second main type of concern that my account will engender: the fear that I must be committed to a spooky metaphysics of agent causation, which, if it is not ruled out by virtue of sheer unintelligibility must at the very least be completely naturalistically implausible.

7.1 Matters of luck

The first objection to my response to the Challenge from Chance alleges that the response I have offered is really no response at all, because the alteration I have sought to make in the libertarian's position is one against which Mele's original objection can simply be raised again. For it might be said that it is *still* a matter of mere luck whether Joe decides at *t* to move in with his girlfriend or does not decide to do so, and that this is inconsistent with Joe's really being in control of whether he decides at *t* to do so or else refrains from making that decision. Mele, recall, justifies his assumption that the difference between the possible world in which Joe decides at *t* to A and the world in which he decides at *t* not to A is a 'matter of luck', by appeal to the idea that 'there is nothing about Joe's powers, capacities, states of mind, moral character, and the like in either world that accounts for this difference'.[1] But it might appear that the very same things might be said of the two worlds now under consideration: the one in which Joe decides at *t* to move in with his girlfriend and the one (or indeed the many, for there are presumably many such alternative worlds, e.g. ones in which he makes the same decision seconds later, ones in which he makes it minutes or hours later, and ones in which he makes it only days or weeks later, as well as ones in which he never makes it at all, perhaps because his girlfriend gets tired of waiting for him to make up his mind and withdraws her offer) in which he does not make this decision at that time. If none of these possibilities is ruled out by the past and the laws and, in particular, if none is ruled out by any feature that Joe possesses at *t*, must it not just be a 'matter of luck' which possibility actually occurs?

This is the point, though, at which to recall the fact that when considering the case of Joe as originally presented in Chapter 6, I rejected these grounds for supposing that which decision Joe makes must be a matter of luck, although I conceded Mele's conclusion. I argued that the Agency Incompatibilist should insist that if it is to be regarded as a sufficient condition of its being a 'matter of luck' that an agent φs rather than ψs that there is no complete explanation[2] of why that agent φs rather than ψs in terms of antecedently existing properties of that same agent, then it is of no concern to the libertarian if it is judged to be a matter of luck, according to this criterion, that the agent φs rather than ψs. For it is simply part of her position that there can be no such explanation. The thought behind libertarian viewpoints in general, after all, is that a single agent at a given moment may have more than one genuinely open possibility before her and indeed *must* have more than one such possibility before her if her action is to be free (according to the traditional libertarian) or if it is to be an action at all (according to the Agency Incompatibilist). It seems simply to *follow* very directly from this thought that there can be no *complete* explanation in terms of antecedently

---

[1] Mele (2006: 9).

[2] By a 'complete' explanation, I mean one which renders it not even partly a matter of luck that the agent φs rather than ψs in the sense explained in Chapter 6.3.1.

possessed properties of the agent for why one outcome occurs rather than the other. This does not imply, though, that it is a matter of luck which decision the agent makes in the problematic sense that the agent has no control over which outcome occurs. It *would* follow if a person's (or animal's) agency was reducible to the causal role played by their *properties*, but that this is so is something I deny.[3] If there are to be true actions, I maintain, we need for it sometimes not to be the case that the way things unfold depends only on the way they already are, even if some of those ways things are, are ways things are *with us*. Action introduces into the world another kind of dependence entirely from the kind that is exploited by explanations of how things turn out in terms of how things antecedently were: dependence on an agent as opposed merely to dependence on the way the agent is. The Agency Incompatibilist should insist that it is not because something *about us* makes us act or because something explains why we act, but simply because *we act* that it is up to us what happens to our bodies.

My grounds for conceding that it was indeed a 'matter of luck' whether or not Joe decided to move in with his girlfriend in the original case, though, had nothing to do with the idea that none of Joe's properties could explain the difference in his decisions in the two possible worlds Mele imagines. I argued that the problem was rather this: that the alternate possibility on which the traditional libertarian insists seems to decrease rather than improve Joe's control over what occurs. Since the relevant alternate possibility, had it occurred, could not have been understood to be any true action of Joe's, given its total lack of fit with his desires, beliefs, reasons, etc., we only seem able to conceive of it as a kind of mad irruption in Joe's psychological life that would simply (if it had occurred) have *prevented* him from making what is, from every imaginable point of view, the right decision. There is simply no coherent way of understanding how Joe, gripped by the excitement and enthusiasm with which he is happily imagining his new life in his girlfriend's beautiful flat, and the relief with which he is contemplating leaving his nasty damp bedsit, and lacking *any* thoughts, emotions, or

---

[3] It does not seem to me that it is true even of inanimate entities, indeed, that they can bring about an event of kind *E* only by instantiating properties that are explanatorily relevant to the question why an event of kind *E* occurred rather than not, provided there exist some genuinely indeterministic occurrences. For instance, suppose a radioactive atom indeterministically emits a particle at *t*. Then the radioactive atom might be said to have brought about certain consequences in the universe (that a particle was emitted at *t* rather than not, for example, together with any possible further consequences of this emission) without any of the prior properties of the radioactive atom having been relevant to the fact that the question of whether or not a particle would be emitted by the atom at *t* was settled with an emission rather than a non-emission. We can, indeed, increase the plausibility of the claim that its antecedently existing properties were irrelevant to the explanation of the fact that it emitted a particle at *t* rather than not, by imagining that any objective probabilities existing and relating to the emission were such that they made an emission at *t* exceedingly *unlikely*. For in that case, it would not even be plausible that we could appeal to the thought that the radioactive atom (and its environment) somehow embodied these objective probabilities to ground the supposition that certain of its properties must have been explanatorily relevant to what happened. There seems, then, to be nothing we can say *about* the radioactive atom which gives us any help with explaining why the particle was emitted at *t* rather than not. And yet the atom emitted a particle all right. *It* brought about consequences in the world by emitting a particle, even though none of its properties was explanatorily relevant to the question why the particle was emitted at *t* rather than not.

motivations that might justify the decision to stay where he is, could nevertheless have made the decision at *t* not to move in after all. We can only conceive of the possibility of such a 'decision' occurring, if we can conceive of it at all, as a kind of random upsurge of total irrationality into Joe's psychological life. And even if such random upsurges are possible, I suggested, they cannot form the bedrock of a sensible libertarianism. How could an insistence upon such possibilities contribute in any way to our control over the course of events?

But the new alternative possibility we are now insisting upon as part of Agency Incompatibilism is a different one. The relevant possibility is merely that Joe should *not* have made the decision to move in with his girlfriend that he in fact made at *t*. And this is an omission, not an act, which changes altogether the nature of the alternative possibility we are being asked to allow for. In the original case, we had to allow for Joe's performing a positive action that he has no reason or motivation whatever to perform and every reason and motivation not to perform. But in the present case, we simply have to allow for the possibility that he might *not* have done something at a given time *t* that in fact he *did* do at that given time. That the world should have gone forward in this way instead of the way in which it in fact went forward, is not something that would have been rationally unintelligible or which we have trouble understanding as anything other than the operation of an alien force, operating counter to Joe's wishes and reasons and hopes. Though he had many reasons, we are supposing, to decide to move in with his girlfriend, Joe need not have had any particular reasons for making the decision *then*. If he had decided at *t* that he ought to put off the decision about moving in with his girlfriend until a later date just in case there were any drawbacks he might not have thought of and notwithstanding his sense that the decision ought to be clear-cut, that would not have been irrational or unintelligible or in the least at odds with our conception of how it is that human beings operate when under the influence of ordinary sorts of human motivation. It is arguable, perhaps (though in fact I should deny it, because of the views on sub-intentional actions I have already expressed in Chapter 3) that anything that counts as an action has to be someone's doing something for a reason. However, even if this is conceded it is not at all obvious that we also have to have reasons for doing the things we do *at the times* at which we do them, as opposed to the numerous other things we might have done at the times in question. Of course we sometimes have such reasons. For instance, if I have promised to telephone you at precisely 12 noon then that is an explanation of why I do so at that time, rather than doing some of the many other things it is in my power to do at that same time. But cases like this are surely the exception rather than the rule. Why, for instance, am I currently still sitting here writing rather than making the cup of tea I have been dimly thinking about for the past hour or calling the bank, which is something I also need to do today? Some will no doubt be inclined to say that I must have wanted to sit here writing more than I wanted the cup of tea and more than I wanted to phone the bank, and that this is the explanation. But if this 'must have' can be justified, it can surely only be by appeal to a conception of desire-strength according to which it simply follows from the fact that I am still sitting here that this was my 'strongest' desire. It can therefore scarcely be a satisfactory explanation of why I am still here; it is merely the analytic consequence of this fact.[4] Of course, there *may* be some alternative and more satisfactory sort of explanation than this—perhaps, for instance, I have been unconsciously influenced by my knowledge that there is a huge pile of washing up in the kitchen that I should prefer to avoid seeing, or by an irrational fear of financial institutions. But does there *have* to be one? Why should it not be that in many such instances there is simply nothing illuminating to say? Perhaps I simply haven't managed to get up and go downstairs to put the kettle on or to telephone the bank and there is nothing particular that explains *why* I have not done so. I could have done either of these things or indeed done a number of other things that I also had reason to do, but I haven't. I have stayed here writing instead. And perhaps that is pretty much all there is to it.

It seems quite plausible in general, indeed, that there are lots of contrastive facts for which there is really *no* good explanation. Consider asking a child why she chose green rather than orange to colour the robot's body in her picture, or the question why I have positioned the bookcase in my room exactly where it is, rather than 2 cm to the right. There may be an explanation. But perhaps there is simply no reason, no explanation at all. And it seems to me especially likely that in cases where we are considering explanations of why someone does something at a particular time rather than doing something else (or nothing) at that very same time, it may be *particularly* rare that there is anything much of an illuminating sort to say. That does not imply, of course, that we cannot explain why that person did that thing *at all*; only that we may not be able to explain why they did it *then* (rather than not doing it then and doing some alternative thing instead). But if there is no particular rational explanation of the fact that Joe decides to move in with his girlfriend at *t* rather than not deciding to do so at *t*, then the possible worlds in which he refrains from deciding at *t* need not be worlds that we need to conceive of as ones in which his control over the course of events has been usurped. They are merely worlds in which he organizes himself a little differently from the way he organized himself in actuality, the ever-present possibility of doing which, according to the Agency Incompatibilist, is at the very heart of the power of agency itself.

There are of course cases in which a decision must be made at a given moment if an opportunity is not to be lost. For instance, Joe might be faced with a situation in which his girlfriend tells him that she requires an instant answer: if he does not agree immediately, the offer will be withdrawn. Suppose he gives an instant positive answer. In such a case as this, it might be said, he *did* have a reason for deciding to move in with his girlfriend at the specific time at which he did so: it would have been irrational to have waited since that would have prevented him from doing what he wanted to do. So under these circumstances, could he have failed to make the positive decision he in

---

[4] See Nagel (1970), Nozick (1981).

fact made at *t*? Does not the argument I used before against the libertarian demand that an agent must always be able to decide for either option in any arbitrarily constructed moral or practical dilemma apply here also?—that because of its irrationality, we cannot conceive of the situation in which Joe fails to make the wanted decision as one in which it was genuinely *he* that failed to make it?

The situation here, though, is not comparable with the one we considered earlier in a number of respects. For a start, the alternative scenario we are trying to imagine is one in which Joe simply does *not* make that decision at the time in question. We are concerned with an omission, a failure to act, not with an action. It may be that it would have been irrational for Joe not to have made the decision then, but there is simply no issue, as there was in the original case, about whether Joe really counts as the agent of an action in the counterfactual scenario in which he fails to decide at *t* to move in with his girlfriend. For we are not, in general, agents of all our non-actions (though we can sometimes be responsible for them). There is no question of its having been possible for Joe not to have made the decision at *t* seeming to entail the possibility that an event beyond his control should have occurred. Moreover, though not deciding at *t* to move in with his girlfriend would have been irrational in one way (because it prevents Joe from doing something he very much wants to do), it is not at all irrational in another. We have a general tendency, if we are prudent, not to rush into irrevocable decisions without careful thought and there therefore *are* reasons speaking for refrainment from deciding in the case imagined, because there are always general reasons speaking for caution and further thought (though of course, they can be outweighed by the need for urgency in a given case). This helps to make sense for us of what might have gone on in a situation in which Joe dithers too long and loses his opportunity. We understand perfectly how faint-heartedness and lack of resolve can enter into situations in which we are robbed of the time to think properly about what we should do. So it seems to me that it is unproblematic to insist that even in situations like this, where time is of the essence, there is no difficulty attaching to the assumption that the agent could have *not* made the wanted decision at the time in question. Though he did indeed make the decision at t, *not* making it then was also within his power and we are not forced into the admission that in saying this we imply that it was merely lucky for him that he was not waylaid by mysterious forces beyond his control at the time of decision. For he remains in control of the question of whether he will decide or whether he will dither. In deciding, he settled at the same time that he would not dither.

It seems to me, then, that for this reason the argument that I conceded went through against the traditional libertarian position outlined by Mele does not go through in the same way against Agency Incompatibilism, because the libertarian possibility on which I am insisting does not have to be conceived of as the operation of a force which, were it to operate, would send Joe off on a course of action he has every reason and motivation not to want to pursue. The possibility on which I am insisting is merely the much more modest possibility that Joe might have organized his life around that moment, *t*, in a somewhat different manner from the way in which he in fact went ahead and organized it. There is no uniquely rational way in which to organize one's life and given that that is so there are, generally speaking and emergency situations aside,[5] *many* courses of action one can take at any given moment without abandoning all one's rights to be called a rational agent. The libertarianism I am insisting upon simply demands that our power to settle *which* of these courses of action becomes the actual one by exercising the two-way power of agency, be conceded.

It is important to my position, though, that this power of agency is a power to *settle*, and not necessarily in all instances a power to *choose*. It is absurd and inaccurate to suppose that we are constantly choosing and deciding between the alternative courses of action that are simultaneously open to us, for not every action we undertake is an action we decide or choose to undertake. We must not be tempted into an over-mentalistic account of our role in our own doings. As I tried to argue in Chapter 3, we are not identical merely with our mental selves and so we must resist the thought that things brought about *by us* are necessarily things that have explanations of a mentalistic sort. Of course, we do choose and decide upon some of the things we do. But the majority of our actions, I would like to suggest, are our settlings of things that we have not explicitly chosen or decided to settle in that way. The occurrence of an action consists merely in the agent's exercise of a power of movement and change with respect to her own body, a power which she need not have exercised in precisely the way or at precisely the time that she did. It is this power that I am suggesting we should insist that Joe exercises when deciding at *t* to move in with his girlfriend. Even a decision represents a power to change an aspect of one's own body, presumably in this case to effect some change (or perhaps a set of changes) in the brain that makes it much more likely that the action decided upon will in fact occur. In exercising this power, Joe exercises a power he need not have exercised, making the world go one way when it might have gone another. Had he refrained from exercising it, that would have been something he need not have done either because he *could* have exercised the power to decide at *t* instead. But neither course of action needs itself to have been chosen or decided upon in order to count as a settling by Joe of what occurs.

The question might be pressed, though: if there is no reason-giving explanation of why Joe decides at *t* to move in with his girlfriend rather than (for example) continuing to deliberate a bit longer as we have said he might also have done, is it not a matter of luck in a still rather problematic sense that he did indeed make this decision at *t*? For what makes the difference between the two situations may simply be some factor that is not under Joe's control at all. For example, he may be struck at *t*,[6] in world W2 but not in world W1, by the sudden thought that caution is often advisable in such matters, which causes him to defer making a firm decision until the next day. Whether or not one is struck by a thought, it is plausible to think, can surely be a 'matter of luck': we do

---

[5] Indeed, even in emergency situations, there are many ways of organizing oneself, as I shall later argue.

[6] It would have to be *at t* (and could not be before) if this description of the situation is to meet the requirement that all antecedent conditions are to remain exactly the same.

not normally control or orchestrate which thoughts it is we are struck by, though perhaps there are various forms of more indirect influence we *can* effect over such matters. One might worry that this just makes the situation directly comparable once again to the original scenario in which Joe 'decides' not to move in with his girlfriend because of the unfortunate irruption of what we seem able to conceive of only as a strange and irrational impetus into his psychological life. But it is very important to see that it does not do so. The crucial difference is the way in which the alternate possibility being insisted upon in each case bears on the conception we have of the *actual* decision made by Joe. In the original case, the alternate possibility being imagined was of no help—indeed, it was a hindrance—in understanding how Joe's actual decision could be an exercise of control on his part. It seemed that it would have been much better for Joe if the alternate possibility simply had not existed at all. But the alternate possibility on which the Agency Incompatibilist insists *does* help. For unless the alternative possibility of refrainment at *t* exists, Joe's *actual* act of decision-making is not properly representable as the active intervention into the world that the Agency Incompatibilist insists all actions must be. The crucial thing is that the *actual act* be something that did not have to happen, for otherwise, in the Agency Incompatibilist's opinion, it simply cannot be an act. But it does not matter a bit if the various *alternative* scenarios do not involve any activity on the part of Joe, for they are simply the foils in the light of which we know that his actually deciding something at *t* was a real intervention in the world on his part. The crucial point so far as the Agency Incompatibilist is concerned is that it does not follow from the fact that there is no reason-giving explanation of why Joe decides as he does *at t* that his actual decision was not an intervention in the world by him. On the contrary, things are, precisely, settled by *Joe*, who, possessed at *t* of the two-way power to decide or not to decide to move in with his girlfriend, goes ahead and exercises his power to decide, thereby settling the matter. He is not simply forced to 'wait and see' whether the alternative possibility occurs. Joe has a role to play precisely because it is his *decision* (a type of *action*) that takes the world in the direction it in fact ends up moving. His acting just *is* his taking the world in the direction it in fact ends up moving, and so it is not a matter of luck *for him* that he acts in the way that he does.[7]

It might be said, though, that even if there does not have to be a contrastive *reason-giving* explanation of why Joe decides at *t* to move in with his girlfriend rather than not thus deciding, there must nevertheless be *some* sort of contrastive explanation here: an agent's φ-ing at *t* is an event and it must have causal antecedents and it is implausible that these causal antecedents might also have been the causal antecedents of S's *not* φ-ing at *t*, but rather, say, of doing nothing or of ψ-ing, where ψ-ing is an action of a completely different type. So it might be insisted that there must be a contrastive explanation of why S φ-ed rather than ψ-ed at *t* in terms of these causal antecedents.

---

[7] I return to say more about these points in Section 7.3.2 below, to which they are also relevant.

However, a great deal of care must be taken with this argument. I have no objection to the claim that actions must have causal antecedents, provided it is not assumed that causation must in all cases be *deterministic* causation. This is because, of course, if this were so the claim that actions have causes would be inconsistent with my claim that they have to be settlings of matters by agents *at the time of action*, and would be merely question-begging. In addition, I accept that there must be a contrastive explanation in terms of events occurring in S's motor cortex, of why S's body moves in the particular way that it does, rather than in some other way, since it is plausible to suppose that similar antecedents could not have given rise to radically different movements. But a bodily movement₁, as I argued in Chapter 2, is not the same thing as an action. An arm rising is not the same thing as an arm *raising*. So it does not follow from the fact that contrastive explanations must be possible for why a certain type of movement occurred rather than some other that contrastive explanations must also be possible for why a certain *action* occurred at a given time rather than some other, or none at all.

Still, it might be said, even if an action is not the same thing as a bodily movement, it must be the same thing as (or must supervene upon) *some* event(s) or other that occurs in the human body. Perhaps it is the same thing as a neural event, for instance, and neural events must themselves have neural antecedents. These, it might be said must surely be usable as the basis of a contrastive explanation that might then serve to explain the occurrence of S's φ-ing at t rather than S's not φ-ing at t. But now caution is needed. For suppose, just for a moment, that the processes that realized actions in the brain were *stochastic* processes. Since where stochastic processes are concerned, different future courses may evolve from one and the same starting point, it need not be true that antecedent conditions would automatically offer an explanation of why a φ-ing of S's occurred at t rather than not. Those conditions might perfectly well be compatible with S's not φ-ing at t, and indeed with S's ψ-ing at t. It would in a sense then be a matter of luck that conditions had evolved in the S φ-ing at t way rather than in the S not φ-ing at t way, since either might have occurred. No impersonally describable set of facts and laws takes the world inevitably from $t-1$ to t. But it is not obvious without further argument that this implies that S *has no control* over the question whether the world evolves in the 'S φs at t' way or the 'S does not φ at t' way. Whether that is so depends on what the relation is between S and the stochastic processes. And I shall be arguing in Chapter 8 that the relation may in fact be such that S can *make* the stochastic processes evolve in one way rather than another—that indeed, the power to do this is what constitutes the power to act.

I conclude, then, that Agency Incompatibilism is not inevitably vulnerable to the Challenge from Chance. The alternative unfoldings of the world on which it insists do not include unfoldings in which the agent's powers of control seem merely to have been usurped; they merely represent different organizational possibilities for the agent. The Agency Incompatibilist insists that it is essential for a true agent to possess such different organizational possibilities as these; it is this that distinguishes something that has a will from something that has none. It is not possible, therefore, to argue that whether or not the agent exercises these powers in a given way and at a given time is a 'matter of luck' in any way that ought to be worrying for the Agency Incompatibilist.

I want now to turn to the second type of objection I envisage being raised to the account I have offered, an objection that is based on what is alleged to be the moral of so-called 'Frankfurt-style examples'. An adequate response to this objection will require a refinement and clarification of one of the central claims of Agency Incompatibilism, namely the claim that a power of refrainment is central to agency. It will be seen that there is more than one power that might be thought relevant here, and it is crucial to developing a version of Agency Incompatibilism that will withstand Frankfurt-style objections to fasten on the correct power or powers.

7.2 Frankfurt-style examples

Frankfurt is the originator of a much-discussed variety of counterexample to what he calls the Principle of Alternate Possibilities (PAP):

(PAP) A person is morally responsible for what he has done only if he could have done otherwise.[8]

Until Frankfurt's article, PAP had been quite widely supposed to be an *a priori* truth, but Frankfurt argued, by way of a now notorious alleged counterexample, that the principle was in fact false, and many others have followed in his wake, providing further examples of a similar sort, often designed to overcome particular objections to the details of Frankfurt's original case. In line with what is now common practice, I term these sorts of example 'Frankfurt-style examples'. PAP itself is, of course, a principle that is centrally concerned with the conditions of moral responsibility, a concept I have attempted to leave largely to one side throughout the preceding chapters. Indeed, I shall not be centrally concerned in what follows with the defence of PAP as such.[9] Nevertheless, Frankfurt-style examples are of significance for my line of argument, since it might be thought that similar examples can be used to show that alternate possibilities must be irrelevant not only to moral responsibility but also to *agency*.

Consider, for example, the following imaginary Frankfurt-style case.[10] Suppose that Gunnar has conceived an intense dislike for Ridley and plans to shoot him. Cosser, who also has reasons for wanting Ridley out of the way, is pleased to hear of Gunnar's plan, but is worried that Gunnar will not carry it through to completion. Being an excellent neurosurgeon, he is able to implant a device in Gunnar's brain that he, Cosser, will activate if there is any sign of Gunnar's resolve beginning to wane.

---

[8] Frankfurt (1969).
[9] Though I have defended elsewhere the view that there is a legitimate interpretation of PAP on which it is true; see Steward (2006a).
[10] Names and the bare bones of the example borrowed from Van Inwagen (1983: 162–3).

Activation of the device will cause in Gunnar an 'irresistible desire' to carry out the shooting. But as it happens, there is no need for the intervention. Gunnar goes ahead and shoots Ridley in any case and Cosser never has to do anything at all.

Under such circumstances as these, it has been argued, Gunnar could not have done other than shoot Ridley. If he had shown any sign of wavering in his resolution, Cosser would have intervened and would have thereby ensured that Gunnar would end up shooting Ridley in any case. But this lack of alternate possibilities, it is argued, does not mean that Gunnar was not morally responsible for shooting Ridley. Since he went ahead of his own accord, Gunnar *is* morally responsible for shooting Ridley, notwithstanding the fact that he could not have done otherwise. And it might be thought that a similar argument could be used to show that the power of refrainment is not essential to agency, either. Gunnar, it might be said, could not have *refrained* from shooting Ridley in the envisaged scenario. But when he does shoot him, it would surely be preposterous to deny that he was, nevertheless, the agent of that action. Therefore, it might be inferred, the power of agency cannot essentially involve, at the same time, the power to refrain.

What is the Agency Incompatibilist to say about this argument? The crucial point to recognize, which I will develop in some detail in the remainder of this chapter, is that the power to do otherwise that is lacking to Gunnar in the above example is not the same as the capacity to refrain that is required for agency on which I have been insisting. Of course, certain powers are lacking to Gunnar under the circumstances imagined, but he *retains* the one that I claim is crucial to the judgement that the action he performs *is* indeed his action. I next want to explain in some detail what this crucial power is and to justify the claim that it is indeed the power that is essential to agency. However, I shall proceed rather indirectly since the general strategy I am pursuing here—of distinguishing the power Gunnar lacks in the envisaged situation from some other power he is alleged to have retained nonetheless—has been quite widely adopted by others writing on the Frankfurt cases. It will therefore be important to differentiate the power on which I wish to focus from some of the others that have been postulated as essential to the judgement that Gunnar is morally responsible for what he has done. It will be vital also for me to respond to a general worry that has been raised about strategies of this kind, namely that they tend to light on alternate possibilities that are insufficiently 'robust' to do the work required of them. I shall not aim at a comprehensive discussion of every move that has ever been made in the Frankfurt literature— that would be a gargantuan task—but I will seek to discuss briefly at least some of the responses that might conceivably be thought similar to my own, in order to explain how I think my own approach succeeds in avoiding the difficulties that have dogged certain others, and why.

Most commentators concede, I think, that Gunnar cannot do other than shoot Ridley under the circumstances imagined. Let us agree, then, that he lacks the power to *avoid* shooting Ridley. But the intuition that there is nevertheless *something* important that Gunnar could have avoided doing in the Frankfurt-style situation in which he finds himself is, I think, one that is both powerful and quite widespread. The difficulty is, though, to say what this something important is that he could have avoided. One quite natural first thought is that though Gunnar lacked the general power not to have shot Ridley, he retains the power not to have shot Ridley *at t*, the precise time at which he did in fact shoot him, and that it is this power that it is necessary for him to have if he is to be morally responsible for the shooting.[11] But this response, though I believe it represents an attempt to capture something that is important about Gunnar's situation, does not succeed by itself. A symptom of its failure is the fact that it appears to be vulnerable to further, more ingenious styles of counterexample. Mele and Robb, for instance, have constructed Frankfurt-style examples on a model that seems to enable us to construct a case in which Gunnar lacks the power even to avoid shooting Ridley *at t*, the very time at which he actually shoots Ridley, although he remains the morally responsible agent of the actual shooting.[12] Here is their example:

At t_1, Black initiates a certain deterministic process P in Bob's brain with the intention of thereby causing Bob to decide at t_2 (an hour later, say) to steal Ann's car. The process, which is screened off from Bob's consciousness, will deterministically culminate in Bob's deciding at t_2 to steal Ann's car unless he decides on his own at t_2 to steal it or is incapable at t_2 of making a decision (because, for example, he is dead by t_2)…The process is in no way sensitive to any "sign" of what Bob will decide. As it happens, at t_2 Bob decides on his own to steal the car, on the basis of his own indeterministic deliberation about whether to steal it, and the decision has no deterministic cause. But if he had not just then decided on his own to steal it, P would have deterministically issued, at t_2, in his deciding to steal it.[13]

But if such a case as this is possible, then it looks, on the face of it, as though Bob could not have done other that decide *at t_2* to steal Ann's car, where t_2 is the time of the actual decision. Yet given that he decides by means of the usual indeterministic decision-making process he always employs when deciding such things, it might seem plausible, nevertheless, that he ought to be held morally responsible for deciding at t_2 to steal it. In which case, it must be possible to be morally responsible for φ-ing at t, even though one could not have done otherwise at t.

It might be doubted, of course, whether it is possible for there to be such a mechanism as P. How could it work? But Mele and Robb's explanation of how we might conceive of such a mechanism is, I think, persuasive. They offer the following description of a machine that produces artistic widgets in order to help explain how the interaction between P and Bob's own decision-making process might be imagined to operate:

The colors of the widgets produced are determined by the color of a ball bearing (bb) that hits the machine receptor at a relevant time. The machine M is surrounded by several automatic bb guns,

---

[11] See Ginet (1996) for a response of this general kind.
[12] Mele and Robb (1998).
[13] Mele and Robb (1998: 101–2).

each containing bbs of relevant colors.....First, if a bb of color x hits M's receptor, and M is not already in the process of making a widget, M at once starts a process designed to result in the production of an x colored widget. Second, because two or more bbs sometimes hit the receptor simultaneously, the artist has designed his machine in such a way that whenever this happens (while M is not busy making a widget) M at once starts a process designed to result in the production of a widget the color of the rightmost bb...

Bob is analogous to M in an important respect. He is physically and psychologically so constituted that if an unconscious deterministic process in his brain and an indeterministic decision-making process of his were to 'coincide' at the moment of decision, he would indeterministically decide 'on his own' and the deterministic process would have no effect on his decision.[14]

With this model in mind, it seems we no longer have any motive for insisting that there is no way of understanding how P could have managed to bring about a decision of Bob's at the very time t_2 at which he actually decides to shoot Ridley by another means. It appears that there could be a mechanism that might intervene should Bob refrain from making the decision in the normal way at t_2, and which would, had it thus intervened, have culminated in an event that would have occurred at the very same time at which Bob in fact decides to shoot Ridley.

I do not think, then, that there is much doubt about the coherence of the idea that there might be a failsafe mechanism which, were it to function, would produce an event that occurred at exactly the time at which the relevant *actual* action occurs. It might be plausibly maintained, though, that there is a more serious worry about Mele and Robb's example. One crucial question is whether anything brought about by a process such as P could really count as a *decision* on the part of Bob. It is simply assumed by Mele and Robb that it is not problematic to suppose that Bob could have been accurately described in the alternative scenario in which P proceeds to its culmination as someone who had decided to shoot Ridley. However, this seems far from obvious. Decisions (unlike, for example, shootings) seem *essentially* to be actions: one cannot decide something without being the decider, the agent of the decision. One cannot decide unintentionally, for example.[15] But when process P culminates in Bob's so-called 'decision', Bob seems to have had nothing whatever to do with the resulting event (except that he has, by refraining from thus deciding 'on his own', inadvertently permitted it to occur). The occurrence of this 'decision' in him, because brought about by a process over which he has no control, seems to be just that: an occurrence *in him* not a decision *by him*. It was not the consequence, for example, of any deliberation on the part of Bob and presumably bore none of the normal sorts of relationship to such

[14] Mele and Robb (1998: 103–4).

[15] Of course, I might decide to wreak revenge on my father's killer not realizing that my father's killer is my mother. One might then say (I suppose) that I had unintentionally decided to wreak revenge on my mother. But (a) this does not seem to me to be a very natural thing to say in any case; and, more importantly (b) the fact remains that anything that is a decision has to be intentional under *some* description. But this is not true of anything that is a shooting or a kicking or a moving or a touching or a pushing ...

things as his emotional state, the content of prior imaginings, etc. Its causal source, indeed, seems to have had nothing to do with him at all, except that some important parts of the process are located within his skin. Why, then, agree that what has occurred is anything that merits description as a decision, on the part of Bob, to steal Ann's car?

Someone might think that it must be possible for Black to ensure that the event produced by process P would be neurologically similar to the events that realize decisions in more usual sorts of case, and that this might be enough to ground the judgement that the event thus produced was indeed a decision. However, this claim is highly tendentious. Even supposing that every token decision is a physical event, it does not follow that one can give sufficient conditions of a purely intrinsic neurological kind for the occurrence of a decision. One must surely respect the conceptual point that in order to count as a decision an event must bear a certain relation to the agent: it must be *the agent's* deciding something. But how could something that was genuinely *the agent's* deciding something be produced deterministically from without, as it were, by another agent in such a way that the first agent has no knowledgeable control whatever over whether it occurs or not? However neurologically similar the resultant event might be to one of Bob's usual decisions, if the unfolding of process P that deterministically produces it is not under his control, then it is hard to see why anyone would want to call the product of the process his 'decision'. I shall say more in Chapter 8 about how I conceive of the relationship between the agent herself and the neural processes productive of the movements and changes that constitute her actions. This will make my views on these questions more perspicuous. For now, though, having explained why I find Mele and Robb's own example unconvincing, I shall leave the point to one side, since I think the issue turns out to be irrelevant to the current question whether Frankfurt cases can be successfully devised that show that an agent may φ at *t* and thereby perform an action, even though she could not have avoided φ-ing at *t*.

I have said that I am not inclined to grant that Mele and Robb's example shows that Bob could not have done other than decide to steal Ann's car at t_2. But the specific difficulty I have highlighted is generated specifically by their focus on an action which is a *decision*. Our original question, recall, was whether Gunnar might have lacked the power not to shoot Ridley at t_2, a question that does not relate, as the case considered by Mele and Robb relates, specifically to a φ-ing which is a deciding. There seems no reason, therefore, why we could not construct a case having the Mele–Robb sort of structure in which the thing that results either from Gunnar's own agency in the actual case, or from process P in the counterfactual case, is simply *Gunnar's shooting Ridley at t_2*. In this case, the objection I raised above would not apply since there is no obstacle to supposing that Gunnar might have shot Ridley at t_2 and yet in such a way that no action of his occurred: it is perfectly possible for there to be shootings that are not actions. But if we were to proceed in this way, we would have constructed an example in which Gunnar lacks the power not to shoot Ridley at t_2, despite having been the agent of the actual shooting. If such examples can indeed be constructed, the power not to have φ-ed at the precise time at which one actually φ-s cannot be a necessary condition of that φ-ing being an action; for it appears that one may be the agent of a genuine action despite not possessing this power. What the possibility of this kind of example reveals, it seems to me, is that the *specificity that* philosophers such as Ginet sought to light upon in considering what Gunnar might have been able to avoid, cannot be introduced by means of times alone. I shall shortly make a different suggestion as to how to introduce it.

However, the point I have just made about the crucial difference between decisions on the one hand, and events such as shootings on the other, leads very naturally to a new thought about how one might try to specify the crucial power of avoidance that is essential to agency. For the possibility of constructing the sort of counterexample I have just considered (and its invulnerability to the worry that arose in the case of Mele and Robb's own example, where the action in question was a decision) turns on the fact that many verbs that can be used to ascribe actions to agents need not be used to do so. 'Shoot' is a good example. I can shoot you quite unintentionally, for instance, by dropping my gun accidentally so that it discharges in your direction. It may be misleading in such circumstances to say that I have shot you, but there seems no reason to insist that it is false. Indeed, I might say things such as that I am sorry that I shot you, I might try to make amends for having shot you or wish that I had not shot you, and so on. Now, it might be said that Frankfurt-style examples simply exploit the fact that we often ascribe actions to agents by means of such verbs. This means that where 'φ' is a verb of the relevant sort, 'S φ-ed' can be true both in the actual and in the counterfactual scenario, even though no true *action* is performed by S in the latter case. For example, in the case in which Cosser intervenes neurologically to see to it that Gunnar shoots Ridley, though Gunnar does indeed shoot Ridley it might surely be denied that he *performed an action of shooting Ridley*, since the shooting does not appear in the counterfactual scenario to have been originated by Gunnar at all, but rather by Cosser. Note that it is not sufficient to meet this point to insist that Cosser can ensure that the shooting is caused by the formation of an intention or a decision, which was in turn produced by an 'irresistible desire' or some such, and so that in virtue of this causal ancestry it *must* be a true action. This claim simply raises the question considered earlier, namely by what right it has been assumed that any events produced by Cosser in such a way that Gunnar has no opportunity to control their production could possibly count as formations of intentions or decisions on the part of Gunnar. But if this is right, then it suggests that we might try to argue that the crucial power possessed by Gunnar is *the power not to have performed an action of shooting Ridley*, a power we might be able to insist that he retains in the Frankfurt-style cases, if it is possible to maintain that he does not perform an action at all when Cosser makes his intervention. We could, if we liked, introduce a subscript '$_A$' for use with the verb 'shoot', to indicate that the shooting was what we might call an 'active' shooting, one that consisted in the performance of an action by an agent. We could then say that the power possessed by Gunnar, and which is essential to his having been the agent of the actual shooting, is the power not to have shot$_A$ Ridley.

A strategy based on this sort of idea is suggested by Maria Alvarez.[16] On her view, Frankfurt-style cases all require a counterfactual mechanism that *could* cause an agent to perform an action that he cannot avoid performing. She argues that given our concept of what it is for someone to act, this requirement is inconsistent. In support of her view, she quotes this remark from Geach:

> If some action on a man's part is wholly determined by (...) events and circumstances in the world over which the 'agent' had no control, then it is quite inappropriate to call him an agent or to hold him responsible for his 'actions'.[17]

Now, Alvarez is obviously right, I think, that there is something deeply problematic about the general idea that the Frankfurt examples seek to exploit that one agent can make another perform an action in such a way that the second agent could not have avoided performing that action. I think her argument does indeed show that Frankfurt-style examples cannot succeed for this reason. But despite my great sympathy for the line she takes here, I still do not think it is safe to conclude that the power not to have shot$_A$ Ridley, or even the power not to have shot$_A$ Ridley at t (though indeed Gunnar has both these powers), is necessary to his having performed an action. This is because, for reasons that have nothing to do with Frankfurt-style examples, these sorts of powers *still* seem to me to be powers that one could conceivably lack whilst remaining the agent of an action.

Some of the examples that seem to me to show that this is so are considered by Alvarez. The cases in question are cases of, for example, obsessive-compulsive behaviour or addiction, which Alvarez imagines being put forward as examples of cases in which the agent acts, even though she could not have done other than perform an action of the relevant type at the appropriate time (and therefore as possible counter-examples to her view). Alvarez comments, rightly, that:

> ...it is not clear that the examples...are really actions that are 'unavoidable' in the required sense. In the case of obsessive-compulsive behaviour, such as compulsive washing, counting, etc, the truth seems to be that, for any particular occasion, the agent can avoid acting. The compulsion, such as it is, lies not so much in each action, but in a pattern of irrational, because unnecessary or harmful, repetition.[18]

But though Alvarez is doubtless correct to point out that the phenomenon of compulsive behaviour is wrongly conceived of in general if it is thought of as involving the occurrence of a succession of strictly unavoidable particular 'actions', it does not seem to me impossible to imagine that there might be a particular compulsive action such that the agent could not have refrained from performing an action of that type (washing her hands, say) at the very moment at which she performs that action, and

---

[16] Alvarez (2009).   [17] Geach (2000: 80).   [18] Alvarez (2009: 73).

yet such that it remained clear that the action *was* an action. Suppose, for example, that one was a compulsive hand-washer. One might be able to hold out for a while, resisting the temptation to wash one's hands. But might there not come a point at which one was strained to breaking point, at which one simply *had* to wash one's hands and could not leave it another moment? Might it not be tempting to say that one could not have done other than wash one's hands at that moment? I do not know whether in fact compulsive handwashers would ever be inclined to describe themselves as quite so powerless in the face of their compulsion as this description suggests, but in fact I am not sure that it matters whether or not they would do so. What seems important is that there seems no reason to think that there *could* not be cases of compulsion in respect of which this description—that the agent could not have done other than φ compulsively at that very moment—was accurate. Nevertheless, it seems to me that the agent under such circumstances really could be the agent of something that really is an action. What makes me inclined to say so is the fact that, even when in the grip of the compulsion, she retains a range of (admittedly minimal) freedoms to act in one way rather than another. She can wash with soap or not, with hot water or cold, for one minute or a bit longer, just the hands or up to the elbows, rolling up one's sleeves or not, moving one's hands in this way or that way, etc. If all of these things are up to her, it seems to me clear that in the hand-washing that results, we have an instance of agency, notwithstanding the fact that the agent could not have refrained from performing a hand-washing action at t.[19] It is these elements of controlledness within the generally restrictive framework imposed by the compulsion that seem to me to make it unarguable that the compulsive washer really *is* the agent of these actions, though no doubt a severely compromised one.

Other possible cases might be provided by examples of what Frankfurt has called 'volitional necessity'.[20] Suppose I am outside a house that I am told is going to explode within three minutes and that I know that my children are inside. Might I not be truly incapable, under such circumstances, of waiting, even for a moment, before dashing in to try to find them? It doesn't seem to me obvious that this description *has* to be inaccurate. But when I run into the burning house I am surely the agent of an action. Though perhaps there is no possibility whatever (short of the occurrence of catastrophes beyond my control, such as my being struck down by a heart attack) that I will not go in to attempt to rescue my children, nor even any possibility that I will not do so there and then, it remains for me to settle all the details of my rescue attempt: do I call out to them from the doorway or run from room to room searching? Do I first search upstairs or downstairs, etc.? Though it is doubtless highly unusual, then, I do not see why there could not be occasions on which I φ_A at t, even though, due to some

---

[19] Of course, there may be cases in which some or all of these details are also fixed by the nature of the compulsion. My claim is only that where at least some of them remain to be settled by the agent, we have a case of action.

[20] See Frankfurt (1982: 86).

addiction or compulsion or volitional necessity, I really could not have refrained from φ_A-ing at t.

Have we reached the end of the line, then, for the idea that acting requires some kind of power to refrain? We have not; on the contrary, the cases we have been considering simply serve to make it clear how to characterize the relevant alternative possibilities. What seems to be utterly crucial, what cannot be entirely imagined away without imagining away agency itself, are the powers of organization and ordering one possesses in the service of one's ends (however unfree one may be with respect to the question how those ends themselves come to be established), of the movements and changes in one's body, the production of which constitutes one's activity. It seems that the possession and exercise of at least *some* such power is necessary for the occurrence of an action. Suppose, for example, that, qua compulsive washer, I could do absolutely none of the following: *stop* washing if the situation suddenly demanded it (e.g. if set upon by a vicious dog), *change* the direction in which my hands rotate, *slow down or speed up* the motions in question, move my hands from under the hot tap when it becomes too hot, turn the tap in the appropriate direction if the water is coming out too forcefully or not forcefully enough, etc. If I simply possessed none of these powers to settle the particular details of the action I execute, I simply could not be said to be its agent at all. My 'action' would thereby be revealed to be no production of mine, but rather of some sort of complex automotive mechanism, not something in which I exert my powers to settle how things will be with respect to a certain part of the world in the service of my ends. The alternative possibilities one needs for action are ones deriving from the necessity, if one is to be an agent, of having power over one's own body: of having the power, in respect of at least some of the particular movings of limbs, digits, or other changes in one's bodily state that constitute one's φ-ing, not to have made those very movements or changes. This implies that even if one is in circumstances such that one cannot refrain from making *some* movements and changes of the sort that go to constitute an action of type φ (because, for example, of some addiction or compulsion or volitional necessity), one always has the power not to make the very ones one in fact makes at the very times at which one makes them, provided one is genuinely acting in the first place. The truth about the relation between agency and alternative possibility is therefore not the simple one that in order for a given φ-ing to count as one's action one has to have been able not to φ. It is the more complex one that in order for a given φ-ing to count as one's action, the φ-ing in question has to have *some* description as a V-ing, say, (e.g. as a moving by S of S's body in precise manner M) such that the agent was able not to V. Let us say that if an agent can be said to have possessed such a power in respect of some given φ-ing of hers, that she possessed a *relevant refrainment power* (RRP) with respect to that action.

Couldn't Frankfurt cases be imagined in which the counterfactual intervener can ensure that one moves one's body in the very way in which one moves it in the actual situation, and so that there is *no* description of one's action as a V-ing from which one could have refrained? They cannot, for the reason highlighted by Alvarez. Cosser might be able to produce the relevant bodily movements₁ but he cannot bring it about that *Gunnar* moves his body in such and such particular ways. Cosser can bring about motions, but he cannot bring about movings-by-Gunnar that are actions. Neural chains that are deterministically initiated from outside the agent and which remain, once initiated, invulnerable to agential control, cannot constitute the actions of that agent. Of course, Cosser's neurological device might be such as to leave many details genuinely up to Gunnar. For example, if Cosser's device simply produces in Gunnar a very strong desire to shoot Ridley, but it remains up to Gunnar to decide on the particular plan by means of which the shooting is to be carried out or which weapon to choose, etc., then perhaps we *could* say that Cosser has caused Gunnar to shoot$_A$ Ridley, though we would likely add that the action in question was not one for which Gunnar has moral responsibility, rather as we might regard the actions of addicts, phobics, etc. But a case like this is not a counterexample to the general principle that action requires the possession of an RRP, since under *these* circumstances, Gunnar still possesses such a power: he has the freedom to settle the details of the movements by means of which the shooting will be effected. On the other hand, if instead the device produces in Gunnar not only a strong desire to shoot Ridley but also produces and controls the many subsidiary intentions and subsequent movements by means of which the shooting is to be accomplished ('I will wait for him after dark in the alley behind his workplace concealed by my black cloak, I will take the Colt 45, I will walk precisely *thus* six paces to the left...'), then we should say that 'Gunnar shot Ridley' does not report the occurrence of any action of Gunnar's at all.[21] What we *cannot* do, I claim, is construct a case such that Gunnar *acts* in the counterfactual scenario and yet which is also such that Gunnar lacks, as he acts, any RRP at all.

Might there be (i) agents so constrained by such things as physical disability and (ii) actions (φ-ings) so simple to execute that there might be only a single bodily means of carrying out one of these simple actions for such agents?[22] If there were, and if such agents might be under the sort of compulsion to φ that I imagined our compulsive handwasher to be under, such that at a particular time t the agent cannot any longer resist φ-ing, might this not constitute an example of a genuine action concerning which the agent possessed no RRP whatever? Imagine, for example, an agent with extremely severe arthritis who presses a button at t. Might it be that such an agent could not have moved her body (owing to the constraints placed upon her by the arthritis) in such a way as to succeed in pressing the button in any way other than the precise way in which it in fact moved? Now additionally suppose that this agent was also subject to a compulsion to press the button at the very time at which she did in fact press it? I think it is in fact very hard indeed properly to imagine an agent subject to such strict constraints as this example is attempting to impose: an agent who genuinely cannot

---

[21] See Alvarez (2009) for a similar argument.

[22] Thanks to Tim Williamson for originally suggesting that I needed to consider the possibility of such a case and to an anonymous reviewer for OUP for reminding me that I needed to do so.

hold back from the button pressing even for a second, even in emergency circumstances, and who could not have moved her finger, moreover, except in the precise spatiotemporal arc in which it in fact moved. However, I would maintain that if we really *do* manage to imagine an agent constrained in all these various ways, we have imagined someone who has not, in this instance, acted. The agent literally cannot prevent the movement of her finger for another second, so the initiation of the action is not up to her. Moreover, we must imagine, if we are to imagine away all RRPs, that she cannot stop the motion once it has begun, even if (for example) threatened with a gun. In addition, she has no means whatever by which to guide and control her finger once its motion is initiated, any more than I can guide and control what happens to my leg when it is hit by a hammer just below the knee and I experience a reflex jerk. In what sense, then, is this agent the agent of an action? Everything that happens is dictated by the occurrence of processes that she is entirely unable to veto, suspend, or otherwise control or alter. That, according to the Agency Incompatibilist, is as much as to say that she does not act, for there is nothing whatever that she truly settles; neither whether, nor when, nor where, nor how she will press the button. And if she settles none of these things, her pressing of the button cannot have been an action.

It might be thought that a Frankfurt-style example of a somewhat different sort might provide a challenge to the suggestion that an agent must have been in possession of at least one RRP with respect to anything that is genuinely to count as an action. Fischer suggests in his (1999) that so-called 'blockage' cases, such as that offered by Hunt in his (2000), may serve to show that there are cases in which an agent remains morally responsible for his action even though he could not have done other than perform that very action. One might think that similar sorts of cases could be used to show that an agent can perform an action though lacking any RRPs with respect to it. In Hunt's example, the actual series of Jones's mental states leading up to his murdering Smith is stipulated to be such that all the necessary conditions on his moral responsibility *other* than those that might pertain to alternative possibilities are met. However, a mechanism is in operation in Jones' brain that blocks neural pathways. Owing to what Hunt calls 'a fantastic coincidence', the pathways blocked by the mechanism on this particular occasion just happen to be all the ones that will be unactualized in any case, and the unique pathway that remains unblocked is precisely the route the man's thoughts would be following anyway. Under these conditions, Hunt claims, Jones appears to remain responsible for his thought and actions, even though he could not have refrained from performing an action having precisely the character and qualities of the one he does in fact perform, owing to the blockage.

Hunt does not tell us whether it is within Jones' power to halt the progression of events along the pathway that leads to his murdering Smith, a power which, one might think, might constitute an RRP with respect to the action he does in fact perform, even if, owing to the blockage, there is nothing else he can do instead. Others who have tried to utilize comparable sorts of case have said more about this. For example, Pereboom's version specifies that 'it is causally determined that she (the agent) remain a living agent, and if she remains a living agent, some neural pathway has to be used'.[23] One might think of responding to the Hunt case, then, by insisting that Pereboom's additional condition renders the pathway a compelled sequence that could not constitute an action, and that if it is lifted it is no longer obvious that Jones lacks an RRP. It might, of course, be asked why a sequence that constitutes an action in the ordinary 'unblocked' sort of case should fail to constitute one when other alternatives are blocked, given that, by hypothesis, the unavailability of the various 'blocked' pathways makes no difference to which sequence occurs. But this question betrays adherence to a particular way of thinking about the relation between neural sequence and action that can be questioned. The thought behind Hunt's example (and also, incidentally, behind Fischer's frequent observation that it is the *actual* sequence that matters) is that *what actually happens* is one thing, and *what might have happened* is simply another. Fiddling with one's answer to the modal question asked of a given 'sequence' what alternative possibilities were around at the time of its occurrence should, therefore, make no difference to the question asked of the sequence, *what actually happened* when it occurred. Thus, on the view being presupposed, we can hold the neural sequence fixed, close off possibilities that were formerly open, but still be sure we have the same 'sequence' and so still be sure we have the same action.

However, we cannot be sure we have the same action, for we cannot be sure we have an action at all. As I have already suggested, it is not obvious that actions can simply be identified with localized neural sequences, any more than it is obvious that substances can be identified with the portions of matter that go to make them up. If there are to be actions, a context must be presupposed in which there is a particular sort of performance by an *agent*, and the existence of agents might bear quite complex relationships to the availability of certain possibilities. One might, for instance, insist that part of what is involved in the occurrence of an action is a context in which an agent may be sensibly regarded as having an ongoing *capacity* to do such things as hold up, reverse, or alter the direction and speed of the bodily movement that constitutes the effect of that action, in response to any of a variety of factors or indeed just because she feels like it. It is not obvious that such a capacity could be attributed to any agent whose brain was suffering from the sort of 'blockage' Hunt envisages. Thus, even if a neural sequence were to occur that was identical in all its details to the sequence that occurs in the case that Hunt refers to as the one that 'would have happened anyway', it might still be argued that the sequence did not on that occasion constitute an action, because crucial modal facts had been altered that no longer supported the characterization of the sequence as the production of an agent. The correct response to Fischer's insistence that it is surely the actual sequence that matters is therefore this: to be sure, but what happens in the actual sequence may not be independent of what powers are exercised there.

---

[23] Pereboom (2001: 16).

The entanglement of modality with the characterization of actuality is, after all, not an unfamiliar phenomenon in philosophy. Where substances are concerned we are used to the entanglement. Suppose one is told to imagine a world that is just like the actual world, except that in the imagined world Tony Blair could have turned into a teapot at any time. Everything *actual*, we are assured, is just the same, and Tony Blair never in fact turns into a teapot. We are only to imagine a world in which it is true that he *could have done*. It is only a *modal* fact that is different. But it is likely immediately to be objected to the coherence of this world-description that, the modal facts having been tampered with in this way, we no longer have something that counts as a world that contains Tony Blair at all. For surely anything capable of turning into a teapot at any moment could not actually be Tony Blair; Tony Blair, one might think, is essentially a human being, and nothing that is essentially a human being is capable of turning into a teapot at any moment. In this case, tampering with the modal facts is enough to alter the intrinsic description we are prepared to supply of the world itself. The lesson is that what can be conceived of as existing in a world is simply not independent of what can happen there.

The same may be true, I should like to suggest, when it comes to considering whether actions exist in Hunt's blocked scenario. Tampering with the available alternate possibilities may affect the question whether something that is genuinely *the action of an agent* may be said to have occurred or not, in a given imaginary case. That Hunt's 'blocked' brain can constitute the brain of an *agent* (at the times at which it is thus blocked) is doubtful, because agents are essentially characterized by their *capacities*, and these have been changed. It is doubtful too, therefore, whether events that are caused by the activity that goes on within the blocked brain can count as the actions of an agent, under those circumstances.

I conclude, then, that an action has occurred only if its agent possessed an RRP in respect of that action. But someone might worry that it is much too easy to possess an RRP and so that an account of action that makes RRPs central embraces alternate possibilities of a sort that are in some way too flimsy or insufficiently 'robust' to do the philosophical work required of them. I want to turn now to respond to that objection by explaining exactly what work my account requires RRPs to do. I shall argue that the role played by these powers in my account is quite different from the role that alternative possibilities are usually expected to play in the accounts of moral responsibility in which they are usually invoked, and that this enables me to escape objections that are often levelled at attempts to defend PAP that might appear, in some ways, to be similar to the account I have offered.

7.3 Refrainment and robustness

The idea that the alternate possibilities condition on free and morally responsible action might be maintained in the face of Frankfurt-style examples, provided it is characterized a little differently from the way it is characterized by Frankfurt's version of PAP, has been made in the literature several times. Van Inwagen, for example, has suggested that though Frankfurtian agents may not be able to avoid bringing about certain *types* of consequence (e.g. 'that Ridley dies'), they might nevertheless retain the power to prevent the *particular* consequences they in fact produce (e.g. the (actual) death of Ridley).[24] Widerker has argued, with respect to Frankfurt's original example in which the action Jones performs is a killing of Smith at a time t_3, that 'though... Jones cannot (at t_1) prevent Smith's death, and cannot avoid exemplifying the property of killing Smith at t_3, he nevertheless can avoid the performance of his *actual* act of killing Smith, or can bring about the non-occurrence of that act'.[25] McKenna makes a similar point in his (1997) when he alleges that 'For each putative counter-example to PAP, the advocate of PAP will argue that indeed there is something which the agent could not have brought about (the act-type); however, in each case there exists something... which the agent could have avoided (the act-token) and that is what explains why we are willing to hold a person responsible in these kinds of cases'.[26]

In some ways, my account has things in common with these suggestions that we should move to focus on *token* actions rather than on types in formulating the alternate possibilities condition, since it rests on the thought that even though the agent might not have been able not to perform an action of type φ on a given occasion her token action might have had *some* description—as a V-ing, say—such that she was able not to V, and that provided this is the case, an instance of action has occurred. There is, then, a focus in my account on the *particular action* viewed as a process of which multiple characterizations can be given, just as there is in these other accounts. However, these sorts of response to Frankfurt-style examples have tended to meet with scepticism in the literature and I think it might be thought that an account such as the one I have suggested might fall to the same sorts of worries. There are, I think, three main difficulties one might have with the move from types to tokens. All of them could be (and have been) characterized as worries about the 'robustness' of the alternative that is represented by the possibility that the agent need not have performed the particular action she in fact performed (or brought about the particular consequence she in fact brought about). However, the worries, though related in various ways, are not the same, and I think it is worth distinguishing them from one another. In general, indeed, it seems to me that a number of rather different concerns have been gathered together under the umbrella of the so-called 'robustness' objection and that the running together of these various sources of unease has not been helpful. In what follows, therefore, I shall try to treat the three concerns as separately as their genuine inter-relatedness will allow.

[24] See his (1978) and (1983).   [25] Widerker (1995: 256).   [26] McKenna (1997: 73).

7.3.1 Robustness and the 'fairness' justification of PAP

The first worry stems from the thought that PAP as originally formulated by Frank-furt—that an agent is morally responsible for what she has done only if she could have done otherwise—ought to be thought of as a principle that is a kind of generalization of the ordinary moral intuitions pertaining to such things as excusability and desert, with which we find ourselves in particular cases. We tend, for example, to excuse those who do wrong when, as we say, they 'could not help it', whether because under the influence of some kind of mental illness, or addiction, or the threats and coercion of others. It is reasonable to think that whatever *prima facie* plausibility PAP might be thought to have must be rooted in such intuitions about the *unfairness* of blaming those who cannot help it (and perhaps also of praising those who could not have done otherwise).[27] Pereboom, for example, in endorsing some of what Fischer says about the need for alternative possibilities to be appropriately 'robust', suggests that any significant principle adverting to alternate possibilities should specify a necessary condition for moral responsibility that:

...plays a significant role in explaining why an agent is morally responsible. For if an agent is to be blameworthy for an action, it seems crucial that she could have done something to avoid being blameworthy—that she could have done something to get herself off the hook. If she is to be praiseworthy for an action, it seems important that she could have done something less admirable.[28]

But if we are operating with this conception of PAP and the source of its justification, it is going to seem beside the point to mention that even in circumstances in which we might be compelled to perform a certain type of morally praiseworthy or blameworthy action, we may retain our freedom to refrain from performing an action of *another* type instantiated by the particular action we in fact perform. For even if it is true that we retain such powers, they do not seem to be powers of the sort that could help explain *why* we are blameworthy or which could help somehow to underpin the praisewor-thiness of our actions. Indeed, the compromised agents who usually serve as illustra-tions of the *prima facie* plausibility of PAP generally possess RRPs in respect of the actions they perform. A heroin addict might be perfectly well able to inject heroin into her arm instead of into her leg at some time *t*, for instance; an alcoholic can pick up his whisky glass, perhaps, with his right hand or his left; someone who is being coerced into killing another person may be able to plan the details of the murder himself and have all sorts of forms of control over the precise details. One might think, then, that such RRPs as these are just not the sorts of power that PAP should be thought of as

---

[27] This is controversial. Many have argued that the situation with respect to blameworthiness and praiseworthiness is not symmetrical. See e.g. Wolf (1990) and Nelkin (2008). I do not enter this controversy here.

[28] Pereboom (2001: 1).

concerned with; they are simply too unimportant and flimsy to serve as the basis for any plausible moral principle relating responsibility to the power to do otherwise.

I think it needs to be conceded that such RRPs as I have insisted are necessary for agency are not the sorts of powers whose presence tends to render an agent responsible for what they have done; they are present in all sorts of cases in which we would not regard the agent as morally responsible including, I would want to insist, cases of animal action. But of course it must be remembered that PAP purports to offer only a *necessary* and not a sufficient condition of moral responsibility. Thus even if one thought of interpreting that principle in such a way that the alternate possibilities to which it alludes related to RRPs, addicts and compulsives would certainly not constitute any kind of *counterexample* to the principle, thus interpreted, for we could agree that the possession of such an RRP is only necessary and by no means *sufficient* for the agent to be accounted morally responsible. Nevertheless, many have argued that any defence of PAP against Frankfurt-style counterexamples ought to enable us to see how it is in virtue of having the alternative possibilities it is alleged she retains, that the agent counts as morally responsible for what she does. This is what might be thought puzzling if the alternative possibilities in question are merely the sorts of RRPs I have suggested. How could the fact that an agent need not have moved in precisely the way she did in fact move, for instance, be morally relevant in any way to the question whether she is morally responsible for what she in fact does? How could the fact (for example) that I could have moved my arm a bit more slowly (say) when I injected the heroin have anything to do with whether or not I am morally responsible for injecting it? Even if it is agreed that an agent in a Frankfurt-style situation does indeed have such RRPs then, it will be said that the possibilities they open up would be too exiguous and insufficiently robust to be the basis of a plausible principle of alternate possibilities.

This worry, however, depends upon a certain conception of PAP and, in particular, on a certain conception of the source of its *prima facie* plausibility. Mostly, PAP has been seen in the literature as a principle that encodes certain of our moral intuitions about *fairness*, in particular, the thought that it is unfair to blame someone if they could not have done anything other than they did. But one need not think of PAP as justified in this way. Intuitions about fairness provide *one* way of connecting moral responsibility with the power to do otherwise; but it is intuitions about *agency* with which I am concerned in this book. These intuitions, I maintain, provide another, quite different means of justifying PAP, conceived of merely as a specification of an important *necessary* condition on moral responsibility. The reason, one might argue, why it is a necessary condition of someone's being morally responsible for something they have done that certain alternate possibilities be available, is that having moral responsibility for something one has done depends upon one's having been an *agent* of the relevant doing in the first place.[29] For someone who supposes that agency requires alternate possibilities,

---

[29] Actually, the truth is somewhat more complex than this, since one can be responsible for doings that are not actions, for example when one spills something accidentally or trips in a case in which one could and

this will provide a second, quite distinct route to the *prima* facie justification of PAP: being morally responsible for something one has done normally requires having been the *agent* of the doing, and if having been the agent of the doing in turn requires alternate possibilities, then moral responsibility will require those alternate possibilities in its turn. However, once one thinks of PAP as justified in this different way—by appeal to considerations that have to do with *agency* rather than ones to do with fairness—it is no longer necessary to insist that the alternative possibilities that it is claimed are present in the Frankfurt situation must 'ground' the agent's moral responsibility in the way imagined by the person mounting the version of the robustness objection currently under consideration: by showing how having these alternative possibilities is connected with the blameworthiness (or praiseworthiness) of the agent. Indeed, it is perfectly possible for someone arguing in this way to accept that the moral of the Frankfurt cases is that PAP *cannot* be justified in this way; that is, in fact, what I myself believe them to show. It is necessary for us only to be able to see how having the alternative possibilities in question might help to ground the thought that the agent really *is* an agent in respect of the relevant action.

But this, I claim, we *can* see. That the agent has certain alternate possibilities at the time of action is essential to her being a *settler* of matters at the time of action. It is thus essential, on the view of agency developed here, to her being an agent at all. Amongst the most basic matters that one must be able to settle at the time of action are those pertaining to the position, speed, direction of movement, etc. of one's body and its parts. If one does not have any powers over the movements and changes that occur in one's body, one can certainly not claim to be an agent in respect of activity that depends on those movements and changes. So the condition that one can have acted only if one's action possesses a description as a V-ing such that one alternatively could have not V-ed is perfectly 'robust' enough to ground PAP once the *prima facie* justification of that principle is thought of in the way I am suggesting it should be thought of: as a justification based on the requirements of agency (which are, in their turn, requirements of moral responsibility).

I conclude, then, that this first version of the 'robustness' objection does not succeed. It is perfectly possible for the possession of an RRP to be a necessary condition of moral responsibility without its also *grounding* moral responsibility directly by means of some principle to do with fairness. The source of the justification of the relevant alternate possibilities principle relates rather to what is required for *agency*. Once this is regarded as its basis it is simply irrelevant to point out (correctly) that the possession of an RRP is both insufficient for moral responsibility and also unconnected with moral responsibility

---

should have avoided the spillage or the tripping by being more careful. But even in these cases, the attribution of responsibility seems to depend on its being possible to see the person as the *potential* agent of some *other* action: one performed with more care or attention, say.

in the way alternate possibilities have traditionally been supposed to be connected with it, by means of any principles that relate to fairness or blameworthiness.[30]

7.3.2 The agent acts unfreely in the alternative scenario

A second worry that has surfaced under the 'robustness' label (one which has been pressed in particular by Fischer) is that in Frankfurt-style scenarios, the particular action that is performed in the counterfactual scenario in which the intervener intervenes is not performed *freely*. It is therefore alleged that the fact that it could have been performed in place of the action that actually occurs seems not to represent the sort of alternate possibility through the possession of which the agent is helped to be morally responsible for what she does. Fischer insists that PAP gains whatever plausibility it has from the picture of reality as constituting a 'garden of forking paths' between which the agent can freely choose, but surely in that case it is most implausible that paths along which the agent *cannot* be said to act freely could help ground the agent's moral responsibility.

Consider, for example, Fischer and Ravizza's complaint about Van Inwagen's response to the original Frankfurt case,[31] a response that depends upon making a careful distinction between what Fischer and Ravizza call 'consequence-universals' and 'consequence-particulars'.[32] In the case being considered by Van Inwagen, which is the same as the one I discussed in Section 7.1, 'that Ridley is shot' and 'that Ridley is killed' would be relevant consequence-universals: they are *types* of thing that Gunnar in fact brings about but which might have been brought about in numerous different ways. However, 'Ridley's death' is a consequence-particular: a particular event that is the consequence of Gunnar's killing Ridley.

Van Inwagen's strategy is to suggest that although it is indeed true that Gunnar could not have done other than *kill Ridley*, it is not at all clear that he is responsible for *the fact that Ridley was killed*—for the consequence-universal. That, after all, is something he could not have avoided, so why should we regard it as his fault that it obtained? What he is responsible for is rather *the death of Ridley*, a particular event that, according to Van Inwagen, he *could* have prevented from happening. Thus, once the confusion between consequence-universals and consequence-particulars is resolved, there are no cases in which an agent is morally responsible for a consequence he could not have prevented from obtaining. PAP is in effect replaced by two more carefully worded principles (in fact, together with a third designed to deal with moral responsibility for omissions):

PPP1 (Principle of Possible Prevention 1): A person is morally responsible for a certain event-particular only if he could have prevented it.

PPP2 (Principle of Possible Prevention 2) A person is morally responsible for a certain state of affairs only if (that state of affairs obtains and) he could have prevented it from obtaining.

---

[30] For a more detailed and thorough elaboration of these points, see Steward (2009a).
[31] Van Inwagen (1978, 1983).   [32] Fischer and Ravizza (1998: Chapter 4).

It is alleged by Van Inwagen that Frankfurt-style examples do nothing to impugn either of these principles.

Fischer and Ravizza dub this strategy 'Divide and Conquer', and they are doubtful about its credibility, placing it in the more general category of 'flicker' strategies: responses to Frankfurt-style examples that highlight alternative possibilities that do indeed seem to remain available under the constraints imposed by a Frankfurt case but which are alleged to be insufficiently 'robust' to ground moral responsibility. For present purposes, I shall focus on what Fischer has to say about Van Inwagen's defence of PPP1. Fischer's worry is that although it may be perfectly true that an agent such as Gunnar could have prevented the occurrence of the particular consequence-particular he in fact brings about, this cannot be the sort of alternative possibility in virtue of which it would be right to hold him morally responsible for what he does. Fisher writes of an imaginary case in which Black, the nefarious neurosurgeon, intends to intervene to ensure that Jones votes for Clinton if he does not do so of his own accord:

> Briefly think about the basic picture of control that underlies the alternative-possibilities view (and thus the flicker of freedom strategy). Here the future is a garden of forking paths. At various points in life, it is envisaged that there are various paths that branch into the future, and one can determine which of these genuinely open pathways becomes the actual path of the future. The existence of *various* genuinely open pathways is alleged to be *crucial* to the idea that one has *control* of the relevant kind. But if this is so, I suggest that it would be very puzzling and unnatural to suppose that it is the existence of various alternative pathways along which one does *not* act freely that shows that one has control of the kind in question...even if it is granted that the terminus of the alternative sequence in the case of Jones and Black is a different event from the actual event of Jones' voting for Clinton, it also is evident that Jones would not be *freely* voting for Clinton in the alternative sequence.[33]

Now, it is true, of course, that Jones would not be freely voting for Clinton in the alternative sequence. Indeed, I would be inclined to go further than this and suggest that it is doubtful that he would be voting for Clinton *at all*, since it is arguable that voting is essentially an intentional action. It is most unclear that Black can arrange for Jones to perform an intentional action (though of course he can arrange for Jones to go through the motions of ticking a box on a ballot paper). But even if one was inclined to deny that voting needs to be intentional, it is certainly true that Jones does not perform an *action* of voting in the counterfactual scenario (even if he votes)—he does not vote$_A$, to use our earlier terminology—and so, *a fortiori*, he does not perform a free action. But this matters not at all to someone whose motivations in insisting on alternate possibilities are those of the Agency Incompatibilist. For her, it is simply not necessary in order for Jones to count as the agent of his action that a rich array of *other* free actions be available to him; that is not the point of insisting on alternate possibilities. It is not important to the Agency Incompatibilist that the agent could have done *otherwise*, if

---

[33] Fischer (1994: 140–1).

that is taken to imply that the agent requires the capacity to perform any of an array of alternative positive actions. All that is necessary, so far as the alternate possibilities required for agency are concerned, is that the agent's *actual* action be a non-compulsory exercise of power on his part. It is only in this way that we can understand his action *as* an action in the first place. A possible world in which Jones does *not* perform the actual action he in fact performs is therefore all we need: we do not need a variety of scenarios in which he does all sorts of *other* things. But this we have, even in a Frankfurt-style situation, provided it is plausible to maintain that the agent does *not* act in the counterfactual situation in which the intervener intervenes. For the possible world in which Jones refrains and thus triggers the intervention will be such a world.

Fischer is puzzled by what he sometimes calls the 'alchemy' involved in the idea that adding possibilities in which an agent does not act freely could transform a situation from one in which an agent does not have responsibility into one in which he does.[34] But the possibility on which the Agency Incompatibilist insists is not, as it were, a separate opportunity or set of opportunities that one 'adds' to what happens in the actual situation in order to ensure that the agent is wandering in a garden of forking paths. It is an opportunity intrinsic to her being an agent of an action in the first place: the opportunity not to exercise the agential powers she in fact exercises in acting. In a sense, indeed, I am at liberty to agree with Fischer in his often-made pronouncement that what matters for responsibility is only what happens in the *actual* sequence and that the existence of various counterfactually available paths is really neither here nor there. That, in a sense, is right: the only thing that matters is what is true of the actual situation, and what would have happened had things been different matters (for its own sake) not at all. But (to repeat a point made above in connection with the discussion of Hunt) it would be more accurate to put the point by saying that actual and counter-factual matters cannot be simply and clearly separated from one another in the way Fisher supposes. What is counterfactually possible matters to the question what *does* happen in the actual sequence, and in particular to the question whether what happens in the actual sequence is the occurrence of an *action* on the Frankfurtian agent's part. The relevant alternate possibility—that is, the possibility represented by the existence of an RRP—is needed not for its own sake, but rather to ensure that what happens in the actual sequence really is characterizable as an exercise of agency in the first place.

7.3.3 *Nothing should turn on abstruse issues concerning the cross-world identity of events*

Fischer has often made a third point in connection with strategies that seek to insist that, although there are types of things the agent cannot avoid doing, there are token events he could have avoided producing. This is that the question whether the agent was morally responsibile ends up turning, implausibly, on difficult metaphysical questions concerning the cross-world identification of events that nobody has any very clear

[34] Fischer (1994: 141).

idea how to answer. Van Inwagen ends up having to rely in his defence of PPP1, for example, on the claim that Ridley's actual death cannot be cross-world-identical with the death of Ridley that occurs when Cosser intervenes. Fischer points out that even if a case can be made for non-identity here, it seems strange that something so important as the question whether Gunnar is responsible for Ridley's death should end up turning on an abstruse metaphysical question (such as whether events have all their causes and effects essentially). But although my response to Frankfurt does depend on a claim about the non-identity of events that occur in the actual and the counterfactual scenario, the grounds on which the non-identity is claimed are neither abstruse nor intuitively irrelevant to the question whether the Frankfurtian agent is morally responsible for what she does. The ground for claiming non-identity is that what actually occurs is an action on the part of the Frankfurtian agent and what counterfactually occurs is not. The only principle relied upon is therefore the claim that no individual action could have had either a different agent or no agent at all. This seems to me quite self-evident, but even if it is not it is not a general metaphysical principle concerning event identity, but rather a principle that specifically concerns *actions* and the sorts of things they are. Even if it is not inconceivable that someone might think to try to challenge the claim, therefore, I think it is clear that the sorts of considerations that would arise in defending the claim are the very sorts of ideas and principles on which I have relied in general to construct my account of agency. So it would not seem strange in the least if those ideas and principles were to resurface in the defence of the claim that the Frankfurtian agent is morally responsible. There is no reliance on any abstruse point in metaphysics, only on a thought about what it takes for an action to occur, which is just as it should be.

I have argued then that the power one possesses in respect of those actions one performs, to have done things differently, in at least some respects, from the way in which one has in fact done them, is utterly crucial to our status as the agents of those actions. To be an agent, I claimed in Chapter 2, is to have the power to settle a variety of matters at the time of one's action and, in particular, matters pertaining to the movements and changes that occur in one's own body by virtue of which one is able to bring about further movements and changes in the world beyond it. I hope it is now clear how that claim is related to the specific version of the principle of alternate possibilities I have defended here. One cannot have this power to settle things if one lacks altogether any RRP in respect of one's particular action. There must always be *some* description of one's token action as a V-ing, say, (e.g. as a moving of one's limbs in this way rather than that) such that one had the power not to V. The supposition that there is no such description is inconsistent with the claim that one's action is a settling. And because all freedoms depend upon our capacity for agency, all freedoms depend upon our possession in respect of all our genuine actions of what I have called RRPs.

8

Agency, Substance Causation, and Top-Down Causation

'…the more the functions of an individual are connected with its organisation, the less is the empire of chemistry over them, and it becomes us to be cautious in the application of this science to all the phenomena which depend essentially upon the principles of life.'

(Chaptal, 1795: lx)

In this chapter, I shall be attempting finally to make good on a number of the promissory notes that have littered the discussions of previous chapters. There are, I think, two main tasks for this chapter to accomplish. The first is a properly philosophical task in metaphysics: to defend the view that one can make *sense* of the concept of agency that has been developed during the course of this book against those who would insist that it must ultimately founder on the shoals of metaphysical unintelligibility. That there will be such objectors I have little doubt, since in many ways my view has much in common with certain versions of the doctrine that has come to be known as *agent causationism*, a view that is widely held, even by some of its most understanding sympathizers,[1] to be exceedingly problematic in a number of important respects. I expect that some of those objections will be thought to apply also to my account of agency. In particular, I accept the agent causationist's insistence that it is utterly fundamental to any possible solution of the free will problem that we be able to find a proper place in our metaphysics for the causation of certain phenomena by *agents*, and not merely by events occurring within them, states of them, facts about them, etc. I also endorse the traditionally agent-causationist thought that it is the event-based metaphysics in terms of which we have come to think about the world in which we live and the engines of production and change within it, which is the most fundamental obstacle in the way of an acceptable solution to the free will problem. Worries about agent causationism that genuinely stem from these central ideas, then, will need to be properly addressed.

---

[1] I have in mind in particular both Bishop (1989) and Clarke (2003), both of whom give agent causationism a very serious run for its money before ultimately (and one senses, slightly reluctantly) rejecting it as unsustainable.

It needs also to be said that much confusion surrounds the notion of agent causation. Not all agent causationists agree with one another about the best way to formulate their fundamental insight, and some versions of the doctrine are unquestionably incoherent. Many agent causationists, moreover, merely reinforce what seems to me to be the mistaken idea that prevents an easy reception for their own views, namely that *regular* causation is always event causation and so agent causation is a relatively rare and exotic exception to the rules governing the world's normal causal functioning. Evidently, this is an unappealing thought for anyone remotely tempted by naturalistic views of human beings. Although it is true that human beings *are* exceptional creatures in all sorts of ways, so that one must not be *too* fearful of all versions of human exceptionalism, it might seem unlikely that their peculiarities include distinctive causal workings, utterly different in their metaphysical basics from any found elsewhere in the animal kingdom. Some work will need to be done, therefore, to distinguish viable from unsustainable versions of the agent-causationist view, before I move on to defend the conception of agent causation I rely upon against objections.

Key to this defence will be some important claims about the concept of causation itself. It is, I think, mainly because we do not understand causation properly and have accepted misleading models of the sort of thing it must be, that we have so much difficulty understanding how agents can be causes. Although there will not be space here to defend a full theory of causation in any detail, I shall describe the outlines of a view for which I have argued more detail thoroughly elsewhere, and try to show how it can help answer some of the worries that have often been raised about the coherence of the very idea of causation that is by a substance rather than an event or fact. I shall also make some suggestions about what has gone wrong with various aspects of our concept of causation that have been orthodox at least since Hume. I will try to show how rejecting these ideas can make the problems surrounding the metaphysics of agency more tractable.

Then, in the second half of the chapter, having made these metaphysical clarifications, I shall embark on the difficult work of trying to explain how the variety of agent causation I endorse (which I prefer simply to call *agency*) could possibly be instantiated in the natural world as our best science believes it to be. I am convinced that to solve the problems surrounding animal agency simply it is not enough to cast off mistaken theories of causation, although it is a good start and a necessary one. It needs also to be shown what real, biological processes might enable us to sustain the idea that an *animal* may be truly in charge of what it does, so that its actions are more than merely the by-product of the complex interaction of its innards and parts. That task requires some reflection on the organizational principles of living creatures, for it is only through such reflection, I think, that we can start to understand where the difference really lies between, on the one hand those things that are true agents, and, on the other, mere machines, entities that nothing will ever be up to, however impressive they may be.[2]

---

[2] Note: this does not imply that no artificially created being could ever be an agent. For we may work out one day how artificially to create something that is not a mere machine.

Scientific as well as philosophical expertise is really needed, I think, in order to make serious progress on these issues. But there are others with such expertise (from whose work I have learned much) currently also taking halting steps in similar directions.[3] I am exceedingly hopeful that the next few years will see the beginnings of a revolution in our conception of the human person, as philosophical and everyday conceptions of the scientific picture of the world are freed from outdated Newtonian ideas and begin to take more note, both of the complexities of science as it really is and of the undeniable fact of our animal nature.

I turn now to the business of clarifying the concept of agent causation.

8.1 Agent causation

Is the view of agency I wish to put forward a version of agent causationism? That depends what one supposes agent causationism to be. Agent causationism is quite often said to be the view that agents cause their actions,[4] but as I have already been at pains to stress, I regard this view as highly problematic. The claim that agents cause their actions simply raises the question: *how* do agents cause their actions? If the answer is: by *acting*, then clearly we are off on a regress. But if that is not the answer, then I concur with the opponents of this version of agent causationism in insisting that it is not clear what the answer could be. There *are*, of course, ways in which agents can cause things other than by acting. For example I can cause a vase to break by tripping over it accidentally, or cause you pain by neglecting you, or cause the oxygen in the room to be depleted by breathing it. But none of these could plausibly be an instance of the kind of causation we are after: the causation of *action* by the agent, were it to capture correctly what we generally take to be the agent's controlling and directive role in acting, would have surely to be a different sort of causation from any of these. Accidents, omissions, and involuntary movements could not possibly offer the right model of what is involved. Only action *itself* seems to have the requisite character.

This recognition, though, it seems to me, is the key to seeing what the agent causationist ought to say instead. What she should do is to *identify* actions with instances of agent causation. Actions should not be regarded by the agent causationist as things *caused* by exercises of agent causation; that just raises the issue what on earth exercises of agent causation are supposed to be (if they are not themselves actions). The question needs to be blocked before it can arise with the recognition that actions are themselves the *active* events in which we need to be interested; they are themselves exercises of agent causal power. Agent causation is needed not to characterize the role played by

---

[3] In particular, I have been helped to think about these issues by the work of Juarrero (2000) and Murphy and Brown (2007).

[4] Or perhaps more usually these days, that they cause their *decisions*. But decisions simply *are* (one kind of) actions, on my view, so everything I say about the agent causation of actions applies equally to the agent causation of decisions. I have already expressed and explained in Chapter 6 my discomfiture with the retreat from action to decisions as the locus of true agency.

the agent in causing her actions (for agents do not cause their actions); it is needed to characterize the role played by the agent *in acting*; that is to say, in bringing about the movements and changes in his or her own body in which acting normally consists. Actions are not caused by agents; instead, they are themselves agents' causings of movements and changes in their own bodies, movements and changes by means of bringing about which agents are able to bring about all kinds of other movements and changes in the world at large.[5]

With this clarification made, however, one might be forgiven at first for wondering what the big deal about agent causation is supposed to be. For there is in a sense, of course, nothing particularly interesting or controversial about the supposition that agents can cause things, including movements and changes in their own bodies. As Chisholm points out, if sentences like 'Jones killed his uncle' and 'Jones raised his arm' are sometimes true, as they surely are, that would seem to imply that agents can cause events and hence that there is agent causation.[6] 'Jones killed his uncle' for example, seems to imply that Jones caused the death of his uncle; 'Jones raised his arm' implies that the rising of Jones' arm was something that was caused by Jones. All languages contain some version of these causative forms, which are used to express the idea of one thing (not necessarily, but very often, an animal agent) causing something to do something or to be in a particular condition, different languages expressing the idea in different ways. One important class of English verbs for which a causative analysis is

---

[5] The negative point that actions must not be thought of as effects caused by agents has been very clearly recognized by many of those philosophers who have attempted to formulate sympathetic versions of agent causationism in recent years (though the precise details of their positive accounts differ in various respects). Bishop (1983: 71), for example, is clear that if there is to be an acceptable version of agent causationism, it cannot hold that actions are caused by agents: 'Since *what constitutes* a basic intentional action, on the agent-causalist view, is the obtaining of an agent–causal relation, the basic intentional action cannot *itself* be the object of this relation. The action *is* the existent relation and may not be collapsed into one of its terms'. O'Connor (1995: 182) is also very clear on the negative point ('...on the agency theory, rather than there being a causal relation between agent and action, the relational complex *constitutes* the action'). But the importance of the point for the coherence of agent causationism has not been universally accepted. Clarke, for example, appears to regard it as a matter of indifference for the agent causationist whether the agent is said to cause the action or whether the action is said itself to be the agent's causing of movements and changes, apparently because he regards this as a merely verbal question concerning how we are to employ the term 'action' (see his 2003: 25). But it is not a matter of indifference. I suppose that we could, if we wished, employ the term 'action' so as to refer to what I would regard rather as the *results* of actions: people's arms going up, their legs bending, their heads turning, etc. But then actions would no longer be *doings*; they would no longer, in fact, be the *locus* of agency at all. The *activeness* of actions would be lost; actions and *acting* would (confusingly) come apart. 'Action' would no longer be the term for an exercise of agency and all our philosophical interest in such exercises would therefore simply have to be recentred on the *actings* by means of which what we are now calling 'actions' are produced. But what would be the point of such a confusing stipulation? We need the concept of action in philosophy because we are interested in the events (or, better, processes) subsumed by words like 'raising', not because we are interested in the events subsumed by words like 'rising'; and it should be reserved for these interesting and special occurrences. The point, incidentally, that actions ought not to be regarded as things which are caused by agents is an old one, Suarez (1994 [1597]: 9), for instance, using the term 'efficient cause' in its Aristotelian sense, to refer to the substantial agent of a change, claims that 'the action is not the efficient cause's effect; instead it is the very nature of the causing...'.

[6] Chisholm (1976b: 199).

possible is the class I have already discussed in Section 2.2, in explaining Hornsby's important distinction between movements$_I$ and movements$_T$: those verbs that occur both transitively and intransitively, the two sorts of occurrence being systematically related to one another in that one may infer from a proposition of the form 'a V$_T$ b' one of the form 'b V$_I$'.[7] It is a widely accepted view that verbs such as these have a causal analysis: it is a necessary condition of the truth of 'a V$_T$-s b' that a cause b to V$_I$.[8] Many of these verbs, importantly, can be used to relate an agent to parts of her own body. 'Shake' for example, is in the relevant class of verbs: if John shook$_T$ his leg then John caused his leg to shake$_I$. So is 'turn': if Susan turned$_T$ her head then Susan caused her head to turn$_I$. Likewise, the more general verb 'move' evidently behaves in just the same sort of way: if Alf moved$_T$ his body or any part of his body then Alf caused his body to move$_I$. It is only a very short step from this admission (negotiable by the invocation of the general idea that the relevant verb predicates should be thought of as introducing implicit event ontology) to the view that there may be causal relations between agents and events. If Alf caused his body to move, then surely he caused an event that was a movement of his body?[9]

Many other transitive verbs also admit of causal analyses, though of somewhat different sorts. 'Knock', 'push', 'lift', and a range of other verbs occur in combination with objective complements[10] in such a way that the objective complement phrase describes the state of the object that results from the action performed. Thus we have, for example, 'John knocked the book on the floor', 'Sue pushed me downstairs', 'Chloe lifted the bowl onto the table'.[11] These, too, have causative implications, though in these cases what is caused is sometimes a state rather than an event, e.g. 'John knocked the book on the floor' implies 'John caused the book to be (or to fall) on the floor'; 'Sue pushed me downstairs' entails 'Sue caused me to be (or to move) downstairs', etc. Such grammatical facts as these suggest that 'cause' is really what Austin calls a 'dimension word'; that is to say 'the most general and comprehensive term in a whole group of terms of the same kind, terms that fulfil the same function'.[12] If one asks the question what that function might be, the answer appears to be that 'cause' is the general umbrella term for a range of transitive verbs that serve to specify the nature of an action brought to bear by an agent on a patient: an action that appears to involve the existence of a causal relation—between agents on the one hand and such

---

[7] Where a and b designate continuants, V$_T$ a transitive and V$_I$ an intransitive, verb.

[8] Hornsby says that this claim is more than three hundred years old, and that as far as she knows, it has never been questioned (see her 1980: 13). Her reference is to Wilkins (1668). Of course, neither I nor, I think, Hornsby, means to deny that many have supposed that 'a cause b to V$_I$' must be *further* analysable somehow in event-causal terms.

[9] That is, a movement$_I$ to use Hornsby's useful terminology. See Section 2.2.

[10] An objective complement is a word, phrase, or clause that follows a verb and gives more information about its object.

[11] See Aronson (1971) for an excellent discussion of these verbs.

[12] See Austin (1962: 71).

things as events or states on the other—the very relation in which agent causation is normally said to consist.

Of course, it will be insisted at this point by the proponent of universal event causation that one must move beyond the surface indicators of ordinary language to divine the underlying event-causal metaphysics in the causal transactions that are adverted to by such constructions. I shall come on to discuss in a moment the suggestion that such an event-causal metaphysics can always be discerned. Nevertheless, I should like to pause to point out before moving on how very important it is that these transitive verbs be clearly in view when one is discussing the role of agents in causation.[13] If one looks primarily to explicit occurrences of the word 'cause' for one's understanding of the sorts of things we regard as causes, one is likely, I think, to underestimate the importance of substances in our everyday causal thinking. For though we do sometimes speak explicitly of persons and physical objects as causes (e.g. 'The director was the cause of the company's downfall'), we are more likely to cite events (e.g. 'the cause of the village's destruction was the volcanic eruption') or facts (e.g. 'the cause of my lateness was the fact that my car wouldn't start') as causes, and are perhaps likely to think also that, insofar as we *do* mention substances as causes this is generally shorthand for a better and fuller explanation in terms of such things as events, facts, or properties (e.g. 'the director's *fraudulent activity* was the cause of the company's downfall'). But one might equally argue, in opposition to this view, that it is not in these relatively sophisticated and explicit explanatory usages of the concept of 'cause', but rather in the use of basic transitive verbs like 'turn', 'push', 'drag', 'open', etc., that we really find the heart of our concept of causality.[14] If we focus instead on these, the linguistic evidence for a serious everyday commitment to substance causation looks immediately far more significant. In these verbs, it might be claimed, we find clear evidence of a commonsense metaphysics that accords to substances, and especially agents, a capacity to wreak effects in the world. Once that is clearly established, the interesting question is no longer whether agents are generally thought by us to cause things; it seems clear that they are thought to do so and indeed perhaps that grammar reveals them to be amongst the causes *par excellence* of ordinary language.[15]

---

[13] Others who have made this point include Anscombe (1971), Aronson (1971), Harré and Madden (1975), and P. F. Strawson (1985).

[14] Why might one think that these verb usages were at the *heart* of our concept of causality? Apart from their very early acquisition (one can talk of pushing and pulling long before one can talk of causing) one might invoke the interesting idea that many abstract concepts (such as causation) are built on the cognitive foundations of concrete ones—see Lakoff and Johnson (1999). There is some evidence of this in the ease with which we adapt these transitive verbs to talk about non-mechanistic forms of causality, e.g. 'the economy was *shaken up* by the application of neo-conservative principles', 'What *turned* him against me?', 'These nations have been *held back* by corruption', etc.

[15] *Pace* Clarke, who writes 'Ordinary human agents, it seems plain, typically lack the concept of substance causation' (2003: 206).

What then *is* the interesting question on which agent causationists and others disagree? I think it is a bit more difficult to say than is sometimes assumed. The question is usually said to be the question of 'whether agent causation can be reduced to "event causation"'.[16] However, this just raises the question of what exactly it would be to 'reduce' agent causation to event causation. Chisholm suggests that such reduction would demand that we be able to convert statements such as 'Jones killed his uncle', 'without loss of meaning into a set of statements in which only events are said to be causes and no one of which presupposes that there is anything of which Jones may be said to be the cause'.[17] Now, it has become (for good reason) much less fashionable than once it was to suppose that metaphysical reductions must turn on the possibility of semantic ones. It might therefore seem desirable to try to find a different definition of what the reduction of agent causation to event causation demands; one that might look more acceptable in the light of developments in metaphysics since Chisholm first propounded his theory. Clarke suggests that what is necessary for a belief in agent causation is belief in the possibility of 'causation by an agent that does not consist at all in causation by events',[18] and perhaps it might be thought that this suggestion, with its reliance on the more metaphysical-sounding 'consists in' relation, would be adequate as a formulation of the agent causationist's view. But the trouble with this definition is that it makes no allowance for the fact that actions *themselves* are thought by many to be events (and certainly are more or less universally supposed to be such by those who believe in the possibility of reducing agent to event causation).[19] Given this premise, those who hold views such as my own, according to which actions are the causings of bodily movements and changes by agents, will have no reason to deny that active causation[20] by an agent in a sense always 'consists in' causation by events, for active causation by an agent will always consist in (because it is the same thing as) causation by one or more *actions*. These views might therefore be thought not to count as agent causationist, according to the Clarke definition. The only views that would *clearly* fit Clarke's characterization of the agent-causationist line would be those that I have suggested are unsatisfactory, namely those that assign to agents a mysterious power of causing *actions*, though not by way of any further action. However, (i) this leaves agent causationism looking to be an altogether hopeless and deeply peculiar position, which seems to countenance the possibility that agents might manage to cause things actively without acting and (ii) excludes accounts such as my own from counting as agent causationist, despite the fact that in many ways my view clearly belongs in the anti-reductionist camp. The reason agent causation cannot be reduced to event

---

[16] Chisholm (1976b: 199). [17] Chisholm (1976b: 199). [18] Clarke (2003: 134).

[19] Though see my reservations about the assumption that actions should be thought of quite generally as events in Section 3.1 and Section 6.6. For the purposes of this chapter, however, I largely ignore these reservations for the sake of being able more easily to engage with a literature that takes for granted a distinction between 'agent causation' and 'event causation'.

[20] The word 'active' is included here to rule out cases where agents cause things by omission, negligence, etc.

causation, I should say, is not that there is any agent causation that does not at the same time 'consist in' event causation. It is rather that if one asks what kind of event an *action* is, the reply ought to be that it is the causing of some bodily movement or change by the agent whose body is in question (or indirectly, by those means, of some further effects in the world). One must therefore appeal to the notion of an agent causing something to *understand* the notion of action in the first place. That causation by agents always 'consists in' causation by actions, then, though true, is not a point that can serve to effect any *reduction* of agent causation to event causation because of the very nature of the events that actions are.

In some ways, then, it seems to me that Chisholm's original criterion actually turns out to be a better classifier of accounts as agent-causal or not than is Clarke's, despite its old-fashioned semantic style. To see this, it is instructive to investigate what happens when one tries to meet Chisholm's original condition for reduction of the sentence 'Jones killed his uncle' to a set of statements in which only events are said to be causes, and no one of which presupposes that there is anything of which Jones may be said to be the cause. One might wonder what would be wrong, for example, with 'Jones's killing of his uncle killed his uncle'? (which would seem to be equivalent, in turn, to 'Jones' killing of his uncle caused the death of his uncle', a formulation that reveals explicitly the event-causal character of the claim). No one would ever say such a thing, of course, because there is too much redundancy in it: once we know that there is an event describable as 'Jones' killing of his uncle' we do not need to be told that this event caused the death of his uncle! But the pointlessness of the statement need not stand in the way of its truth. We can assume, for present purposes, that 'Jones' killing of his uncle'—his action—is an event. So have we not succeeded in converting 'Jones killed his uncle' without loss of meaning into a statement in which only events are said to be causes? Indeed we have done so, but what seems very doubtful is that we have met the *second* of Chisholm's two conditions. 'Jones' killing of his uncle' is arguably unsuitable to be the wanted event because it is an event whose occurrence simply presupposes that *Jones* caused the death of his uncle: the event causation we have brought in simply presupposes agent causation in the first place.

It might be wondered whether it might not likewise be argued that Jones could not cause his uncle to die without there being an *event* describable as Jones' killing of his uncle, so that the presuppositions go both ways here and neither agent nor event can be said, at any rate on these semantic grounds alone, to be more fundamental than the other. However, it may be pointed out, in opposition to this suggestion, that since one can cause people to die by *not* doing things, as well as by doing them, the second inference does not go through. Jones might, for example, have caused his bed-ridden uncle to die simply by not feeding him over a period of several weeks, in which case there would have been no event describable as Jones' killing of his uncle.[21] So it does

---

[21] I would strongly resist the claim that Jones's not feeding his uncle should itself be characterized as an action, although it may nevertheless be something for which Jones is responsible. NB, the *imperfect* nominal,

indeed seem true that there is a reason for regarding 'Jones killing of his uncle killed his uncle' as a statement that presupposes that *Jones* caused the death of his uncle—and not vice versa—since the entailments go in only one direction.

However, it is *not* true that there is ever agent causation in the absence of something that could also be called event causation. An agent never causes anything actively (rather than e.g. by accident, omission, or involuntary movement) except *by acting*. There are no causal relations between agents and events that are not accompanied by causal relations between events and events (on the assumption than actions are events). The agent causationist therefore need not endorse the peculiar idea that agents somehow have the power to cause actions by means of some bizarre 'exercise of agent causation' that takes place prior to the action and which is not itself an event. However, this just raises the question what *kind* of events actions *themselves* are and whether they can be understood independently of the idea of agent causation. It is here, I think, that we are able finally to locate the substantive and difficult issue on which we need to focus. For though I am assuming, for the purposes of this discussion, that actions *are* events, they are events of a very special sort. They are events that are causings of bodily movements and changes *by agents*. Causation by actions is therefore just causation by causings by agents. No *real* reduction, then, of agent causation to a notion of causation that dispenses entirely with the idea of agents causing things can be effected by the mere observation that causings by agents are always at the same time causings by actions: the idea of a causing that is by an agent remains at the heart of the concept of an action. What we would need to do to effect such a reduction, one might think, would be to show that causation by action can, in its turn, be understood as a kind of causation that consists somehow in causation by *other* sorts of events, such as those occurring in a person's brain and central nervous system prior to the muscular movements in which most of our actions result. It is, then, to the question whether causation by action can indeed be so understood that we now need to turn.

8.2 The reduction of agent causation to event causation

The thought that, given what we know about the provenance of motor activity in the body and brain, the causation of bodily movements and changes that is involved in action must indeed reduce to the causation of such movements and changes by lower-level physiological events, such as neural firings, is a very tempting one. However, it is not an idea that sits at all easily with the claim that I have tried to defend throughout this book that actions must be settlings *by agents*, at the time of action, of what is to occur subsequently with respect to some particular question or range of questions. For

---

'Jones' killing his uncle'(without the 'of') would still be in order under such circumstances for it would still be true that Jones had killed his uncle, merely not by means of an *action*. See my (1997: Chapter 4) for a detailed discussion of the distinction between different sorts of gerundive nominal.

if causation by actions *did* reduce in this way to causation by such things as neurological events, it would seem as though we would have to accept that actions must themselves *be* neurological events (or mereological sums of such events), events that in turn have their own causes, which in turn must be such things as *prior* neurological events, since neurological events, one might think, must have neurological—or at any rate, broadly physiological—causes. But in that case, how could an action manage to be a settling by the agent, at the time of action, of such matters as what she will do, how and when she will do it, etc.? Must not those matters have been *already* settled by the prior neurological causes? If they have not been, how can the lack of such settledness amount to anything other than sheer randomness in the causal process of a sort that could hardly amount to agential freedom? To defend the view that actions are settlings, then, it looks as though we will need to defend the idea that the causation involved in agency does *not* reduce to causation by lower-level events in the brain and central nervous system.

However, in considering this question of reduction, I think we need to distinguish two issues that are often run together. One issue is about whether substances (as opposed to events) can really be causes of anything at all. The main problem with agent causation, on this view, is that it is a sub-species of the problematic genus of *substance* causation. This is the line taken by Clarke, who concludes his book on libertarian accounts of free will with the suggestion that 'The sticking point for an agent-causal account is the notion of...causation by a substance...there are, on balance, reasons to think that substance causation is impossible'.[22] I shall try to suggest, in the next three sections of this chapter, that on the contrary, there is no particular reason to worry about the notion of substance causation—that substance causation is both omnipresent and utterly unproblematic—and hence it is not because agent causation is a species of this genus that we should wonder whether it can really be instantiated. The other issue is, however, by no means so easily dispensed with. Supposing that substance causation does indeed make sense, there is a question whether substance causation by a big and complex substance like an animal could ever fail to be constituted by causation going on at the level of the much smaller and simpler substances that are the animal's *parts*—neurons, muscles, etc.—that is to say, whether we can really understand what might be called *top-down* causation, where causality by the complex does not merely reduce to the sum total of a lot of causality by the simple. I shall come onto this issue in Sections 8.6–8.8, where I shall make some suggestions about how we might try to understand the possibility that complex things might come to have powers not exhausted by the powers of their parts and innards. But it is here, I think, that the serious thinking needs to be done, and science as well as philosophy needs to contribute to that thinking.

---

[22] Clarke (2003: 221).

8.3 Agent causation and substance causation

Perhaps the main worry about agent causationism is the fear that it is committed to the existence of 'two types of causation':

i. event causation, in terms of which we are to understand the occurrence of events in the inanimate universe and perhaps also the behaviour of most animals
ii. agent causation, in terms of which we are to understand human activity.

It is feared by many that to accept this picture is to set humans apart from the rest of nature in a way that is wholly unacceptable to the naturalist. Now, if this *were* the picture to which the agent causationist was committed, I would agree that it should be wholeheartedly rejected. But the agent causationist need accept no such picture. In this section of the chapter and the next, I want to set out some of my views on causation in general and explain how they enable the agent causationist to avoid the objection that she is committed to a peculiar divide in nature between different types of causation.

The first and most crucial point to be made is that *it is simply not correct to suppose that the ontology of most non-human causation is an event ontology.* Causation by substances is utterly ubiquitous. Inanimate substances can cause things just as well as animate ones can. A ball can break a window, a mass of water can burst a dam, one hot object can cause another to heat up. Of course, in all these cases, we can find events, too: the ball's colliding with the window, the mass of water's coming to be in the lake behind the dam, the hot object's coming into contact with the second object. But as I have emphasized, this is true also in the case of agency. When an agent causes something (by acting), her action also does. Thus far, there is no difference to be discerned between cases in which agents act and cases in which other sorts of substances bring about effects.

It might be thought, however, that while there is a problem about the reduction of agent causation to event causation, no such problem exists in other cases of substance causation. Substance causation, one might suppose, can always *normally* be reduced to event causation. Indeed, the idea seems to have become very prevalent in philosophy that where an inanimate substance may be said to cause something, it is always 'really' some event involving it that is the cause. This view is often made even more tempting by a liberal conception of events, whereby they are understood to be exemplifications of properties at times, so that even where it is an intuitively static property of the substance that seems relevant to the effect in question, it can still be an 'event' that is the *cause* of the effect—since on the liberal conception 'A's being F at *t*' may be accounted an event, whatever 'F' is in question. For example, 'this rug's being red at 12 noon today' would count as an event, on the liberal view. Against this background, the agent causationist might put her view by saying that this type of reduction to events is not possible where active causation by agents is concerned. Indeed, it is not true where agents are concerned, but why should we think we have to accept it even in the case of causation that is not agency? Why, for example, when a ball breaks a window, must we accept that this causation 'reduces to' event causation?

The main line of reasoning that is generally offered in the literature for this supposition is fallacious. The suggestion that is usually made appeals to the fact that in a case in which we are inclined to say that a substance has brought about some event, it is usually true that the object would not have caused the effect in question had it not been involved in some relevant event. We can therefore safely say that it was the event and not the object that was 'really' the cause.[23] For example, suppose a ball is thrown at a window and breaks it. It might be said that since the ball would not have broken the window had it merely continued resting on the grass as it was doing prior to being thrown, or if had it been placed gently in contact with the window, it cannot really be the cause of the window's breaking. But does this reasoning really stand up to scrutiny?

What principle does the reasoning invoke? Why should it be thought to follow from the fact that the ball would not have broken the window if it had not been thrown at it, that the ball was not really the cause of the window's breaking (i.e. didn't really break the window)? We cannot *usually* infer from the fact that A would not have V-ed if such and such had not been the case, that A did not V. Why here, in the case of causation, should it be thought to follow?

The reason it has been thought to do so, I think, stems ultimately from the fact that *causation* and *explanation* are closely related concepts. This means that in our assessment of what is 'the real cause' in instances of causation, there are often methodological principles at work that sustain an understandable preference for causal explanations that mention events over those that mention only substances. It is certainly not hopeless, when confronted with the question, say, why the window broke, to say 'the ball broke it': that is a causal explanation of sorts. But we definitely do better from an explanatory point of view if we can say, in addition, something about how the ball *came* to break the window: what happened to it such that it came to be in a position to realize its window-breaking power. Many inanimate objects tend just to sit there unless something happens to them so if they manage to produce an effect that is an event,[24] there is usually some *other* event one can point to which explains why the object has come to have the effect it did in this instance. Events in the inanimate world are usually precipitated by preceding trigger events: either events that consist in something's stimulating the object to behave in a particular way (as when, for instance, the sun warms a seed and makes it germinate) or in clearing away some obstacle or impediment to the activity of a particular (as when a crucial pillar collapses and allows the gravitational power of the earth to bring a roof crashing to the ground). In seeking a cause, we

---

[23] See, for example, Humphreys (1989) and Campbell (1990) for examples of the form of argumentation in question.

[24] Objects can produce effects which are *not* events even when they are 'just sitting there', e.g. a plant pot can be flattening the grass (= causing it to become flatter (a process?) or remain flat (a state?)).

are often in search of the trigger, the event that moved the object in question from a state of inertia into a state of activity, or which allowed the object to realize one of its pre-existent powers.[25] Even where the inanimate world is concerned, there seem to be exceptions to the rule that there must always be some such trigger (e.g. the emission of a particle from a piece of radioactive material may occur, it appears, in the absence of any particular trigger), but, on the whole, most of the inanimate substances with which we come into everyday contact seem to possess only one-way potentialities and thus, if one of these substances ever manages to exert one of its powers on some occasion, this is rarely a *spontaneous* matter: there is usually some change in the circumstances or in its own properties that can be regarded as the triggering cause of that exertion. For example, suppose my alarm clock goes off at 7am. This particular event, we suppose, is caused by some preceding event in the interior mechanism of the clock—say, a circuit's being completed—which makes my alarm clock's going off inevitable in the circumstances. Since we normally assume that alarm clocks do not have any two-way potentialities, we expect that there must always be an explanation such as this for anything it does. This being so, it might appear that the alarm clock itself drops out, to all intents and purposes, of the explanation of occurrences involving it. The event, it is sometimes claimed, is the thing that 'does the causal work'.

But we must be careful here not to mix up metaphysics and epistemology. It may be right to say that if we want an explanation of why the alarm clock went off, it will be best to cite the event that triggered it, or better perhaps the *fact* that an event of that kind (a circuit-completing event) occurred at the relevant time. Does that mean, though, that the event 'does the causal work'? Certainly it means that it, or facts involving it, do the *explanatory* work in accounting for why the alarm clock went off at the particular time that it did. But as Lowe has powerfully argued, it may be a category mistake to suppose that events do causal work, since they are not the sorts of things that have causal *powers*. It is Lowe's view that only substances have causal powers.[26] I am not sure whether I would wish to agree with Lowe about that, since I am not sure whether or not there might be reasons to suppose there are things other than substances that have such powers (perhaps fields or energy), but it ought surely to give us pause for thought. How can something to which it does not make sense to attribute a causal power do causal work? Isn't doing causal work the same thing as exerting causal power?

Lowe's view is that it is *substances* and not events that are the relata proper of the causal relation. To say this would be to overreact to the worry about causal power, as

---

[25] See Aronson (1971) and Harré and Madden (1975).

[26] 'It seems proper to say that *events of themselves possess no causal powers*. Only *persisting objects*—that is, individual "substances"—possess causal powers, and indeed causal liabilities. It is such objects that we describe as being magnetic, corrosive, inflammable, soluble, and so forth' (Lowe, 2008: 138). A similar view is expressed by Ayers (1968: 8): 'events neither have nor lack powers, except perhaps such odd powers as the power to surprise people'.

Lowe himself, I think, realizes in some places.[27] For even if events do not have causal powers, it need not follow that they cannot be causes: perhaps there are kinds of causes, the kind that events are, that cause things in ways other than by exerting causal powers. Perhaps, for instance, there are causes that trigger other events by *occurring*, and to occur need not be to exercise any kind of causal power. But still, Lowe is surely right to question whether we can move smoothly from the observation that it is often appropriate and useful to cite an event as the cause of something to the conclusion that it is always really the event that 'does the causal work', that the substance simply drops out of the causal metaphysics, giving way gracefully to the event that precipitates its activity.

My own view, in fact, is that the question what the relata of the causal relation are, though often posed, is simply not a sensible one. It is not true either that events are the relata of the relation, nor that substances are, nor indeed that any other of the multifarious candidates that have been proposed (e.g. facts, processes, properties, tropes, etc.) are its relata. There simply is no single relation that is *the* causal relation. Nor indeed is causation always and everywhere a relation at all. Causation is best thought of as a *category*: a large and ontologically flexible umbrella concept under which we bring a wide diversity of ontologically various relations and relationships, unified only by their connections to our interest in the explanation, prediction, and control of phenomena. We need to ask why it is obligatory to suppose that causation *has* an ontology in the first place. After all, as is frequently observed, items in almost all the ontological categories it is possible to think of are *spoken* of as causes: objects, persons, events, facts, states, properties, and so on. Why should one think that any of these ways of speaking can be sensibly thought of as revelatory of *the* ontology of causation? Might not the simple truth be that we need a plurality of irreducibly distinct ontological categories to do justice to the totality of causal phenomena?

In insisting that this is indeed the simple truth I do not mean to offer merely a counsel of despair with respect to the question whether we can, as philosophers, bring any order to the chaos of causal discourse. On the contrary, there *is* plenty of order to be discerned; I only wish to claim that it is not order of the sort that can be dealt with by means of the invocation of entities of an entirely homogeneous sort. What I suggest is that we need to recognize at least a three-fold ontological categorization to capture and account for the different types of thing we call 'causes' (and, relatedly, the different sorts of relationship we recognize as causal).[28] I call these three types of cause *movers*,

---

[27] 'I speak of "causal relations" in the plural here advisedly, because I think it is tendentious to assume that there is such a thing as "the" causal relation, although this assumption is very widespread amongst contemporary analytical metaphysicians…some causal statements undoubtedly have an event–causal formulation…However we also have what might be called "mixed" causal statements, such as "The bomb caused the collapse of the bridge" in which the grammatical subject of the verb "to cause" is a noun-phrase denoting a particular persisting object or individual *substance*…' (Lowe, 2008: 142).

[28] I focus here on causes. Effects can, I think, be readily accommodated within the ontological categories I shall argue are needed to deal with causes. Indeed, they can be more simply dealt with, for in their case, I do not really think there is anything which corresponds properly to the category I call 'mover'.

matterers, and *makers-happen*. None of the types, I maintain, can be dispensed with in favour of the others ('reduced to' the others), although there are important relations between the types that can, to a certain extent, be mapped. But the really important thing, in my view, is that we must not get the categories *mixed up* and assimilate them wrongly to one another in the service of a chimerical uniformity.[29] An honest recognition of the multiplicity of ontological categories we need in order to catalogue all the sorts of causal relationship there are, is preferable to an attempt to iron out the differences in favour of an entirely spurious standardization. In particular, it is absolutely essential to recognize that some types of cause (both the movers and the makers-happen) are proper spatiotemporal *particulars* while others (the matterers) relate to *general* factors (properties, features, aspects, etc.) and we only make a horrendous hash of our causal thinking if we fail to recognize that we are interested, when looking for causes, in *both* things that are particular *and* things that are general. If we do not recognize this, we shall have things that are general or propositional, and therefore utterly unsuited to *doing* anything, in the role of exerter of causal power. We shall also have things that are particular, and therefore utterly unsuited to serving in the formulation of laws and generalizations, outlawed as non-causes just because they *are* thus unsuited. It is utterly imperative to recognize that causal thinking involves a concern *both* with particularity *and* generality. If we do not recognize this, we shall soon find ourselves mired in absurdities of various sorts, as I shall shortly attempt to show.

The main intellectual obligation of the causal pluralist is, I think, the explanation of what *unites* these ontologically various categories of cause. It is an obligation I cannot fully discharge in a book whose main concerns are elsewhere, but one needs to say *something*. My own current favourite hypothesis is the one already adumbrated above in note 14 and defended in enormously convincing detail by Lakoff and Johnson, namely that the relatively sophisticated talk of causation in which we engage as seekers of knowledge in disciplines as diverse as chemistry, history, and economics is a cognitive achievement that builds on the simpler grasp embodied in our basic understanding of the transitive verbs we use to express agent–patient relations. Our thinking about the relatively abstract causes involved in functional relationships—between, say, rates of inflation and interest rates or levels of concentration of a substance in a solution and rates of reaction with another reagent—utilize the cognitive resources—the very same neural structures—as we first utilize in our early thinking about the mechanistic relations: pushing, pulling, lifting, turning, squeezing, and the like. It is this that makes us think of all these relationships as ultimately causal. But the defence of this hypothesis is a controversial matter, and evidently one which goes beyond the scope of this book. So, having gestured briefly at the direction in which I would hope to look

---

[29] In my view, it is our having got them mixed up that is largely responsible for the existence of a number of artificial ontological categories for which I have yet to be persuaded that there is any genuine need: token states, tropes, and facta, to name but three.

for an understanding of what unifies the three sorts of cause I wish to invoke, I turn next to explain the three categories.

8.4 Movers, matterers, and makers-happen

What, then, are these three categories of cause and how do they work? Roughly speaking, movers are *things*: usually substances, or collections of substances, although, as I have already said, I would not want to rule out the possibility that less familiar sorts of endurant, such as fields, might also be movers of a sort.[30] They are such entities as stones and masses of air and water, animals and persons, as well as some of the smaller entities that go to make them up, like molecules and ions. It might be objected that fundamental physics may ultimately recognize no entities of the sort we generally suppose enduring things like this to be, but I reply that fundamental physics, as is often observed, has little use for the concept of causation either. I claim only that at the levels at which we *do* find it useful and important to speak of causation, we also find it useful and important to single out powerful particulars that *do* things, and which act and are acted upon. It is these things that are the possessors *par excellence* of causal powers and liabilities in the true sense—such things as solubility, abrasiveness, magnetism, etc.— and hence they are the primary doers of so-called 'causal work'. Usually, though, so far as inanimate entities are concerned, their production of any event-effect requires a *trigger* of some sort; some particular event that initiates a causal process within the object or which constitutes or effects the removal of some barrier to the exercise of one of its causal powers. In such cases we may also speak of this triggering event as the cause of the subsequent one. But that is no reason to deny that the substance is also a cause of a sort (but in this case, a mover, as opposed to a maker-happen).

Makers-happen, roughly speaking, are the proper Davidsonian events[31] that trigger substances into action. Since they are triggers, they must be happenings. Strikings of matches, for example, are makers-happen, although the fact that a match was struck is not. It is perhaps necessary to caution that of course my terminology here is technical: not everything of which we might say in everyday life that it made something happen counts as a maker-happen, in my sense. We might, for instance, say that a stone (which, in my terminology, is a mover) made the breaking of the window happen or that the fact that the match was dry (which in my terminology is a matterer) made it light. But these things are not makers-happen in my technical sense. A maker-happen, in my technical sense, can only be a particular event.

Often, the particular event that triggers a mover into action is the impact of some *other* substance such as a kick, a blow, a heating, etc. It is thus easy to come to think of

---

[30] For the purposes of my interests here, it will not be necessary to settle the question what *exactly* are the bounds of these various categories.

[31] As opposed to such things as exemplifications of properties at times, which are, in my view, not really events at all but are better conceived of as facts. See my (1997) for a detailed defence of this claim.

causality as essentially a sort of *external* business, whereby an event kicks an essentially inert bit of matter into motion or change. This is particularly tempting if the phenomena that seem, on the face of it, most clearly to constitute counterexamples to this general idea, namely biological phenomena, such as growth, development, and many instances of agency itself, which occur apparently without the need for any such strictly *external* stimulation, are thought of as constituted essentially by lower-level processes that involve the same sorts of external impacts on the fundamentally inert inner *parts* of a biological organism, culminating eventually in basically mechanistic relations between atoms or their sub-atomic constituents. This thinking is no doubt part of what encourages the idea that it is *events* that are the real causes, substances always needing a kind of injection of kinetic oomph from somewhere, if they are ever going to move or change. Poorly comprehended ideas about conservation principles no doubt add to the temptation to think of substances as entities that essentially require some sort of input from without if they are ever to get into motion.[32] But if we ought *not* to think of these various biological phenomena as reducible to lower-level processes, as I shall argue later, then that puts into question this externalized view of the essence of causation and helps with the idea that there may be substances that need no external impetus to get into motion, but which can provide the needed resources entirely from within themselves.

Matterers, finally, are *facts*. They are the causes we advert to by means of basically sentential expressions and which we link together with their effects by means of sentential connectives like 'because'. 'The disease spread quickly because the weather was unusually hot', 'the match did not light because it was damp', 'I took an umbrella because I thought it would rain': all these are causal explanations that claim that a certain fact is causally relevant to, *matters* causally to, another one.[33] These are the causes in which science tends to be interested, for science, on the whole, is interested in generality and it is these mattering causes in terms of which we talk about the general factors, properties, and features that are causally relevant to the production of effects of

---

[32] Sometimes it is suggested that the idea that there might be such self-moving substances might somehow contradict some conservation law. But conservation principles apply only to closed systems. An animal in its environment is not a closed system.

[33] A similar caution applies here as was mentioned in the previous paragraph, i.e. we use the verb 'matter' of course in connection also with movers and makers-happen: the stone (a mover) matters, in a sense, to the breaking of the window (if it breaks it) and so does my throwing of it (officially, a maker-happen). But one can perhaps get a sense of my motivation for employing the word 'matterer' specifically to pick out causes that are facts, or equivalently, causes that are aspects, properties, or features of things or situations, by reflecting on the naturalness with which we might say that it was not really the individual stone that mattered to the fact that the window broke, nor the individual throwing; it was really the fact that a projectile of a certain mass was thrown at a certain speed at the window. The particularities of individual stone and individual throwing are neither here nor there. Another projectile and another throwing meeting given criteria would have done as well. It is fact that those criteria were met, we might say, that is really what matters for the production of an effect of the kind in question.

certain sorts.[34] Much of what has been written about the relation of causation to such other concepts as law, counterfactuals, and probability really relates to these mattering causes.

Just as some have suggested that causation by substances should really be dispensed with in favour of causation by particular events, so others have suggested that causation by substances should be dispensed with in favour of causation by those causes I call 'matterers'. These confusingly are sometimes also called 'events' by those who use the term 'event' to refer to something like an exemplification of a property at a time. But the arguments that are regularly put forward for this conclusion seem to me to be confused. Here is an example of such an argument, taken from Humphreys' book, *The Chances of Explanation*. Objects, says Humphreys, although attributed causal efficacy in ordinary talk, as in 'The car demolished the wall', cannot really be causes. It always turns out really to be some *aspect* of the thing in question that was the real cause, for example the high momentum of the car. Clearly, then, says Humphreys, it was not the car per se that demolished the wall, since a car parked touching the wall has no effect and moreover any object of a similar size moving at similar velocity would have done as well as the car. But this is a non-sequitur, produced by the fact that Humphreys has invoked methodological principles (in this case, Mill's 'Method of Difference' and his 'Method of Agreement')[35] that apply only to what I call *matterers*, to causes that are of another sort. Where matterers are concerned, we look for difference-making, and if we treat the car as though its causal role were that of a matterer, we will reject it because we will find that its mere presence in the situation is not what makes the difference between demolition and non-demolition of the wall. It is perfectly true, of course, that had the car been parked touching the wall, it would have had no effect (Method of Difference), and moreover it is true also that had an object of similar size and velocity impacted the wall the wall would have been demolished (Method of Agreement); the car's presence is not even a *necessary* condition of the wall's being demolished. But it simply does not follow from any of these counterfactual considerations that the car did not in fact demolish the wall. The car is not being presented by the original claim as a causally relevant factor or an aspect—as what I call a *matterer*. It is being presented as

---

[34] I see no real distinction between the idea that a *fact* is causally relevant to the explanation of some effect and the idea that a *property* is thus relevant. For a property must be a property *of something*, and so where F-ness is relevant to some effect one can always speak alternatively of 'the fact that S is F' being relevant. These seem to me to be simply alternative ways of speaking about causal matterers, and there is no point in insisting that it is 'really' the property or 'really' the fact that is the cause. We can talk equivalently in either way, and since neither facts nor properties are causal *agents* there is no question which type of entity is better suited to 'do causal work'. Neither is suited to *doing* anything. What they are suited to is *mattering*.

[35] Mill's 'Method of Difference' states that 'If an instance in which the phenomenon under investigation occurs, and an instance in which it does not occur, have every circumstance in common save one, that one occurring only in the former; the circumstance in which alone the two instances differ is the effect, or the cause, or an indispensable part of the cause, of the phenomenon' (Mill, 1970 [1872]: 256). His 'Method of Agreement' states that 'If two or more instances of the phenomenon under investigation have only one circumstance in common, the circumstance in which alone all the instances agree is the cause (or effect) of the given phenomenon' (Mill, 1970 [1872]: 255).

a *mover*, as the particular *agent* of the demolition. And indeed it *was* the agent of the demolition. That it would have had no effect had it been merely parked touching the wall is neither here nor there. For it was not in fact merely parked touching the wall; it was in fact driven into it at high speed, and in being thus driven into it, served as the agent of its collapse.

Here, then, is a type of fallacious argument that is directly traceable to the assumption that all causes must be of the same ontological type. Humphreys' book presents an excellent account of the causes I call matterers, but he fails to recognize that not all causes *are* matterers and he therefore ends up denying, in my view absurdly, that cars can, under certain circumstances, demolish walls.

Another area in which it seems to me it is helpful to accept a diverse causal ontology is in connection with the various puzzles posed by phenomena like overdetermination and pre-emption. For example, those who are attracted to an account of causation like Mellor's, on which causes are said to raise the chances of effects, face difficulties in cases of causal pre-emption.[36] Suppose, for example that two assassins A and B are taking aim at their victim C at the same time. A shoots first, his bullet hitting its mark. On seeing A fire, B desists, but he would certainly have fired, let us suppose, if A had not, and being a crack shot would certainly have hit his target. We now cannot say, it seems, that A's shooting raised the chances of C's being assassinated, since those chances, we are supposing, would have been just as good if A had not shot. But we surely want to say that A's shooting was the cause of C's death.

A pluralistic ontology of the sort I have suggested enables us easily to see what is going on here. The idea that causes must raise the chances of their effects is an excellent account of what it is to be a cause that is a matterer, but it is not an excellent account of what it is to be a cause since not all causes *are* matterers: some are movers and some are makers-happen. This realization enables us to say that A's shooting C indeed *was* the cause of his death, unequivocally and unproblematically. It was the maker-happen, the individual event that brought about that death.[37] But the fact that A shot C was not a fact that mattered (in my technical sense) to the fact that he died that morning, for it was not a fact that raised the chances of that outcome: C would have died anyhow.

With this three-fold causal ontology in place, we are in a position, I think, to meet very many of the worries that have been raised both concerning substance causation in general and agent causation. For many of those worries stem entirely from the assumption that all causes must be of the same ontological type and thus that substances, if they are to be causes, must meet some criterion or other that applies, at best, only to one of the other sorts of cause. To show that this is so, I shall turn now to consider the objections to the notion of substance causation considered by Clarke in the final chapter of his (2003). I shall try to suggest that most of these worries can be answered

---

[36] See Mellor (1995).

[37] C.f. Armstrong (1999), who suggests a very similar way of dealing with such cases.

easily by a proper recognition and understanding of the pluralistic ontology for which I have argued.

8.5 Objections to the possibility of substance causation

8.5.1 Laws and conditionals

Clarke considers briefly, only to dismiss, an objection to substance causation based on the idea that causation is connected to laws and to conditionals, and that these connections might stand in the way of a view of causation according to which substances can be causes. Clarke does not really explain *how* exactly the idea that causation is connected to laws and conditionals is supposed to stand in the way of substance causation, but presumably the idea is that there are no laws connecting particular substances to particular event-effects and furthermore that since the antecedent of a conditional must always be propositional in structure, it will always be a propositional sort of thing (such as a fact, state of affairs, or exemplification of a property at a time, e.g. 'S's being F at *t*') that will always be highlighted as the relevant cause by such conditionals, rather than a mere substance. Clarke's own reason for dismissing the worry is that 'If a substance causes something, then it does so in virtue of having some causally relevant property'. We might therefore still find laws relating the instantiation of the relevant property by some substance to the occurrence of some relevant event-type (e.g. 'all pieces of sodium that are immersed in water catch fire'). Likewise, there will be conditionals of the form 'if S hadn't been F, E wouldn't have occurred'. Clarke is evidently right about this, but he does not explain how he means to resist the inference, made very commonly by others writing on causation in the literature, that it is therefore 'really' these propositional sorts of thing that are the causes of metaphysical reality, since it is these that the laws and counterfactuals relate. One may only do so convincingly, I would suggest, if one is prepared to recognize a pluralism of types of cause of the sort I have suggested above. Otherwise one is always open to the objection that it is, for example, 'the magnesium's being immersed in water at *t*', and not the magnesium or the water, which is the *real* cause in such a case. But once one *is* an ontological pluralist about causation, one may happily accept that though causation *is* connected to laws and conditionals, the ontology of law and counterfactuals is the ontology of *matterers*, and that no mover ought to be denied its status as mover by the mere observation that referring expressions for particular substances tend not to figure in laws and are unsuited to serve as the antecedents of counterfactuals.

8.5.2 Broad's objection

Broad's objection to substance causation is one of the most popular and widely endorsed objections to agent causationism. It may therefore be useful to quote in full the central argument:

The putting forth of an effort of a certain intensity, in a certain direction, at a certain moment, for a certain duration, is quite clearly an event or process, however unique and peculiar it may be in other respects. It is therefore subject to any conditions which self-evidently apply to every event, as such. Now, it is surely quite evident that, if the beginning of a certain process at a certain time is determined at all, its total cause *must* contain as an essential factor another event or process which *enters into* the moment from which the determined event or process *issues*. I see no *prima facie* objection to there being events that are not completely determined. But, in so far as an event *is* determined, an essential factor in its total cause must be other *events*. How could an event possibly be determined to happen at a certain date if its total cause contained no factor to which the notion of date has any application? And how can the notion of date have any application to anything that is not an event?[38]

Is Broad's objection a worry for my view? I have argued for a view of actions according to which they are precisely *not* determined by any sort of prior cause and so one might think that the whole of Broad's argument here is simply beside the point, since it appears to be meant to apply only to events that *are* determined. I have insisted, in addition, that actions should not be thought of as caused by agents, so the idea that I am committed to the view that the total cause of an action includes no factor to which the idea of date has any application, in virtue of being committed to the view that *agents* are the causes of actions, would also be a mistake. Nevertheless, the question might be pressed what exactly I *do* want to say about the causation of actions, and here may be the place to begin to address that question. If they are events (as I have said I am prepared to allow for the purposes of this chapter) and if they are not to be consigned simply to the realm of the random and chancy, must they not have causes that are also events?

Some elements of my response to this question must await the discussion of top-down causation in Sections 8.6–8.8. But this may well be the place for some preliminary clarifications of some areas of agreement and disagreement between my view and that of some other agent causationists. Many agent causationists claim that actions simply do not have causes at all; that the cause of an action is neither the agent nor any event. Lowe (2008), for example, claims that *free* actions, at any rate, 'are *completely uncaused*'[39] and O'Connor's position seems to be that an agent's exertion of active power is an event of a sort such that 'there cannot, in the nature of the case, be a cause that produces it'.[40] But I think one must be rather cautious about such claims as these. It seems right that the agent causationist ought to believe that actions do not have prior *necessitating conditions*, and indeed that follows from the conception of actions as settlings of matters by agents that has been developed during the course of this book. But in recent times, many philosophers have been encouraged, both by the development of probabilistic conceptions of causality and also by other ontological considerations,[41] to

---

[38] Broad (1952: 215).   [39] Lowe (2008: 7). Italics in original.   [40] O'Connor (2000: 61).
[41] In particular I am thinking of the distinction pressed by Davidson (1967) between necessary and sufficient conditions, on the one hand, and particular event-causes on the other. Davidson stresses that a particular cause is something ontologically quite different from a sufficient condition and provided one

accept that causation and necessitation are not the same thing. As a result, these philosophers are happy to embrace the idea that there can perfectly well be causes that do not necessitate their effects. And if this were right, it would not be obvious what would be wrong with admitting that a particular action may have a certain *kind* of cause. For example, suppose I see a pound coin on the ground and stoop to pick it up. Is there anything wrong with saying that my noticing the pound coin—a particular event, let us assume—caused my stooping to pick it up—another particular event? This claim need not imply that I could not have done anything else or that my stooping was necessitated by some set of prior conditions that was completed by my noticing the coin and which therefore led inexorably to the stooping event. All that need be meant is that the noticing was an important *prompt* or *trigger* for the stooping (though not one that led to it *inexorably*, since it remains *up to me* whether or not I stoop). In a similar way, we can allow that a contact with the carrier of a contagious disease caused the onset of my fever, without supposing that the fever was *necessitated* by the contact and even without supposing that the fever was necessitated by the contact *in conjunction with* numerous further unknown conditions. It is a mere assumption that there must be some total set of conditions that together necessitates each actual effect produced in our complex world, not something of which we have any a priori assurance.[42] If we reject this assumption, as many philosophers have suggested we ought, we might think we could accept the existence of particular event-causes for actions, even though their *necessitation* by prior circumstances is ruled out.

Of course, there is a difference between the case of the contagious disease and the case of the stooping. In the first case, if there are no necessitating conditions, we are likely to think that it is partly a chance matter whether or not I catch the fever. In the second, meanwhile, we are likely to think it is *up to me* whether or not I stoop and pick up the coin. This is an important difference, but not one, it seems to me, which rules out the claim that my noticing the coin can be the cause of my stooping to pick it up. Though I have to exercise a power I need not have exercised if there is to be a stooping by me, I do not see why this should preclude there being a particular event-cause of my exercising it, provided we do not mean by 'cause', 'sufficient condition'. However, we cannot mean this literally in any case, for a particular event-cause is *never* a sufficient condition:[43] it could only ever be the fact that an event of a certain type had occurred *in conjunction with a large range of other conditions* that literally necessitated something. Moreover, it seems to be a mistake to suppose that a particular event-cause always owes its status as a cause to its participation in any such giant conjunction, given that caused and yet indeterministic phenomena are possible. My meeting with the carrier of the

accepts this then obviously one will accept also that there can be causes which are not sufficient conditions. See my (1996) for an argument for the conclusion that this distinction in effect undermines the whole idea that there might be something thinkable of as the 'whole' cause of some effect, a giant conjunction of particular events and standing conditions 'added together'.

[42] As pointed out by Anscombe (1971).   [43] See Davidson (1967).

disease I catch can be the cause of my catching it, whether or not there is any set of prior conditions that *necessitates* my catching it.

Might it not be wondered though, how, if there is an event-cause of my action, I can also be the *agent*-cause of its results (e.g. the bending$_i$ of my knee as I stoop)? Does not the event cause, in causing my action, also cause its results (by transitivity) and therefore prevent *me* from doing so? No. For the event-cause in this case is a cause of *my action* and only achieves those results in a way mediated by that action: it is a cause of my causing something. In so far as it has effects that are movements and changes in my body, it operates *through* my agency, not in competition with it. I see, then, no reason to deny that there can be causes of my actions, provided they are not necessitating causes; provided, that is, it is left to me to settle what will occur as a result of the event-cause in question.

Moreover, there seems no reason why there cannot, in addition, be a causal explanation[44] of *why an agent has done what she has done*. As argued in Chapter 6.4.3, we must distinguish between giving the cause of a particular action and causally explaining why an agent did what she did: the first concerns a *token* event, the second why someone did some *type* of thing.[45] But the latter seems possible as well as the former, provided we do not read too much into the claim that the explanation *is* causal.[46] On the assumption, for instance, that to offer a causal explanation of something is merely to say something illuminating that consists in attributing one phenomenon to derivation from another, it seems perfectly all right to suppose that if I say, for example, that I washed my hair because my head felt itchy, I have offered a causal explanation.

I do not think, then, that there is any need for the agent causationist to deny that actions may have causes. Particular actions may perfectly well have particular causes and there may also be perfectly good causal explanations of why agents do things in cases where their doings of those things are their actions. But what is not possible is that an action should have a *necessitating* cause, a sufficient condition that brings the action inexorably in its train. For if this were so, the agent could not settle at the time of action what is to occur. This insistence might be thought to cast doubt on the compatibility of the version of agent causationism being defended here with basic facts already known about the nature of human beings, and this is a charge that I shall shortly consider. But it seems to leave us utterly immune to Broad's worry, since actions are *not* determined and hence fall outside the category of events that require an event-like cause.

---

[44] In some suitably broad sense of 'causal'.

[45] I am trying, for the purposes of this book, not to take sides on the question whether rational explanation is a form of causal explanation. I am inclined to think it is, because I am inclined to interpret the concept of 'cause' very liberally. But I think the main theses outlined in this book are probably consistent with either position.

[46] See Section 6.4.1.

8.5.3 Explanation

This objection contends that substances can contribute little or nothing to causal explanation and therefore cannot be causes. The simple response to this, which I have already outlined, is that the premise is false and that the inference is in any case faulty. Substances can and do contribute to causal explanations although, as explained earlier, it is generally possible to say much more than is said when the substance responsible for some effect is named. For example, one can normally say what it was that triggered the substance into action or what it was about the substance that mattered causally. However, more importantly, one cannot infer from the fact that something contributes less to a causal explanation of some phenomenon than does some other thing that it is therefore less of a cause, much less that it is not a cause at all. Substances are simply causes of a different ontological type than either makers-happen or matterers, and it is entirely unsurprising that they do not play exactly the same role in explanation as causes of these other sorts.

8.5.4 Time

Clarke considers what he calls a 'modified version' of Broad's objection, according to which every cause of an event must be an entity that occurs at a time. On his own so-called 'integrated agent-causal view', when a substance causes an event it does so in virtue of having some causally relevant property and hence, when it causes that event to occur at a certain time, it does so at least partly in virtue of having that property at a certain, slightly prior time. His account is therefore not without the resources to explain why events occur when they do but, as he notes himself, this point 'comes perilously close to acknowledging that it is the substance's having the property at the time in question that is the cause' and he concludes, for this reason, that 'The fact that events...but not substances, are directly in time...appears to count against the possibility of substance causation, even if not decisively'.[47]

But the agent causationist can do better than this. It seems to me that what is required to see off the objection is the ontological pluralism about causation for which I have argued, plus a bit of additional clarity about events. The causes that genuinely have to *occur* in time are those I have called 'makers-happen', and the reason they must be occurrences is that these are the things to which we accord the privilege of *prompting* or *triggering* further events. Evidently, nothing can count as a trigger that was there all along. But the agent causationist must insist that not all causes *are* triggers and so it is simply not true that *every* cause of an event must be an entity that occurs at a time. It may well be true that it is usually the case that there *are* such triggering causes when events occur. But as well as triggers, there will be movers and there will be matterers; there will be things exercising their causal powers and there will also be causally relevant facts. In fact, Clarke's 'events'—such things as 'the substance's having the

[47] Clarke (2003: 202).

property at the time in question'—are not particular events at all. They are better regarded as facts; facts that may well be causally *relevant*, which *matter* to some outcome, but which are not the sorts of things at all that could actually *do* anything, not being particular, spatiotemporal entities in the first place. 'S's being F at *t*' is a *sentence* nominalization (it is a nominalization of the sentence 'S is F at *t*'), not a referring expression for a particular.[48] The idea that when a substance causes an event it is always 'in virtue of having some causally relevant property' just means that when a substance causes an event, some of its properties matter, and some don't, to the nature of the outcome when that outcome is described in a particular way. It does not imply in the least that the substance did not cause the event (c.f. the diagnosis of Humphreys' fallacious argument above).

8.5.5 Probability

Clarke considers the popular idea that causes are the sorts of things that can affect the probabilities of their effects. This idea, he argues, has 'considerable plausibility'. He also argues that substances do not appear to be the sorts of entities that could affect the probabilities of subsequent events in this way. Here again, then, he discerns a consideration that is 'of significant weight, even if nothing that is by itself decisive, to place in the balance against the possibility of substance causation'.[49]

But the response to this is more or less the same as to the worry about laws and conditionals. Indeed, it has already been broached in the discussion of causal preemption above. The idea that causes must raise the probability of their effects is a very appealing account of *mattering* causes. What it is for a fact to matter causally to the occurrence of an effect of a certain kind may indeed be for that fact to raise the probability of an effect of that kind's occurring.[50] My not wearing a seat belt was causally relevant to my being badly injured in the car crash, for example, because my not wearing a seat belt raised the probability that such serious injuries would occur. But the *movers* in the case were the glass from the shattered windscreen and the sharp shards of metal that pierced my ribcage. It is these things, properly speaking, which 'did the causal work'. These, it is true, are not the sorts of entities of which it can sensibly be said that they raised the probability of anything, since we need propositional structures to express such relationships. It was not the shattered glass itself that raised the probability that serious injuries would occur but rather, say, the fact that the glass shattered. But still what injured me was the glass itself, and not facts concerning it, since these are simply not the sorts of entities that can injure people![51]

---

[48] For a detailed defence of this view, see my (1997).   [49] Clarke (2003: 204).

[50] Though I do not here wish to commit myself to that particular account of causal mattering. I only wish to insist that what it is, *is* an account of causal mattering.

[51] C.f. Lamprecht, criticizing Schlick's view that causation implies nothing but regularity of sequence: 'Sitting in my home at night, I may hear a knock at the door. Someone might chance to tell me that, always and invariably, according to a law of nature, sound results from the reverberation of a solid block of wood which is disturbed by blows upon it, and that this explanation is the full and entire causal account of the

8.5.6 Structure

Clarke considers—and rejects—the claim that only structured particulars, 'structured as events are structured' can be causes. He points out that when an object stands in the relation 'bigger than' to another, it does so in virtue of having a certain property (its size). He also notes that, for all that, it really is the object and not the object's having that size that stands in the 'bigger than' relation to the second object. Presumably, this reasoning is supposed to make available the parallel thought that when a substance causes an event, though it does so in virtue of having a certain property, it really is the substance that stands in the causal relation to the event. This is all perfectly correct. What is puzzling is only that Clarke does not see that the same point will serve to block the worry about time, which he seems to consider serious. When a substance S causes an event E, it may indeed be in virtue of the fact that S possesses some property P at an immediately preceding time t, that it is able to effect the causation. But it does not follow that the substance therefore does *not* stand in the relation of causation to the event E.

8.5.7 Directedness

The worry here is that the specific sub-type of substance causation that is constituted by *agent* causation is peculiar, in that the property that confers on an agent the power directly to cause certain sorts of event confers no *determinate* tendency to cause those events since everything is supposed to be left 'up to the agent'. The question is whether we can really understand how a property of something could 'carry a directedness of no determinate degree' toward certain effects. Clarke himself dismisses the worry on the basis that there seems no reason to suppose that a property should not carry a directedness of no determinate degree toward certain effects, even where the property in question is a property of an event. There is therefore no reason either to suppose that it could not do so when the property is a property of a substance.

I confess to being a little unsure, here, of what the objection really amounts to, perhaps because I do not really accept Clarke's vision of the role played by properties in conferring powers on things. Of course, it would be silly to deny that in a loose way: properties of things in a sense 'confer' powers on them; if I didn't have the property of having a brain and fingers, for example, I wouldn't be able to type. But the idea that this general thought can be tightened up so that an exact relationship between any given power and some property or set of properties can be formulated seems misguided to me. What is 'the' property in virtue of which I am able to walk, say? Does Clarke

knocking. Would I be satisfied? Would you? Would even Moritz Schlick? The laws of nature in terms of which a particular knocking might be adequately described would probably not be of much interest to you or me or Schlick at that moment. I am sure that I should want to know who or what concretely was making blows on the door. I should want to identify the specific agent who or which did the knocking...That there would be uniformity of result in similar cases would be of no account to me at the moment.' (Lamprecht 1967: 121–2).

seriously think there must be one? Even if we are allowed a giant conjunction of everything that could possibly be relevant, how on earth are we to decide on the criteria for relevance? Does the property of having a heart count, for example? Under certain circumstances, things can walk without having hearts (e.g. robots) so perhaps it should be excluded. On the other hand, if you were to take my heart out, I wouldn't be able to walk any more, so perhaps it should be included. What about having feet? In a sense that seems very important to walking, but a person can lose a foot and still manage to walk. Maybe having at least one foot is the thing to go for, then? But perhaps even that is not strictly necessary? Such reflections lead me to think there could be no principled way whatever of arriving at a definitive characterization of 'the property' in virtue of which I have the power to do each of the various things I can do. I am therefore inclined to reject the whole idea that there is any *particular* property (even a giant conjunctive one) that confers agent-causal powers of any sort.

8.5.8 Discovery

Clarke here considers the objection that there could be no evidence for the existence of substance causation. We discover causal relations, the objection goes, by finding patterns in the course of events. However, these relations are always evidence for *event* causation, and it is unclear, what, if anything could ever give us evidence of substance causation.

Clarke's own response to this objection is the surely rather feeble riposte that even if agent causation were undiscoverable, that would not show that it did not exist. The agent causationist ought not to rest content with the possibility that the relation she contends for exists as an empirically unverifiable phenomenon. Fortunately, she need not do so. The correct response to the worry has already been made several times in the literature, by a number of authors arguing against the unobservability of causation in the particular instance, and it is that the objection presupposes a Humean epistemology of causation to which the substance causationist ought to be in any case completely opposed. Although perhaps it may be conceded that in certain difficult and abstruse cases we have to resort to 'patterns in the course of events' to look for causal relationships—for example, we may not realize the link between mosquitoes and malaria until we discover that the eradication of mosquitoes in a particular area leads to a decrease in malarial related deaths—the substance causationist will want to insist that there are many far more basic cases of observable instances of causation in which a substance is seen to act on another. We can *see* an engine pulling a carriage, for instance, or a wave wetting a bystander, or a cog moving another. We also experience the relation in the case of our own actions: as we pull a suitcase behind us, for instance, or push a button. As Anscombe remarked: 'This often happens in philosophy: it is argued that "all we find" is such-and-such, and it turns out that the arguer has excluded from his idea of "finding" the sort of thing he says we don't "find"'.[52]

---

[52] Anscombe (1971: 137).

8.5.9 Immanent substance causation

The worry here is that agent causation would have to involve a substance's directly causing a change in *itself*—so called 'immanent' substance causation (as opposed to 'transeunt' causation, whereby a substance brings about a change in an entirely distinct substance). Clarke says he sees no reason to rule this out, provided we eschew certain reductive accounts of causation. I, on the other hand, think that this is where all the real difficulty with the notion of agent causation lies. The problem, though, is not with the notion of substance causation *as such*. It is rather with the notion of causation of motion and change in the *parts* of a complex, organized substance by the whole substance. I shall treat this issue in Section 8.8.2; I set it aside for now since I do not regard it as a worry specifically about substance causation: it is a particular concern about the specific sort of substance causation that agency seems to be.

8.5.10 Uniformity

The objection from uniformity is the one I have alluded to already at the beginning of Section 8.3, namely that it seems implausible that there should be two utterly different types of causation. Clarke finds this objection to be an important one and indeed, I think it would be if it could be sustained. But I have already offered my response, which is simply to deny the crucial premise that 'causation in familiar cases…is event causation',[53] or at least to deny it in the sense that would be needed to sustain the conclusion. For though causation in many familiar cases *is* event causation, it is *also* substance causation (and fact causation). All three categories are required to do justice to what we need to say about causation across the board, both in the animate and in the inanimate world.

It seems to me, then, that contra Clarke, there is simply no general issue about substance causation. Substance causation is simply everywhere, and the idea that it can always be 'reduced to' event causation is based on the fallacious application of methodological ideas about the discernment of causes that are appropriate when one is trying to discriminate effectively amongst various possible candidate *matterers* in scientific contexts, to cases in which the competition is rather between causes that are in utterly different *categories*. But this competition is spurious. It is simply silly to ask whether it was the ball or the ball's being thrown at the window that caused it to break. The ball caused the window to break all right, and so did its being thrown at the window. We can and should say both things without fear of being committed to some bizarre kind of overdetermination.

I regard concern about the notion of substance causation, then, as a red herring. But that is not to say that there are no genuinely puzzling questions about agent causation. There *are* such puzzling questions but it is important that we get clear about where the genuine puzzle lies.

---

[53] Clarke (2003: 208).

What, then, is the genuine puzzle, if it is not the question how substances can be causes? It seems to me that we have no real difficulty understanding the possibility that a substance may act on *another*. Water may dissolve sodium chloride, my pen may produce an impression on some paper, some moving air may move a leaf. But what we have to make sense of in the case of agent causation is the possibility that a whole substance (an animal) may somehow come to act on its own parts, and yet not in such a way that its action can simply be reduced to the action of *parts* on parts. But how can that be? Doesn't the action of a complex whole have to consist in the combined actions of its parts? But if the action of an animal simply consists in the combined activities of its neurons, muscles, organs, etc., must its action not be governed by the laws of chemistry, electricity, etc., which determine when neurons will fire, when muscles will contract, etc? How on earth could this really amount to the *animal's* being in charge? It is this question that I now take up.

8.6 Top-down causation

I have just raised the question how an animal could possibly bring about a movement or change in a part of its body in such a way that its causing that movement or change did not simply amount merely to *another* part or parts of its body causing that movement or change (and therefore being governed merely by the laws and principles pertaining to the behaviour of those parts). This is closely related to a number of issues that have been discussed in the philosophical literature under the heading of 'top-down', or sometimes 'downward', causation. It might not be immediately evident, however, quite *how* my question relates to some of the more common formulations of the top-down causation issue that have appeared in the literature, which do not very often characterize top-down causation in quite this way. Recent discussions, in particular, have tended to characterize what would be involved in top-down causation (were there to be any) as essentially something that would have to involve the existence of so-called 'emergent', higher-level properties acting back down upon lower-level ones. It is perhaps difficult to see straight away how exactly this issue connects with my question about causation *by wholes* and its relations to causation by parts. Emergent properties are evidently normally characterized as properties that can be properties only *of* rather complex wholes, but that might not be to say that causation by emergent properties is entirely the same thing as causation by that whole itself.

My own view (as already explained, to some extent, in Sections 8.4 and 8.5 above) is that the ontological preference for properties over the things that possess them that one can discern throughout many recent discussions of causation, is based on motivations that are ultimately confused. Properties are universals and their role in causality is therefore quite different from that of the *efficacious* causes that are the real agents of change in our universe. Properties have causal relevance, they *matter,* but they do not (literally) do causal *work,* for a universal is not the sort of entity that *could* do work. Sometimes, admittedly, the fact that properties are universals is mentioned as an obstacle to regarding them as legitimate agents of change, but then the solution provided is to introduce property exemplifications or property instances, entities that are alleged to combine the fine-grained relevance appropriate to a property with the particularity that many judge necessary for real efficacy. But by my lights, this 'solution' is simply the result of an attempt incoherently to combine in a single ontological category requirements of efficaciousness that are rightly judged to attach only to particulars with requirements of counterfactual relevance that are (again rightly) judged to attach only to such entities as properties or facts. In fact though, it is to ontological *diversity*, not to hybridity that we should look in order properly to understand how to fit together these different aspects of our concept of causation. Moreover, it seems to me quite obvious that we shall not satisfactorily solve the free will problem unless we can understand the idea of causation that really is *by the animal* rather than by the animal's *properties,* however 'high-level' and 'emergent' those properties may be. How could I be held responsible for what my properties (or instantiations of them) have brought about (even if it were right to think of properties as the things that 'bring about' effects) unless the fact that those properties are instantiated is, in some way or other, down to *me*? I shall therefore not follow the literature in its characterization of top-down causation, preferring my own formulation in terms of causation by wholes and parts respectively. Nevertheless, I should like to *connect* my discussion to some of the existent literature on top-down causation, since some of the issues that have arisen there are unquestionably relevant to the issue I wish to discuss. In the current section, then, I want to try to explain how I see my question and those that are generally considered under the head of top-down causation as related, and to provide some defence of the way in which I prefer to formulate the crucial issue.

The idea of a form of causation that is 'top-down' evidently exploits a metaphor of ascending levels. For the purposes of this discussion, I shall simply accept without argument the claim that it is best to think about the relevant levels in a *relative* rather than an absolute way; that is to say, that we need not commit ourselves to the idea that there are monolithic divides across the whole of nature of which there is a single correct account to be given, but merely that so far as the explanation of the workings of any given complex system is concerned, it may be useful to consider those workings as, in a certain sense *stratified*. Thus, for example, so far as animals are concerned, at the bottom level there may be sub-atomic particles, moving up through atoms and molecules, to such things as cells, tissues, and organs, culminating ultimately in the top-level system that is an organized animal. The workings of each different level may be the subject of study by different sorts of disciplines, but, ultimately, understanding the behaviour of the whole animal will demand an understanding of how the different levels relate to one another. In particular, so far as animals are concerned, we will need to understand how the way in which we tend to think and talk of the motions and changes of the whole animal as due to actions on the part of that animal relates to what the study of the workings of the lower level *parts* of animals reveals about their role in the production of these higher-level motions and changes.

The challenge, as I see it, is to understand how on earth it can be that the animal has any real, independent efficacy *of its own*: any efficacy that does not merely reduce to the efficacy of its various parts. Consider, for example, the phenomenon of bodily action. In acting, I make my body move in certain ways: I raise my arm, I bend my leg, etc., and perhaps by means of these bodily movements I bring about further effects in the world. But my body cannot move in these various ways unless certain things first happen in my brain and central nervous system. For example, certain neurons must fire in my motor cortex. It would seem, then, that in order to bring about the resultant bodily movement I must either bring about the prior activity in my motor cortex as well, or the activity in my motor cortex must simply *be* (at least part of) the process that constitutes my bringing about the bodily movement in question. If we choose the former answer—that I must bring about the activity in my motor cortex—the question merely arises again how is it possible for me to bring about *this* activity, and the answer would seem, again, to be the disjunctive one that it is possible only if I am able to bring about still *prior* neural activity that produces the activity in the motor cortex, or if the prior neural activity is at least part of a process that *constitutes* my bringing about the activity in the motor cortex. If we choose the former answer, once again the question will be raised of how on earth is it possible for me to bring about this prior neural activity, and again the same disjunctive reply seems inevitable. We do not seem to be able to end the impending regress without at some stage either concluding that the whole chain of neural activity must be initiated ultimately by an ethereal input from something like an immaterial self that sets off a whole chain of physical causes, or else that my activity is at the end of the day entirely constituted by the activity of certain of my functionally significant smaller parts on other such parts: neuron on neuron, synapse on synapse, and so on. Since I take the former solution to be unacceptable for a variety of reasons sufficiently familiar from the literature that I hope I need not rehearse them, *some* version of the latter must be the right thing to say. In some sense or other, my activity must always be realized in the activities of parts of my body: there is no acting on my part that is not realized in some way by these lower-level events. Action, after all, is not magic; it needs a physical realization if it is to create physical effects such as bodily movements. But the question is whether it is possible to say this and yet avoid the conclusion that it is not really me but rather my *parts* that are doing all the important causal work. If my actions are simply constituted by neural and other bodily activity, where am I to be found in the causal story? It is hard to see how, if the story is correct, the agent herself can be anything more than a kind of epiphenomenon, arising out of the hive of activity taking place in the cells, muscles, blood vessels, etc.

There are those who will say that to talk of epiphenomena here is to make a premature and rather silly mistake. My activity, they will say, is just the *same thing* as the activity of my parts; there is no question of my agency having been usurped. We have simply said something about what constitutes that agency and have thereby *reduced* rather than eliminated it. It does not follow from the fact that my actions are constituted by neural firings, etc. that I do not really raise my arm, bend my leg, and so on, any more than it follows from the fact that my washing machine's activities are constituted by various movements of the drum, switch, pump, etc. that it (the machine) does not really wash my clothes. But merely to say this is, I believe, to say much too little to answer the concerns that the reductive picture tends to engender. We do not generally think that we relate to our parts in the way that a washing machine relates to its parts. We are really in *charge* of at least some of our parts, we tend to feel—the ones that respond to our voluntary control— and we initiate, orchestrate, and organize their movements into the patterns that are demanded for the execution of our plans in a way to which nothing corresponds in any inanimate entity. We are happy to concede, I think, that nothing is really up to the washing machine; its activities really *are* the sum total of the connected activities of its parts and there is no *further* sense in which *it*—the whole machine—can make anything happen. But with us, it is different. We feel that certain things are truly up to us; that our input can genuinely settle which way things will go. It is this idea that is so difficult to square with the picture according to which our activity is simply constituted by a maelstrom of neurological processes. And it does not help, I think, with the basic difficulty, to insist that a movement's being 'up to me' is a matter of its being caused by some appropriate mental state or collection of states, such as a desire or an intention or cluster of such things, something that, it is then supposed, must have a neural realization in the brain. For if desires and intentions are just names for certain neural states, the problem remains that it seems to be those neural states, not me, that are calling the shots. Given that I am in those states, what I will do, it would seem, is settled by them. It is not settled by me. And yet we think of actions as settlings of matters by agents *themselves*, settlings that occur at the time of action and not before.

What would have to be true if it really were to be the case that I myself could settle how precisely my body is to move and change in various respects? I think we would have to be able to make sense of a conception of a human being as a creature with powers to affect (by means of its own agency) the processes that go on in its own small parts, such as its neurons. It would have to be possible for the whole human being somehow (by acting or trying to act) to make a difference to what goes on at the level of such things as neurons and hormones. But is this idea coherent? I want next to consider what I regard as the major challenges to such a conception of what a true agent must be able to do. What I shall aim to show is that there is nothing about this idea that is demonstrably at odds with any metaphysical picture we have good reason to embrace, but only with metaphysical prejudices with which we have grown over-familiar and over-comfortable. I shall try to tell a story about how we might think about the causal metaphysics involved in agency that is naturalistically acceptable and does not involve anything spooky, magical, dualistic, or otherwise metaphysically problematic, but which also allows for the existence of a conception of agency that meets the requirements of the Agency Incompatibilist. Let me be clear that I do not think this story is easy to tell. If it were easy to tell and to understand it would already be part of our orthodox way of thinking. Learning to tell and to understand it is a task with which I think philosophers of mind, action, and biology will probably be heavily preoccupied over the next few years. But I have no doubt that it *can* be told, no doubt better than I have managed to tell it here. What I offer is, I suppose, a first attempt at making some of the moves I think will need to be made if we are to formulate a conception of the animal agent that better captures what we already know about such agents.

8.7 Breaking the laws

One idea that has often surfaced in the literature on top-down causation is that if such a thing existed, it would have to involve suspension of, or interference with, the laws in operation at the lower level (for example, the laws of physics). Here is Kim, for example, explaining the idea of downward causation as it pertains to a case of animal motion:

> The idea is that when certain wants and needs, aided by perceptions, propel a bird through the air, the cells and molecules making up the bird's body, too, are propelled, willy-nilly, through the air by the same wants, needs and perceptions. If you add to this the further thesis…to the effect that these psychological states and processes, though they 'emerge' out of biological and physicochemical processes, are distinct from them, you are apparently committed to the consequence that *these "higher-level" mental events and processes cause lower-level physical laws to be violated*, that the molecules that are part of your body behave, at least sometimes, in ways different from the ways they would if they weren't part of a living body animated by mental processes.[54]

There are two important questions arising from this passage. The first is how the 'apparent commitment' to law violation is supposed to arise from the mere assumption that certain psychological states and events (when regarded as distinct from any biological and physicochemical ones) can cause the cells and molecules in a bird's body to move. The second is how what follows the italicized phrase is supposed to relate to the italicized phrase itself. I take the second of these two questions first.

Kim's suggestion seems to be that if it were to turn out that the molecules that are part of a human body behaved, at least sometimes, in ways different from the ways they would if they weren't part of a living body animated by mental processes, then that would amount to a violation of physical law. But this is surely highly questionable, at least if taken at face value.[55] Why should the physical laws be such that they do not allow for any variation of behaviour according to contextual setting? After all, the physical influences on a molecule embedded in a cell, say, will be different from the

---

[54] Kim (1992: 120).

[55] This point is well made by Moreno and Umerez (2000) in a discussion of this same passage from Kim: 'the rephrasing takes for granted that if "the molecules that are part of your body behave, at least sometimes, in ways different from the way part of a living body animated by mental processes" that implies the presumed violation of lower-level physical laws. This is totally unwarranted because for a molecule to behave differently within a living organism does not, by itself and without further argumentation, imply that a violation of physical laws is being committed' (102).

physical influences on one that is not so embedded. This may allow perfectly well for consequent differences in behaviour without any violation of physical law, simply because the relevant causal (and, for all that has been said, physically describable) factors impacting on the molecule are different. Indeed, one need not enter the biological realm at all to see that the idea that a thing might behave differently in one context from the way it behaves in another must involve law violation is confused. The molecules that make up a door no doubt behave very differently from the way in which they might behave if they were not part of the door, e.g. regularly moving backwards and forwards on familiar trajectories as the door opens and closes. But surely no one thinks that any physical laws are violated when doors are opened.

It may be that Kim has mis-stated the point he really wished to make here and indeed I think he has done so. I shall come back shortly to speculate about what he might really have meant. But let us turn first to the other question raised by the passage: how the 'apparent commitment' to law violation is supposed to follow from the idea that psychological states and processes might bring about movements of the cells and molecules making up a bird's body. Presumably, the thought must be something like this: purely physical laws (i.e. laws expressible using only the concepts of *physics*) are sufficient to dictate completely the movements of all physical things. Cells and molecules are certainly physical things, and so purely physical laws ought to be sufficient to dictate their movements too. But then, unless psychological states and processes are themselves describable in physical ways, so that their influence on events, such as it is, can be found simply to be a form of influence that comes within the ambit of those physical laws, their having an impact on the way the cells and molecules move is inconsistent with the assumption that everything is dictated by the physical laws. There will be extra, non-physical influences to take account of in the story of what causes motion in our universe. And that is something that many naturalistically inclined philosophers will be very disinclined to accept.

I think something like this line of thinking is what motivates Kim's worry about top-down causation. It is, moreover, a line of thinking that has been extraordinarily influential more generally in philosophy of mind. It has many formulations and manifestations, some more convincing than others. But in its current form, at least, it surely begs the question against the defender of top-down causation who will wish to reject the first premise of the argument above. Indeed, that the first premise should be rejected is at the heart of her position. It is simply *not* true, according to the friend of downward causation, that the laws merely of *physics* are sufficient to *dictate* in all their myriad details, the movements and changes that will occur as the result of any particular collocation of circumstances. What the physical laws (at any rate, those that we know of) do, she will say, is rather to *constrain* those movements and changes—they place limits on the possible—but they need not be conceived of as dictating every detail of what occurs. A free-falling tennis ball, if left to fall by itself, for example, will have to obey Newton's law of gravity. But it can never be predicted, simply on the basis of the law of gravity, that any given individual tennis ball will hit the ground at such and such a velocity given such and such a starting position, since the law applies only *ceteris paribus* and hence can be used to predict a precise outcome for a given, individual ball only where no interference is envisaged—no person or animal to step in and catch the ball, no gravitational or other forces to draw it away from the line of freefall, no tennis racket to swipe it away in a different direction, no sudden explosion to cause it to break into smithereens, etc. Now, it might be retorted that all these various interfering influences must be representable in their turn as physical interventions that can themselves be brought within the purview of other physical laws, so that the *overall* physical outcome will be a result dictated by the entirety of physical laws that apply in any given situation. But it is most important to be clear that it is sheer speculation that there really is such a complete set of laws, a set that not only *constrains* but also *dictates* the entirety of what happens (or even a set that dictates the probabilities of different things occurring). It is quite possible that in supposing it must be so, we simply let our imaginations run away with us—extrapolating from the closed and ideal systems that physics and mechanics give us to think about to the huge complexity of the real world—in ways that are inadmissible. This is suggested, for example, by Cartwright, in describing her vision of what she calls the 'dappled world':

The laws that describe this world are a patchwork, not a pyramid. They do not take after the simple, elegant and abstract structure of a system of axioms and theorems. Rather they look like—and steadfastly stick to looking like—science as we know it; apportioned into disciplines, apparently arbitrarily grown up; governing different sets of properties at different levels of abstraction; pockets of great precision; large parcels of qualitative maxims resisting precise formulation; erratic overlaps; here and there, once in a while, corners that line up, but mostly ragged edges; and always the cover of law just loosely attached to the jumbled world of material things. For all we know, most of what occurs in nature occurs by hap, subject to no law at all. What happens is more like an outcome of negotiation between domains than the logical consequence of a system of order. The dappled world is what, for the most part, comes naturally: regimented behaviour results from good engineering.[56]

Now, Cartwright's vision of the universe might, of course, be mistaken and there is not space here properly to engage in her defence. Perhaps the cover of law is less loosely attached to the jumbled world of material things than she surmises. But my point is merely that at the moment we are not in a position to know this to be so. Moreover, I am in agreement with Cartwright that such empirical evidence as we have bearing on this issue rather points in the opposite direction. So far as I am aware, then, there is absolutely no *scientific* reason to endorse the claim that purely physical laws are sufficient to dictate the movements of every physical thing (or even its indeterministic cousin— that they are sufficient, at any rate, to fix the probabilities that any given movement should occur). There is only the grip of a mesmerising world view. And a mesmerising world view cannot be allowed to win the argument merely because it is mesmerising.

---

[56] Cartwright (1999: 1).

The defender of top-down causation, then, ought not to be moved by the argument above; she should simply stick to her guns and reject its first premise, insisting on the distinction between physical laws regarded as *constrainers* of reality (which she accepts) and physical laws regarded as *dictators* of reality (which she denies).

8.8 Causal exclusion

Sometimes, the concept of supervenience (or some closely related idea of upward determination of the macro by the micro), rather than the concept of law, is used in the attempt to say what it is that seems to be in tension with the idea of downward causation. Here, for example, is Searle, arguing that there is no room for free will on what he thinks of as the contemporary scientific view:

Our basic explanatory mechanisms work from the bottom up. That is to say, we explain the behaviour of surface features of a phenomenon such as the transparency of glass or the liquidity of water, in terms of the behaviour of microparticles such as molecules. And the relation of the mind to the brain is an example of such a relation. Mental features are caused by, and realised in, neurophysiological phenomena...But we get causation from the mind to the body, that is we get top-down causation over a passage of time: and we get top-down causation because the top level and the bottom level go together. So for example, suppose I wish to cause the release of the neurotransmitter acetylcholine at the axon end-plates of my motor neurons, I can do it by simply deciding to raise my arm and then raising it. Here, the mental event, the intention to raise my arm, causes the physical event, the release of acetylcholine, a case of top-down causation if ever there was one. But the top-down causation works only because the mental events are grounded in the neurophysiology to start with. So corresponding to the description of the causal relations that go from the top to the bottom, there is another description of the same series of events where the causal relations bounce entirely along the bottom, that is, they are entirely a matter of neurons and neuron firings at synapses, etc. As long as we accept this conception of how nature works, then it doesn't seem that there is any scope for the freedom of the will.[57]

Why does Searle think that accepting this conception of how nature works leaves no scope for freedom of the will? Presumably, the thought it this: though it may be admitted that there is top-down causation *in a way*, there is no *irreducibly* top-down causation according to this picture. Intentions can cause physical events to happen in the brain, to be sure, but only if they are themselves thought of as 'grounded in the neurophysiology to start with'. And that leaves no room for freedom of the will, Searle thinks, because the neurophysiology ultimately settles everything. To use his words, 'corresponding to the description of the causal relations that go from the top to the bottom, there is another description of the same series of events, where the causal relations bounce entirely along the bottom'. There is in that case no room for *me* to settle anything because my neurons have done it for me. Compatibilists will tend to think this picture confused: my neurons settling things *just is* my settling things, they

[57] Searle (1984: 93).

will say (or at least can be, when things are going well). But I think Searle is right. If there is no irreducibly top-down causation, it is utterly puzzling how I am supposed to be anything other than a *place* where certain lower-level events produce others, how anything can ever really count as having been 'up to me'.

Is there any way to resist the picture of reality that generates the difficulty? The only real hope, it seems to me, is to be found in the suggestion that perhaps it is not really so obvious as Searle thinks it is that all 'explanatory mechanisms' have to work from the bottom up. There are at least two possible routes of resistance here. One is to wonder whether Searle may be overstating the extent to which the explanation of movement and change in our world is 'bottom-up' *in general*, even in the case of the sorts of basic inanimate physical systems that we think we understand reasonably well. The other is to question whether, at any rate, it must be so throughout the whole of nature. I am inclined to think there is merit in both approaches and that they may perhaps be combined in the idea that (i) there is a certain amount of 'top-down' causation throughout the whole of the natural world, but that (ii) the extent to which top-down causation is able to usurp and replace bottom-up explanation increases exponentially with animacy and further still with the increasing complexity of animal life. I shall proceed to look at the two distinct parts of this suggestions in turn. By the end of the chapter, I hope that by means of showing what can be said in favour of each I shall have made out the case for the view that there is scope to challenge the very widespread idea that top-down causation is not a phenomenon we can readily countenance.

8.8.1 Top-down causation in the inanimate world

Roger Sperry is perhaps the most determined and explicit recent defender of the reality of downward causation throughout our universe. He notes that when a wheel rolls downhill, 'the molecules and atoms...are carried along...regardless of whether the individual molecules and atoms happen to like it or not'[58] and he intends this, as he makes clear in a later paper, not merely as an *analogy* for the kind of downward causation of brain events by conscious phenomena in which he is really interested, but as a 'direct, simple, objective, physical example of macro-causation illustrating the universal principle of how the emergent properties of an entity as a whole exert downward causal control over the parts and the trajectories of the parts through space and time without interfering with the causal interactions of the subentities at their own lower levels'.[59] His idea seems to be that unless we understand that a given molecule is part of a *wheel,* there is no hope of predicting or explaining its course through the world. It is the fact that it is a part of this particular type of larger whole that governs the path it takes through reality. Moreover, Sperry appears to believe that this influence—of wheel on part—cannot be captured properly by any mere account of the

---

[58] Sperry (1969: 534).   [59] Sperry (1986: 266).

influence of *parts* on part. Without reference to the role played by the wheel, the idea must be, we would be unable to give a proper account of why the molecules move as they do.

One might try, of course, to argue that the appearance of macro-determination here may be explained away. Klee, for example, commenting on Sperry's wheel example, writes as follows:

The motion of the whole wheel clearly does affect the motion of any individual molecule in it…How and why is it able to do this? By what means does it effect this influence? It seems to me that the higher-level motion of the whole wheel…has an influence on the lower-level individual molecule through the fact that the molecule bears individual structural micro-connections with neighbouring molecules in the wheel…It's not as though there is some setting in motion of the molecule by…the wheel's motion (in a direct property-to-property interaction) but rather, that the molecule is intimately connected in a physical sense to all the other molecules that make up the wheel…and so the motion is 'dictated' to the molecule in virtue of its participation in the total micro-structure of the wheel…[60]

Klee's idea seems to be that insofar as the wheel's motion affects the molecules within it, this is an interaction that is ultimately entirely explicable in terms of molecule-to-molecule relations at the lower level. But is this true? What Klee explicitly says about the nature of the relationship between higher- and lower-level entities seems true enough, i.e. that the higher-level motion of the whole wheel has an influence on the lower-level individual molecule *through* the fact (among other things) that the molecule has individual micro-connections with neighbouring molecules in the wheel, in the sense that if there were no such connections there would be no possibility that the wheel should transmit its motion to the molecules—indeed, there would be no possibility of there being a wheel in the first place. But it does not seem to follow merely from *that* that the influence of the higher-level motion just *consists in* the influence of the lower-level molecules on each other. Lower-level connectedness of this sort amongst the molecules might be a *necessary condition* of the existence of the relevant higher-level causal factors without itself constituting the totality of causal forces relevant to the understanding of why the molecules are moving as they are.

Another important question is what Klee means by saying that 'it is not as though there is some setting in motion of the molecule by…the wheel's motion (in a direct property-to-property interaction)'. What is a 'direct' property-to-property interaction, exactly? Properties do not seem to be the most obvious candidates for literal interaction. As I have stressed above, they are universals, and it seems very doubtful that a universal can literally *act* (and *a fortiori*, doubtful that it can *inter*act). Perhaps Klee would say that he is really talking about interactions between property *instances*. But it is not really any more obvious that property instantiations can interact than that properties can. On the view for which I have argued very extensively elsewhere, [61] they are best

---

[60] Klee (1984: 60–1).   [61] See my (1997: Chapter 1).

regarded as facts, and facts are no better at interacting than are properties. The things that (literally) *interact* are the same as the things that *act*, which means, so it seems to me, that they have to be *things*.

What *is* indisputably true, though, is that the molecule is not set in motion by the wheel in the way in which one inanimate thing most usually sets another in motion, i.e. by colliding with it. Perhaps this is really what Klee means when he speaks of a direct 'property-to-property' interaction. Our standard model for causation involves one object impacting on another and thereby producing a change in it, usually a change in properties that relate to its motion (though perhaps not only those). The wheel certainly does not impact upon the molecule in *this* way, but must that be the only kind of causal interaction we can envisage? Might there not be types of causal affecting that obtain only in the special case where one object is a *part* of another? It does not seem straightforwardly obvious that a wheel might not, by moving, bring about effects in its parts that are of a somewhat different character from the effects it is able to produce by interacting with *other* objects. Of course, its capacity to do so is bound to be reliant, in many ways, upon the relationships between its parts, not least because its own existence is reliant upon those relationships. But it does not seem to follow merely from this that the wheel is unable to affect a molecule within it in such a way that this influence is no mere resultant of the individual influences on that molecule of other molecules within the wheel.

A better challenge to the possibility of such irreducible top-down causation comes, I think, from the thought that it is not merely true that the existence of molecules with certain sorts of structural micro-connections to one another is *necessary* in order that the motion of the wheel should produce motion in the molecules; it is also true that it is *sufficient*. All one needs, the thought goes, is the molecules arranged wheelwise and one gets the wheel 'for free' as it were, which makes it seem as though any effects that the wheel might then be said to have on anything are really attributable to the molecules arranged wheelwise. As Kim puts it: 'the difficulties [with downward causation] essentially boil down to the following single argument. If an emergent, M, emerges from basal conditions C, why can't C displace M as a cause of any putative effect of M? Why doesn't C do all the work in bringing about the putative effect of M and suffice as an explanation of why the effect occurred?'[62] Why, for instance, can we not attribute an effect on the trajectory of a given individual molecule, which we might initially be inclined to attribute to the wheel, to the molecules arranged wheelwise instead? Surely, if the existence of the wheel is emergent with respect to these lower-level entities, the lower-level entities ought to be regarded as the ultimate repository of the causal powers of the higher?

---

[62] Kim (2000: 318). Kim is, of course, utilizing a different ontology—an 'emergent', for him, is an emergent *property*—and hence it would be the property of wheel-shapedness or some such thing that was the emergent entity in the case. But I think it does not matter, for present purposes, if we simply speak of the wheel as the emergent. The general issue seems to be the same, whatever the ontological framework.

To answer this question, what is required, I think, is a challenge to the appealing presupposition that underlies it, namely that an effect of any kind is always fully accounted for, metaphysically speaking, once proximal causally sufficient conditions for its occurrence have been provided. For it is this assumption that makes it seem as though causal efficacy will always have to drain down to the lowest level once we have conceded (as commitment to something like supervenience seems to require) that certain lower-level arrangements are constitutively sufficient for the existence of certain higher-level phenomena. If the lower-level arrangements give rise constitutively to the higher-level ones, the thought goes, then they are all we need for the generation of the causal effects of anything we might have wanted to attribute to the higher-level entity. It is quite true that the lower-level arrangements (once we have them) are 'all we need', but the crucial question is how the requisite causally proximal lower-level arrangements are to be provided for in the first place. It is in thinking about this question that one can begin to see why we might need to appeal to top-down causation.

The key to the solution to this puzzle about top-down causation, I think, is the phenomenon of *coincidence*. For in general, the 'basal conditions' from which complex entities may be said to 'emerge' tend to be complex conditions, which require for their generation that a great many quite separate things occur *together* or else in some particular precise order, or (more usually) both. To take Sperry's example, if we are fully to account for the motion of a particular molecule within a wheel, we are going to have to account at some point for the existence of the *wheel*: for the arrangement of molecules that then governs the motion imparted to an individual molecule contained within it. It is not enough, in order to provide this account, merely to say that the wheel 'emerges' from certain basal conditions, for it is not as though the molecules that go to make up the wheel simply form themselves spontaneously into the wanted arrangements. Wheels have to be *manufactured*.[63] This implies that a person with a certain skill is required and they need to have appropriate tools for making the wheel. The material from which the wheel is to be made needs to be in the same place as the person and the tools. Then, all this being in place, numerous different kinds of event have to occur together in the person's brain; events relating to tactile and visual perception, memories of previous attempts to make similar items, judgements about the best means to various ends, etc. In order to *get* molecules arranged wheelwise, in other words (and hence, ultimately, to generate the effects that will eventually be

---

[63] Of course, there are entities which do *not* have to be manufactured whose shape and size also affects the motion of their component molecules, e.g. boulders. Here too, the size and shape of the boulder affects how the molecules that compose it move, and indeed whether it will move at all. But it is less obvious in this case that there is anything wrong with thinking of the causal powers of the boulder as in some sense just a resultant of the causal powers of molecules arranged boulder-wise because there is no temporal coincidence involved in its production that demands appeal to a higher-level cause. Such temporal coincidences as are required to produce a boulder of this particular size and shape can be just that: coincidences, accidents. But those required to produce wheels cannot be accidents.

attributable to the wheel, such as the trajectories of individual molecules within it), an enormous number of separate transactions, interactions, collocations of phenomena, etc. have to be in place, some occurring together, some sequentially, in the right order, and all harmonizing in such a way that a manufactured wheel is the eventual result.

But from the point of view of low-level physics (say), it is just not possible to gain any understanding of how the co-occurrence of these different phenomena required for the production of a wheel has been provided for by the universe. Though we know that they *have* been thus provided for (because the phenomenon has actually occurred—a wheel has actually been produced), the co-occurrences in question just look utterly coincidental when looked at from the lower level: there is nothing to explain how it has come to pass that everything has worked out so well, how all the co-ordination, the harmonization has arisen. It is only when we raise our view to the higher level that we begin to find the resources to make sense of what has occurred, when we can speak, for example, of persons and their plans and designs and see the whole of what has occurred as something that someone has orchestrated in order to achieve an end. In one sense of the word 'emerge', indeed, it is more accurate to say that the basal conditions emerge from factors favouring the existence, in these circumstances, of the higher-level entity, rather than the other way around. The requisite basal conditions are only produced when somebody wants a *wheel* and therefore goes about the business of making it the case that certain molecules are arranged wheelwise. That the molecules are in this kind of arrangement, that they are ordered in the necessary way, is a fact that is to be causally explained by appeal to someone's plans and designs: a wheel was wanted and so a wheel got made. Without this part of the causal story, it would just be an enormous and totally inexplicable coincidence that the universe had managed to throw up molecules arranged wheelwise.[64] One might think, then, that the answer to Kim's question about why C cannot displace M as a cause of any putative effect of M might, at least in some sorts of circumstance, be this: C can hardly be allowed to usurp M entirely in the causal order unless we can understand how C came to be without invoking the fact that C constitutes M. For C may be an exceedingly complex condition, the generation of which itself requires to be explained in such a way that its existence not appear to be the most enormous and inexplicable *coincidence*. In many cases, it may be that C would not have come into existence in the first place, were it not for the fact that C constitutes *M*. To understand how C can fail to be an enormous and inexplicable coincidence, that is, we may need the view from the higher level.

---

[64] A caution in case my intentions here are misunderstood: with respect to the question, how did these molecules come to be arranged wheelwise?, the answer involves an appeal to design. But I do not mean to imply that the answer to *all* such questions about how complex arrangements of things have arisen must involve an appeal to design. There are many higher-level resources for the explication of what might otherwise look like coincidence. Design is one. Natural selection of the biologically more fit is another.

Of course, once we *have* the basal conditions C requisite for an M, then we can say that M's existence 'supervenes on' those basal conditions—and so it does—in the sense that reproducing those basal conditions C would obtain for us another M, and in the sense that we could not cease to have an M without making some alterations that would involve an alteration in those basal conditions. But the question is how you get those very specific and complex basal conditions to arise in the first place? Why have they arisen? Moreover, I suggest, it may be impossible to answer this question in terms merely of *prior* basal conditions, because those prior conditions may themselves simply be just as coincidental as the ones we are currently trying to explain, in the absence of the resources provided by the fact that these conditions are constitutive of certain higher level facts. To explain one coincidence in terms of another, prior coincidence is clearly no real progress at all. What we need is to understand the forces and pressures that create and sustain a chain of lower-level activity that from the point of view merely of the lower level consists simply of a succession of giant coincidences.

Kim's supposition—and indeed the supposition of many writing in the literature—is that the causal generation of any given set of 'basal' conditions is a matter that can itself be understood in terms entirely of some prior set of circumstances, also characterizable in 'lower-level' terms, a description where 'the causal relations bounce entirely along the bottom', to use Searle's phrase. But from the point of view of the 'bottom level' the collocations of circumstances required to generate the basal conditions for a wheel are themselves, once again, giant coincidences: molecules arranged person-wise and others arranged knife-wise; interactions between the molecules arranged person-wise and those arranged knife-wise of—strangely—just the right kind to produce a wheel. No matter how far back we go along the chain, if we never raise our eyes from these lower level events, we will lack what is requisite to explain why these conditions are (at any stage in the chain) produced *together*. And yet this is what is extraordinary; it is what needs to be explained. How on earth can it be that all these lower-level events in brain matter, in muscles, in metal or wood, are happening together in just the right way to enable a wheel to be produced? What explains the co-ordination, the collocation? What we need to know is how it has come about that all these conditions have managed to obtain so fortuitously together. Merely stating that they *have* managed to so obtain (which is what one does when one offers up the conjunction of all the various relevant proximal lower-level conditions in explanation of the effect) is not enough to provide this explanation.

In *Metaphysics* VI, 3, Aristotle considers the case of a man who dies at the hands of ruffians because he goes out to the well for a drink at the wrong moment.[65] Perhaps there may be a sufficient condition for his being at the well at that time: he was thirsty, perhaps, and knew he could quench his thirst by going to the well, or perhaps we could give a sufficient condition in neurophysiological terms. Perhaps there may be a

---

[65] Aristotle (1984b: VI, 3).

sufficient condition for the ruffians being at the well, too. This would imply that we could give, if we would like to do so, a sufficient condition for the man's being at the well at the same time as the ruffians. But for all that, it may just be a coincidence that they are there together, making the man's death an accident, an unfortunate piece of happenstance. There may be nothing to explain the simultaneity of the man's arrival and the ruffians' arrival at the well. In particular, the sufficient condition we are able to give does not explain that simultaneity, for all that it is sufficient for it.[66] There *could* be such an explanation. An accomplice to the ruffians might, for instance, have inveigled himself into the man's company and suggested to him that he go to the well at just the right time to coincide there with the ruffians. But the mere existence of a sufficient condition does not by itself imply that the question how it was that these phenomena obtained *together* has a satisfactory answer or any answer at all. However, in the case of the complex phenomena of which our world consists—in the case of such states of affairs as the existence of wheels, for instance—we surely have the right to demand that there be such an answer. If we cannot get such an answer from low-level physics then we will have to look to higher levels to supply it for us.

Is this just a point about *explanation*, though, thought of as a phenomenon related merely to the requirements of human enlightenment and understanding, rather than a point about the hard metaphysics of the matter? Perhaps it will be said that in order for we humans to be satisfied a story might need to be provided from the higher-level perspective; that in order to understand how a wheel has come into existence, for example, we humans will need to be told about its manufacturer and his skills and plans and intentions. But nevertheless, so far as the causal metaphysics is concerned, it is all just causally sufficient conditions described in lower-level terms and giving rise inexorably to others. But this cannot be the right way to think about the matter. Causation is about how things come to be. Where certain things require for their coming to be that complex synchronous arrangements are brought into being, then whatever sustains or enables the complex synchronous arrangements to exist has to be part of the causal story, part of the relevant *metaphysics* of causation and not just part of what is required to satisfy the intellectual curiosity of a human investigator (though it will be required for that, too). It will not do simply to suggest that we need the higher level only to give ourselves intellectual satisfaction. Without appeal to the higher level, there is actually nothing to *cause* the synchronicities required for the phenomena we are trying causally to account for. Without an agent, for instance, there is no one to manufacture the wheel, no one to ensure that the causally sufficient conditions for its emergence (including e.g. successive states of tools, materials, etc.) come about. The explanation of how things come to be co-ordinated is part not only of the explanatory but of the causal story.

---

[66] This point is well made by Richard Sorabji in his (1980: Chapter 1).

From a certain point of view, though, this can seem terribly puzzling. Surely causally sufficient conditions are *sufficient*—that is the whole point of them. So how can more than what is causally sufficient for something be causally required for it? But this is the place to note two things. One is an observation made by Anscombe about the concept of a sufficient condition. 'Sufficient condition', she notes, is a term of art,

…whose users may therefore lay down its meaning as they please. So they are in their rights to rule out the query: 'May not the sufficient conditions of an event be present, and the event yet not take place?' For 'sufficient condition' is so used that if the sufficient conditions for X are there, X occurs. But at the same time, the phrase cozens the understanding into not noticing an assumption. For 'sufficient condition' sounds like: 'enough'. And one certainly *can* ask: 'May there not be *enough* to have made something happen—and yet it not have happened?'[67]

What Anscombe notes here is that we may, if we wish, define 'sufficient conditions' to be *necessitating* conditions, conditions such that, once they are in place, nothing else could possibly have happened. But if we take the concept in this way, we have to concede that we are in no position to know whether everything that happens *has* sufficient conditions (let alone ones that can be described entirely using physical vocabulary). The assumption that everything does have such conditions, indeed, would seem to amount precisely to the assumption of determinism, and so cannot be taken for granted in a context such as this where the truth of determinism is precisely what is in question. We cannot just help ourselves to the assumption that everything that happens is inexorably necessitated by some prior state of the world. We *do* know, of course, that in another sense of the word 'sufficient', anything that actually happens must have had causally sufficient conditions, i.e. conditions that were 'enough' to allow for its occurrence, which is to say that nothing strictly requisite for the occurrence of anything that actually occurs could have been lacking. But that is different from there being conditions in place such that nothing else could then *possibly* have happened. It is only if one is operating with the stronger concept of a causally sufficient condition as a necessitating condition, one might think, that one is entitled to the supposition that once we have causally sufficient conditions there could be nothing more to be said about the metaphysical aspects of the causality by means of which some particular effect came to be. Perhaps if there truly were *necessitating* microphysical conditions in existence for the next global state of the universe at every stage, it really would be true that there was nothing more to be said about the causal metaphysics of any matter once the proximal sufficient conditions were given, they being in their turn secured by *prior* and once again entirely necessitating conditions. Here one can indeed see no gap into which a phenomenon like top-down causation might be fitted. But to suppose that this is so is precisely to insist upon the thesis of determinism, the thesis that I have been insisting throughout this book that we do not

---

[67] Anscombe (1971: 135).

know to be true and indeed which the phenomenon of agency gives us every reason to believe not to be true.

The second thing that helps with the puzzle about sufficiency, I think, is reflection on the fact that supervenience is a thesis that generally relates to one or another properties or states of affairs or facts that obtain at the same instant in time, so that in order to think of the relationship between higher-level conditions and the lower-level conditions that the supervenience thesis alleges are always constitutively sufficient for them, we are often thinking of the world in a kind of instantaneous, freeze-frame, snapshot view. There is something deeply misleading about this snapshot view, I think. It makes it seem as though an entity that exists only for an instant could do causal duty for one that is a persisting object. At the higher level, for instance, we might speak of 'the existence of the wheel at t' supervening on a momentary molecular arrangement that also exists 'at t'. But we have to remember that an instantaneous molecular arrangement does not in fact, of course, guarantee, by itself, the existence of *a wheel*. A wheel is a *persisting* entity and so its existence requires that the molecular arrangement that exists at t either maintains itself or manages to be succeeded in time by a whole series of appropriate further molecular arrangements. The causation of the right sort of succession of arrangements may be something that can only be understood by abstracting away from individual molecules and their interactions—not because of some fact to do with what is required to give a human being intellectual satisfaction, but because of facts to do with what is actually required metaphysically in order that an entity should persist.

To see this, consider the phenomenon of a *whirlpool*. Individual molecules of water may become caught up in an already existent whirlpool, and once they are so caught up, are subjected to the forces that keep the whirlpool in existence. But to understand these forces and how they work, we do not look to each momentary individual supervenience base and consider how it generates the next. The persistence of the whirlpool is a phenomenon entirely blind to the details of individual molecules. It may indeed be a complete accident that any given individual molecule is part of the supervenience base of the whirlpool at any given moment. Remember that unless we beg the question in favour of determinism from the outset, we have no right to the assumption that each momentary individual supervenience base necessitates the next. Perhaps, for instance, there are pairs of molecules existing in positions such that either might possibly be sucked into the whirlpool at a given moment, and it is an entirely chance matter which in fact ends up inside it. Or perhaps there are possible interferences we can envisage: interferences that could have happened but did not, which would have led to molecules other than the ones in fact inside the whirlpool at any given time being inside it at that time. If either of these things is possible, we have no right to help ourselves to the idea of necessitation. What helps us understand how it might come about that the right kind of *succession* of molecular arrangements occurs to constitute a whirlpool is a story that abstracts entirely from each individual supervenience base; a story that is indeed, in this case, entirely physical but which is 'high level' at least in the sense that whatever *actual* succession of molecular arrangements

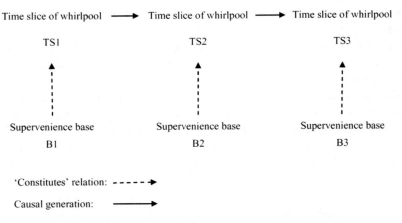

Figure 8.1 Causality and constitution relations for a whirlpool.

realizes the whirlpool may be coincidental. What is not coincidental—what can be explained by physical causes—is only that there is *some* such succession.

If the causality and constitution relations relating to the whirlpool were as depicted in Figure 8.1, then it would not be true that, as Searle has it, 'corresponding to the description of the causal relations that go from the top to the bottom, there is another description of the same series of events where the causal relations bounce entirely along the bottom'. In Figure 8.1, there are no causal relations bouncing along the bottom, since no momentary supervenience base is presumed to necessitate its successor. So far as causality is concerned, the pertinent fact is that once a whirlpool has formed certain forces tend to sustain it in existence unless and until the delicate equilibrium that maintains the whirlpool is disturbed by the intervention of some further factor. The complex arrangement that constitutes each individual momentary supervenience base therefore has a cause only in so far as it is a whirlpool-instantiating phenomenon; further details of the nature of the base (such as which individual molecules it contains) may be accidents relative to antecedent circumstances. So it is more accurate to think of the causality here as a kind of causality in which the phenomenon of the whirlpool creates the subsequent supervenience bases that then contribute to sustaining it, rather than the other way around.

What I am suggesting, then, is that appeal to higher levels of organization may be required in order to serve the coincidence-resolving function we require of a causal explanation adequate to the evolution of complex effects. This is not just a matter of what is required to help a human being understand why a certain effect has come about. It is a matter of what was actually required to *make* the effect come about; that is, it is a matter of causal metaphysics. So far as I can see, there is absolutely nothing incoherent about the idea that there could be such top-down causation, provided we reject (i) the assumption that there is necessitation at the lower level of each momentary supervenience base by the next and (ii) the idea that a succession, $C_1....C_n$ of momentary supervenience bases for a higher-level entity M could do the causal work done by the persisting entity M itself. It could not do so, I maintain, because the coincidence that is represented by the succession $C_1 \ldots C_n$ cannot be resolved without appeal to forces, principles, or regularities that apply only *because* $C_1 \ldots C_n$ constitute an M. The existence of M therefore answers causal questions that the existence of its successive supervenience bases does not.

Reflection on examples such as this can help us begin to see, I think, how we might come to shake ourselves free of the idea that all causation is ultimately due to the smallest things, even when it comes to the inanimate world. But it is when we begin to consider the innovations that nature has injected into the universe by means of the evolution of life, and in particular of complex animacy, that we see top-down causation really come into its own. I turn now, then, to consider the particular issue of how we might think about the top-down causation that makes animal agency possible.

8.8.2 Top-down causation and animacy

In the phenomenon of action, I have alleged, we see a situation in which a complex whole entity—an animal—is able to produce effects—in the first instance, movements of and changes in its own body by means of which it is then able to bring about further effects in the world. But how can this be? Surely movements and changes in the body that are of a physical sort are brought about by prior movements and changes in that same body, movements and changes that are also of a physical sort. If something happens to a neuron, for instance, that will surely have to be because the neuron has been physically affected, perhaps for example by an adjacent neuron. The question is how on earth a whole person or animal could manage to have effects on its own parts in such a way that that causation does not simply reduce to the causation of parts on parts? It is of course not possible for me to give a full account here of what the causation of human action actually involves, for that is a scientific question to which there will have to be scientific answers. But I would like to try to provide a sketch, at least, of how it might be conceivable that an animal could affect things without its role collapsing into the role played by the various lower-level entities out of the activities from which its own doings emerge.

In considering the question how we are to think of the relation between animal action and neural and muscular activity, it is essential, first of all, to avoid thinking of the animal's input as something *prior* to whatever neural processes initiate and then monitor and control the relevant bodily movement or change. That just leads to the dilemma mentioned in Section 8.6 above: either the prior input is itself a neural process, in which case we just face the same question again about how that prior neural process has been produced by the animal, or it is not, in which case it is hard to see how we could be doing anything other than flirting with dualism. The key must be to see the animal's input as a matter not of *prior* intervention but of *top-down* control of lower-level processes (such as the firings of individual neurons) by higher-level ones (such as the maintenance of particular wave patterns). This is the solution to the slightly different question how consciousness could be relevant to action that is suggested by Sperry, and it seems to me that it remains the most promising way of thinking about how top-down causation of the sort instantiated in agency might be possible. Nothing problematically ethereal is then involved; just as a whirlpool could have no effects were it not for the molecules of which it is composed having effects, so the way is clear for the straightforward admission that an animal could do nothing unless its parts simultaneously did things. The action of an animal is indeed constituted in this way by the actions of its parts. But as with the whirlpool, the key to seeing how the action of the animal is more than the sum of the actions of its parts is, I think, likely to be the idea that higher-level processes can dominate and dictate the evolution and distribution of certain lower-level ones, so that, so far as the important causal metaphysics is concerned, the explanation of how a certain complex neural state of affairs has come to be depends upon higher-level processes and ontologies. And as with the whirlpool, we avoid the puzzle about how there could be anything more to be said than what is given by the low-level neural story (or indeed than by what is given by stories told at much lower levels than the neural) by simply refusing the assumption that each momentary lower-level supervenience base necessitates the next. Insofar as there is constraint of the future by the past, the constraints are general and operate at multiple levels; there is simply no necessitation of an entire, detailed, global, microphysical arrangement by any prior arrangement of the same sort. It is perfectly possible that many of the important processes involved in the production of action are stochastic, i.e. are such that more than one conceivable future may evolve out of one and the same state. As with the whirlpool, we need to move up to higher levels of organization to understand how the coincidences and sequences that are required for action are orchestrated; how the *actual* evolution of what occurs is selected out of the range of possibilities left open by the microphysical laws and conditions.

In order for any kind of action to occur, it is obvious that an enormous amount of *co-ordinated* activity has to occur in the brain. Think about my typing, for example. I have to think about what I want to write and then separate messages must go to all the right fingers at the right time. My command of English will need to be engaged. My eyes need to be kept focused on the words as they appear on the screen and feedback from them needs to be utilized so as to enable corrections to be made. My body has to maintain itself upright and balanced in my chair. My brain may need to screen out disturbance from noise so that I can continue to focus on what I want to say. And so on. Something must account for this co-ordination, for the fact that all this activity occurs at the right time and in the right order, and is properly targeted at its goal. What does?

Some parts of the answer to this question will not require the invocation of the idea of the whole animal as a source of co-ordination; in some very simple animals, perhaps the idea of the whole animal as a source of co-ordination is never required. For much—indeed, in some ways, most—of what is achieved in the way of co-ordination and integration in an organized creature is achieved sub-animally by things it is natural to think of as *subsystems*. Complex animals are hierarchically organized entities: cells are organized into tissues, tissues into organs, organs into systems (e.g. the digestive system, the circulatory system, the visual system). Much of what has to be done in the way of co-ordination is achieved entirely by these subsystems, operating without any help at all from the creature itself. That I will remain balanced in my chair as I type, for example, is something that will be ensured by the operation of various sub-personal processes over which I have no direct control. Even here, I would want to insist, there will be something it is worth calling top-down causation; each level of the subsystemic hierarchy will generate processes that are able to dominate processes at lower levels. Campbell, for example, characterizes downward causation as something that involves a higher-level selective system determining the distribution of lower-level events and substances.[68] It seems clear that this is something that exists in hierarchically organized biological systems of all kinds, including plants. For example, a cell is a structure that, once formed, can be a source of control over the chemical processes that go on within it in the sense that laws and principles that belong to the level of the cell overtake those that belong to the level of the molecule when it comes to understanding how those lower-level processes are integrated and harmonized to serve the purposes of the cell. There need be nothing incoherent about this idea, provided we hang onto the idea we have already insisted upon: that lower level laws are only *constrainers* and not *dictators* of the future development of the things to which they apply. But in simple creatures, where there is little scope for distinguishing the contributions of different systems one from another (e.g. single-celled creatures like the paramecium) or else where the effective integration of different subsystems one with another can be achieved by such automatic mechanisms as feedback loops, there may be no need at all for the animal *itself* to be a source of co-ordination. It is these creatures for which the owner–body distinction I discussed at the beginning of Chapter 2 is *de trop*; there is no need to move beyond an explanation of their activity that invokes a range of simple subsystems interacting in ways that are self-regulating.

In more complex animals, though, it seems that the need to respond swiftly to the ever-changing demands of an unpredictable environment has made it imperative that the integration of subsystems be organized overall by a top-level system that differs from the other systems that operate beneath it in a special way. The important new feature of the top-level system is *discretion*: the creature itself becomes a special sort of object with a power selectively to control certain of its own subsystems in the light of constantly updated information, in such a way (roughly) as to optimize its chances of survival and success. In particular, it has this discretionary power over the systems that control its *movement*, for the sorts of responses to environmental changes that it needs to be able to effect are most usually responses that depend upon its being able either to get itself from one place to another or to causally affect parts of the world by way of the

----

[68] Campbell (1974: 180).

movements of its own body. It can stop eating, for example, if it suspects danger, and flee to hide itself. It can abandon a plan that does not seem to be working, to try another. It can stop playing the piano in order to talk. And so on. Much can be achieved in the way of teleological appropriateness by self-regulating and automatic systems. But, I suggest that for a mobile creature with many needs and many competing ends, some way of integrating the operation of these various systems so that the right range of things can be done in a sensible order is required, and for that, nature has found that a different kind of system is needed. What it has found, I surmise, is that the type of system needed is precisely the type that I have here called an agent; i.e. to repeat the characterization I gave in Chapter 4, a creature that can move the whole or at least some parts of something we are inclined to think of as *its* body, that is the centre of some form of subjectivity, a creature that is something to which at least some rudimentary types of intentional state (e.g. trying, wanting, perceiving) may be properly attributed, and a creature that is a settler of matters concerning certain of the movements of its own body.

In the case of such objects as these, the idea of causation that is irreducibly *by the object itself* and which does not simply reduce down to causation by properties of, fact about, or events occurring in the agent, finds a proper home precisely because of the *discretionary* aspect that is involved. It really is *up to the agent* which selections are made from the large repertoire of possible actions available: the agent counts as the settler of what is to happen with her body and thereby as the settler of what will happen to those parts of the world on which her body is able to impinge. In this way, as mentioned before, two conditions that have often been separated from one another by incompatibilist treatments of the free will problem—the 'leeway condition', which insists that a free agent must have alternate possibilities available, and the 'source condition', which insists that an agent must be an ultimate arché, or origin, in some sense, of what she does—are seen to be connected to one another. The agent can be the arché, precisely because she is a settler: because the chain of conditions from which her action results cannot be traced back along lines of inevitability beyond her. She really is an initiator, in a sense, of what happens; not in the sense that her action has no causes but in the sense that it has, at any rate, no prior necessitating conditions.

I have not attempted here to argue by means of empirical findings that agency has to be conceived of in the way I have suggested here. My aim has been much more modest: to try to show that there is at least nothing incoherent or manifestly at odds with anything we know to be a scientific truth in supposing that agency might be the kind of evolved capacity for discretionary control that I have here suggested it might be. The Existence Question, recall, as characterized by Kane, was the question whether the freedom postulated by the incompatibilist actually existed in the natural order and, if so, where it might do so. My suggestion is that there is every reason to think it does indeed exist, and that the most promising idea about where it is to be found is that it is to be sought in the hierarchical nature of biological organization, which, when it reaches a certain level of complexity and requires to be responsive to highly complex and rapidly changing information, turns what are already complex, self-organizing systems in which top-down causation already occurs, into creatures for which the owner/body distinction makes sense: creatures that are 'selves'. I am under no illusion whatever that I have properly explained how such creatures have come to exist; that is an enormous task that requires the co-operation of many different types of science. But I hope I may have said enough to make it seem plausible that it is quite possible that the pressures of natural selection should have produced creatures with the characteristics I have insisted must be ascribed to agents and that nothing we know about laws, causation, supervenience, emergence, or anything similar means that it is out of the question that there should be such things.

Conclusion

In this book, I have tried to make out the case for a certain sort of libertarianism, which I have called 'Agency Incompatibilism'. I have tried to defend the idea that action, properly conceived of as a kind of input into the world that is essentially *by its agent*, an input which is such that it is genuinely up to the agent whether or not it occurs, is inconsistent with determinism. I have offered arguments for this view, and also arguments against the Causal Theory of Action, which I take to be its main compatibilist competitor. I have suggested that non-human animals above a certain level of complexity (as well as human beings) must be accounted agents; and have defended the idea that the cognitive systems by means of which we organize and conceptualize the world are already disposed to recognize this fact. I have tried to argue that determinism ought not to be thought of as a purely empirical thesis that only a scientist could ever have the right to deny, but rather as a metaphysical thesis, vulnerable to challenge on grounds that are perfectly accessible to any of us. Moreover, I have attempted to defend my version of libertarianism against what I take to be the two main sources of objection to libertarianism of any sort: (i) the idea that libertarianism merely introduces unhelpful randomness into the causal processes that constitute our activity and that such randomness could never help us see how an agent could be in control of anything; and (ii) the idea that it is naturalistically incredible that there should be any such thing as I have alleged an animal must be: an object, a substance, that things can genuinely be up to.

I am sure there are flaws in my argumentation, and I look forward over the next few years to discovering from communication with some of you, my readers, what some of them have been, and attempting to remedy the deficiencies. But I remain very confident that something like the view I have offered here must be, in general, the right way to think about some of the most basic of the conditions that are required, metaphysically, for freedom. Much more of course, might also be required, and much more certainly *is* required in order for the related concept of moral responsibility to be applicable. I have not so much as begun, here, to consider what those extra conditions might be. But agency, as I have frequently said, is a *sine qua non* of any richer conception of freedom, and unless we can see how agency is possible, we will not be able to understand how any of the more impressive forms of liberty can be instantiated. What I hope I may have done in this book, even if imperfectly, is to have sketched, in broad outline, a picture of the metaphysical conditions that would be required to sustain agency and to have made it plausible to think that these metaphysical conditions might be met by the unquestionably indeterministic world in which we live.

References

Alvarez, M. (2009). 'Actions, thought experiments and the "Principle of Alternate Possibilities"'. *Australasian Journal of Philosophy*, 87: 61–82.

—— and Hyman, J. (1998). 'Agents and their actions'. *Philosophy*, 73: 219–45.

Anscombe, G. E. M. (1957). *Intention*. Oxford: Blackwell.

—— (1971). 'Causality and determination'. In: Anscombe (ed.), *Metaphysics and Philosophy of Mind, Collected Papers Vol.II*. Oxford: Blackwell, 133–47.

Aristotle (1984a). 'Eudemian ethics' tr. J. Solomon. In: Barnes (ed.), *The Complete Works of Aristotle Vol, II*. Princeton: Princeton University Press.

—— (1984b). 'Metaphysics', tr. W. D. Ross. In: Barnes (ed.), *The Complete Works of Aristotle Vol II*. Princeton: Princeton University Press.

Armstrong, D. M. (1999). 'The open door: counterfactual versus singularist theories of causation'. In: Sankey (ed.) *Causation and Laws of Nature*. Dordrecht: Kluwer Academic Publishers.

Aronson, J. L. (1971). 'On the grammar of "cause"'. *Synthèse*, 22: 414–30.

Austin, J. L. (1962). *Sense and Sensibilia*. Oxford: Oxford University Press.

Ayers, M. (1968). *The Refutation of Determinism*. London: Methuen.

—— (1991). *Locke* Vol II: Ontology. London: Routledge.

Barnett, S. A. (1958). The 'expression of emotions'. In: Barnett (ed.), *A Century of Darwin*. New York: Books for Libraries Press.

Bekoff, M., Allen, C., and Burghardt, G. M. (eds) (2002). *The Cognitive Animal*. Cambridge, MA: MIT Press.

Belnap, N., Perloff, M., and Xu, M. (2001). *Facing the Future: Agents and Choices in our Indeterministic World*. New York: Oxford University Press.

Bíró, S. and Leslie, A. M. (2007). 'Infants' perception of goal-directed actions: development through cue-based bootstrapping'. *Developmental Science*, 10: 379–98.

Bishop, J. (1983). 'Agent Causation'. *Mind*, 92: 61–79.

—— (1989). *Natural Agency*. Cambridge: Cambridge University Press.

Broad, C. D. (1952). 'Determinism, indeterminism and libertarianism'. In: *Ethics and the History of Philosophy: Selected Essays*. New York: Humanities Press, 195–217.

Broadie, S. (2002). 'Alternative world histories'. *Philosophical Papers*, 31/2: 117–43.

Campbell, D. (1974). '"Downward causation" in hierarchically organised biological systems'. In: Ayala and Dobzhansky (eds), *Studies in the Philosophy of Biology*. Berkeley and Los Angeles: University of California Press, 179–86.

Campbell, K. (1990). *Abstract Particulars*. Oxford: Blackwell.

Carey, S. (1985). *Conceptual Change in Childhood*. Cambridge, MA: MIT Press.

Cartwright, N. (1999). *The Dappled World*. Cambridge: Cambridge University Press.

Chaptal, J. A. (1795). *Elements of Chemistry Vol. I*, 2nd edn., tr. W. Nicholson. London: G. G. and J. Robinson.

Chase, A. and Glaser, O. (1930). 'Forward movement of paramecium as a function of the hydrogen ion concentration'. *Journal of General Physiology*, 13: 627–36.

Chisholm, R. (1966). 'Freedom and action' in Lehrer (1966): 11–44.

Chisholm, R. (1971). 'Reflections on human agency'. *Idealistic Studies*, 1: 36–46.

—— (1976a). *Person and Object*. LaSalle, IL: Open Court.

—— (1976b). 'The Agent as cause'. In: Brand and Walton (eds), *Action Theory*. Dordrecht: Reidel, 199–212.

Chomsky, N. (1959). 'A review of B. F. Skinner's *Verbal Behavior*'. *Language*, 35: 26–58.

—— (1965). *Aspects of the Theory of Syntax*. Cambridge, MA: MIT Press.

—— (1975). *Reflections on Language*. New York: Pantheon.

—— (1980). *Rules and Representations*. New York: Columbia University Press.

—— (1988). *Language and Problems of Knowledge: the Managua Lectures*. Cambridge, MA: MIT Press.

—— (1991). 'Linguistics and cognitive science: problems and mysteries'. In: Kasher (ed.) (1991).

Clarke, R. (1993). 'Towards a credible agent-causal account of free will'. *Nous*, 27: 191–203; repr. in O'Connor, (ed.), (1995).

—— (1996a). 'Agent Causation and event-causation in the production of free action'. *Philosophical Topics*, 24: 19–48.

—— (1996b). 'Contrastive rational explanation of free choice'. *Philosophical Quarterly*, 46: 185–201.

—— (2003). *Libertarian Accounts of Free Will*. New York: Oxford University Press.

Crist, E. (1999). *Images of Animals: Anthropomorphism and Animal Mind*. Philadelphia: Temple University Press.

Dancy, J. (1993). *Moral Reasons*. Oxford: Blackwell.

—— (1995). 'Why there is really no such thing as the theory of motivation'. *Proceedings of the Aristotelian Society*, 95: 1–18.

Darwin, C. (1881). *The Formation of Vegetable Mould Through the Action of Worms with Observations of their Habits*. Whitefish, MT: Kessinger Publishing.

—— (1965) [1872]. *The Expression of Emotions in Man and Animals*. Chicago: University of Chicago Press.

—— (1981) [1871]. *The Descent of Man and Selection in Relation to Sex*. Princeton: Princeton University Press.

Davidson, D. (1967). 'Causal relations'. *Journal of Philosophy*, 64; repr. in Davidson (1980): 149–62.

—— (1971). 'Agency'. In: Binkley, Bronaugh, and Marras (eds), *Agent, Action and Reason*. Toronto: University of Toronto Press. Repr. in Davidson (1980): 43–61.

—— (1973). 'Freedom to act'. In: Honderich (ed.) *Essays on Freedom of Action*. London: Routledge and Kegan Paul, 137–56. Repr. in Davidson (1980): 63–81.

—— (1980). *Essays on Actions and Events*. Oxford: Oxford University Press.

—— (1982). 'Rational animals'. *Dialectica*, 36: 317–27.

Dennett, D. (1971). 'Intentional systems'. *Journal of Philosophy*, 8: 87–106. Repr. in Dennett (1978): 3–22.

—— (1973). 'Mechanism and responsibility'. In: Honderich (ed.), *Essays on Freedom of Action*. London: Routledge and Kegan Paul. Repr. in Dennett (1978): 233–55.

—— (1978). *Brainstorms*. Montgomery VT: Bradford Books.

—— (1981). 'True believers: the intentional strategy and why it works'. In: Heath (ed.) *Scientific Explanation*. Oxford: Oxford University Press. Repr.in Dennett (1987): 14–35.

—— (1984). *Elbow Room*. Oxford: Oxford University Press.

Dennett, D. (1987). *The Intentional Stance*. Cambridge, MA: MIT Press.

—— (2003). *Freedom Evolves*. London: Penguin.

Dretske, F. (1988). *Explaining Behavior: Reasons in a World of Causes*. Cambridge, MA: Bradford Books, MIT Press.

Ekstrom, L. (2000). *Free Will: A Philosophical Study*. Boulder, CO: Westview Press.

Fischer, J. M. (1983). 'Incompatibilism'. *Philosophical Studies*, 43: 127–37.

—— (1994). *The Metaphysics of Free Will*. Oxford: Blackwell.

—— (1999). 'Recent work on moral responsibility'. *Ethics*, 110: 93–139.

—— (2006). *My Way*. Oxford: Oxford University Press.

—— and Ravizza, M. (eds) (1993). *Perspectives on Moral Responsibility*. Ithaca: Cornell University Press.

—— —— (1998). *Responsibility and Control: A Theory of Moral Responsibility*. Cambridge: Cambridge University Press.

Fodor, J. A. (1987). *Psychosemantics*. Cambridge, MA: Bradford Books, MIT Press.

Frankfurt, H. (1969). 'Alternate possibilities and moral responsibility'. *Journal of Philosophy*, 89. Repr. in Frankfurt (1988): 1–10.

—— (1971). 'Freedom of the will and the concept of a person'. *Journal of Philosophy*, 68/1. Repr. in Frankfurt (1988): 11–25.

—— (1982). 'The importance of what we care about'. *Synthese*, 53: 257–72. Repr. in Frankfurt (1988): 80–94.

—— (1988). *The Importance of What We Care About: Philosophical Essays*. Cambridge: Cambridge University Press.

Geach, P. (2000). 'Intention, freedom and predictability'. In: Teichmann (ed.) *Logic, Cause and Action: Essays in Honour of Elizabeth Anscombe*. Cambridge: Cambridge University Press, 73–81.

Gelman, R., (1990). 'First principles organize attention to and learning about relevant data: number and the animate-inanimate distinction as examples'. *Cognitive Science*, 14: 79–106.

—— ,Durgin, F., and Kaufman, L. (1995). 'Distinguishing between animates and inanimates: not by motion alone'. In: Sperber, Premack, and Premack (eds) (1995): 151–84.

Gergely, G. and Csibra, G. (2003). 'Teleological reasoning in infancy: the naïve theory of rational action'. *Trends in Cognitive Sciences*, 7: 287–92.

—— Nádasdy, Z., Csibra, G., and Bíró, S. (1995). 'Taking the intentional stance at 12 months of age'. *Cognition*, 56: 165–93.

Ginet, C. (1966). 'Might we have no choice?'. In: Lehrer (1966): 87–104.

—— (1996). 'In defense of the principle of alternate possibilities: why I don't find Frankfurt's argument convincing'. *Philosophical Perspectives*, 10: 403–17.

Glaser, O. (1924). 'Temperature and forward movement of paramecium'. *Journal of General Physiology*, 7: 177–88.

Goldman, A. (1989). 'Interpretation psychologized'. *Mind and Language*, 4: 161–85.

Golinkoff, R. M. (1981). 'Infant social cognition: self, people, and objects'. In: Liben (ed.), *Piaget and the Foundations of Knowledge*. Hillsdale, NJ: Lawrence Erlbaum Associates, 179–200.

Gopnik, A. and Wellman, H. M. (1994). 'Why the child's theory of mind is really a theory'. *Mind and Language*, 7: 145–71.

Gordon, Robert (1986). 'Folk psychology as simulation'. *Mind and Language*, 1: 158–71.

Griffin, D. R. (1981). *The Question of Animal Awareness*. Los Altos, CA: William Kaufmann Inc.

Harré, R. and Madden, E. H. (1975). *Causal Powers*. Oxford: Blackwell.

Harris, P. L. (1992). 'From simulation to folk psychology: the case for development'. *Mind and Language*, 7: 120–44.

Hillel-Ruben, D. (1991). 'Review of John Bishop: *Natural Agency*'. *Mind*, 100: 287–90.

Hirschfeld, L. A. and Gelman, S. A. (eds) (1994). *Mapping the Mind*. Cambridge: Cambridge University Press.

Hobart, R. E. (1934). 'Free will as involving determination and inconceivable without it'. *Mind*, 43: 1–27.

Honderich, T. (1988). *Mind and Brain: A Theory of Determinism, Vol. 1*. Oxford: Oxford University Press.

Hornsby, J. (1980). *Actions*. London: Routledge and Kegan Paul.

Humphreys, P. (1989). *The Chances of Explanation*. Princeton: Princeton University Press.

Hunt, D. (2000). 'Moral responsibility and unavoidable action'. *Philosophical Studies*, 97: 195–227.

James, W. (1968). 'The dilemma of determinism'. In: James, W., *Essays in Pragmatism*. New York: Hafner, 37–64.

Johnson, S. (2000). 'The recognition of mentalistic agents in infants'. *Trends in Cognitive Sciences*, 4: 22–8.

Juarrero, A. (2000). *Dynamics in Action: Intentional Behavior as a Complex System*. Cambridge: MIT Press.

Kane, R. (1996). *The Significance of Free Will*. New York: Oxford University Press.

——(2000). 'Responses to Bernard Berofsky, John Martin Fischer and Galen Strawson'. *Philosophy and Phenomenological Research*, 60: 157–67.

Kant, I. (1960) [1793], *Religion within the Bounds of Reason Alone* tr. T. Greene and H. Hudson. New York: Harper and Row.

Kasher, A. (1991) (ed.) *The Chomskyan Turn*. Oxford: Blackwell.

Kenny, A. (1975). *Will, Freedom and Power*. Oxford: Blackwell.

Kim, J. (1992). '"Downward causation" and emergence'. In: Beckermann, Flohr, and Kim (eds), *Emergence or Reduction?: Essays on the Prospects of Nonreductive Physicalism*. Berlin and New York: Walter de Gruyter, 119–38.

——(2000). 'Making sense of downward causation'. In: Andersen, Emmeche, Finneman, and Christiansen (eds), *Downward Causation*. Aarhus University Press: Aarhus.

Klee, R. L. (1984). 'Micro-determinism and concepts of emergence'. *Philosophy of Science*, 51/1: 44–63.

Klein, M. (1990). *Determinism, Blameworthiness and Deprivation*. Oxford: Oxford University Press.

Lakoff, G. and Johnson, M. (1999). *Philosophy in the Flesh*. New York: Basic Books.

Lamb, J. (1977). 'On a proof of incompatibilism'. *Philosophical Review*, 86: 20–35.

Lamprecht, S. P. (1967). *The Metaphysics of Naturalism*. New York: Appleton-Century-Crofts.

Lehrer, K. (ed.) (1966). *Freedom and Determinism*. New York: Random House.

Leibniz, G. (1956) [1707]. *The Leibniz–Clarke Correspondence*, ed. H. G. Alexander. Manchester: Manchester University Press.

Leslie, A. M. (1982). 'The perception of causality in infants'. *Perception*, 11: 173–86.

——(1984). 'Spatiotemporal continuity and the perception of causality in infants'. *Perception*, 13: 287–305.

Leslie, A. M. (1994). 'ToMM, ToBY and Agency: core architecture and domain specificity'. In: Hirschfeld and Gelman (eds) (1994): 119–48.

—— and Keeble, S. (1987). 'Do six month old infants perceive causality?' *Cognition*, 25: 265–88.

Levy, N. (2005). 'Contrastive explanations: a dilemma for libertarians'. *Dialectica*, 59: 51–61.

Lewis, D. (1981). 'Are we free to break the laws?'. *Theoria*, 47: 113–21. Repr. in Lewis (1986): 291–8.

—— (1986). *Philosophical Papers, Vol. II*. New York: Oxford University Press.

Libet, B. (1985). 'Unconscious cerebral initiative and the role of conscious will in voluntary action'. *Behavioural and Brain Sciences*, 8: 529–66.

—— (1993). *Neurophysiology of Consciousness*. Boston: Birkhäuser.

—— Gleason, C., Wright, E. W., and Pearl, D. K. (1983). 'Time of conscious intention to act in relation to onset of cerebral activity (readiness-potential): the unconscious initiation of a freely voluntary act'. *Brain*, 106: 623–42.

Lowe, E. J. (2008). *Personal Agency*. Oxford: Oxford University Press.

Lycan, W. (1988). 'Dennett's instrumentalism'. *Behavioral and Brain Sciences*, 11: 518–19.

McCann, H. (1974). 'Volition and basic action'. *Philosophical Review*, 83: 451–73.

McKay, T. and Johnson, D. (1996). 'A reconsideration of an argument against compatibilism'. *Philosophical Topics*, 24: 113–22.

McKenna, M. (1997). 'Alternative Possibilities and the Failure of the Counterexample Strategy'. *Journal of Social Philosophy*, 28: 71–85.

Magill, K. (1998). *Actions, Intentions and Awareness and Causal Deviancy*. ΠΑΙΔΕΙΑ, http://www.bu.edu/wcp/Papers/Acti/ActiMagi.htm.

Massey, C. and Gelman, R. (1988). 'Preschoolers' ability to decide whether pictured unfamiliar objects can move themselves'. *Developmental Psychology*, 24: 307–17.

Mele, A. (2006). *Free Will and Luck*. Oxford: Oxford University Press.

—— and Robb, D. (1998). 'Rescuing Frankfurt-style cases'. *Philosophical Review*, 107: 97–112.

Mellor, D. H. (1995). *The Facts of Causation*. London: Routledge.

Mill, J. S. (1970) [1872]. *A System of Logic*. 8th edn. London: Longman.

Moreno, A. and Umerez, J. (2000). 'Downward causation at the core of living organization'. In: Andersen, Emmeche, Finnemann, and Christiansen (eds), *Downward Causation*. Aarhus: Aarhus University Press.

Murphy, N. and Brown, W. S. (2007). *Did My Neurons Make Me Do It?* Oxford: Oxford University Press.

Nagel, T. (1970). *The Possibility of Altruism*. Princeton: Princeton University Press.

—— (1986). *The View from Nowhere*. Oxford: Oxford University Press.

Nelkin, D. (2008). 'Responsibility and reason: defending an asymmetrical view'. *Pacific Philosophical Quarterly*, 89: 417–515.

Nichols, S. (2004). 'The folk psychology of free will: fits and starts'. *Mind and Language*, 19: 473–502.

—— and Stich, S. (2003). *Mindreading: An Integrated Account of Pretence, Self-Awareness and Understanding of Other Minds*. Oxford: Oxford University Press.

Nozick, R. (1981). *Philosophical Explanations*. Oxford: Oxford University Press.

O'Connor, T. (1993). 'Indeterminism and free agency: three recent views'. *Philosophy and Phenomenological Research*, 53: 499–525.

—— (1995). 'Agent causation'. In: O'Connor, (ed.) (1995), *Agents, Causes and Events*. New York: Oxford University Press, 173–200.

—— (ed.) (1995). *Agents, Causes and Events*. New York: Oxford University Press.

—— (1996). 'Why agent causation?' *Philosophical Topics*, 24: 143–51.

—— (2000). *Persons and Causes: The Metaphysics of Free Will*. New York: Oxford University Press.

O'Shaughnessy, B. (1980). *The Will*. Cambridge: Cambridge University Press.

Peacocke, C. (1979). *Holistic Explanation: Action, Space, Interpretation*. Oxford: Oxford University Press.

Pears, D. (1975). 'The appropriate causation of intentional action'. *Critica*, 7: 39–69.

Peirce, C. S. (1892). 'The doctrine of necessity examined'. *The Monist*, 2/3: 321–37.

Pereboom, D. (2001). *Living Without Free Will*. Cambridge: Cambridge University Press.

—— (2003). 'Source incompatibilism and alternative possibilities'. In: McKenna and Widerker (2003) (eds), *Moral Responsibility and Alternative Possibilities*. Aldershot: Ashgate, 185–99.

Perner, J. (1991). *Understanding the Representational Mind*. Cambridge, MA: MIT Press.

Pink, T. (2004). *Free Will: A Very Short Introduction*. Oxford: Oxford University Press.

Pinker, S. (1994). *The Language Instinct*. London: Penguin.

Poulin-Dubois, D. and Schultz, T. R. (1988). 'The development of the understanding of human behavior: from agency to intentionality'. In: Astington, Harris, and Olson (eds), *Developing Theories of Mind*. Cambridge, MA: Cambridge University Press.

Premack, D. (1990). 'The infant's theory of self-propelled objects'. *Cognition*, 36: 1–16.

Pylyshyn, Z. W. (1984). *Computation and Cognition: Toward a Foundation for Cognitive Science*. Cambridge, MA: Bradford Books, MIT Press.

Reid, T. (1858) [1788]. *Essays on the Active Powers of the Human Mind* in *The Works of Thomas Reid, D. D.*, ed. Sir William Hamilton. 5th edn. Edinburgh: Maclachlan & Stewart.

Ryle, G. (1949). *The Concept of Mind*. Harmondsworth: Penguin.

Searle, J. R. (1984). *Minds, Brains and Science*. London: Penguin.

—— (1992). *The Rediscovery of the Mind*. Cambridge, MA: MIT Press.

—— (2001). *Rationality in Action*. Cambridge, MA: MIT Press.

Slote, M. (1982). 'Selective necessity and free will'. *Journal of Philosophy*, 79: 5–24.

Smith, L. B. (1989). 'A model of perceptual classification in children and adults'. *Psychological Review*, 96: 125–44.

Smith, M. (1994). *The Moral Problem*. Oxford: Blackwell.

Snowdon, P. (1998). 'Strawson on the concept of perception'. In: Hahn (ed.), *The Philosophy of P. F. Strawson*. Chicago: Open Court, 293–310.

Sorabji, R. (1980). *Necessity, Cause and Blame*. London: Duckworth.

Spelke, E. S. and Van de Walle, G. A. (1993). 'Perceiving and reasoning about objects: insights from infants'. In: Eilan, McCarthy and Brewer (eds), *Spatial Representation: Problems in Philosophy and Psychology*. Oxford: Blackwell, 132–61.

—— ,Phillips, A., and Woodward, A. L. (1995). 'Infants' knowledge of object motion and human action'. In: Sperber, Premack, and Premack (eds) (1995): 44–78.

Sperber, D., Premack, D., and Premack, A. J. (eds) (1995). *Causal Cognition: A Multidisciplinary Debate*. Oxford: Oxford University Press.

Sperry, R. W. (1969). 'A modified concept of consciousness'. *Psychological Review*, 76/6: 532–36.

—— (1986). 'Macro- versus micro-determinism'. *Philosophy of Science*, 53/2: 265–70.

Steward, H. (1996). 'On the notion of cause, "philosophically speaking"'. *Proceedings of the Aristotelian Society*, 97: 125–40.

—— (1997). *The Ontology of Mind: Events States and Processes*. Oxford: Oxford University Press.

—— (2006a). '"Could have done otherwise", action sentences and anaphora'. *Analysis*, 66: 95–101.

—— (2006b). 'Determinism and inevitability'. *Philosophical Studies*, 130: 535–63.

—— (2008). 'Fresh starts'. *Proceedings of the Aristotelian Society*, 108: 197–217.

—— (2009a). 'Fairness, agency and the flicker of freedom'. *Nous*, 43: 64–93.

—— (2009b). 'Animal agency'. *Inquiry*, 52: 217–31.

—— (2009c). 'Sub-intentional actions and the over-mentalization of agency'. In: Sandis (ed.), *New Essays on the Explanation of Action*. New York: Palgrave Macmillan.

Stout, R. (2004). 'Internalising practical reasons'. *Proceedings of the Aristotelian Society*, 104: 229–43.

Strawson, G. (1986). *Freedom and Belief*. Oxford: Oxford University Press.

—— (1994a). *Mental Reality*. Cambridge, MA: MIT Press.

—— (1994b). 'The impossibility of moral responsibility'. *Philosophical Studies*, 74: 5–24.

Strawson, P. F. (1959). *Individuals*. London: Methuen.

—— (1962). 'Freedom and resentment'. *Proceedings of the British Academy*, 48: 1–25. Repr. in Watson (2003): 72–93.

—— (1985). 'Causation and explanation'. In: Vermazen and Hintikka (eds), *Essays on Davidson: Actions and Events*. Oxford: Oxford University Press.

Suarez, S. J. F. (1994) [1597]. *On Efficient Causality: Metaphysical Disputations 17, 18 and 19*, tr. Alfred J. Freddoso. New Haven and London: Yale University Press.

Taylor, R. (1966). *Action and Purpose*. Englewood Cliffs, NJ: Prentice Hall.

—— (1992). *Metaphysics*. 4th edn. Englewood Cliffs, NJ: Prentice Hall.

Tinbergen, N. (1989) [1951]. *The Study of Instinct*. Oxford: Oxford University Press.

Van Inwagen, P. (1978). 'Ability and responsibility'. *Philosophical Review*, 87: 201–24.

—— (1983). *An Essay on Free Will*. Oxford: Oxford University Press.

—— (1989). 'When is the will free?' *Philosophical Perspectives*, 3: 399–422.

—— (2000). 'Free will remains a mystery'. *Philosophical Perspectives*, 14: 1–19.

Velleman, J. D. (1992). 'What happens when someone acts?'. *Mind*, 101: 461–81. Repr. in Fischer and Ravizza (1993).

Vihvelin, K. (1988). 'The modal argument for incompatibilism'. *Philosophical Studies*, 53: 227–44.

Warington, R. (1852). 'On the habits of the water-snail and stickleback'. *Annals and Magazine of Natural History*, 2nd Series, 10: 273–80.

Watson, G. (1975). 'Free agency'. *Journal of Philosophy*, 72: 205–20.

—— (1987). 'Free agency and free will'. *Mind*, 96: 145–72.

—— (2003). *Free Will*. 2nd edn. Oxford: Oxford University Press.

Weatherford, R. (1991). *The Implications of Determinism*. London: Routledge.

Wellman, H. M. (1990). *The Child's Theory of Mind*. Cambridge, MA: MIT Press.

Widerker, D. (1987). 'On an argument for incompatibilism'. *Analysis*, 47: 37–41.

—— (1995). 'Libertarianism and Frankfurt's attack on the principle of alternative possibilities'. *Philosophical Review*, 104: 247–61.

Wiggins, D. (2003). 'Towards a reasonable libertarianism', revised version in Watson (2003): 94–121.

Wilcox, S. and Jackson, R. (2002). 'Jumping spider tricksters: deceit, predation and cognition'. In: Bekoff, Allen, and Burghardt (eds) (2002): 27–33.

Wilkins, J. (1668). *An Essay Towards a Real Character and a Philosophical Language*. London: Printed for Sa. Gallibrand.

Williams. B. (1985). 'How free does the will need to be?', Lindley Lecture, The University of Kansas. Repr. in Williams (1995): 3–21.

—— (1995). *Making Sense of Humanity*. Cambridge, Cambridge University Press.

Wittgenstein. L. (1953). *Philosophical Investigations*. Oxford: Blackwell.

Wolf, S. (1990). *Freedom within Reason*. Oxford: Oxford University Press.

Woodward, A. (1998). 'Infants selectively encode the goal object of an actor's reach'. *Cognition*, 69: 1–34.

Index

Lightning Source UK Ltd.
Milton Keynes UK
UKOW04f0014080814

236572UK00001B/2/P